Equals and Partners:

A Spiritual Journey Toward Reconciliation and Oneness, Wazin Îchinabi

PATRICIA VERGE

*To dear Gail,
Warmest wishes,
Patricia*

 FriesenPress

Suite 300 - 990 Fort St
Victoria, BC, V8V 3K2
Canada

www.friesenpress.com

ISBN
978-1-5255-1867-6 (Hardcover)
978-1-5255-1868-3 (Paperback)
978-1-5255-1869-0 (eBook)

1. BIOGRAPHY & AUTOBIOGRAPHY, PERSONAL MEMOIRS

Distributed to the trade by The Ingram Book Company

Table of Contents

ACKNOWLEDGEMENTS

First and foremost, I would like to thank my husband Harry, who has always supported my writing ventures wholeheartedly, both in spirit and in practical terms. Many thanks to Deloria Bighorn, for suggesting the Bahá'í history of Stoney Nakoda Nation be written. Dear friend Beverley Knowlton unfailingly supported the project from start to finish. Many thanks to the friends who read the manuscript, or parts of it: Tyson Bearspaw, Deloria Bighorn, Chantelle Carlston, Dr. Roshan Danesh, Drew Erickson, Tina Fox, Beverley Knowlton, and Louise-Profeit LeBlanc. Special thanks to Roshan for clarifying legal terms and making suggestions for content. Deepest thanks to Bob Watts Jr. for a beautiful Foreword and for reading the book twice. Marcia Veach did a most helpful manuscript edit. I also want to acknowledge my dear sister Allison Healy, who has given so much of her heart to Stoney Nakoda Nation.

There are so many friends to thank for being able to serve together among the Indigenous peoples of Canada, in a field of service so dear to the heart of 'Abdu'l-Bahá. I chose the form of memoir, so that I could "own" the story of my spiritual journey and my learning. But in doing so, there is always the danger of focusing too much on the self. There are presently, and have been, many people, both on and off reserve, who have contributed to help build cross-cultural understanding between Indigenous and non-Indigenous people.

Thank you to members of the Stoney Nakoda Nation who have shown me such kindness, friendship and understanding. Your names are mentioned throughout the book, as are the names of those wonderful friends from both on and off reserve who continue to regularly support the community-building activities going on today. Some of those who visited over the years, but whose names are not mentioned in the manuscript, include Teddy Anderson, Farid Astani, Benjamin Berteig, Garry Berteig, Jordan Bighorn, Jenn Bopp, Diane Brown, Mansoor Derakhshan, Patrick Deranger, Laila Eiriksson, Gerald Filson, Massoud and Victoria Forouzan, Richard Forsberg, Chuck and Joan Haigh, Darren Hedley, Jean Hedley, Hannon Jaberi, Shirley Lindstrom, Esther Maloney, Clint and Jenny Munkholm, Farhad and Lois Naderi, Sadigheh and Mohammad Naderi, Frank Royal, Karim Rushdy, Andrew Ysselmuiden, Dolina and Ross Watson.

For talks, for encouragement, for suggestions for books and articles to read and subjects to research, I am indebted to Helen Mirkovich Kohm, Reggie Newkirk, Janet Embacher, Kamao Cappo, Nancy Ackerman, Bahram Gustaspi, and Louise Mandell. Thanks to Joan Young and Wilma Rubens for writing feedback; to Chris Pike for materials from the Cochrane Women's Conference; to Anisa White for providing a copy of Doug White's talk at Harper Mountain.

Jill Bennett and Jeff Wilson of Klondike Ventures near Rocky Mountain House rented me their amazing cabin for several weeks, which allowed me to focus on the book.

Thank you so much to Nikki Clarke for the cover photo, and to Mehran Imamverdi for other photos.

Foreword to the Foreword

I just finished reading Pat's book for a second time. As I closed the book, the silence surrounding me started to whisper in my ear. It was clear that I was a witness to something really special. Pat called this treasure a memoir. It is a memoir, it's also prescription for the ingredients of reconciliation, it's a love story and it's an invitation to look at the world through the loving eyes that are Pat Verge's eyes. I feel very inadequate to write the foreword to such a beautiful story, but here goes.

Foreword

I remember how excited my Mom was when a woman named Pat Verge agreed to help Mom write the book *Return to Tyendinaga*. I have to confess I was happy but not overwhelmed at the prospect of someone outside of our family helping on a project that had become sacred to many of us. It became clear that Mom knew exactly what she was doing when she asked Pat to help her. There was a special connection between the two of them, they were spiritual sisters. As Mom's health began to fail, Pat grasped the pen they both shared more firmly and ushered into reality a beautiful book about my grandparents, Jim and Melba Loft. Our family fell in love with Pat and witnessed first-hand her kindness, faith, dedication, love and determination.

When Pat asked me if I would write a foreword to her own story, I agreed immediately. When her book arrived in my in box, I decided to wait for a special time so I could immerse myself in her words. Pat paints vivid images with words and within the words sounds, sights and feelings jump off the page. After my first reading, I almost asked Pat to let me take my agreement back. And then I was at a meeting with a number of Indigenous Elders and something very special happened.

Diane Longboat, a wisdom keeper and traditional teacher from Six Nations, addressed the issue of reconciliation. She said, we will never have reconciliation in this country until those that came here from somewhere else love the land the way that we do; reconciliation starts with our relationship with the land and then is further manifest through us as we look at each other as brothers and sisters. Those words really stuck with me, but something about the significance of the words was evading me. When I started reading Pat's book for the second time, I realized that Pat personified the Elder's words in every way. Pat's descriptions, of the places she lived, traveled through and the people she met all oozed with love.

The historical journey and national and international events, as told by Pat, take on a special significance. Pat learned the importance of "looking for signs" and her beautiful interpretations of the many signs she discovered cannot help but fill the reader with hope and joy. Into every life some tragedy visits. The life lessons Pat shares, born in both joy and sadness, really show the fortitude and beauty of the human spirit and her own faith. Pat's description of her journey to discover her own heritage is precious. Irish philosophy and culture remind me so much of my Indigenous worldview. Pat's exploration of her Irish roots made me experience our common themes of misery, hope, strength, freedom and justice and I feel in love with the Irish as "mystical attitudes toward the world were taken for granted." Maybe that's part of why Pat has had such strong bonds with the Indigenous peoples in Canada.

Pat's story is timely given we are just starting on our journey of reconciliation as a country. Pat shows us signs we should watch for. Through her humility, her passion and her love she shows us that reaching across cultural boundaries is really building bridges of understanding. As someone who worked on setting up the Indian Residential Schools Truth and Reconciliation Commission and who teaches a course on Reconciliation, I often get asked, "what can I do to contribute to reconciliation?" The answer to that question has been made easier for me by reading this book. I'm looking forward to telling people about the ingredients for reconciliation contained in this book. I often speak of the TRC's 94 Calls to Action; in my view Call to Action number 95 is to read the book you're holding. Enjoy the journey....

Robert (Bob) Watts Jr.

Equals and Partners[1]

A Spiritual Journey Toward Reconciliation and Oneness, Wazin Îchinabi

---

1   Wazin Îchinabi is the Stoney Nakoda word for oneness. The title of the book is partly taken from this quote: "The goal should be all-Indian assemblies, so that these much exploited and suppressed original inhabitants of the land may realize that they are equals and partners in the affairs of the Cause of God, and that Bahá'u'lláh is the Manifestation of God for them." (From letter dated July 28, 1957, written on behalf of Shoghi Effendi to the National Spiritual Assembly of Central America and Mexico), *A Special Measure of Love*, p. 19.

PROLOGUE

Deloria Bighorn, a member of the National Spiritual Assembly of the Bahá'ís of Canada,[2] was visiting the Stoney Nakoda Reserve at Morley Alberta, located approximately one hour west of the city of Calgary towards Banff National Park in the Rocky Mountains. We were preparing for a children's camp to be held at the Bearspaw-Chiniki Elder's Lodge on the reserve during the summer of 2011 and visiting families to invite their children. At one point Deloria turned to me and said, "Pat, you know so much about the (Bahá'í) history of Morley. You should write about it."

I resisted the idea a little, because though fortunate to have a relationship with the Stoney Nakoda people for over thirty years, I wasn't sure I had much knowledge or wisdom to share. But Deloria's encouragement stuck and I began to write my memories. It came to me strongly that I needed to know much more, both about the history of the Stoney Nakoda First Nation and of Canada and its Indigenous peoples. I felt entirely inadequate.

Harry and I went on a pilgrimage[3] to the Bahá'í World Centre the next February (2012), with Blackfoot Bahá'í Beverley Knowlton. There, I confided to Beverley about the wish to do this writing. She wholeheartedly supported the idea, because she felt the Bahá'í community, like most Canadians, remains ignorant of Canadian history with respect to its Indigenous peoples. On the last day of Pilgrimage, we went to the resting place of 'Amatu'l-Bahá Rúḥíyyih Khánum,[4] the wife of the Guardian of the Bahá'í Faith. She was a prominent Bahá'í greatly admired by Indigenous people. While praying there, I remembered two very brief dreams where this beloved soul had encouraged my writing. So, this gave courage to begin.

With a deep need to learn, I then spent several years researching and reading Canadian history. As a slow reader and learner, no doubt I only touched the surface of this complex history. I was also worried about appropriating stories that rightfully belong to the Indigenous people of Canada. I read an indignant remark about this in *They Called Me Number One: Secrets and Survival at an Indian Residential School*, by author Bev Sellars. She wrote:

> I really get angry when non-Aboriginal people become "experts" on Aboriginal people. They come into our territories and gather information for four or five years and they become the experts and our elders like Gram, who have lived the life of a First Nations woman, become mere footnotes. Aboriginal people are the only experts on Aboriginal people. I don't care how many years people go to school to learn about us. Unless they have lived our lives, they are not the experts.[5]

Despite this worry, my reading led to much more clarity for me on why conditions are the way they are in Indigenous communities and the nature of the spiritual challenges faced by both settler and Indigenous communities in coming to true healing and reconciliation. In my travels and reading, I often heard that reconciliation is something that must be worked for by both Indigenous and non-Indigenous people. No matter how late in my life, I feel the learning I did was essential for me. In sharing, I hope it will be useful to any "would-be warrior" in this community-building work to bring together peoples long separated from each other. As well, I believe the Bahá'í Faith, as the newest of the world's religions, may have much to offer in reconciliation, as its desire is to serve with others to promote the oneness of humanity, share the spiritual revitalization offered by Bahá'u'lláh's[6] teachings and walk with Indigenous friends as they strive to apply those teachings in their own cultural setting.

While beginning to write, I realized how closely my personal spiritual journey has been molded by a connection with Indigenous peoples. Along the way, I also began to explore my own cultural roots. This took me on five trips to Ireland, where my father's parents had begun their earthly journey. In addition to finally wholly embracing this side of my heritage, I discovered a surprising number of commonalities with the First Nation tribes I have become acquainted with and found this a rich avenue for reflection.

In trying to find a format in which to write, I finally settled upon the memoir. I attended a writing workshop with western Canadian author Sharon Butala about memoir, not because of interest in memoir, but because I love Butala's writing, especially *The Perfection of the Morning: An Apprenticeship in Nature.*[7] But I came out of the workshop with my head spinning. Memoir seemed to be a flexible medium to write about one's own life, but focused on a particular theme.

Molly McCloskey, in offering a workshop on memoir in Listowel Ireland, referred to memoir as "consciousness contending with experience." Memoir, she wrote, needs to grapple with such issues as the unreliability and patchiness of memory, and how to construct a coherent narrative of the past. It needs to ask what "true" means and how we write about the lives of other people in a way that is ethical and accurate. Writers also need to ponder how much of themselves they will give away.[8]

There is a huge body of scholarly work on Indigenous issues and many people working on reconciliation and decolonization. So, while the purpose of this book is not to offer solutions to the many-faceted social and political issues now before Canada, I believe we need to know what those challenges are, and to delve into how spiritual principles can raise the level of discourse about them and guide action.

A book that influenced me a great deal was *Unsettling the Settler Within: Indian Residential Schools, Truth Telling, and Reconciliation in Canada,* by Paulette Regan.[9] A non-Indigenous writer who worked as director of research for the Truth and Reconciliation Commission of Canada (TRC), Regan consulted with Indigenous scholars and residential school survivors about her writing.

"Without exception, they all encouraged me to tell my own story, not theirs."[10] Regan writes about her own decolonizing journey. This is called, in academia, auto-ethnography, to document and analyze one's own lived experience. The Stoney Nakoda people have always told their own stories and will continue to do so. Regan's work has given me courage to tell my own story, what I have learned and how much it has enriched my life. In gratitude, I dedicate this writing to the people of Stoney Nakoda First Nation, who have so kindly welcomed and allowed me to feel part of their community, and especially to the youth, who will bring the fruits of their learning and service, and the richness of their cultural background, to both their own people and the world community.

Note on the use of terms: Terminology for the Indigenous peoples of America has changed regularly over the years and many tribes have returned to their original names for themselves as people. These are used wherever possible. Because of older sources referenced, the terms First Nations, Indian, Indigenous, Aboriginal, Native, Native American, and original inhabitants are used interchangeably in this book.

Chapter One

The Sacred

It was a startling question. During a writing workshop, the instructor asked, "What was your first experience with the sacred, your first intimation of God?" Startling not because the question was out of place—it was after all a workshop about the spirit and writing—but because, despite professing a strong faith, I had never really thought about where my faith journey had begun.

Faith — what I think of now as believing in the Creator, sensing the constant presence of the divine in daily life, and having a defined moral standard in which to weigh my actions — hadn't begun with bedtime prayers with my parents as faith had for many young children. In fact, there were never any discussions of spiritual matters in our home, though our family, nominally Roman Catholic, did occasionally go to church.

The earliest memory I have of being in a church was in Bassano, a small rural Alberta town where we lived for three years, from the time I was eight. Faith hadn't started then, nor at the time of my first confession and first communion a few years later.

No, reaching back in my memory, I found it had begun far before that, in the earliest memories I have. My first intimation of something sacred, beyond the physical, had happened in the yard of our family home in Williams Lake, a small town in the interior of British Columbia, about 600 km north of Vancouver, where my dad worked as the district agriculturalist and where I was born in 1948. Our home sat on a small hill, which overlooked the Williams Lake Stampede grounds. During those years from 1948 to 1957, when we lived there, the stampede was much smaller than it is now (today it is second in size only to the famous Calgary Stampede). But then, as now, there were people camped on the grounds of the stampede. My memory is too dim to remember many details. But as a young child of four or five, I found myself attracted to the people, the First Nations gathered there from the many surrounding reserves in Cariboo Regional District.

I stood in our yard smelling smoke wafting up from the fire pits. Children ran shrieking with abandon between the square canvas tents and teepees, long braids flying in the gentle summer breeze. Older women, dressed in hide moccasins that wrapped their legs, and colourful print dresses, bent over the fire making fry bread. It would be decades before I knew what the traditional food was called and learned to savour its buttery flavour. The men worked with horses, washing them down, putting bridles on and saddling them up.

Though only a child, from observing the people camped below our house, I felt their spirit, and perceived in that spirit a mixture of pain and joy. Perhaps it was the bent shoulders of the older people. Or the drumming heard once or twice at night, the high voices wailing. Little else but this remains in my memory after sixty years. But having learned that the nature of most drum songs is spiritual, and about the First Nations' respect and attachment to the land, my sense of the sacred started, I believe, with this experience. As an adult, my spiritual journey over many years has come to be intertwined with First Nations people and much of my learning and growth has depended on this connection.

I was happy to find these early memories confirmed by writer Liz Twan who grew up in the Williams Lake area. In an article entitled "Tent City," she writes:

> I was a local girl, and in my mind I can still see the canvas tents covering that hillside. Driving by the grounds in the darkness of evening, looking down into the Stampede bowl from Highway 97 you could see the flickering campfires and imagine the camps' occupants visiting over campfire coffee in the cool of the evening. There were native campers, ranchers and cowboys as well as spectators, who all pitched their tents and made camps on various areas of the grounds...

The most interesting travelers to see were the First Nations peoples who traveled in from their various homes around the Cariboo, usually arriving a day or two before Stampede. In the early years the only mode of travel was by horse drawn wagons and saddle horses as very few country people owned automobiles. The wagons were of all shapes and descriptions with the most common type being the rubber tired wagon with a bench seat across the front, some were covered but the majority were open.[11]

The First Nations people came in to the stampede from places around Williams Lake. They were known then as Alkali Lake, Dog Creek, Canoe Creek, Anahim, Redstone, Toosey, Soda Creek, and Sugar Cane. These reserves today take their Indigenous names of Esketemc First Nation (FN); Stswecem'c Xgat'tem FN (Dog Creek and Canoe Creek); Tl'etinqox FN; Tsi Deldel FN; Tl'esqox FN; Xatśūll FN and T'exelc FN.

My dad's work as a district agriculturalist took him all over the Cariboo region, to ranches and small towns, to reserves and in the back country. He often took the family for drives down gravelly back roads. I sat in the back-seat with my two sisters and brother. Frequently it was hot and dusty in the old station wagon and one or another of us kids got sick to our stomachs. The whole car reeked of vomit.

But the memory of those car trips is precious and happy. I credit my deep love of the land and of nature to those long days driving in the country and my dad's passion for the land, people and animals he felt responsible for as the district agriculturalist. We visited tiny communities with such names as Horsefly and Lac La Hache, and most of the First Nation communities.

The Cariboo is ranching country, semi-arid and hilly. To the east of Williams Lake spread the Cariboo Mountains. To the west is the powerful Fraser River, the longest river in British Columbia, which has its source at Mount Robson on the western slopes of the Rockies. To the west also spreads the ranching country of the Chilcotin, today called Tsilhqot'in by the several First Nations who live there. In my mind's eye, I can still see the rolling dry sand-coloured hills backed by dark stands of trees. The mountain pine beetle has today decimated much of the once-abundant forest and devastating forest fires destroyed more in the summer of 2017. There are "hoodoos," natural rock formations carved by rain and wind, near the Fraser River.

In the ranching country south of Williams Lake, I saw a slough without water and covered in a white sediment. The sediment was alkali, a soluble mineral salt that occurs in arid soils and some natural waters. My dad often visited Esketemc or Alkali Lake Reserve. This First Nation community, I was to learn, was the first reserve in Canada that began to deal with its huge rate of addiction and became a role model for many other communities to emulate in the healing movement among Indigenous people.[12]

My dad had great respect for the First Nations people he met when travelling through the Cariboo. Having grown up on a farm on the Prairies, he felt a kinship with people living close to the land. He helped people buy horses, deliver calves and repair wagons. (A favorite family story has Dad missing the birth of my sister Coleen, because he was out helping deliver a calf while Mom laboured at the hospital.) Dad took us to springtime bull sales. The pungent odour of manure and sage and the brawling and mass of the heavy beasts are indelibly stamped on my memory.

***

When the final meeting of the Truth and Reconciliation Commission (TRC) was held in early June 2015, I watched the extensive coverage with intense interest. By this time, I had spent several years researching the history of Canada's relationship with its Aboriginal people. On one broadcast, I saw a photo of St. Joseph's Mission (residential school) in Williams Lake, notorious for the sexual abuses of children that took place over many years. Years before, my mother had sent me a newspaper clipping from the June 18, 1998, edition of *The* (Vancouver) *Province* newspaper. The front-page article covered the apology of former Roman Catholic bishop, Hubert O'Connor, principal of the school from 1961 to 1967, for sexual abuse of students. The complicated trial brought out the overall legacy of the residential school, including years of lost culture, language and traditions. The last step in the long legal process with the former bishop was a traditional Aboriginal healing circle, which took place at Esketemc First Nation.

This troubling history was all in the background when I was a little girl. But it may well have contributed to the feeling of pain and suffering I felt when looking down at the people gathered at the stampede. Then in 2016, I read Bev Sellars' memoir about her time at St. Joseph's Mission, *They Called Me Number One*, which exposed for me much of the cause of that anguish. I also thought of my childhood in 2014 when the Supreme Court of Canada ruled in favor of the Tsilhqot'in Nation in a ground-breaking case that established land title for the First Nation.

After we left Williams Lake, I didn't have any significant communication with First Nations people for many years. But when I did reconnect, it shaped the rest of my life.

Chapter Two

Early Years 1948-1961

Reprinted from a slide, the 1950s photo has the look of sepia, brown and cream, yet there are other subtle colours, blue, orange and green. My mother kneels in the centre of the photo. Stunningly beautiful, she wears blue pedal pushers and a sleeveless white blouse with a delicate blue motif. Her hair is parted down the middle and pulled behind her ears into a bun. She's holding a posy of cut white lilacs and smiles happily.

I stand to the left of Mom, the only child who isn't dressed yet for the day. I'm wearing boxy, two piece pyjamas in a blue and white plaid and the pant legs are rolled up. My bangs are long, my hair doesn't look combed. There's a sweet, vulnerable look on my face as I smile into the camera. Many people, viewing the picture, think I'm a boy. I'm about seven years old.

My sister Coleen, five years my junior, kneels below me in the photo. She's wearing a short-sleeved T-shirt and her brown hair is pushed to the side of her forehead. She has a strained look, not quite a smile. Is she squinting at the sun or preoccupied with some worry?

Tom, aged four, is to the right of Mom. He has a chubby face and a big smile that looks just like Mom's. He's wearing shorts and an orange, plaid, long-sleeved shirt.

Dad must have taken the photo. Lilac bushes at our home on the hill in Williams Lake are the blurry backdrop to the photo.

Continuing to gaze, I feel an intense mixture of emotions. Gratitude for the happiness and stability of my earliest years. Grief that the little girl I was didn't develop confidence and acceptance of herself until way past midlife.

There are four more children to come in our large family, Tanya born in 1956, Mark in 1958 and twins Carmen and Karen in 1961. The peacefulness reflected in the photo changes as Mom and Dad have to work hard in a family business to support all of us. This robs us of our family life. As Dad's work history becomes more erratic and his drinking progresses, Mom remains the stability of the family. As in the photo, she stays in the centre. She is the rock.

***

Beginnings: Mom

My mother Katherine, "Kitty", Mesich was born in Croatia (then Yugoslavia) in 1925 and came to Canada with her mother and younger brother in 1929 to join her father who had homesteaded to the Smithers area in the Bulkley Valley, northwestern British Columbia, a couple of years before.[13]

My grandparents, Mike and Yvonne Mesich, were from a small village not far from Zagreb, the capital of today's Croatia. While visiting Yugoslavia in 1973 with my parents, I learned some history of the country, including the centuries-long feuds between the Serbs and Croats. A tour guide told us about the influence of the communist dictator Josip Broz Tito, who had managed to bring six states, several language groups, and a variety of religions under one federation to form Yugoslavia. But it all dissolved into great conflict between its diverse peoples after Tito died in 1980.

Because of the longstanding animosity between the Serbs and Croats, with the Serbs dominating much of the time, my grandfather didn't see a future for himself in the country, so he decided to emigrate. Within my grandparents' extended family that still remained in Yugoslavia, there were marriages between Serbs and Croats. During the Balkan wars in the 1990s, it became extremely difficult for these relatives, as they felt pressured by the conflicts to choose nationality over love.

Grandpa and Grandma Mesich eventually had five children, four boys and a girl, and were respected farmers always willing to help others. The family first lived at Lake Kathlyn in the rural area outside Smithers. My grandfather had purchased the land, which needed a great deal of clearing. He hired First Nations people to help him clear the land and later with the haying. The work was hard, clearing bush and cutting wood with saws. The people pitched their tents, worked for a couple of weeks, and then went back to their homes to rest, and another crew came in. Grandpa built them a cookhouse. My grandmother had a garden and gave the workers pots of food and her homemade bread. Grandpa had great affection for the First Nations people he knew and treated them as equals. It was a lifelong connection. When Grandpa died and also when one of my uncles passed away, several Indigenous people came to the funerals.

The family then moved to two different farms outside Smithers. My mother rode to school on a horse, hitching it up in a field not far from the one-room school at Glentanna. She spoke only Croatian when they arrived in Canada and entered kindergarten with no English. She picked it up quickly. When she came home speaking English, my grandparents learned it, though they always spoke broken English. Mom felt "backward" as a young person, being raised out in the country. She believed she got a much wider view of the world through marrying my father.

At one point, when Mom was in grade four and her brother in grade two, my grandfather bought a little house in Smithers so they could go to school there. Hard to believe in today's world, but during the winter months, the two young kids lived by themselves during the week, with neighbours looking in on them.

Throughout the years, my grandfather met the train as it came into Smithers to see if there were any Croatian immigrants on board. He helped them get started in a new land. Some years after my grandfather died, my mother was at a Croatian gathering in the Okanagan. When she told a guest she was from Smithers, he asked if she knew Mike Mesich.

"Do I know him?" she laughed. "He was my father." The man broke down in tears as he recalled my grandfather meeting him at the train and his kindness as he adjusted to life in the Bulkley Valley.

My grandparents bought their last farm from an Irish woman, Katie Chapman. Katie was a widow, well-educated and well-read, who drove her own car, unusual in those days. She took a special interest in my mother and was upset when my mother quit school after grade nine to help on the farm. Katie was also upset when she heard my mother was getting married, having heard she was marrying an Englishman. With her strong Irish identity, she phoned my mother and chastised her. Mom said, no, Joe was Irish, and Katie immediately responded, "Well, bring him right over!"

***

One summer, when my husband Harry and I were settled in southern Alberta and our son Isaac was living in Ontario, he came for a visit with his family. I invited Mom to fly over from British Columbia to join us. One day we visited Heritage Park in Calgary, an historic re-creation of pioneer days in southern Alberta. We saw horseshoes forged in the blacksmith's shop, a young woman in a long dress churning butter, a barn and other homestead buildings. I thought Mom would enjoy the park, and though she enjoyed being in the company of her children, grandchildren and great-grandchildren, she wasn't keen on the park because it brought back memories of a tough early life. There was no "romance" about it.

***

Privilege and Permission

In recent years, as my awareness has grown of the massive injustices towards Indigenous people that characterized the settlement of Canada, I began to wonder about the land my grandparents settled. Sitting down with my mother to see how she would react to my new learning, I thought she might be defensive. Her upbringing was harsh. She lived virtually in the bush, felt gauche compared to the young people in town and had suffered being called such pejorative terms as "Bohunk."

"Mom, you know I think my family and I have a lot of comfort, because Grandpa and Grandma left the old country," I said. "And they worked so hard on the land in Smithers. Then you and Dad worked for years to raise all of us. I never had to carve out a homestead, always had enough to eat, had access to a good education. Together with Harry, we've been able to offer the same to our children.

"All this privilege has a basis on the land you grew up on. I've asked myself if that was land unjustly taken from Aboriginal people. You know, so much land was cleared by the government for settlers in the early history of Canada."

My mother didn't flinch. "Why," she asked, "are we so concerned about ensuring rights to all those who come here from elsewhere, when we haven't provided the same for the first peoples? You tell that story."

Mom's wholehearted response gave me courage to pursue my own learning journey about Indigenous people and the true history of our country, through the lens of my spiritual beliefs. I will likely never know the exact history of the land Mom grew up on. I heard a non-Indigenous speaker at the TRC's national meeting in Edmonton say that we "shouldn't throw our ancestors under the bus." While I honour the hard work and sacrifice of my grandparents, I believe they would want me to work towards justice and reconciliation in this country.

***

Beginnings: Dad

My father, Michael Joseph Walsh, "Joe," was born in 1919 in Altario, a tiny prairie town near Provost on the border of Saskatchewan and Alberta. His parents, Michael Walsh and Hannah Sheehan, were from Grenagh, County Cork, Ireland. Before emigrating to Canada, they had lived in England for a year where their first son, Tom, was born. The bald Prairies were a rude shock for my grandmother, who had worked in a pub in the lush green surroundings of Ireland. She raised her seven children in Altario. To make ends meet, my grandfather, always known as "Pop," had to work away from home much of the time. He had gone to San Francisco and also worked in Canada's north. In 1913, he worked for the railroad on the Connaught Tunnel, in the Selkirk Mountains near Revelstoke, British Columbia.

Dad told Mom that hunger was a constant presence in their lives during the Depression and drought on the Prairies. He remembered freight trains dropped off potatoes and apples for the starving people.

My grandmother Hannah was driven by the thought that her children should grow up to have more opportunities, so she pushed them to go away for education. My aunt Elizabeth, "Lil," the oldest daughter, became a nun. I learned that many Irish Catholic families of the time expected at least one child to have a "vocation" and enter religious orders. But Lil eventually realized it was not for her, left the convent, and later married.

After Grade 12, my dad went to Big Valley to work on a dairy farm and complete grade 13. A relative once told me that Dad was always the "angry" one, even as a young child. Throughout his life he was a passionate man, railing against injustice. He must have known these characteristics of himself and witnessed the fights between his parents, because when he and Mom got married, he told her that they should never fight. Unfortunately, through the years of financial struggles and bringing up their own seven children, they did fight a lot. After Big Valley, Dad got a scholarship and did a year of engineering at the University of Alberta in Edmonton. For money, he took care of elderly men at a local hospital. Then when the war broke out, he signed up. He worked in radar for four years and was posted in Great Britain. When he returned, he went to the University of British Columbia in Vancouver and took a degree in agriculture.

***

Williams Lake

Mom and Dad met at the fall fair in Smithers when my father, fresh out of university, went to replace the district agriculturalist while he was on holidays. Dad already had a job to go to later in Williams Lake. They eloped to Vancouver to get married, then spent the first eight years of their marriage in Williams Lake. Because Dad worked as a professional, he and Mom met many interesting people who became life-long friends, such as the newspaper editor, school principal, teachers and local ranch owners. My dad loved arguments and had many heated discussions about politics and life with these friends, but my mother said they never lost a friend. Everyone saw the discussions as the sport of debating and no one took it personally.

The years in Williams Lake were both wonderful and difficult for my mother. As the wife of the district agriculturalist, she was expected to take part in regular functions as well as tea parties with other women in town. She learned to bake fancy squares and get dressed up, even wear a hat to the parties. This was extremely stressful for her, because she had grown up milking cows, tending to the garden, helping her mother in the kitchen, and delivering food to men labouring in the fields. She felt awkward, though it is unlikely anyone else saw her that way.

In Williams Lake, our family had relative financial stability, and though government wages were low, we enjoyed the ebb and flow of life in a small interior town. My parents always had a garden and beautiful flowers. Lilac bushes surrounded the house and gladiolas grew in the front yard. Mom and Dad took part in the annual fall fair that Dad started, where townspeople showed off the fruits of their gardens. During an autumn occasion in our back yard, my parents put corn and potatoes in tin foil and buried them in a bonfire. I can still taste the burnt, ashy sweetness.

As the first child, I was the apple of my dad's eye, loud and chatty. A family story has it that my parents were dining in a nice restaurant. I ran around, talking in a loud fog-horn voice. My dad either didn't notice or looked on with indulgence. A couple sat stiffly at a nearby table and at one point, the lady said, "What an atrocious child!" Mom had to restrain Dad from jumping up and decking the lady.

**

I learned guilt at an early age. We had a bird nesting in our yard and Dad warned me not to let the cat out of the house or it might get the eggs. I was remiss in my duties and the cat got out. Dad hauled me out to the yard to show me the remains of the robin's eggs. A painful lesson indeed.

**

To this day, I don't know why I wanted them, but in grade three I started stealing textbooks from school, carrying them home under my sweater, then hiding them in my chest of drawers behind my sweaters. I think the school principal might have been on to me. He looked at me very strangely. Maybe he spoke to my parents but they never said anything to me. And shortly after that our family moved.

Those stolen books came along when we moved to Alberta and then back to British Columbia several years later. Any pleasure that I might have derived from them was overwhelmed by the guilt I felt for five years. When

I was thirteen, I saved up and got a money order for $12, a lot at the time, and sent it to the Williams Lake Elementary School, explaining in the letter that it was for books for the library. I even took the bus to Calgary from Golden where we were living to mail the money order to disguise where it was sent from. Ironically, the secretary of the Williams Lake school, a friend of my parents, visited our family in Golden within a year of that. She said the school had received the money order and asked if it was from me. I lied and said no. The theft of the books and my lie stayed with me for a long time. I'm sure the experience contributed to my drive to find a moral code to live by. I wanted to avoid those feelings of guilt and shame.

***

At least once a year we visited my Croatian grandparents on their farm. As we approached, we saw the aluminum farmhouse roof from afar. Once, when my mother was due to give birth, she sent my brother Tom and me to Smithers alone. We flew to the nearest airport at Prince George. I was nervous when my grandfather picked us up; he seemed so different from most of the people we knew in Williams Lake. He had a heavy accent and mustache, and brought out funny food like smelly sausages to eat. I was scared the whole way, wondering if he really was my grandfather. Scared, that is, until we approached the farm and saw the aluminum roof.

My grandparents were extremely hard workers and expected it of their family. As a child, I saw my grandmother as a tough woman, with her constant emphasis on working. As a teenager wanting to fit in, I was ashamed of their broken English, something that brings me shame today. The last time I saw Grandma in 1989, I had taken my two children, ages seven and nine, to visit my sister Carmen and her family in northern British Columbia. On the way home to Alberta, we stopped at the old age home in Smithers where my grandmother was. She was over ninety by this time and in a wheelchair. Though I was her oldest grandchild, it had been many years since I'd seen her and I wasn't sure whether she would even know me. I introduced myself as "Patty," the name the family knew me by. We had an awkward conversation, and the kids, hyper from the long trip, were rambunctious and ran around, adding to my stress. When it was time to go, Grandma gave me a gift, in her still-tough voice. She said gruffly, "nice kids," as we left, a kindness for which I thanked her and that came as a flow of relief over my tensed body.

I have few memories of my Irish grandmother Hannah. Once she and Grandpa joined us during a holiday we took in the Okanagan. My Aunt Lil and a friend brought them from Edmonton. We took a ferry over Okanagan Lake at Kelowna and stayed in Peachland, in a motel not far from the beach. I remember little except the warmth and enjoyment of sandy beaches, but I have a lasting impression of my grandmother's unhappiness. She had become blind by then. After her death, Dad said he deeply regretted not taking her back to Ireland for a visit. She pined for Ireland most of her life in Canada. For the last ten years of her life, Grandma had Alzheimer's disease and was confined to a hospital in Edmonton. When Mom and Dad visited, she didn't know them. Much later, when I was in my fifties, I would decide to explore the Irish side of my heritage.

***

My parents made a friendship in Williams Lake that lasted their lifetimes and influenced me greatly. Urban Guichon was an agriculturist and managed the Alkali Lake Ranch, near Alkali Lake. His wife Mary came from an Alberta family with Irish roots. She was born Mary McCormick. Her mother had died at birth, and she was brought up by her father and a series of housekeepers. She had trained as a social worker, but only practiced for a while before she and Urban began their family. Mary was intuitive and interested in my family. Not having a mother to help her develop practical household skills, she stood in awe of my mother's ability to cook, tend house and garden.

Mary became an important person in my life, a mentor and friend. Her training in psychology, interest in the journey of immigrant families, and intuition gave her particular insight into the patterns developing in my family. She often recalled one of her first memories of me. Coming down the back alley in Williams Lake towards our house, I stepped in every single mud puddle along the way. When I got home, covered with mud, my mother rushed to clean me up. Mary asked what I was doing jumping in all the mud puddles. She was amazed at my answer. I told her I was looking for the sky.

Musing on this now, it's intriguing to think a little girl would look for the reflection of the sky in a mud puddle. Was it part of my beginning spiritual search at a young age?

***

Bev Sellars, author of *They Called Me Number One* and former chief of the Xat'sull First Nation (historically known as Soda Creek Indian Reserve), was born in 1955, two years before my family moved away from Williams Lake. She grew up around twenty kilometres from where I did, and spent part of her childhood in a happy and stable way, in the home of her grandparents at Deep Creek. From the ages of seven to twelve, however, she was forced to go to St. Joseph Mission, near Williams Lake. Sellars takes pains to recount some positive experiences at the school and friendships she made with other children. But her description of the abusive treatment of the children echoes testimonies from other residential school survivors across Canada. She writes about getting the strap:

> One of the first times I was in line to get the strap, one of the other kids told me not to cry. But the pain was like taking a knife and slicing your hands and arms. I was always ashamed if I cried too soon. Some of the reasons I remember getting the strap were for getting a ball that fell on the other side of the fence, talking in church, being too close to the boys' side of the playground, not moving fast enough for the nuns, and being late.[14]

Sellars says the disempowering effect of such regimentation and discipline is fear, being afraid to do anything at all. This lasted into her adult years.

"Even though I knew I wasn't going to get the strap once I left the Mission, the fear of being punished for the smallest things took years of hard work to overcome." Sellars believes the violence by the nuns and other students also conditioned her to step right into an abusive relationship with her first husband.[15]

While reading the book, I couldn't help but compare my childhood with hers. Her family and mine lived within a short distance of each other. My upbringing was by no means perfect, and alcoholism eventually affected the whole family. But I was not taken away from my family for months at a time and subject to abuse, and we had much freedom of choice. What I admire deeply in the story of Sellars' life is the strong family and community bonds that existed in her community, despite injustice and unacceptable social conditions, as well as her journey to overcome her timidity and fear to become a strong advocate of Indigenous rights.

***

CHAPTER THREE

The Prairies and the Mountains

Bassano and Countess

By 1957, my father was becoming restless with his government job and sought a job in the private sector. So we moved to Bassano, Alberta, 140 km (eighty miles) east of Calgary on the TransCanada Highway. He managed XL Feeds, a grain elevator. At first, we lived in the little town of 700, in a tiny house with two small bedrooms. In the summer, we kids slept on the floor to escape the extreme heat. Already nine, I helped with the younger ones and began to take more responsibility. When my mother announced she was pregnant with her fifth child, I was furious and self-righteous, thinking there couldn't possibly be room for another child in that tiny house. One day my mother climbed up on the freezer to retrieve something that had fallen behind. Big with child, she got stuck up there and couldn't get down. I was tasked with running to a neighbour's. He came over promptly and helped Mom off the freezer. I got over my anger quickly when my little brother Mark, cute and cuddly, was born.

Within a year, my parents purchased a farm at Countess, nine miles from Bassano. We bused to school in Bassano. We kids joined the 4-H and each had a calf to look after, helped collect eggs from the chicken house and loved the freedom of roaming the fields in the countryside. There was an old train stop across the road, and a station house built from oiled planks. One night we kids slept over in that house, creeping back home in the middle of the night after being spooked by the shadows and sounds of a prairie evening.

While much of the surrounding land was flat, in Countess, rolling hills dominated. Arid like the Cariboo, the fields required irrigation. Our family still drove through the land: trips back and forth to Calgary, out through the countryside to see the irrigation canals, to the cattle sales in Brooks.

***

We kids wrapped sausage, cheese and Mom's homemade buns in bandanas, slung our packs over our shoulders and headed out. The blistering August mid-day heat rolled over us, drawing sweat, but denting not a bit our enthusiasm for adventure. Crossing the gravelled country road, we began to climb the dry hills. I breathed pungent sage, dropped down to sniff, then cradle in my hands, first wild roses, then black-eyed Susans, their petals dropping in amber streams as I carried them. Stretching limbs over boulders, we found the hidden path long since nearly erased by winter snows and spring rains. Cresting the hill, we found it: a shallow valley that reeked of dinosaurs. How did I know this? I just knew. I knew we would find fossils. We scrambled down the dry hill, kicking up dust, loosening pebbles that rolled away ahead of us, reaching the bottom where tall grass broke their fall. Above a crow cawked.

All afternoon, we combed the hills, searching for evidence of our ancient fellow creatures. We didn't find anything except what might be an arrowhead, which I carefully slipped into my pocket.

The Canadian writer W. O. Mitchell beautifully described his experience growing up on the prairies and how it had affected his whole life, in *How I Spent My Summer Holidays*.

"Here was the melodramatic part of the earth's skin that had stained me during my litmus years, fixing my inner and outer perspective, dictating the terms of the fragile identity contract I would have with myself for the rest of my life."[16] I so love the term "litmus years." In a physical sense, litmus tests whether a solution is acidic or basic. In the spiritual or metaphorical sense, for me, it evokes the image of the child absorbing their surroundings, especially their natural environment, like a sponge. The process is mostly unconscious, but surprisingly enduring. Even today, I feel at home in arid climates, where scrubby bunch grass, sage brush, and cactus meet the sky.

***

August, 2013

The long windbreak of poplars is still there after more than fifty years. The trees, fully matured, in some cases haven't been pruned so their branches spill out in unseemly disarray. A few are dead. But the windbreak cuts across the horizon as it did back then, breaking up the treeless undulating prairie. A landmark for me as we traveled the highway from Calgary to Bassano in the late 1950s, the windbreak stands a few kilometers before the Bassano turnoff, just south of Highway 1.

We turn down the road shaded by the poplars. On the left, combines move across the fields, supplying evidence this is still working farmland. We see a sign posted by an oil company. Halfway down on the right, there it is, one of the ubiquitous oil wells dotting the southern Alberta landscape. I hold my breath, wondering if the house is still there. If so, this will confirm a strong childhood memory.

Indeed it is. Once a luxurious ranch-style split level built near a humble little town not used to wealth, the house now looks shabby and rundown. The shape is as I remember, however, with a south-facing window on one end and a shop or garage on the other. What had intrigued me as a girl of nine or ten was that, over the garage, the lady of the house had her own studio. A painter, she had a room of her own where she could create. I have never forgotten gazing up to that room.

A long stone wall still stands along the road and, at the entrance to the driveway to the house, a smaller wall of stone carved with the dates, "1867 to 1967," no doubt marking Canada's centennial year. Not even remembering the family name, I'm too shy to inquire into details of the property's history. But the house has all the signs of being inhabited, with baskets of flowers and lawn furniture in the front yard. Farther down the road, we find a newer machine shop and another house.

When I phone to ask, my eighty-seven-year-old mother can't remember this place our family had visited in the three years we lived in Bassano from 1957 to 1960, or the name of the family. It's strange how this house is one of my strongest memories of those years and how excited I am to explore the road today with my fourteen-month-old grandson, Cedar, on one of our summer meanderings. The windbreak is as long as I remember, and the house has the same shape. Though neither is as elegant any more as my childhood memory conjures up, the idea—in the fifties—that a woman could have her own space to do important artistic work, had clearly sunk deep into my psyche.

***

My first memory of organized religion goes back to the Roman Catholic church in Bassano. We kids were getting ready for First Communion. To do so, we had to prepare for our first confession. I rehearsed my litany of sins to tell the priest. I can't remember what they were, though perhaps they included the stolen school books. There are family photos of Coleen and me wearing white dresses outside the little church.

My religious training didn't include much of the story of Jesus Christ. I flirted during those years with the idea of becoming a nun, probably after seeing the movie *The Nun's Story* with Audrey Hepburn. My mother strongly discouraged the idea. While she made sure we followed a few church rituals, my mother didn't like any kind of extremism in religion, a moderation for which I am thankful today. She had seen my aunt Lil unhappy as a nun and did not see this as a choice for her children. Later, Mom became extremely disillusioned with the Catholic Church after hearing about abuse of children at the hands of clergy. Though she contributed to charitable projects run by the church, she never attended Mass again.

***

I had always enjoyed school and done well at it. One of my teachers wanted me to skip a grade. But my mother felt that because of my small physical size, I'd have a difficult time socially with older children. With her practical nature, she got me to do painting lessons with a lady who lived down the gravel road from the farmhouse. I had no talent for visual arts or for the later piano lessons, but they did keep me busy.

My bedroom in the farmhouse at Countess had a slanted roof and a window overlooking the farm. Here I discovered a love of reading, especially the *Anne of Green Gables* books by L.M. Montgomery. I absolutely loved Anne, her enthusiasm and assertiveness, love of words and the land, lively imagination, exaggerated and sometimes overdone descriptions. This series of books added to my love of nature, and Anne's optimism and indomitable spirit in the face of many disappointments offered hope during low times. I reread some of the books as an adult and became aware of a thread of small town parochialism and racism towards immigrants, unnoticed as a child.

At Countess, we got our first television, a small black and white. My dad loved watching the Saturday evening boxing matches. We used to laugh that Dad always cheered for the underdog. If the underdog started to win, Dad changed sides. He could never be happy just to be on the winning side.

Dad's youngest brother, Gerald, was born when my Grandmother Hannah was fifty years old. He had a mental illness and struggled all his life. Though he was bright and volunteered for the Salvation Army, he had a hard time with pressure. His first marriage broke up when their child died, after falling down stairs while in the care of a babysitter. A barber, Gerald struggled with work. Mom and Dad had him come and live with us for a time, both in Williams Lake and at the Countess farm. There was a feeling of desperation about Gerald and, in fact, he scared me a little. He didn't live with us long, but for years my dad sent him a little money every month to get by on.

***

At the Countess farm, we kids used to set up a house and office under the trees using hay bales. I loved play acting as secretary and organizer. Being the oldest, I always organized the other children. At one point my brother Tom, three years my junior, decided he was tired of being bossed around. He was getting taller and bigger and, after the ensuing fight, I knew I was beat. I couldn't dominate him anymore!

***

My first memories about alcohol come from this time. One Christmas we made the long trip to Edmonton to spend the holiday at the home of our aunt and uncle. The bedrooms for the children were in the basement, and all the kids bunked down there. Our Walsh grandparents and most of our

Walsh aunts and uncles were there. Late at night, everyone was arguing and yelling, fueled by drink. I crouched in the basement, maybe the only child still awake, and fretted. I don't remember ever talking with anyone about that night, but its uncertainty and insecurity are seared in my memory. A second clear memory I have is of being in the car outside a house in Gleichen, not far from Bassano. I don't know whose house it was, just that my dad had gone in to visit and didn't come out for a very long time. I suspect he was drinking. Whenever I hear of children being left in cars while their parents are partying or gambling at a casino, the memory of that night's fear comes back. And this was a tiny fraction of what many kids go through while their parents are drinking.

*****

Calgary

Late one evening, we woke up to the phone ringing and ringing. We found out XL Feeds was on fire, started by internal combustion within the grain elevator. We could see the flames and red sky all the way from Bassano out to our farm in Countess. My dad lost his job after that, and we moved to Calgary for a year.

My father's good friend from our Williams Lake days, Urban Guichon, offered him a job as a travelling salesman for his western wear company, Riley and McCormick. Dad travelled around northern British Columbia and to Yellowknife. My parents rented a duplex off Macleod Trail in the Stanley Park area of Calgary. We kids went, for the first time, to a Roman Catholic School called St. Anthony's. This was the first time I had any kind of formal religious training. Catechism was part of the curriculum. I must have been spiritually thirsty and dove into learning catechism. No doubt I also felt at a disadvantage to the other kids who had been in a parochial school all along, and a need to catch up. There were pages and pages of stuff to memorize. It's hard to believe now, but quite a lot of it was in Latin. I memorized passages like the Apostle's Creed and the Nicene Creed that form part of the Roman Catholic Mass, but I don't remember asking what it meant or being encouraged to understand the meaning of the passages. It was simply rote memorization.

Under the influence of Urban's wife, Mary, who had taken me under her wing with my mother's tacit approval, I began going to Mass regularly. Mary gave me my first Bible, a Roman Catholic version. I never, however, actually studied the Bible with others. Neither my father nor my mother shared my interest in religion. Dad was busy trying to make a living and Mom had five kids to watch over.

One night, we heard our parents laughing hysterically in the kitchen of our tiny duplex. When asked what the big joke was, they told us Mom was expecting twins. They knew she was pregnant, but had just found out they were having twins. Mom's grandfather had been a twin, but there hadn't been twins in the family for a couple of generations. I didn't find the news funny at all. Once again, I was outraged at the continuously proliferating number of kids in our family. Maybe, being the oldest, I already felt responsible for them.

***

We struggled off the bus on Elbow Drive. I had three of my younger siblings in tow for a visit to the dentist. I rounded them up, cajoled them to the corner with the traffic lights, and we crossed. It was bitterly cold, and we'd left school early. Mom was feeling too sick to accompany us. I sat in the waiting room as each child went in for a check-up. Finally everyone was back in the foyer, and we all donned our parkas. The receptionist looked over at me kindly. "You know, dear," she said, "you're a real lady." I never forgot her comment and how much it meant to a twelve-year-old burdened with responsibility. It showed me how much a simple act of kindness could solace a human heart.

***

Golden

While we lived in Calgary that year, Dad searched for where he could start a business. He heard that the TransCanada was to be built through a high mountain pass, the Rogers Pass, west of Golden, British Columbia. This would be a shortcut for the highway that until then had to go around a particularly difficult stretch called the Big Bend highway. He also learned about a general store for sale in Golden, which he felt would be a good opportunity. Dad bought the store and renamed it Walsh Mercantile. It had groceries, dry goods, hardware and the services of a butcher.

Golden, at the confluence of the Columbia and Kicking Horse Rivers in the Columbia Valley, is nestled between the Rocky and Columbia (Selkirk and Purcell) mountain ranges. When we moved there in the early sixties, Golden's population was well under 5000. My parents bought a small three-bedroom house near the high school. When we first arrived, Dad took us to the store, and gave us all responsibilities. I don't remember what mine was, but Tanya, then age five, was to be "vice-president in charge of the chocolates." Dad saw the new business as an adventure and at first I think we kids did too.

My parents soon bought a larger house for their growing family, with a carport, three bedrooms upstairs and a basement they later developed. The living room window had a breathtaking view of the Selkirk mountain range.

***

In retrospect, like many youth, I entered a dark period of life beginning during my adolescence, whose shadows didn't lift until I graduated university some ten years later. My mother went to work at the store soon after we arrived. Our baby twin sisters, Carmen and Karen, were just a few months old. Mom's Croatian cousin Fanika lived with us at first to help with the twins. Then, as they grew, my sister Coleen, five years my junior, and I took over the care and nurturing of the twins when Mom began to work more. Though I was completely unaware of it at the time, my sister Carmen later told me that Coleen and I were the only mothers she knew. In our adulthood, most of us made peace with our upbringing, but at the time, it laid a heavy burden of responsibility on us kids.

***

The sun burned hot in the summer sky. No hint of a breeze relieved the close air.

"Please, please, please God," I breathed. "Help us find him."

My brother Mark, then four, had disappeared from the yard. Preoccupied with the twins who were just learning to walk, I had completely forgotten about him. Mom was at work, so I yelled at Coleen to watch the twins and took off down the alley. Scouring the landscape, I couldn't see a trace of Mark.

Our house in Golden was three long blocks away from the Kicking Horse River, which wound its way through town. All I could think of was the worst, Mark drowning in the river. Rushing down the sidewalk, panting, drenched in sweat, wave after wave of heat flowing over me, I experienced what I now think was my first panic attack. I yelled out Mark's name. By the time I got to the river, my damp hair clung to my head. I was shaking all over. I walked along the bank searching for someone in the churning waves. No one there. Still terrified, I next started to wonder if Mark had been kidnapped. I turned back towards the house. When I got near home, Mark came out of the nearby apartment block. I almost fainted with relief.

"Where have you been, Mark? I thought you'd drowned in the river. I nearly called the police."

"I was just at Bryce's house. He wanted to play trucks," Mark said, his freckled brow furrowed, his lips trembling.

"Don't you ever, ever do that again without telling me," I burst out. "You have to ask first." I started to cry, then I sat down on the grass. Mark looked so distressed. He was the kind of kid who wanted to please. I reached out and hugged him as hard as I could.

***

Today I feel compassion for my fourteen-year-old self and the burdens I took on growing up. Though I had no doubt exaggerated the danger Mark was in, I felt completely responsible for my siblings. The anxiety I felt would later transform into trust as I developed spiritual practices, but some traces of anxiety and trauma still remain at my core. I've spent much time struggling to let go of the overly responsible role, so engrained in me as the oldest child in the family and because of my own nature. Of all the characteristics of co-dependents listed in various sources, this one fits me best: "Having an exaggerated sense of responsibility for the actions of others."[17]

Much later I discovered the word "catastrophize" in *Learned Optimism* by Martin Seligman.[18] I learned this was the tendency to make a huge deal out of every event and to predict the worst, like Mark being drowned. Later, when our son, Isaac, first tried alcohol, in my mind I already had him being a bum on the street.

Learning, also much later, about the characteristics of alcoholic families, I felt it was my responsibility to educate my mom and siblings so we might do something together about Dad's drinking, such as an intervention. My family wasn't interested in my new-found knowledge. Now I see how naïve my hope was. But I played my role to the utmost, forging ahead trying to find solutions and fix problems.

***

Throughout high school, I worked in the Mercantile every Friday night and on Saturdays, and, during the summer, I often worked during the week. Mostly I worked on the cash, though all of us learned about stocking shelves and helping customers.

Mom had excellent cooking skills developed over years of feeding a large family. In the winter, when the store was closed on Mondays, she spent the day baking and cooking. She often made homemade buns and cinnamon buns, sometimes a banana cream pie, sometimes cookies, sausage rolls and cheese buns. We binged on the sweets that day. On other days, before she left for work, she often started supper for us. I marvel today at how she kept it all together.

Mom came home exhausted at night. In the summer, the store was open seven days a week, 9 a.m. to 9 p.m.; in the winter, it was closed Sundays and Mondays and evenings, except Friday. My parents discovered disillusioning things about human nature during the eleven years they had the store. Though they had good hard-working employees, they learned they couldn't trust everyone. One particular older woman set out groceries under empty cardboard boxes at the back of the store, which she then took home without paying for. When Mom discovered this, she fired her on the spot.

They also found many of the town residents weren't loyal customers. Some ran up their credit, then when they owed a lot, went to a competing store to buy their food rather than come to ours. When a chain grocery store came in, many people abandoned my parents' store. My parents had a few lean years before they sold the business.

Dad hired the bank manager's son because he felt indebted to the manager for a loan he had taken out. The son was chronically in trouble with the law. My parents were away on holiday leaving me in charge of the store (I was probably no older than fifteen). I caught the young man stealing a rifle, so promptly fired him. My parents found it funny and were also grateful to me for doing something they couldn't have done themselves.

***

I credit Mom for keeping the family—and the store—together. Dad was always anxious about money. Besides working in the store, he tried different things. He bought a grocery store in Invermere, two hours south of Golden in the Columbia Valley, which they later sold. He got into a contract to clear land on the Big Bend Highway, cleaning up debris from a large forest fire. In both cases, Dad's business partners didn't pull their own weight. Dad broke a rib doing some of the work on the Big Bend.

After Mom and I had seen the movie *A Beautiful Mind*, about the brilliant mathematician John Nash and his battle with mental illness, she said Dad had probably struggled with some form of mental illness most of his life. On my father's Irish side of the family, several relatives have suffered from mental illnesses. It makes sense to me that Dad struggled with anxiety, depression, and the after-effects of drinking. I can't imagine the difficulty of having seven children and being worried about feeding, clothing and educating them. My mother likely sensed that Dad couldn't be a completely stable provider and stepped into the void, becoming the pivot around which turned the family and the store.

***

Dad's voice reaches a higher and higher pitch. He shouts at Mom. Tonight it's about people who haven't paid up the credit the store has extended to them.

"We've sent them bills every month. What do they think, that we don't have to pay our own bills for everything we bring into the store?" he rants.

Downstairs in my bedroom, I cower under the blankets.

"Why doesn't she say something?" I fume. "She's so damn passive."

Many nights I hear great commotion in the kitchen after my parents get home from the store. Dad gets keyed up, Mom just listens. Later I see that her choices are limited—jump into the fray and argue with Dad and inflame things even more—or just let him blow off steam.

I fret that my parents will split up. I take everything personally. If I can just be the best girl, the best student, do everything perfectly, our family will be okay. Of course, this is an illusion.

***

Added to this mix was the normal teenage challenge of dealing with hormones and trying to fit in. Not a popular student in school, I had a couple of friends to hang out with who weren't in the in-group either. Once when I went to meet them, they didn't answer the door. Later I saw them running away together out the backyard. Their rejection hurt. Another girl who stayed a friend over many years was one of the most ignored and picked-on students. She was very bright, and I've wondered if she might have achieved much more and made a happier marriage, if she'd had a chance to be accepted.

***

We had one family vacation while we lived in Golden. We went to Invermere and stayed in a cabin on the lake. While there, I read about Eleanor Roosevelt in a magazine and became inspired by her example of community service. Dad had a strong sense of social responsibility and a great interest in politics and, for most of their lives, he and Mom were members of a political party, though they changed their allegiances several times when they got disillusioned. Dad worked on one election campaign for my friend's father who was running in the Columbia Valley. I helped stuff envelopes and put up posters. Dad also served on the town council and helped get a sewage system into Golden.

Dad loved the family, and I know that everything he did in his work was to give us a good start in life. He loved family dinners on Sunday, the only day we could have them. And he enjoyed Christmas tremendously, when he could play Santa Claus and distribute gifts.

***

One teacher in high school, Mr. Dyck who taught French, greatly influenced me. We all learned French in high school and probably had never heard it spoken by a native speaker. I don't think Mr. Dyck's French was particularly fluent. But he loved the language and communicated his enthusiasm to us.

Mr. Dyck's life took a tragic turn when I was in grade nine. His wife was driving home from Calgary on a treacherous winter highway. Coming down the twisty Kicking Horse Pass, she lost control of the car, which went into the river. One of their children, a baby, was lost and never found. We saw Mr. Dyck in the river, in hip waders, searching desperately for the baby. He came back to school after a few weeks, and began again right where he had left off, cheerfully, never mentioning the loss of his child. Nowadays, we might bring grief counsellors in to the school. I greatly admired his courage and ability to carry on. I studied French when I went to university, in no small part because of his example.

***

Dad taught me to drive, a process that involved a lot of head-butting and struggle between us. But I got my license at sixteen and drove the various cars my parents owned, though in some I could barely see over the steering wheel.

My favorite vehicle was the 1948 pick-up. The shocks were almost completely gone and when I drove over the railway tracks, my head hit the roof in the cab. My friends and I used to drag race down on the small airport in Golden and the pickup held its own. I used to tell myself that if I had only a few months to live, I'd become a race car driver!

I first heard about John Lennon's controversial remark that the Beatles were more popular than Jesus Christ, while driving that truck. I loved the Beatles but was shocked. As it turned out, his remarks were taken out of context, but they flamed a big controversy. On March 4, 1966, an article appeared in the London *Evening Standard* by journalist Maureen Cleave. Here's what Lennon actually said.

"Christianity will go," Lennon said. "It will vanish and shrink. I needn't argue about that. I'm right and I'll be proved right. We're more popular than Jesus now. I don't know which will go first, rock 'n' roll or Christianity. Jesus was all right but his disciples were thick and ordinary. It's them twisting it that ruins it for me." The controversy spread far beyond the London paper.[19]

***

Not yet thinking of myself as a spiritual being, I did go to Mass each Sunday. I didn't question what I believed, but followed the rituals. A girl my age sat up in the choir, joked and ate sunflower seeds during Mass. Her disrespect bothered me, like John Lennon's did, though I couldn't have said why. The few times my father went to church, I noticed he was completely bored and skeptical of what the priest said. Sometime during high school, I got close to the priest for a short time. He took me for a ride somewhere and gave me a necklace with a bejewelled cross. I felt extremely uncomfortable being in the car with him. I think my mother spoke to Mary Guichon about it, because on one of my trips to visit her in Calgary, Mary warned me about getting close to the priest. I'm grateful she overrode her own loyalty to the Church to warn me.

***

I often took refuge in the hills behind our house. When we first moved to Golden, my parents bought two Samoyed husky puppies, Nikki and Chief, which we kids loved dearly. Those days you didn't keep dogs on a leash nor pick up their poos after them! As they grew, the dogs ganged up on other neighborhood dogs, so we had to find another home for Chief. Nikki lived with our family to an old age, dearly loved by all of us. He was my constant companion as I walked the hills behind the house.

Those hills became my place of solace. While there is now a subdivision on the hill, back then there was only a narrow, rutted dirt road up to the cemetery. I was drawn to the graveyard, though at the time I didn't know a single soul who had been buried there. The gravestones under a canopy of trees looked out over what we now call a slough or wetland, named Reflection

Lake. At its prettiest in the fall, the lake mirrored the mountains and the deep goldens of the aspens for which the town had befittingly been named.

***

May, 2013

We drive up to the Golden cemetery. I jump out and pass through the gate with our Corgi, Meghan, totally missing the sign that says no dogs. The graveyard is still, without a breeze, serene with no background noise. Only two other people are here, at the far end. My sister, who has a broken knee, stays in the car.

This spring day is sunny and cool. A circle of multicoloured daffodils surrounds a few flat grave markers. The grass is shimmering green and trimmed. Spruce and fir border the open fields. The dog and I wander into the grove of trees that looks down over Reflection Lake. The old upright graves are here, weather-beaten, covered with lichen, the lettering completely worn off most of them by the elements. The odd one sports a date. 1921 says one, well before Golden became a town.

Memories flood back of wandering, as an adolescent, through this graveyard, now greatly changed by the clearing of large spaces to contain the modern flat markers. But it's still an utterly tranquil place, cocooned by the tall trees from the bustle of the mountain town.

Had they known, my high school classmates might have found my behaviour ghoulish back then. But I took all my troubles up that hill and walked the trails and slopes and pathways of the hill and graveyard. Whether weighted down by family tensions or boyfriend troubles, I always came back with peace of mind. The trees, fresh sweet air, plants and birds—and the gravestones—drew me away from my burdens. I've often wondered since if the souls of early Golden residents influenced my later direction in life. Did someone I had never met in this life intervene for me when I most needed it? Some musings while I wandered the hills found their way into an assignment for my English class. I waxed philosophical about the meaning of life, and the teacher got excited that I was even asking such questions.

***

At the end of grade twelve, two schoolteachers offered to take a group of students to Europe for six weeks—I wonder now what they were thinking! But they had done it before. With the help of my parents and some of my own savings, I was able to go. The group went to seven countries in six weeks: England, Scotland, France, Switzerland, the Netherlands, Germany and Italy. We stayed in youth hostels and went to many tourist sites. Three memories remain strong.

***

We visited York, a walled city in the northern Lake District of England. The youth hostel, in an old castle, had windy stairs and turrets. Our group came in from a long day's walking tour and flopped down in the common room. Though we were enjoying ourselves, it was standard to grumble about the packed schedule we had every day. Our teachers got us up at the crack of dawn and herded us through activities the whole day. In the midst of the muttering, I glanced over at a young couple seated by a window table poring over maps. They traced a route on one map and both nodded in agreement. I tried not to stare.

"Wouldn't it be fabulous to be here with someone you love?" I thought longingly.

Seven years later, I found myself back at the same youth hostel with my husband Harry. We were on a hitchhiking trip around Europe. We pulled out our maps and guidebooks. I made sure we sat at the table right by the window.

***

Joan, another Catholic on our school trip, and I sat in the pew of a small church along a canal in Venice. It was Sunday Mass. I couldn't understand what the priest was saying in Italian. He was shouting and flailing his arms. But what shocked me most was the attitudes of the people in the congregation. They were ignoring the priest completely. Some were standing, some sitting, one couple was kneeling. And several were talking to each other. I felt sick to my stomach.

***

Our group crossed the threshold into St. Peter's Basilica at the Vatican, famous as a place of pilgrimage. As a Roman Catholic, I had been looking forward to visiting one of the great centres of the faith. As we stood beneath the soaring dome, the tour guide pointed to gold lines on the marble floors inside the entrance.

"This is the size of St. Paul's in London," she said, pointing to one line. "And this is the size of Notre-Dame in Paris."

I was horrified. Her point was that St. Peter's was much larger than these other well-known churches. What does size have to do with anything? I thought, sickened by the superficial approach. I could hardly bear to tour the rest of the ornate grandiose building. There was some relief when we saw the exquisite "Pieta" sculpture by Michelangelo. Mary was holding the lifeless body of Jesus on her lap, after the Crucifixion. The grief in her face nearly brought me to tears.

CHAPTER FOUR

University, The Search Intensifies

My fragile system of spiritual belief continued to undergo shocks. I broke up with my boyfriend right after I got back to Canada from Europe. The relationship wasn't going anywhere; after all the places I'd seen, my world had opened up past Golden.

Now I was in my first year at the University of British Columbia (UBC) in Vancouver, staying at the Totem Park residence on campus. It was surrounded by walls. Sometimes I felt like a prisoner. Everyone else seemed confident of what they were doing. I felt like just what I was, a small-town unsophisticated girl.

I took French and other arts courses and met Vivienne in the philosophy class. She was nice and thoughtful and told me she didn't believe in God. I'd never met an atheist before. I was reading James Joyce's *A Portrait of the Artist as a Young Man* in English class. He questioned everything about the Catholic Church, its rituals and sacraments, such as confession, communion and the Mass, and its institutions. He wanted to put his faith in art.

I nearly freaked out in the philosophy class one day. The bald-headed professor looked straight at me.

"You're a deist, aren't you?" he bellowed. Well, maybe he didn't bellow, but it felt like it. I was so embarrassed. What kind of look did I have on my face for him to single me out? Skeptical, questioning, vulnerable?

I stayed silent after his question. Of course, I did believe in God, but I didn't have the courage to stand up and say so. The way he dismissed religion, he probably would have ridiculed me. And the truth be told, I didn't know what I could have said. I was questioning everything.

***

The arts faculty at UBC was huge, and life in Vancouver was lonely. It rained all the time, or so it seemed. That first fall, it rained for forty days straight. I phoned home a lot and told Mom I wanted to quit. I was depressed, sure I had mononucleosis. Mom told me to hang on for a few more days. If I still felt I had to, I could come home then. By the end of the weekend, when I was supposed to phone back, I felt better.

***

At the end of the school year, I went home to Golden and told my mother I didn't believe in God any more. Mom wasn't a rigid Catholic, but she burst into tears. But what she did about it was shocking to me. The next day, she told me the Catholic priest was coming in on Sunday to talk with me.

I was furious. How dare she? I couldn't look her. But I had a niggling feeling she was doing this out of love and because she was worried about me.

The priest came in Sunday afternoon. Ironically, his name was Father Patrick Walsh and mine was Patricia Walsh. We sat around the living room and nobody said much. But when Father Walsh was leaving, he said to Mom that I would be all right, I'd come back to the fold. He metaphorically patted me on the head.

I seethed. How patronizing. How dare he presume anything?

***

Father Walsh never knew how much his visit propelled my spiritual search. It started my resistance to the priesthood. I strongly felt I had a right to choose myself what to believe.

Though furious, I was also completely miserable as an atheist. I had boxed myself into a corner with little air. I took refuge in the Romantic poets, Wordsworth, Shelley, Byron. Their passion for nature deeply attracted me.

I began regular visits into Calgary to see Mom's friend Mary Guichon. We often talked into the wee hours of the morning. That year, she managed to talk me into returning to the Catholic Church.

"Mary, how can I go back when there are so many things about the Catholic Church I can't accept?" I argued.

"Well, can't you go back to the church and just pick out the things you can accept?" Mary asked.

Seeing how unhappy I was, Mary offered a compromise, which I accepted. For several years I went back to church and hung on to whatever spiritual truth I could glean. Most often, I found words of inspiration during the reading of the Gospel. Since the accounts of the Apostles are the nearest thing to the actual words of Jesus Christ that exist, they felt more like the true essence of Christianity than did the rituals of the Mass.

In my last year at university, I found a Catholic church on campus, avant-garde for the time, where the priest invited those present to gather around the altar during Mass. The guitar music and singing, the absence of Latin, and the participatory feeling all attracted me. After leaving university, I never again found a church that open or participatory.

**

After my first year at UBC, I went back to Golden to work in the store. That summer I started going out with a fellow from Vancouver working in the area. He had a sports car, was kind of wild, and once when he was drinking, fell down a long flight of stairs. Another night, he hit the ditch in his fine car. The relationship didn't last.

Later that summer, I met Jack, a twenty-three-year-old RCMP officer who had been posted to Golden. He had been part of the RCMP Musical Ride. He showed interest in a long-term relationship. I wasn't interested at first but later became the one more interested. Jack took me to a few parties with his colleagues. They were older and I felt out of place, so I drank too much. Once I had to be driven home in a police car. Much later, when I quit drinking altogether and examined the roots of alcoholism in my family, I realized I had the drinking pattern of an alcoholic. I never had just one drink but kept drinking and often mixed my drinks.

I returned to school that fall and stayed with my friend Ella in a basement apartment. It was dark, damp and depressing. To this day, I hate basement rooms. Jack came to Vancouver for the RCMP ball, and I wore a formal outfit, a long skirt and my mother's fancy sequined top. My long hair was piled in an up-do.

Deep down, I had doubts about Jack, though I thought of him for years after he broke up with me. His ideas were conservative, understandable given his work. Though I was never comfortable with much of the 1960s thinking, I was influenced by the times, especially the music of the Beatles, Bob Dylan, Joan Baez, Gordon Lightfoot and Ian and Sylvia. The lyrics of protest resonated with me. I couldn't call myself a hippie. I was far too steeped in the responsibility inculcated in me from an early age to join in anarchistic movements. Later I would joke that I was more of a hippie in my sixties than then, if being a hippie meant believing in peace, non-violence, and universal reconciliation.

After my second year, I planned to go to Ottawa to spend the summer with Jack. I felt uneasy about it but was determined to go anyway. But Jack sent me a letter before university was out, saying he had met someone and gotten married. Heartbroken, I didn't want to stay in Golden that summer. So I decided to make the trip east anyway, to Québec. Since childhood, I had always wanted to go to Québec. I loved the French language and had a very sketchy idea of French-Canadian history.

***

In the summer of 1968, I took the Greyhound bus across Canada, stopping overnight in Winnipeg and Sault Ste. Marie. This was my first trip across the country, and making it alone gave me confidence. The first night in Montréal, I met a young woman, Lyse, in a bar. She was Québécoise and when she realized I wasn't a native French speaker, spoke English. She was experiencing marriage problems and living alone. She invited me to stay at her house. I wasn't there long, but her kindness helped me get a start. I went through a couple of jobs that summer, working for a pharmacy and later as a nanny for three kids living in the suburbs. The children were spoiled and, not being used to this, I lasted only three weeks, before heading back west on the train to Edmonton. I stayed with my uncle and aunt there for a day or two before taking the bus to Golden. I was gone a total of five or six weeks. But it was enough to deepen a love for Québec and to know I could handle myself in different cultural situations.

I couldn't adjust to being home and working in the store again. My mother was angry with me for being bitchy and influencing my younger sister. After that summer, I never went back to work in the store. During my third year, I met someone who worked at a truck stop along the Alaska Highway in the Yukon during the summers. So I wrote and got a job at Mendenhall Camp Lodge, north of Whitehorse on the way to Haines Junction. Later that summer I moved to Smith River and the following year to Muncho Lake, both near the British Columbia/Yukon border. I cleaned cabin rooms, made pastry and waitressed.

The hauntingly beautiful surroundings cemented my love of mountains. When we first got to the Yukon in May, people were using snowmobiles and nights came early. But summer arrived suddenly with its long days and beautiful magenta purple fireweed. On a break, I travelled to Haines Junction and on to Haines, Alaska. At a summit on the road, patches of snow still glistened, but when we descended to the town, we met an almost tropical climate of greenery and ferns.

On July 21, 1969, we watched Neil Armstrong walk on the moon on the small black and white TV in the café. That summer, I explored yoga and meditation through a book.

I was aware only at a superficial level of the Indigenous people who lived in the Yukon. A few First Nations people came to the restaurant from the bush, and one woman sold me a smoked leather hanging for a wedding present for my university friend Vivienne who got married at the end of the summer.

***

At some unconscious level, I took university courses that reflected my spiritual search. I studied the existentialist writers Simone de Beauvoir, Albert Camus and André Gide, as well as Shakespeare, comparative religion, the history of art. At one point, steeped in the existentialist philosophy of the French writers, I called myself an existentialist Catholic. Almost a contradiction in terms, to me it meant a belief in God, but also a moral responsibility for my own actions.

During the comparative religion course, we studied several universal religions including Judaism, Christianity, Buddhism and Islám. My term paper was on Buddhism. I also learned much from a course on the history of art.

Intrigued with how art reflects the great developments in religion and civilization, the period after 1000 AD when Christianity in Europe was influenced by Islám and the Moors held special interest for me.

***

I met Marlies Schoenfeld at a social gathering hosted by the professor of a senior level English course. Marlies was in her thirties, older than most of our classmates. She and her husband Hans had emigrated from Germany a few years before.

"Do you believe in God?" was my first question to her.

She nodded, with a surprised look on her face. As we chatted, we quickly became close and she invited me several times to visit with her family in North Vancouver. Marlies, a mother of two daughters, was a brilliant scholar who went on to get a PhD in comparative literature in Michigan.

The Schoenfeld living room looked out over Vancouver Harbour. On the wall was an evocative abstract painting, a ball of light of many hues of gold and peach. Marlies shared that she belonged to Rosicrucianism, a philosophical secret society said to have been founded in late medieval Germany by Christian Rosenkreuz. I was intrigued but never got into the teachings with her. I enjoyed the wonderful German cuisine Marlies prepared, especially the layered hazelnut torte, and the freedom to speak about God openly.

***

"Do you really believe it's a mortal sin not to go to church on Sunday?" my roommate asked.

Her question unnerved me. It was my last year at university, and I'd discovered the campus church that I enjoyed for its participatory atmosphere, faithfully attending each Sunday.

My roommate was a Swedenborgian, a Christian denomination that developed as a new religious movement, based on the writings of the Swedish scientist and theologian Emanuel Swedenborg who died in 1772. He claimed to have received a new revelation from Jesus Christ through continuous heavenly visions.

I started to cry, much to the dismay of my roommate, who had only asked a simple question. I couldn't answer her. I still had not deeply questioned some beliefs I grew up with, such as "once a Catholic, always a Catholic," or the infallibility of the Pope, or that partaking in communion was taking the body and blood of Christ. Or indeed if missing Mass on Sunday was a mortal sin.

My faith stood on an unstable foundation.

***

After four years of university in Vancouver, I finished an arts degree with a focus on French literature. I lined up a job with a company based in Québec City to teach conversational English to francophones. My dad planned to give me a car after graduation, and it was waiting at the end of the summer when I returned from the Yukon.

In retrospect, it's clear that my parents' hard work and staying together, despite their tumultuous life, gave me privilege. They helped with university so I had no debt at the end of the four years. Dad's gift, a brand new 1970 orange Volkswagen Beetle, gave me freedom. I had privilege because my grandparents emigrated from Ireland and from Croatia to make a life in Canada. Though both generations had to work hard, they made it possible for me to get an education.

Until recently I didn't see these things as privilege, because I felt the burden of being from a troubled family that didn't really fit in, and because of my own insecurities, timidity and lack of confidence. But I see now that just by virtue of being white and the stable middle class economic base from which I came, I had privilege.

CHAPTER FIVE

Québec and Halifax

Québec

My sister Coleen and I travelled across Canada in the fall of 1970 in my new car. Dad had added a radio, camping pots and a tent when we were heading out. Though I had gotten my license at sixteen, I never drove in Vancouver, so only had experience with small-town driving. On a side street to the Palliser Hotel in downtown Calgary, I freaked out when I had to use a manual transmission, while trying to stop and start again on a hill without rolling backwards.

We camped across the country and frequently our tent blew down in the prairie winds. We braved the 401 highway in Ontario to visit a friend's family in Toronto. In Montréal, we got on a roundabout and drove around it several times before learning how to get off. I seriously knew how to drive by the time we got to Québec City!

After Coleen flew home from Québec City, I stayed in a small room within the old walled city while getting training to teach conversational English. After three weeks, I moved to Rimouski, a small city on the southern shore of the St. Lawrence River on Québec's Gaspé Peninsula and found a room in a boarding house. At night, I offered conversational classes to adults at several different levels. The company had provided me with an audio-visual program with the goal of having people speak only English in class. I called my car "Clémentine," its colour in the French language, and "Clémentine" became a featured topic of conversation, especially for the classes with an elementary level of English.

At the end of the initial three months, the students wanted to continue but the company needed to move me on to another town. People had been kind and hospitable to me in Rimouski and I didn't want to leave. One of my students offered me his dance studio to conduct the classes, and we made that arrangement.

***

I stumbled over my words trying to respond to Huguette's question. We had met in the hallway of the boarding house where there was a tiny kitchen and stove shared by the boarders. Huguette Rioux and her younger sister Hélène were students from a small town who were attending Rimouski's college, the CEGEP. They had spoken to me in French. As soon as they realized I was an anglophone, they spoke more slowly.

Rimouski was a francophone, not bilingual, city, so in my classes I spoke only English to give my students exposure to the language. Through buying groceries, getting my new car serviced and going to the post office, I had brief chances to practice my French. Though I had a university degree in French and my grammar was quite good, the different accent and unique character of Québécois French challenged me. I often had to ask people to repeat what they'd said. But it was with Huguette and Hélène that I could practice the most. They were infinitely patient as I tried to express myself.

***

It was October 1970. Huguette and Hélène seemed tense when I met them in the hallway. Though I listened to the radio from time to time, I hardly understood what I was hearing. They took the time to share with me the October 5 kidnapping of James Cross, the British trade commissioner in Montréal, by members of the Front de Libération du Québec (FLQ). The October Crisis, as it became known, had begun. Over the next few weeks, whenever I saw them, Huguette and Hélène shared what had been happening. Another official, Minister of Immigration and Minister of Labour Pierre Laporte, was kidnapped as he played with his nephew on his front lawn.

Huguette and Hélène were nervous and strained. There was no evidence of the crisis in Rimouski, but in Québec City there were soldiers on the streets. Prime Minister Pierre Trudeau had brought in the War Measures Act, the only invocation of the act during peacetime in Canadian history. There were armed soldiers on Parliament Hill too.

My parents began phoning from British Columbia. Worried, they kept repeating that I could come home any time. I felt perfectly safe in Rimouski, and my friendly students had been inviting me to dinner.

On October 17, the body of Pierre Laporte was found in the trunk of a car left near Saint-Hubert airport. In early December, police discovered the cell holding James Cross and negotiated his release in return for safe conduct to Cuba for the kidnappers. Invoking the War Measures Act remained controversial for years.[20]

***

That fall, I often turned on the radio to get the time, but two hours later I still didn't know what time it was. Huguette and Hélène's coaching helped a lot. At Christmas, I visited a friend in New Brunswick with whom I had taken training, and we made a trip to the New England states. Amazingly, after the break when I returned to Rimouski, I understood much more of what was said in French.

I made only eighty dollars a week with the language company, but I was supporting myself. Later, when Dad found out how much I'd been making, he was upset and said I should have let him and Mom know. But I felt independent and loved living in Québec.

Huguette and Hélène invited me to their home for the weekend. They told me their parents had a new house. I was nervous, but eager.

***

The Rioux family lived on a farm just outside Trois-Pistoles, thirty-five miles from Rimouski. When we arrived, I saw their new farmhouse, a small simple two-storey home with a front veranda in the Québecois style. They lived on one of the historic farms along the shores of the St. Lawrence River, part of the seigneurial system that played a major role in traditional Québec society. I learned about the system in school and was thrilled to meet a family who still lived on the land. The Rioux farm was a long, narrow rectangle facing the St. Lawrence. It was less than half a kilometre wide and three or more kilometres back from the river. On another visit, I snowshoed up the gently graded hill behind their house.

Later, when I understood spoken French better, I learned that the Rioux family history goes back to the early days of French colonization in Canada when Jean Rioux, the son of a labourer from Brittany, exchanged property on île d'Orléans, near Québec City, for a seigneurie at Trois-Pistoles in 1696. Over 10,000 Rioux family members descended from this humble man who became a seigneur.[21]

***

I immediately felt at home with the Rioux family. I met parents Louis-Philippe and Madeleine, and Huguette and Hélène's siblings, Jean Guy, Christian, Francis and Marielle. The house was small inside and life revolved around the kitchen. Love and unity seemed to emanate from the very walls. What amazed me most was when supper was done, everyone got up and helped clear the table and they did the dishes together, all the while chatting and laughing. At my family home, we always fought about who would do the dishes.

Food was a big part of the Rioux family life. Their food was so delicious, I could hardly stop eating. They grew their own vegetables and raised dairy cattle. The table was always set for every meal, there was no grab and go. It was a very simple setting, often with a tablecloth. They ate lightly at breakfast and always had "dîner," their big meal, at noon. They started with simple soups, then wholesome meat and vegetables, then delicious desserts.

My bedroom was at the front of the house. I never slept so well as I did there. Several layers of thin blankets or handwoven spreads and flannel sheets kept me warm. The room was tiny, with old fashioned furniture and narrow windows, one on the front and one on the side. I loved to gaze out over the St. Lawrence River. There was such comfort falling asleep in that house, surrounded by loving people.

***

Mr. Rioux normally spoke very quickly and I sometimes had trouble discerning what he was saying. When he saw I didn't understand, he tried to slow down. Quite short of stature, Mr. Rioux had a straight nose, clear eyes, and was slightly balding. He had an inherent dignity that never wavered, whether he was wearing the overalls that he put on to milk cows or a suit for Sunday Mass. Over time, I became very close to Mr. Rioux. He had only grade four education, but was one of the most knowledgeable people I had ever met. He was self-educated, read widely and was completely informed of current events. He was active in several agricultural organizations and cooperatives to do with dairy farming.

I was used to Dad who was often passionate and liked to argue. With Mr. Rioux, no matter how fervent his beliefs were, it never degenerated into arguing, though I probably wouldn't have been able to anyway, given my French. To me, Mr. Rioux had a pure spirit and I felt we had a strong bond of affection.

Mrs. Rioux was effervescent and always happy. She loved nature and delighted in looking out her kitchen window to the fields stretching the length of the property behind their house. She took endless delight in everyday things, like a warm breeze, or the leaves waving in the wind or the first carrots pushing through the ground.

The Rioux were strong practicing Roman Catholics. But Mrs. Rioux's faith seemed to be firmly based in the things of everyday life.

***

My French gradually improved with the Rioux family's patient help, though I have always had an accent. Today, I see the guiding hand of God in my life when I met the Rioux family in my early twenties. Louis-Philippe was a male father figure who was strong, pure-hearted and moral, as well as being fully engaged with everyday life. The family presented a model of simplicity in living, unity and kindness.

We visited often that year. As we got to know each other, we laughed about the stereotypes French and English sometimes have about each other. They told me, "tous les Anglais ont le tableau de la reine sur les murs" ("all the English have a picture of the Queen on their walls"). Of course, coming from a Croatian and Irish background, my family definitely did not have a picture of the Queen on our walls! We joked about anglophones calling French-Canadians "grenouilles" or frogs, again something neither I nor my family did. I learned it was this close contact, this true friendship between people on a one-to-one basis, that could demolish prejudices and misconceptions we have about each other.

The Rioux lived in a rural area, but neighbours dropped in on them quite often. There were always discussions about current events with these neighbours and within the family. At the time, in the early seventies, the church still provided a lot of cultural support. I wondered if this rural life hadn't changed much in the past three centuries. All the Rioux children got a good education and had careers, moving away from farming life, though several still live in rural areas.

When I became a Bahá'í in 1975, I especially wanted to share this wonderful news with the Rioux family, and did so, a bit at a time, over a few years. I gave Louis-Philippe and Madeleine a French language book of Bahá'u'lláh's Writings. The last time we visited, Mr. Rioux seemed to have deeply grasped the essence of the Faith. I shared then that it was partly my meeting them that had prepared my heart to accept the Bahá'í teaching of the oneness of humanity when I encountered it. Reflecting on this, I believe their loving-kindness to a complete stranger, especially someone from the dominant culture in Canada, opened my heart. Through them, I developed a love and respect of their culture, particularly their strong family ties and sense of community.

The story of friendship with the Rioux family spans several decades to the present day. In the summer of 1971, I took my sister Tanya and the youngest Rioux daughter, Marielle, on a camping trip around the Gaspé Peninsula. I also travelled with Huguette and Hélène to Nova Scotia. After I had moved from Québec to Nova Scotia, I went back for the wedding of Huguette to Gilles Lebel. And after I got married a few short months later, Harry and I went to the Rioux home at Christmas during our honeymoon. While we lived in Nova Scotia, we went camping with Gilles and Huguette.

Other visits followed through the years, including a visit of Mr. and Mrs. Rioux to our home in Alberta. Some of their children and grandchildren also visited us in Alberta and visited my parents in British Columbia. I also visited the Rioux family in Trois-Pistoles with my mother, when she, Louis-Philippe and Madeleine were all in their eighties. Though she spoke no French and the Rioux elders spoke no English, they seemed to have a wonderful connection of hearts. Pierre-Louis, Hélène's son, did a little translation for Mom, and I brought out my rusty French.

***

Summer, 2001

We drive along the St. Lawrence River past the town of Trois-Pistoles, and I watch anxiously for the Rioux driveway. MaryAnne DeWolf and I are just starting out on a travelling-teaching trip to Bahá'í communities around the Gaspé Peninsula. The *Angus* book[22] came out a year ago, and we are visiting small Bahá'í communities to share stories from the book and other deepening themes we've developed. I lost my father to bone cancer just a few weeks ago.

I catch sight of the Rioux farmhouse and draw in my breath quickly. There, on the front veranda, are Louis-Philippe and Madeleine, sitting in their rocking chairs. Mr. Rioux, wearing his beret, rocks back and forth. They see us and begin to wave. We pull into the driveway and drive around to the back of the house. Louis-Philippe and Madeleine come through the house and out the back door. It has been eleven years since I've seen them. It seems a lifetime. I begin to cry.

Mr. Rioux, his face expressing concern, gives me a hug.

"Je t'ai toujours considerée comme ma quatrième fille (I've always considered you my fourth daughter)," he says gently. The Rioux were my French family.

***

Early in summer 1971, when I travelled to Halifax with Huguette and Hélène, I dropped in at *The Fourth Estate* newspaper, an alternative weekly paper. Nick Fillmore and his father, seasoned journalists, had started the newspaper in 1969. The co-editor was interested in me as a reporter, as I had some experience with high school and college newspapers. But they were on a shoestring budget and weren't hiring.

There was a job opening teaching English at the CEGEP back in Rimouski and I applied. I badly wanted a permanent job and to stay in Rimouski, and arranged to take over an apartment lease from a friend and to share this accommodation with Huguette and Hélène in the fall. Weeks went by, and I didn't hear anything about the job. I got a contract for a three-week course at the University of Rimouski to help teachers of English improve their spoken language. When it was over, still hearing nothing, I became increasingly anxious about not getting a job.

One of my adult students in Rimouski welcomed me to stay with her family temporarily. They invited me to a weekend Christian gathering called "La Rencontre" ("The Gathering"), a marriage retreat. That weekend, I had the first of what might be called mystical or spiritual experiences. During Mass, I felt connected to sky and earth, as if a thread of light passed through, binding me to both. In my vulnerable state and unsure of what the future held, this sensation confirmed to me that I was in God's hands though I probably wouldn't have put it in those words at the time.

Following the retreat, I decided I couldn't hold on to the apartment anymore and broke the lease, packing all my stuff up in the Volkswagen. I decided to move to Halifax and volunteer for *The Fourth Estate*. My mind was made up and just a few days before leaving, the CEGEP called and offered me the job I had wanted. By this time, my mind was already halfway to Halifax, so I turned it down.

***

Halifax

Late that summer, I moved from Rimouski to Halifax. I felt uprooted as I had dearly wished to remain in Québec, but the call from the CEGEP had come too late. Little did I know that the move would set my life in a completely new direction.

Margie, a friend I knew in Québec who also taught English there, moved to Halifax before me. We stayed in the YWCA for a few days and took a few days to camp on Nova Scotia's south shore. Then we found a small bachelor apartment to share in Rockingham, a suburb of Halifax. Three days later, we decided to go to a movie. I drove my orange Volkswagen Beetle with Québec plates on it down Gottingen Street, a main thoroughfare in Halifax, the windows wide open to let in the warm breezes. A car with Ontario plates pulled up on the right side, and Margie started talking to the two young men in the other car. We ended up going to a bar with them.

At one point, I talked with the young man from Ontario who owned the car, then we changed places and I started talking with Harry Verge, who lived in Halifax and worked for the Nova Scotia government. Harry and I ended up talking for days and days, and within a very short time, we decided to get married.

My mentor Mary Guichon had given me advice about choosing a marriage partner. She said "choose someone who would make a good father for your children." Looking back, I see this meant a focus on values and spiritual qualities. I intuitively knew when I met Harry that he would make a good father. Though our meeting seems like the classic pick-up story, we have been married for decades and Harry has been a kind and supportive husband, father and grandfather.

My roommate became quite possessive of me and anxious about my relationship with Harry, and it wasn't too long before she moved out. Harry and I got married just before Christmas that year on December 18, 1971, and he moved into the Rockingham bachelor apartment. Our wedding was small since none of my family could come from British Columbia; Christmas was a busy season in the store. I had started volunteer proofreading at *The Fourth Estate* newspaper, and the co-editor, Brenda Large, agreed to be my matron of honour.

We got married at the Catholic church in Rockingham. The priest did not insist on Harry, who was from an Anglican background, becoming a Catholic or even studying it. I sewed my wedding dress in a cream brocade, using a Vogue pattern, and drove myself to the church in my little Volkswagen, with flowers and corsages for the best man and matron of honour. With Harry's family, we were an even dozen. We drove to New England for our honeymoon and motored to Trois-Pistoles to spend Christmas with the Rioux family.

***

Early in the new year, I began a journey of intense learning. *The Fourth Estate*, which did investigative reporting into issues such as slum landlords and conditions in housing projects, found the money to hire me as a journalist. It was fascinating work, and Brenda worked closely with me to improve my writing. It was also stressful because the newspaper had set itself up to uncover issues and challenge the status quo, which ruffled feathers.

I was still searching for an inner sense of direction and security and wasn't finding it through work. My parents had given us a generous monetary wedding gift, and Harry wanted to travel. So we decided to go to Europe. After a year at the newspaper, I gave my notice; Harry gave his notice at the government, and we prepared to leave.

Before leaving for Europe, we made a trip out west for Harry to meet my family for the first time. We flew into Calgary, and my parents and Mary Guichon met us. They liked Harry immediately. We travelled from Calgary to Golden over snowy, icy roads. I was extremely nervous about Dad's driving, even though he was a competent driver and never had a major accident in his life. But the conditions were treacherous. We spent a couple of weeks in British Columbia and travelled out to Vancouver, again on icy roads.

CHAPTER SIX

Europe and The Search Continues

Returning to Halifax, we joined up with Harry's friend Greg Giffin, who had been his best man, and flew to England in January 1973. A high school friend, Heather, lived there and had married Stewart, an Englishman. We visited with them in Devon and then parted ways with Greg, who continued travelling for a number of years. My dream was fulfilled when we stayed in the same York youth hostel as I had just after high school. York is a beautiful walled city and we explored it and the Lake Country with Heather and Stewart.

Harry and I carried on to continental Europe after our English visit. I was surprised to find in our travel journal, unearthed recently, mention of my deep belief in God. While I think of my Catholic upbringing as mostly ritualistic, I had picked up a spiritual thread, however fragile, after my happy year in Québec and the marriage retreat in Rimouski where I felt connected with a greater power than myself. And then I had met Harry so soon after being "kicked out of Québec," which I did not think had been a coincidence.

I noted in the diary that our trip across the English Channel was a low point of the trip so far. We had hitchhiked to Dover and stayed overnight in a hostel. Then we decided on a whim that, unlike most tourists who took the ferry to Calais, France, we would go to Dunkerque, a town ten kilometres from the Belgian border. Though we were an hour early for the trip, the ferry left two hours late, and because of docking through the lock system in Dunkerque, we didn't arrive until 6 p.m., too late to change our money to francs. We walked from the port into town–really quite a long walk–and started to look for hotels, beginning with a little Chinese one and going the gamut. They were all full; Dunkerque is very industrial, and while it doesn't have a lot of tourists, there are many people continuously coming in on business. I described the evening:

> It started to hail and was very cold, and I was getting down a lot. One hotelier sent us to the police—they were totally unhelpful about cashing cheques...we went to a tobacconist and he wouldn't change the money—said the value of the American dollar was steadily dropping...so that got us down more. We literally didn't know what to do so we went to the church (no one will EVER take my faith away from me)...In the church a concert had just been cancelled so we slipped in and sat down to try and get warm. We hoped the last people would leave but they didn't so we went out again but it was so cold we went back to the church. I told the men our problem so one of them in a Citroen (posh) drove us to a number of hotels (all full). We were just about despairing completely when we landed on one—Hotel Modern near Rue Louis Vanraet. It was expensive...because she charged us for two beds but we were really thankful and fell asleep promptly without supper.

I find it interesting that in this entry I attribute the help we got to God.

Harry and I hitchhiked through France, staying in youth hostels, some quite dirty. In one hostel, I awoke to find someone tugging at my pillow, under which I had hidden my passport and money. Responding quickly in French, I frightened him off. Rainy grey days followed us, but we enjoyed when we got rides that took us along treelined roads, and delighted in fresh French bread and café au lait at bed and breakfasts when we didn't stay in hostels.

A highlight for me was visiting the cathedral at Chartres southwest of Paris. Chartres, one of the finest examples of French Gothic architecture, has a vast nave and beautiful stained-glass windows that filter light into the building. I was impressed by the primitive sculptured characters on the outside, whose emotion-filled faces looked awestruck. Building started in 1145 and stretched over many decades. I marveled at the selflessness of the nameless people who had worked on the building, had subjugated their own egos, and worked so physically hard, with no cranes or big machines. They had received no personal recognition; all was done to pay homage to God.

***

Because of the cold, Harry and I determined to get to the south coast of Spain as soon as we could. Our goal in going there was to go into Africa, to Rabat, Morocco, where we were to meet my university friend, Marlies Schoenfeld, who was very ill.

Our hitchhiking adventures took us south through Bordeaux, to a city called Pau on the northern edge of the Pyrenees. We travelled into Spain through the Basque region and were lucky enough to get a ride to Tordesillas—only 179 km from Madrid—with a French truck driver. Because it was winter and cold, we couldn't appreciate the beauty of the areas we were travelling through. Having been able to speak French in France, it was much harder to communicate when we reached Spain. In Tordesillas, we had no idea what to order from the menu. We ordered "sopa" and the soup that arrived was, in the words of Harry, "about the same constitution as Grade D axle grease!" Fortunately, the rest of the meal was tastier; we were nearly hysterical laughing over the soup.

We spent several days in Madrid, visiting the famous Prado museum, going late at night to a special Spanish dance performance, and walking a lot. We both came down with bad colds. Then we took the train to Malaga, on the Costa del Sol on the Mediterranean Sea. We went on to Estepona to visit friends. I was surprised to see in our journal that these friends lived in an area called Bahai Eldorado. The word "Bahai" never twigged on me then. I may have spelled the name wrong, and it should have been Bahia. Perhaps a spiritual thread still followed me. We spent three weeks in Estepona while waiting to go to Morocco to visit with Marlies. My cold developed into bronchitis, which I finally got treated with antibiotics.

In mid-March, we took a bus from Estepona to Algeciras, a port city in the south of Spain on the Bay of Gibraltar. From there we took a ferry to Tangiers, Morocco, then a train to Rabat. I wrote about my first encounter with Africa, the only time I have been to that continent. The ferry ride was rough, and we passed Gibraltar, the boat following both the coast of Spain and North Africa.

Surprising to me, the coast of N. Africa is mountainous, it seemed exciting coming to another continent...the (train) ride took us through some terrific country—quite mountainous and green at first, then gradually flattening out. Such a change—small, primitive houses, some just shacks, mosque-like architecture, camels, many people in the long cloaks, women with veils. Often a lone shepherd, people in the fields, most roads not paved. A beautiful day and sunset across the plains.

***

My friend Marlies was visiting her sister and family in Rabat where her brother-in-law worked for the Goethe Institute. Shortly after receiving her doctorate in comparative literature, Marlies was diagnosed with a terminal form of cancer. We found her in constant pain. Marlies had a strong willpower and took codeine to keep going. The first day we went sightseeing in Rabat, to the famous Hassan Tower, the unfinished minaret for a mosque that was not completed because of the death of the Sultan; the Mausoleum of Muhammad V, king of Morocco; and the Chellah, a necropolis and complex of ancient Roman ruins. Over the next few days, Harry and I explored Rabat on our own and saw Marlies and her family from time to time. They were kind to us and let us do our laundry at their home. Marlies gave me an envelope with money for a meal that she asked us to enjoy on her behalf. But she wasn't well enough to leave the house again.

***

I visited Marlies for the last time in her sister's home. She planned to leave early to return to Canada because she couldn't get the medication she needed in Rabat. She was having unrelenting pain.

When I came into the room, Marlies was in her bed. The curtains were closed; only a gloomy light filtered in. Marlies smiled weakly and welcomed me.

Marlies was in her early forties, in the prime of her life, and she had reached the pinnacle of her career. She said with a trace of bitterness that she was dying just when things should be getting started. I felt sad and disturbed, having nothing to offer, nothing that could bring comfort. We shared a love of literature and spiritual ideas, but I had no wisdom or insights that would sound like anything more than platitudes. I was haunted by this.

***

Marlies died a few months after returning to Canada. How relieved I was to find, some years later, a wealth of wisdom about the eternal journey of the soul and the existence of worlds beyond this world, as I delved into the Bahá'í Writings. I never again wanted to be bereft of spiritual medicine when encountering a heart in distress.

***

After saying goodbye to Marlies and her relatives, we travelled to Fes, then north to Ceuta and across to Algeciras in Spain. We took a bus to Estepona, spent a few nights, then set out to travel north by hitchhiking.

We had Canadian flags on the knapsacks we carried, as we didn't want to be mistaken for Americans. But through our travels, we met some young Americans who were sensitive over the "Ugly American" stereotype about arrogant Americans abroad, and humble and open to learning. We also met a few obnoxious Canadians in some hostels. This began to blow our stereotypes.

We found hitchhiking in Spain difficult and made it up the coast of Spain slowly, taking buses out of large cities to smaller places where it was easier to hike. In two days, we hitched for twenty hours and only covered about 200 kilometres. But outside of Barcelona, we got lucky. A couple who were with the Canadian army in Lahr, Germany, picked us up and drove us all the way to Freiburg, Germany. They even put up with the fact that at the Swiss border, the guards took apart their tail lights and went through the car, no doubt because they had hippie hitchhikers with them. Through this Canadian couple, we learned that civilians could get jobs on Canadian military bases in Germany. This proved providential for us later. After they dropped us off, we spent a few days in Freiburg, a lovely town in Germany's Black Forest region. We then decided to hitchhike to Rotterdam to try our luck getting work on a ship to Australia.

***

Harry and I quickly found out that the only available ship jobs were for dog-handlers, for which neither of us qualified. After several weeks in Rotterdam, we decided to look for work on the Canadian base. Our good luck hitchhiking held, and we got a ride right on to the Canadian Air Force base at Baden-Sollingen in the Black Forest region. Our first stop was the base's newspaper, where we met Corporal Ray Schuler, a Canadian Indigenous man who was in charge of the paper. He gave us information about jobs for civilians and kindly invited us to stay at his home for a couple of days, as his wife Rhonda, also a soldier, was away on a military exercise. Within a couple of days, Harry had a job as a clerk in the base's auto club that sold auto parts, and I had a job as a clerk in the Canex warehouse. We found a small apartment one kilometre from the base, in the tiny village of Hugelsheim, and bought secondhand twin-size beds, one saggy and soft, the other lumpy and hard, and pushed them together. A small table, two chairs and donated dishes and pots expanded the contents of our knapsacks.

Our employers knew we were there to travel and generously gave us time off in the fourteen months we stayed on the base. We bought a small Renault sports car through the auto club and travelled frequently to France, Switzerland and throughout Germany. We took bus trips offered to military personnel or to their families, to Florence, Italy and another to Russia (still behind the Iron Curtain). My sister Coleen came to Germany, and we travelled through Austria and France and over to England.

***

Work in the warehouse was boring and I struggled to understand what path I should be taking. On the side, I took on a night course teaching English to francophone wives of Canadian soldiers. Though we had an exciting life on the surface, inside, my sense of self was battered. Angst simmered underneath the surface of work, travel and friendships. I didn't find comfort in attending the Catholic church on the base and stopped going.

It was an easy drive to France, only a few kilometres over the border from the base, to explore the countryside. Strasbourg is a city in the historic area of Alsace-Lorraine, which changed hands between France and Germany many times over the years. Its crown jewel is the magnificent Cathedral of Our Lady of Strasbourg, one of the most beautiful Gothic cathedrals of Europe, constructed of pinkish sandstone, all its contours pointing to the sky. In its hushed interior, I bathed in the reflected light of its stained-glass windows and towering arches.

***

I wake suddenly in the middle of the night in our tiny upstairs apartment. I am quivering, and uttering the words "joie, joie, certitude:" joy, joy, certainty. What have I just experienced? Was it a dream or a vision?

Whatever it was, I found myself in Strasbourg Cathedral under the beautiful stained glass window. But unlike the deep blues, yellows, greens and reds of the stunning rose window of the actual cathedral, the window panes in my dream were clear. The light reached through them and shone through me. I became the light. Then I woke up or came to, uttering the words.

***

I had no idea why the words in my dream/vision came to me in French, except that they were words I had read while studying maxims of a seventeenth century French writer at university. I had a similar other-worldly feeling to the one I had at the marriage retreat in Québec. There was some hope in the words "joy, certainty." It was another thread in my search.

***

Maddie and Ray Wingett were Canadians who came to live and work in Germany. Ray worked at the warehouse repairing stereo equipment. He was quiet and wore a ring with a large ringstone symbol. In the warehouse coffee room, there was always a lot of gossip. One of the employees said Ray belonged to a weird religion. I was definitely not interested in a weird religion. "Once a Catholic, always a Catholic" was still my credo, despite my struggles with the Church. Maddie stopped by the warehouse every once in a while. Very friendly, she was seventeen years older than me. But we soon found plenty in common, especially from our similarly troubled childhoods.

She had discovered the book *The Primal Scream*,[23] which she loaned me. By Arthur Javov, it has become one of the classic explorations into the causes and cures of neuroses and the use of primal therapy. Our discussions may have started me on a lifetime of browsing through psychology articles and books. I heard the name of their religion, Bahá'í, but I wasn't interested in even inquiring. But I always looked forward to chats with Maddie.

***

Maddie and Ray lived in the beautiful spa city of Baden-Baden. One night they invited Harry and me to their tiny second-floor apartment. I was struck by the warmth of their welcome and the brightness of the place despite its size. And Maddie had baked homemade cookies, one sure way to get to my heart. Sitting in the living room, I noticed a notepad on a side table with a long, handwritten letter to a friend. I didn't know what the letter was about, but secretly wished someone would write long letters like that to me.

At the end of the pleasant evening, with my hand on the doorknob so I could bolt if necessary, I asked Maddie about her faith. She sensed my resistance and didn't jump in with a bunch of information. She mentioned two names, of the co-founders, the Báb and Bahá'u'lláh. I remembered my Swedenborgian friend from university, equated the strange names, and thought cynically to myself, "Oh sure."

But then Maddie said something else. "This is a religion for humanity in its maturity," she stated. This bothered me very much. I was twenty-six-years-old and not feeling mature in my dead-end job, interesting but unfocused travels, and underlying discontent.

***

The Wingetts were returning to Canada that fall as we were. We had one more visit with them at our home before they left. Though we had some unnerving experiences running into smug Canadian travellers at hostels while hitchhiking, I still spouted off proudly how great it was to be Canadian, not American. Maddie spoke up.

"You know, I'm very grateful to have been born in Canada," she said humbly. "But I consider myself a citizen of the world."

I drew my breath in sharply and felt momentarily ashamed though Maddie didn't intend to shame me. She was simply stating truth and my heart recognized that truth. My trumped-up patriotism crumbled. Later we found out Maddie and Ray were Bahá'í pioneers[24] to Baden-Baden. They had followed their daughter Sharon and her husband, who were travelling as musicians through Europe. Maddie and Ray had left a large home and comfortable middle-class life in Canada to pioneer twice, first to Iceland, and then to Germany, where they lived on a shoestring. But I didn't know any of that right then. Maddie had planted a few seeds in ground thirsting for truth.

***

After several weeks travelling in Scandinavia and Québec, we returned to Halifax that fall. When we arrived, a letter was waiting from Maddie. She and Ray had moved back to Ontario. She casually asked if I could look up how many Bahá'ís there were in Halifax, because she felt a bit isolated where she was and wanted to know how communities were doing in other areas. I liked Maddie a lot, but as much as I wanted to respond to her request, I knew I couldn't find out what she wanted to know without actually looking into the religion. And I wasn't ready to do that.

My restlessness continued. We stayed with Harry's parents for several months in their small cramped home. Harry soon had a job with the Bedford Institute of Oceanography, and we found our own apartment near Dalhousie University. I dropped into *The Fourth Estate* and Brenda asked me to do a freelance article on multicultural education. I put in resumés around town and tried writing fiction.

After resolutely leaving the Catholic Church during our European stay, I felt compelled to go back. Curiously, though so much troubled me about the Church, I never thought of investigating a Protestant denomination. The church was walking distance from where we lived. The presiding priest was the Bishop of Halifax. Though he had never spoken to me personally, one day during the sermon, he looked straight at me and said in a thundering voice, "We must REALLY pray to God and then REALLY listen to what He says."

Thunderstruck, I began questioning myself. Why is he staring at me when he says this? What shows in my demeanour? Do I look so needy? So pathetically searching for truth? The man might have only been randomly looking at me, but in my state of mind, I was shaken. That it bothered me so much only underlined my deep distress.

Seemingly random things happened in the next few weeks. I attended a women's conference at Mount Saint Vincent University. We moved into small groups and I found myself attracted to the energy of the facilitator of my group, Joyce Edmonds. She mentioned doing service in Preston, a predominantly African-American area near Halifax, close to where Harry and I had lived before leaving for Europe. At lunch, I sat down with her and asked, "Joyce, whatever possessed you to go out to the Preston area?" Her answer: "Well, I'm a Bahá'í." That word again.

I was excited to meet another Bahá'í and again, wisely, Joyce didn't tell me too much. I was intrigued by people who reached out to another population. This would later become a main thrust of my life.

***

It took several months to finally decide to contact the Bahá'ís. I noticed an ad in the daily Halifax paper, *The Chronicle Herald*, for a Bahá'í public meeting in January. So I finally called the Bahá'í number in the phone book and found out the weekly informal "fireside"[25] meetings took place on Bishop Street in Halifax. "Fireside" is an interesting word, I thought. I knew the Lieutenant-Governor's residence, a fine old classical building in the Georgian style, was at the corner of Bishop and Barrington Streets. So I was thinking we would sit in front of a fireplace, sip tea and talk intellectually about religion. Probably there would be middle-aged people there. And that was okay with me.

But that wasn't what happened. The fireside was in the home of Spencer and Bonnie McCleave, young university students, and it was in a tenement building at the other end of Bishop Street. Harry and I climbed up to the third-floor apartment. The living room had no furniture; we sat on the carpet and leaned back on cushions. A picture of a man with a white beard hung on the wall as we entered. I later found out it was 'Abdu'l-Bahá, the eldest son of the founder Bahá'u'lláh, who is considered the perfect exemplar of the Bahá'í teachings.

Young people filled the room; they had come to hear about the Bahá'í Faith as an assignment for their university course. Spencer had a flip chart and gave a concise talk about the history, principles, and laws of the Faith. The students took notes; then they stood up and left.

Harry and I were left sitting with a few young people. I pounded them with questions about Jesus Christ. They said Bahá'ís revere Jesus as a Manifestation (or Messenger) of God. They said this new revelation of Bahá'u'lláh fulfilled all of Christ's promises about His Second Coming and the building of the Kingdom of God on earth, prophesied by all past religions.

Then I asked my most burning question: "What are we supposed to be doing with our lives?"

The answer was completely unexpected. A young man with his long hair in a ponytail replied, "We should become channels for the light." Stunned, I was immediately taken back to my vision/dream in Germany of the rose window at Strasbourg Cathedral, the feeling of being part of the light, and the Québec marriage retreat where I felt one with earth and sky.

Then Bonnie McCleave said, "Of course, our purpose is to know and to love God." I thought to myself, "I have heard that all my life, almost as a platitude. But this young woman is saying it with sincerity."

It felt like I was coming home. All my questions had been answered. Spencer loaned me an introductory book. As we left, Harry asked what I thought and I replied, "I think I'm already a Bahá'í."

***

All week I devoured the book Spencer loaned me, *Bahá'u'lláh and the New Era*, by John Esslemont. I was ecstatic. God had not left humanity alone; we hadn't been abandoned. There was a new Messenger of God and new teachings to bring about a united world, one in which all people see themselves as one human family in its glorious diversity. A few days later, I phoned Bonnie and asked how a person became a Bahá'í. She said that when we recognize Bahá'u'lláh as the Manifestation of God for today, we are already a Bahá'í in our heart. There was a declaration card I could fill out for administrative purposes. I was eager to do so and filled out the application for enrollment on January 19, 1975.[26]

One of the Bahá'ís told me later she thought I'd never become a Bahá'í, because I had so many questions that first night. But I had received satisfying answers to all those questions.

CHAPTER SEVEN

Immersion in the Ocean and Yellowknife

"We have created you from one tree and have caused you to be as the leaves and fruit of the same tree, that haply ye may become a source of comfort to one another."[27]

My spiritual journey, begun in Williams Lake while gazing down on the people at the Stampede grounds, now took a leap forward. The Halifax community actively nurtured me and my participation in gatherings. A reader, I plunged into any available books and kept coming across ideas that made sense. With respect to how humanity can understand God, I found great clarity and comfort in the concept that the Creator is essentially unknowable.

> ...God is almighty, but His greatness cannot be brought within the grasp of human limitation. We cannot limit God to a boundary. Man is limited, but the world of Divinity is unlimited. Prescribing limitation to God is human ignorance. God is the Ancient, the Almighty; His attributes are infinite. He is God because His light, His sovereignty, is infinite. If He can be limited to human ideas, He is not God.[28]

I found the Faith's teachings freed the mind of confining thoughts and concepts. One day, while walking along Spring Garden Road in Halifax, I saw a little church. The realization dawned that it wasn't necessary to be in a particular building to pray. Any spot on the planet "where mention of God hath been made" is blessed. A prayer by Bahá'u'lláh, *Blessed is the Spot*, seemed to exemplify this new understanding.

> Blessed is the spot, and the house, and the place, and the
> city, and the heart, and the mountain, and the refuge, and
> the cave, and the valley, and the land, and the sea, and the
> island, and the meadow where mention of God hath been
> made, and His praise glorified.[29]

The doors of my mind were flung wide open. I also found beautiful explanations of the oneness underlying all religions in such words as these: "The foundations of the divine religions are one. If we investigate these foundations, we discover much ground for agreement, but if we consider the imitations of forms and ancestral beliefs, we find points of disagreement and division; for these imitations differ, while the sources and foundations are one and the same."[30] The quote went on to state emphatically that if we lack love for humanity or show hatred and bigotry to anyone, this violates the foundations of our own beliefs.

Bahá'u'lláh strongly advocated independent investigation of truth, so important a practice that it will pave the way to harmony between religions as humanity discovers the truths brought by all the divine Prophets. Later I learned that Bahá'í teachings recognize the existence of messengers or holy people who brought teachings to Indigenous peoples.

A course I had enjoyed at university and that made the most sense to me was art history. I learned there are patterns to history that are reflected in the artistic expressions that endure: paintings, ceremonies, sculptures, cathedrals, mosques, cave drawings, music, poetry and literature. Now my understanding of and interest in history took a giant leap forward. I saw that the rise and fall of civilizations had a direct correlation with the advent of a Manifestation of God and that, indeed, all the revelations are connected. These words from a summary presented by the Guardian of the Bahá'í Faith, Shoghi Effendi,[31] to the Special UN Committee on Palestine in 1947, clarified this concept of "progressive revelation."

> The fundamental principle enunciated by Bahá'u'lláh, the
> followers of His Faith firmly believe, is that religious truth
> is not absolute but relative, that Divine Revelation is a con-
> tinuous and progressive process, that all the great religions
> of the world are divine in origin, that their basic principles

are in complete harmony, that their aims and purposes are one and the same, that their teachings are but facets of one truth, that their functions are complementary, that they differ only in the non-essential aspects of their doctrines and that their missions represent successive stages in the spiritual evolution of human society.[32]

History, which had been the most boring subject to me in high school, suddenly came alive.

***

Within a short time of enrolling, I phoned Maddie and shared that I had joined the Faith. She burst out in tears and soon began to write long letters to me, filled with encouragement and wisdom. Maddie wrote letters to me for years, sharing mutual spiritual struggles and relevant teachings of the Faith, imparting health advice and supporting my spiritual journey. Today we would call it "accompaniment." I cherished those letters. My secret wish, made in Maddie and Ray's Baden-Baden apartment, for someone to write long letters to me, had come true.

I had been actively looking for work since getting back from Europe. Not long after I enrolled as a Bahá'í, the Canadian Broadcasting Corporation (CBC) called me to come in for an interview. The interviewers said they never looked at resumés, but this time they had, and flagged mine. They hired me to work as a program assistant with "Information Morning," the radio breakfast show with hosts Don Tremaine and Russ Kelly, helping set up interviews, writing introductions for the hosts to read, and occasionally doing studio direction. It was exciting and stimulating work.

Several months after joining the Faith, during the National Bahá'í Convention at the university in Guelph, Ontario, I met up with Maddie and Ray for the first time since we'd all returned from Germany. Despite my delight in having encountered the Faith, I was plagued with a deep sense of unworthiness due to my background and weaknesses. My roommate in the dorm at the convention came from a prominent Bahá'í family, was younger than me, upbeat and full of confidence. One morning, she said she'd had a dream about me the night before. The message from the dream was, "If Pat can be here, anyone can be here." I think her dream was true, and, no doubt she meant it to sound encouraging, but the remark exacerbated my sense of worthlessness.

Maddie and Ray insisted that, no matter what the weakness or struggle, I had a right to be there like everyone else. I wasn't inherently defective. No one else was perfect, either. A beautiful teaching about the nobility of human beings has sustained me since.

"O Son of Spirit! Noble have I created thee, yet thou hast abased thyself. Rise then unto that for which thou wast created."[33]

Maddie bolstered my fragile self-worth for years through her letters, love, and understanding of complicated human backgrounds. In Halifax, Fran Maclean, a Bahá'í several years older than me with a background in journalism, took me under her wing. We met regularly at a vegetarian restaurant for lunch, and she gradually helped deepen my faith through her example and character. The friendship reminds me of Bahá'u'lláh's *Hidden Word*, "Treasure the companionship of the righteous and eschew all fellowship with the ungodly."[34] Association with Fran, Sarah Lynk and Shirley Macdonald, backbones of the Halifax community for years, burnished my soul and began to cleanse it of the rust of ego and attachment to worldly things, a process that is ongoing to this day. Many years later, I thanked Fran for her kindness in deepening me. In her humble fashion, she replied that she saw it as "sharing."

Up to then, drinking had been a big part of our social life. But because of the Bahá'í law prohibiting alcohol and drug use for non-medical purposes, I stopped immediately. Shortly after, Harry and I went to dinner at a friend's. I was apprehensive about telling anyone I no longer drank, and there were a few people I didn't know at the supper. When the host offered me wine, twice, and I refused, she said, "What's the *matter* with you, Pat?" I mumbled that I'd become a Bahá'í. No one said anything.

A few days later, one of the Halifax Bahá'ís told me his business partner had been at the dinner and met me. "He was really impressed," he said. My worries about not drinking disappeared after that.

***

I was elected to the local nine-member Spiritual Assembly[35] on a by-election sometime during that first year, and the friends gently educated me on Bahá'í administration. Then, for the celebration of World Religion Day 1976, Fran put forward my name to be the Bahá'í speaker on a panel about the meaning of worship in our respective faiths. Fran herself would have been a wonderful speaker, but she coached me, a new Bahá'í, by suggesting references from the Writings to prepare the talk. Panel members included a Mi'kmaq elder, a Jew, a Muslim and a Christian. The Christian speaker was the Bishop of Halifax whose church I had attended. I had never done public speaking before and was the only woman on the panel. The Hand of the Cause of God Ramatu'lláh Muhajir[36] was travelling through Halifax at the time. On the day of the event, when someone suggested he do the talk instead of me, he declined, saying that since I had prepared, I should do it, another example of encouragement and humility. I was very nervous, but the whole time I was speaking, Dr. Muhajir kept nodding his head, and I was filled with energy. He helped with wisely answering audience questions after the panel members spoke.

Adrienne Reeves, who served as an Auxiliary Board member,[37] came to give a talk in Halifax and focused on the wonderful Tablet of Bahá'u'lláh with the words "Release yourselves, O nightingales of God, from the thorns and brambles of wretchedness and misery, and wing your flight to the rose-garden of unfading splendor."[38] Her passion for the Writings and joyfulness were contagious. She later attended the unit convention, and when she saw I hadn't contributed to the consultation, encouraged me to speak up. It was easier to speak the next time, after her little push. I share these few stories to show how kindly and practically the Bahá'ís helped my first steps in the Faith.

At the unit convention I met Greg Johnson, a Mi'kmaq Bahá'í from the Eskasoni Reserve on Cape Breton Island, a First Nation community that has had an active Spiritual Assembly for many years.[39] Greg married Linda Gray who coincidently was a cousin of Julie Gray, Harry's sister-in-law, married to his brother Ken Verge. We were moving to Yellowknife, and when I told Greg, he said, "Oh, there's a lot of Indians up there." I was finally going to re-connect.

***

Harry had been offered a job working for the Territorial Government in Yellowknife, Northwest Territories. When my colleagues at the CBC learned we were moving, they wanted to take me out for lunch. My departure fell within the Bahá'í Fast in March,[40] and I explained why I couldn't make it to lunch. A few days before leaving, I got a call at five in the morning. The director of the show said they wanted me to come in and work. I groaned.

"Oh, I can't lie to you," she said. "We're having a going-away breakfast for you in the studio."

I hurriedly got dressed and rushed down to the studio to find my colleagues making pancakes and bacon. Show host Don Tremaine explained the noise in the background by saying, "Don't worry about the noise in the background. We're having a going-away breakfast for Pat Verge. She belongs to a weird religion where they starve all day and eat all night."

We had a great breakfast before the sun came up, and I was so happy he didn't name the religion!

***

After I became a Bahá'í, my enthusiasm boiled over and I shared my new-found faith with as many friends and family as possible. I was most vulnerable to how Mary Guichon, my mentor and a lifelong Catholic, might react to me changing faiths. When I visited her on my way to Yellowknife, she listened respectfully and accepted a gift of Bahá'u'lláh's writings. I was grateful she didn't criticize or minimize what was a huge discovery in my life.

***

Yellowknife

We moved to Yellowknife in 1976. My first real contact with First Nations and Inuit people began there. Many political changes were going on in the Indigenous community at this time. In 2012, at the Association for Bahá'í Studies conference in Montréal, lawyer and Indigenous rights activist Louise Mandell told us of the important activism of the late 1970s and early 1980s in Indigenous communities to make sure they were included in constitutional talks as the constitution was being "patriated" from Great Britain.[41]

Back then, I kept somewhat aloof from Native politics, trying to follow the Baháʼí principle of non-involvement in partisan politics. But I now believe that non-involvement is no excuse for ignorance! Setting myself to learn, so many years later, I see that many things would have made so much more sense had I known Canadian history. For example, Roy Daniels, an Indigenous believer originally from Manitoba, planned a workshop for the Yellowknife Baháʼís to increase our awareness of Indigenous history and issues. It took place at the Tree of Peace Friendship Centre. Though it was a full day, I remember being surprised when Roy expressed a bit of frustration at the slow pace we were going. Now I understand why—how much there is to learn and how ignorant we were.

I became aware at this time of an astounding promise in the *Tablets of the Divine Plan*. These Tablets, addressed by ʻAbduʼl-Bahá to the North American Baháʼís between 1916 and 1917, provide a vision of the world's spiritual revival. They hold a special message about the destiny of the "original inhabitants of the Americas."

> Attach great importance to the indigenous population of America. For these souls may be likened unto the ancient inhabitants of the Arabian Peninsula...When the light of Muhammad shone forth in their midst...they became so radiant as to illumine the world. Likewise, these Indians, should they be educated and guided, there can be no doubt that they will become so illumined as to enlighten the whole world.[42]

This quote has propelled many generations of outreach to Indigenous people in the Americas. Not until I later did research on the life of Angus Cowan did I find out how many efforts had already been made by the Canadian Baháʼí community in many areas of Canada and in Yellowknife itself.[43]

I first worked for the *Yellowknifer* newspaper owned by Jack "Sig" Sigvaldason and his wife, Mae. Jack hired me and encouraged me to do human interest stories on some of the early Yellowknifers still living in town. Later I wrote stories for the magazine *Arctic in Colour*. The paper at that time covered Indigenous issues to a lesser degree, but this has changed dramatically in the subsequent years as Sig's company *News North* has spread, with outlets in many Northwest Territories and Nunavut communities. Due to Sig's leadership (and later Mike Scott's), the company has kept up with the times. As a reporter, I had the opportunity to travel to the Eastern Arctic and to the Mackenzie Delta to cover some stories.

In the mid-70s, the Mackenzie Valley Pipeline Inquiry, also known as the Berger Inquiry,[44] was held in the North. Justice Thomas Berger consulted extensively with Indigenous peoples and at its conclusion, called for a moratorium for twenty years on development of the Mackenzie Valley pipeline.

A strong sense of community develops in isolated areas, and we found ourselves attached to our life and friends in Yellowknife. Not surprisingly, we felt the underlying tension between the Indigenous inhabitants and those who had come from "outside." Those tensions made me nervous. I visited, with other Bahá'ís, in the nearby village of Dettah (Yellowknives Dene First Nation) and participated in tea dances. Some Yellowknife Bahá'ís made trips to Rae-Edzo, now known as Behchokǫ̀, where Bill and Cindy Gilday worked as school teachers. The Gildays opened their home and provided wonderful breakfasts to people who came out from Yellowknife. We sometimes stayed over and made a few home visits to local residents. People were living traditional lives, hunting and speaking their language. Some Bahá'í teaching had been done in earlier years, and we contacted a few people who had become Bahá'ís. Because we weren't consistent and didn't have tools to deepen, our contact with the local Indigenous people was somewhat superficial.

***

In 1977, Harry took a trip on his own to Australia and New Zealand, and I made a travelling-teaching trip to Québec during the Fast. I visited Québec City, Rimouski, Trois-Pistoles to once again see the Rioux family, Rivière-du-loup, Sherbrooke and Montréal. It was a wonderful opportunity to reconnect with old friends, share my new-found faith, and make a small contribution to the teaching work in Québec.

***

Pilgrimage

When I first joined the Baháʼí community and people spoke of the Shrines and historical buildings in the Holy Land, I had no interest in going on a pilgrimage. During our time in Europe, I had my fill of cathedrals, churches and museums and thought it would be more of the same. But one day during prayers, it came to me to apply for pilgrimage. I received an invitation to the Baháʼí World Centre in Israel in February, 1978. Harry decided to go to Egypt and Kenya during this time, so we flew together from Yellowknife to London. I was nervous about going on to Israel alone. Harry joked about my fears.

"Oh, you'll be so busy meditating and praying, you won't have time to be nervous." I thought to myself, nine days of praying. That sounds tedious.

***

There was nothing boring about Israel as I feared. I was intoxicated by its beauty, especially in the Baháʼí Holy Places. The air seemed rarified, shot through with sacredness. I had never experienced anything like it before. None of the cathedrals I visited in Europe had such spirit. It was February and the temperatures were in the mid-teens Celsius, a far cry from the deep cold of Yellowknife. The fresh, crisp colours of the trees, grass and flowers shimmered.

The simplicity touched my heart. We first visited the Shrine of the Báb, the forerunner of the Baháʼí Faith, who sacrificed his young life at age thirty to announce the coming of a Divine Educator who would bring the peoples of the world together. In the Shrine, there were beautiful Persian carpets, on which we could stand, sit or kneel, but no furniture, few ornaments. The threshold, behind which the Báb's remains were entombed, was covered with fresh rose petals.

Later, in the Shrine of Baháʼuʼlláh at Bahji, I felt like I'd come home. Being a fairly new Baháʼí, I knew little history of the Faith, but the beauty of the holy places filled my senses. Harry and I later were fortunate enough to make two more pilgrimages, in 2003 and 2012. During those visits, we noticed how industrial and built up the Haifa-Akká area had become. But in 1978, visiting Akka and Bahji took us far out into the countryside.

At a gathering in the Pilgrim House one evening, I heard a prayer recited in an Indigenous language. I met Alice Bathke, a Navajo believer, her husband, Jerry, and her family. The Navajo language forms part of the Na-Dene First Nations language group, to which languages spoken in the Northwest Territories belong. We listened to radio programming in the Dene languages in Yellowknife, so the tones sounded familiar to me. This was the beginning of a lovely friendship with the Bathkes that has spanned decades and distance.[45]

***

On this first pilgrimage I was greatly moved at the resting places of the wife of Bahá'u'lláh and of his son Mírzá Mihdí, known by the title the Purest Branch. Mírzá Mihdí was the younger brother of 'Abdu'l-Baha. When Bahá'u'lláh was first exiled by the Persian government in 1853 from his homeland of Írán to Baghdád, Iráq, the conditions were severe, as the family had to walk over mountains during an exceptionally cold winter. Mírzá Mihdí was a young child and had to be left in the care of relatives in Írán. He was separated from his family for seven years, only rejoining them in 1860. A Bahá'í author has written that the agony and heartbreak of the separation from his beloved parents at such an early age was preparing his soul "through pain and suffering to play a major part in the arena of sacrifice and to shed an imperishable lustre upon the Cause of his heavenly Father."[46]

Bahá'u'lláh was exiled three times more, and finally arrived in Akká, Palestine, in 1868. Mírzá Mihdí shared the imprisonment and served Him devotedly as an amanuensis (secretary). One evening, while chanting his prayers on the rooftop of the prison, he fell through a skylight on to a crate below, which pierced his body. While he was dying, his Father came in and asked what his wish was. Mírzá Mihdí begged to sacrifice his life so the gates of the prison could be open to the many believers who wished to visit Bahá'u'lláh but were prevented by authorities from doing so. He died on June 23, 1870. Soon the restrictions on visitors were lifted.[47]

I began learn about how all the Manifestations of God have suffered in order to bring a message to humanity. 'Abdu'l-Baha described the sufferings of Bahá'u'lláh, which lasted sixty years.

There was no persecution, vicissitude or suffering He did not experience at the hand of His enemies and oppressors. All the days of His life were passed in difficulty and tribulation—at one time in prison, another in exile, sometimes in chains. He willingly endured these difficulties for the unity of mankind, praying that the world of humanity might realize the radiance of God, the oneness of humankind become a reality, strife and warfare cease and peace and tranquility be realized by all.[48]

***

The 1979 historic Egypt-Israel peace treaty signed by Egypt's Anwar Sadat and Israel's Menachem Begin (for which they won the Nobel Peace Prize) was still a year away, so Harry couldn't fly directly from Egypt to Israel. Instead, he visited Kenya after Egypt, and then flew to Israel at the end of my nine days of pilgrimage. The Universal House of Justice[49] kindly gave permission to stay for one more day in Haifa, so Harry could visit the Shrines. Following this stay, we took three days to travel in Israel, to the Golan Heights and the Sea of Galilee, and to the holy places associated with Judaism, Christianity and Islám in Jerusalem.

We stopped over in Greece on our way home from Israel. Our travel agent in Yellowknife had booked us into the Hilton Hotel in Athens. We only stayed one night; then we moved to a less expensive hotel in the inner city closer to the Parthenon. But we were determined to get our money's worth from our Hilton stay. We received two coupons for ouzo, an anise-flavoured aperitif widely consumed in Greece, to be imbibed on the rooftop café. So I ordered an ouzo for Harry and an orange juice for me. The waiter gave me a funny look. When the drink came, I belted back a large mouthful of orange juice. It tasted awful and we realized it was orange juice mixed with ouzo. No wonder the waiter gave me such a look. That one taste was the first and last time, God willing, I broke the Bahá'í prohibition against consuming alcohol!

***

After pilgrimage, I left the *Yellowknifer* newspaper and worked for the Native Friendship Centres in the North, coordinating training workshops for their staff. I was ecstatic when I got pregnant that year and excitedly shared the news with my friends. The pregnancy resulted in a miscarriage, however. Devastated, I lay in a hospital bed, reciting *The Tablet of Aḥmad*[50] by Bahá'u'lláh. When I came to this line, "Remember My days during thy days, and My distress and banishment in this remote prison," I knew the Author understood my grief.

This test was the beginning of learning that, in times of difficulty, I could remember the many sufferings of the Manifestations of God, so much greater than my own. During the years to come, I dove more into the history of the Faith and learned of the tremendous sacrifices that have been made, not only by its Central Figures, but by generations of believers since its beginning in 1844.

***

The Institute and Outreach

The most significant Bahá'í activity for me in Yellowknife and one that has had an impact ever since, came at the end of the Five Year Plan in 1978-1979.[51] Goals for the Faith's expansion had not been met in Canada, and from the senior institutions came encouragement to reach out to those around us. We had a visit from National Spiritual Assembly member Jamie Bond during this time. As was happening in other areas of Canada,[52] Bahá'ís focused on outreach to First Nations. In early 1979, a nine-day training institute was set up in part of the school at Rae-Edzo, where Bill and Cindy Gilday worked. Nine-day teacher training institutes had been started in Alaska by Jenabe Caldwell. The main focus for the friends was to have deep contact with the Sacred Writings of the Faith to gain inspiration for the teaching work.

Hazel Lovelace, a Tlingit Bahá'í originally from the Yukon, but who lived in Alaska, came to facilitate. After becoming a Bahá'í, Hazel had taught herself to read and immersed herself in the Bahá'í Writings. She had much experience in teaching the Faith and using the nine-day training materials developed in Alaska. She came to the Northwest Territories with her cousin from the Yukon, Mark Wedge.[53]

We recruited friends who could dedicate their time to the training and a follow-up teaching campaign. Our group of ten[54] included two Indigenous Bahá'ís from Rae-Edzo and Fort Wrigley-Fort Simpson area who lived in Yellowknife. Bernice Boss from Yellowknife prepared all the food for the nine days to send with us.

During the institute, we spent much time in prayer and then in studying the Writings word by word. In the evenings, we gathered, told stories and sang, sometimes inviting in members of the community. For all of us, it was an in-depth study of passages, many relating to Bahá'í ideals of behaviour as well as teaching the Faith. The power of the Word of God, which few of us had studied so closely before, forged deep bonds of unity between us. It was a foretaste for me of the joys we experienced some twenty years later, when Bahá'ís of all ages around the world embarked on systematic training in the Word of God through the institute process based on the Ruhi Institute curriculum.[55]

> ...in the spiritual realm of intelligence and idealism there must be a center of illumination, and that center is the everlasting, ever-shining Sun, the Word of God. Its lights are the lights of reality which have shone upon humanity, illumining the realm of thought and morals, conferring the bounties of the divine world upon man.[56]

The institute tested us all in different ways. One new Bahá'í commented at the end of the nine days that now she wouldn't be ignorant any more, but this carried responsibility. The intensity of the study grounded us in the Writings and in the certainty that if we did arise to teach and serve, we would be confirmed. For me, a lasting impact was meeting Hazel and Mark, Indigenous Bahá'ís strong in their culture and the Faith. I would meet both of them again in the following years and derive fresh inspiration from their devotion to the Faith.

Following the institute, we had a two week teaching project in the Northwest Territories. We had a rented van and visited Kakisa; Zhahti Koe or Zhahti Kue (Fort Providence); Liidli Kue (Fort Simpson); Xátł'odehchee

(Hay River); Deninu Kue (Fort Resolution) and Thebacha (Fort Smith). During that time, over 100 people responded to the teachings of Bahá'u'lláh through direct teaching, some of them relatives of our Indigenous friend from Fort Wrigley. Though MaryAnne DeWolf and I followed up later that year by going out to the communities to visit and form Assemblies where there were enough believers, we didn't have the ability to deepen the new believers. The distances were great. We didn't have the methods of the institute process we have now, but most importantly, we didn't have personal relationships with the people.

Once a young person whom we had met in Fort Resolution called me in Yellowknife. The phone call was awkward and I didn't feel able to make a good connection nor help her in any meaningful way. That year, I sent out cards with a Bahá'í quote to each of the new believers.

We left the North a year later. It's now over thirty years since this experience. I carried guilt for many years that we had been unable to give the new believers the attention and deepening they deserved. The experience did, however, propel my future efforts to serve the Cause, to connect with, and learn about, Indigenous people.

In 2000, the Universal House of Justice commissioned a work called *Century of Light*, which reviewed the processes of the twentieth century, both within the world and within the Bahá'í community. The book discussed what had been learned from the challenges of expansion and consolidation of the Faith over the course of many decades.

> It is safe to say that during these years there was virtually no type of teaching activity, no combination of expansion, consolidation and proclamation, no administrative option, no effort at cultural adaptation that was not being energetically tried in some part of the Bahá'í world. The net result of the experience was an intensive education of a great part of the Bahá'í community in the implications of the mass teaching work, an education that could have occurred in no other way. By its very nature, the process was largely local and regional in focus, qualitative rather than quantitative in its gains, and incremental rather than large-scale in the progress achieved. Had it not been for the painstaking, always

difficult and often frustrating consolidation work pursued during these years, however, the subsequent strategy of systematizing the promotion of entry by troops would have had very little with which to work.[57]

What I understood from this was that the experience of large scale enrollment in communities all over the world had brought similar challenges to the ones we faced in the North. Only later would the tools and methods become available to properly reach out and assist in developing human resources among the new Bahá'ís. Only after reading this was my guilt finally assuaged.

***

I was invited to a Native Council after Christmas that year, at Silver Creek Guest Ranch outside of Cremona, Alberta, along the foothills of the Rocky Mountains.[58] This was the first national Native Council in a series held over the next few years.[59] The setting was magical, in a heavily wooded area with stunning views of the Rocky Mountains. Friends—both Indigenous and non-Indigenous—who had been involved in the teaching work, gathered to celebrate and deepen together. Fortunate to attend several Native councils, I caught a vision of the Indigenous friends taking their rightful place in the affairs of the Bahá'í community and offering their unique contributions and spirit.

***

Our first child, Isaac Hussein Verge, was born in Yellowknife on February 25, 1980. Isaac was several weeks overdue, so Harry and I welcomed his birth with great relief. I didn't anticipate the joy I would feel nor the depression. Having been used to being out in the community for many years, staying at home with Isaac, which I wanted to do, seemed impractical, because the long months of winter in the North would be isolating for a mother at home. That summer, friends from British Columbia drove to Yellowknife to visit us. Harry had recently received an offer from an oil company in Calgary, Alberta Gas Trunk Line Company Ltd, later known as Nova Corp. He had turned down the offer because he was making more money working for the

Territorial Government. The supervisor called back while our friends were there and said Harry was the preferred candidate and asked him to reconsider.

We had been in Yellowknife for four and a half years and loved the frontier spirit and the close bonds of friendship we had made. Our visiting friends helped us create lists of the pros and cons of moving. We came up with two lists almost equal in length. In the end, we decided to move, but not right into the city of Calgary. I got in touch with the regional Baháʼí committee who recommended checking out a couple of small communities outside Calgary.

Late that summer, while we looked for where we would live, Farhad and Lois Naderi hosted us in Airdrie, a small town thirty kilometres north of Calgary on the Queen Elizabeth II Highway. After looking at a couple of other small communities, we decided on Airdrie, and took possession of a bilevel house on Ashwood Road, on September 1, 1980.

CHAPTER EIGHT

Airdrie, First contact with Stoney Nakoda people

"Each Bahá'í is part of a continuum of believers that reaches back into the past and stretches forth far into the future, called upon to carry out the tasks set before his own generation, while conscious of the contributions of those who came before."[60]

Sometime that fall, Arthur and Lily Ann Irwin visited and stayed in our home. I had known about the Irwins, early teachers of Indigenous people, from Fran Maclean who had mentored me in Halifax. Fran knew the Irwins while she worked in Yellowknife. In July 1976, I had attended an intercontinental Bahá'í conference held in Anchorage, Alaska and met Lily Ann there for the first time.

The Irwins shared many stories of their days teaching the Faith among Indigenous people. Lily Ann told a touching story of how she had been inspired. Arthur worked as a geologist in Yellowknife. Lily Ann did not feel accepted by the women in the circles of white people in town. One day, while walking in downtown Yellowknife, she felt depressed. An Indigenous woman she met along the street smiled at her warmly. The kindness of that gesture became the impulse for decades of service among First Nations people.

Arthur and Lily Ann were the first to have started an Indian/White friendship group in Calgary. This initiative eventually grew into the Friendship Centre movement across Canada.[61] They had taught the Faith to the first members of the Siksika (Blackfoot), Piikani (Peigan) and Stoney Nakoda First Nations.[62] In 1961, Piikani had the honor of forming the first Spiritual Assembly on a First Nation Reserve in Canada.[63] Arthur and Lily Ann had tried to help the friends on the Stoney Nakoda First Nation at Morley west of Calgary form a Spiritual Assembly there. But they found a lack of unity among the people, particularly since there were three different bands and, in consultation with the local believers, decided it wasn't timely to do so.

When they visited us in Airdrie, the Irwins were living in the Okanagan. They slept on our pull-out bed in our small living room, as we only had two bedrooms. They must have noticed our lack of good pillows, because in the mail a few weeks later came some brand new pillows.

Arthur came back some weeks later to do contract work. He stayed with us and invited me to visit Stoney Nakoda Reserve with him. The day we went out, it had snowed. We drove from Airdrie through the back road of Highway 567 to Cochrane and then took Highway 1A out to the Reserve. Arthur introduced me to the first believer in Bahá'u'lláh on the Reserve, Judea Beaver,[64] who had come into the Faith in the 1950s through the efforts of Noel Wuttunee, the first Indigenous person to have become a Bahá'í in Canada.[65] Judea greeted us warmly and we visited. Though Arthur was leaving the area, I promised to come back to visit the next weekend. But there was a huge storm the next weekend and I didn't make it. The following weekend, when I arrived at the home, I found out Judea had passed away during the snowstorm.

I continued to visit his family and eventually met most of their children and grandchildren. Since I was just getting to know the Reserve, I found a marker on the highway, a white canister on a fencepost with a number on it, so I could find my way back to the home. The driveway in was just across the road from the canister.

***

On the Stoney Nakoda Nation website,[66] the Nakoda Nation is described in these words: "We are the original 'people of the mountains' known in our Nakoda language as the Îyârhe Nakoda and previously as the Iyethkabi. We are called by many different names historically and in current literature: Stoney Nakoda (incorrectly as Stony); Mountain Stoneys (or Sioux); Rocky

Mountain Stoney (or Sioux); Warriors of the Rocks; Cutthroat Indians (in Plains sign language, the sign of cutting the throat); or wapamathe.

"Historically, our neighbouring tribes designate the Stoney Nakoda as 'Assiniboine,' a name that literally means 'Stone people' or 'people who cook with stones.'"

Early traders gave this name to Stoney groups because of the unique method of boiling food with hot stones.

"In order to boil meat a fire was first made, and round stones placed in a fire so that they would become very hot. Nearby, a small hollow was dug into the ground and lined with rawhide to form a large bowl. Food, such as meat and wild vegetables, was placed in the bowl and water added; the hot stones were then taken from the fire and placed into the broth to cook the food. The stone would not burn holes into the rawhide, but only make the water very hot."[67]

After the signing of Treaty 7 in 1877, the Nakoda received land in the Bow Valley, which stretches from near Cochrane Alberta, at the Star Ranch, along the Bow River to Seebe at Highway 1X.[68]

Highway 1A is the old road from Calgary to Banff. It starts in the northwest of Calgary, now Crowchild Trail, and makes its way west through a picturesque landscape towards Cochrane. Descending the steep Big Hill into the Town of Cochrane, the visitor sees a panorama of foothills to the south and west and, in the distance, the majestic Rockies themselves. The townsite of Stoney Nakoda First Nation is about a twenty-minute drive from Cochrane.

***

I began to travel out to Morley on a regular basis. I got to know Randall Brown, who lived in Calgary and had reached out to First Nation reserves in southern Alberta. He was very systematic and kept meticulous records of the various trips out to Morley. He enlisted Baháʼís to go out to Morley on a rotational basis. At that time, we had very little idea how to share Baháʼí teachings with people, or deepen them if they were already Baháʼís. Most of the visits tended to be friendship visits. Sometimes we were invited into homes, oftentimes we weren't. Once, I took a young Baháʼí couple to a home to visit. I had heard that white people talk too much and silence was a part of Indigenous culture. So we sat in the living room for at least a couple of hours and very little was said. The lady with me started to yawn. Looking back, it's actually quite hilarious, but at the time it was simply awkward. That couple never expressed an interest in going to the Reserve again!

Not yet knowing many people, I visited one extended family for years even though they never seemed particularly happy to see me. One especially painful time happened while I was pregnant with our second child, Zara. When I visited the family, their daughter showed an interest in the pregnancy, as did other family members. A few weeks after Zara was born, I drove to Morley with Deb Clement, a Bahá'í friend of Cree ancestry, to introduce the baby to the family. We sat in the living room, and although we heard everyone talking in the kitchen, no one, except the daughter, came out to see the baby. I was terribly hurt, as I thought I had made a connection with them around the baby. Later, Deb told me they were drinking in the back. She said she could tell because people would usually buy pop for the kids while they were drinking. Knowing this took the sting out of what felt like personal rejection.

Deb and I travelled regularly to Morley from Airdrie for several years, usually with Isaac and Zara. In August 1982, we took three young children from Morley to the Continental Indigenous Council, a spiritual gathering for Indigenous Bahá'ís, on the Blood (Kainai) Reserve near the Alberta-Montana border. We hauled a large borrowed tent trailer. Between our two vehicles, we had the three children from Morley, our son Isaac, two-and-a-half, and baby Zara, just five months old. On the way, we also picked up an elder from the west coast, Dorothy Francis.[69] It was at least a four-hour trip, added to the time spent picking up the children from the Reserve. We camped outside the conference location on the Reserve, the site of a former residential school.

Once at the Council, my days were completely tied up with our two little children. The three children from Morley, who were six or seven years old, attended children's activities. I was exhausted and unable to attend any of the council sessions. A young First Nation woman, Cheryl Ogram, came up to me at one point over the three days and said she thought what I was doing was too much for me. Of course it was. But in those days, I didn't think twice about taking on trips like this. Through my experiences in the North and at the Silver Creek Indigenous gathering, I had caught a vision of the eloquence, devotion, and unique contributions Indigenous Bahá'ís made to the Faith and wanted to assist others to be part of it, as well as partaking in the spirit myself. I did catch a sense of the elevated nature of the gathering by hearing fragments of talks and watching the pow-wow held outside at night, one of the first pow-wows I'd seen. The Indigenous friends wore beautiful regalia of many colours and everyone joined in a circle and moved to the drum beats.

***

At the end of the Indigenous council, we brought the kids home safely to Morley. We arrived late at night. When we got there a family member, prompted I think by the three children's grandmother, asked if the Bahá'ís would pay for a headstone for the grandfather's grave, since he had been an early Bahá'í on Morley. This was one of the material tests we often faced going to the Reserve—the expectation that there were material benefits that came with being part of a faith community. This had been the legacy of churches around the world, which built hospitals, schools and orphanages, in exchange for people's allegiance to their faith. What would take many years for us as Bahá'ís to understand clearly ourselves, let alone convey to others, was that the mission of Baha'u'llah's revelation is to empower people to take charge of their own spiritual and material affairs, rather than be recipients of charity. Non-Indigenous Bahá'ís frequently were asked for "loans" and it was hard to be firm about not contributing to a habit of dependency.

I didn't know how to respond to the request for the headstone, but promised to find out. I took the matter to our local Spiritual Assembly, which referred it to the National Spiritual Assembly. A few weeks later, we received the reply that buying the headstone was the responsibility of the family, but Bahá'ís could help arrange a memorial gathering for their grandfather or help design a headstone. I went out with Deb to deliver the message. A daughter and granddaughter came out to receive the message and were clearly not too happy about it. The family eventually did raise their own headstone, with a Christian cross on it.

Reflecting now, it's surprising, yet reassuring, to me that the family let the children go with us to these gatherings, given the legacy of residential schools. I learned that the Nakoda adults often would not come out themselves, but rather send their kids out to survey the scene, so to speak. During this period, we also organized for some older youth from an extended family to attend a summer school session at Sylvan Lake Bahá'í Centre in central Alberta. Though they were homesick during the session, these children spoke of it later with awe, saying they had felt in a place of peace. They no doubt were touched by the tranquility and beauty of the Sylvan Lake property, which sits right on the lake surrounded on three sides by trees. One of the youth who attended died later in a tragic bull-riding accident.

***

Feeling the mercy of the Creator and watching for signs

Global unity is the goal of Baha'u'llah's revelation and His comprehensive teachings are designed to create a world that reflects the oneness of humanity. There are strong prohibitions against backbiting, which undermines our work towards oneness at any level. The Writings are replete with admonitions such as: "Breathe not the sins of others so long as thou art thyself a sinner." "How couldst thou forget thine own faults and busy thyself with the faults of others? Whoso doeth this is accursed of Me."[70] The language is very strong, and everyone struggles to overcome this habit, so ingrained in our society. At one point I was feeling burdened with the knowledge that I had betrayed this strongest counsel of Bahá'u'lláh.

Harry and I had a rare weekend together without the children, who were staying with friends. It was fall and we were at the historic Prince of Wales Hotel in Waterton National Park near the Alberta-Montana border. I didn't sleep well and woke up early. I decided to go down to the lake that surrounded the hotel on three sides. From there, I wouldn't be seen from the hotel. Mist rising from the lake encircled me. With my eyes closed, I began to say the Long Obligatory Prayer,[71] which has a series of movements accompanying the words and has many lines about forgiveness. Partway into the prayer, I heard a sound of splashing water and looked up to see three deer emerging from the lake and making their way up the hill. I've always loved deer, and this unexpected appearance gave me hope. I took it as a sign of the mercy of God that I had been forgiven and must try to do better. My burden lifted.

I began after this to watch for signs in nature and in everyday life. From the Baháʼí writings I found this:

> I am well aware, O my Lord, that I have been so carried away by the clear tokens of Thy loving-kindness, and so completely inebriated with the wine of Thine utterance, that whatever I behold I readily discover that it maketh Thee known unto me, and it remindeth me of Thy signs, and of Thy tokens, and of Thy testimonies.[72]

Another quote from the Qurʼán speaks about how frequently I could miss these signs. "How many a sign there is in the heavens and the earth which most men pass by and ignore."[73]

One of the first signs that came up was a writing project.

***

Beginning to write

Angus Cowan, who had been a close friend of Indigenous peoples since the 1950s and had served as a Counsellor of the Baháʼí Faith,[74] died in 1986, after a long battle with cancer. From Scottish, Irish and American background, Angus reminded me of my own father. Though I never spent much time with Angus, his kindness, sensitivity and love touched my heart. He humbly accepted when I shared that I considered him my spiritual father, though he hadn't initially taught me the Faith.

When Angus died, I felt a book should be written about him. He had served ceaselessly among First Nations people across the Prairies, was deeply loved by them and had been adopted by the Tlingit people of Alaska and the Yukon who gave him the name Yik-Gah, "Great Great Grandfather."[75] I urged other Baháʼís to take the task on, until one day my friend Joanie Anderson[76] suggested perhaps I should do the book. That night, I couldn't sleep. Despite my writing background, I remembered an incident with Angus that had rather shocked me and made me hesitant to consider writing about him. He had a habit of introducing people in a group to each other, by telling stories of each and focusing on one of their strengths. For example, he'd say,

"This is Randall Brown, he has a whole houseful of books on Native history. This is Allison Healy, she's very dedicated to visiting all the people on her reserve." And so on.

Well, I was at a meeting with Angus in Calgary where we were sitting in a circle. He went around the room talking about each person and when he got to me, he said, "This is Pat Verge. She's a really good writer. I just wish what she wrote was true!" Then he laughed and laughed and went on to the next person.

I was flabbergasted and never did find out what prompted that comment from Angus. The only thing I could come up with was that once in Yellowknife when he had visited, I wrote a story about him for the local paper and sent him a copy. It might have been too flattering for his taste, knowing Angus's deep humility. I never could find the clipping in my files to verify this one way or the other. Nonetheless it made me nervous to think of writing a book about his life. The night after Joanie spoke to me, I realized that whatever I wrote, it had to be a truthful story, one that didn't gloss over the challenges of the times or of Angus's own life. So I set myself a few hurdles; if I got through them, this would be a confirmation to write the book. The first was asking Harry. When Angus first met Harry, perhaps intuitively knowing how much Harry supported me in Bahá'í service, he said to him, "You must be a very special man." Harry agreed with the idea of writing Angus's story right away. Then I asked two Bahá'ís who had at one point contemplated writing the story, if it was all right for me to go ahead. They both encouraged me, and Gordon McFarlane gave me research he had already gathered on Angus.

The next step was to talk with Dr. Jamshid Aidun, a close Bahá'í friend of Angus who had been his doctor during his long illness. He immediately jumped on the idea and offered a video he had done with Angus towards the end of his life. The last and scariest step for me was to talk with Angus's wife, Bobbie. I didn't know Bobbie well; she had often stayed in the background supporting Angus as he travelled widely to encourage the Bahá'í community. When I phoned her, she said, "Yes, I've been thinking something should be done. You know, Angus wasn't an intellectual, he was a man of the heart."

Bobbie's blessing, both on the phone, in a subsequent interview, and during the time she herself was ill with cancer, gave me courage to move ahead, though the whole process of researching and writing the book took some eleven years. It also gave me the title for the book, *Angus: From the Heart.*

***

Maintaining vision

Throughout their childhood, my children and I benefited from Baháʼí summer schools at Sylvan Lake Baháʼí Centre, west of Red Deer in south-central Alberta. In the mid-eighties, I attended a session with Earl McAuley that had a significant impact on my faith and conviction. When I became a Baháʼí, I was ecstatic with the Faith's vision that the next step for humanity is its unification into one global community. As humankind has successively organized itself by unifying in clans, tribes, city-states, and nations, Baháʼuʼlláh's revelation is destined to unify the human race globally while preserving its marvellous diversity. But truth be told, nine years after joining the Faith, I felt a little jaded. Our Baháʼí communities were still small and struggling; for the most part, society seemed quite unaware of the Baháʼí teachings, and the "golden age" of civilization promised in the Writings didn't seem to be anywhere on the horizon.

Earl made a big sacrifice to drive to Sylvan Lake every day from further west, to facilitate a discussion based on the book *The Advent of Divine Justice* by Shoghi Effendi, the Guardian of the Faith. I will always be grateful for that, because during the course, we studied a passage that put our current efforts into perspective. It described the stages the Faith will go through until its teachings are accepted by the masses of humanity. Calling the Faith "sore-tried," Shoghi Effendi talked about "the obstacles that must be overcome, and the responsibilities that must be assumed" to enable the Faith "to pass through the successive stages of unmitigated obscurity, of active repression, and of complete emancipation." These stages would lead to the Faith being acknowledged as an independent religion with full equality with its sister religions, eventually assuming "the rights and prerogatives associated with the Baháʼí state....(and) ultimately culminate in the emergence of the world-wide Baháʼí Commonwealth."[77] Someone in our study group made the comment that each generation's progress rests on the efforts of those who have come before. If we don't do our part, the next generations won't have the foundation to stand on. I suddenly realized that our services, no matter how humble and insignificant they might be, would be the basis for future progress.

***

Cochrane

By 1989, I felt stagnant in Airdrie and began to have itchy feet about moving. Harry wasn't as keen, neither were the kids. But one Sunday afternoon, I set out alone for Cochrane, a small town on the west side of Calgary, to look at real estate. At an open house, the realtor told me there were only two homes in Cochrane in our price range. One was a two-storey with dormer-type windows. The house backed on to a park flanking Big Hill Creek that flows through Cochrane to the Bow River. Driving by it, I had a special feeling about the house. At home in Airdrie, Harry, who had been reluctant to come with me, coincidently had found the same house advertised in the paper. By Tuesday, we had made an offer that went back and forth with the owners, one of whom was in Europe at the time. They accepted our offer on Friday, we put the Airdrie house up for sale Friday night and it sold Saturday morning. It felt like a huge confirmation of our move to Cochrane, where we have lived ever since.

We moved in July 1989. I made plans to travel while the new house was repainted. Having decided to proceed with the *Angus* book, I travelled to the "Spiritual Unity of the Tribes" gathering on Pasqua Reserve, a Saulteaux/Cree First Nation located sixty kilometres northeast of Regina and fifteen km west of Fort Qu'Appelle, Saskatchewan. The ten-day meeting, held to share spiritual beliefs and culture, was planned by a group of First Nations Bahá'ís and others. I hoped to gather material for the book and had a list of Bahá'ís to interview.

I travelled with Peggy Ross,[78] an Auxiliary Board member from British Columbia, already quite elderly, whom I hadn't met before. Peggy was intuitive and observed me closely during the ten days we travelled together. I found it impossible to interview the people on my list; most of them were busy with organizing the gathering that had attracted hundreds of people. I was frustrated, had car trouble and was on the verge of tears half the time. Then one day, nearly at the end of the gathering, I went to the graveyard on the Reserve and said a prayer for selflessness. Suddenly everything changed. Walking away from the graveyard, I ran into a number of people who could be interviewed, including some from Alaska and the Holy Land, a rare opportunity that wouldn't happen again. I did eventually interview the people on my list, but not until the next year.

At the end of the trip together, while we were visiting with friends in the Okanagan, Peggy said I would write a beautiful book about Angus, but would have to get myself out of the way and let Angus show me the path. What a lesson in detachment. After all the frustrations of the trip, it was clear I'd have to let go of my plans and become more open. Peggy's wisdom has helped in learning to let go of control. So has this quote about being open to the promptings of the spirit.

"O thou handmaid of God! In this day, to thank God for His bounties consisteth in possessing a radiant heart, and a soul open to the promptings of the spirit. This is the essence of thanksgiving."[79]

***

Now from Cochrane, I continued to visit Morley sporadically. It was a much shorter drive than from Airdrie, less than half an hour. We tried hard to find a location to have children's classes, sometimes having short classes outside a home when we found kids there, but the classes weren't regular. Around 1990, a daughter of a family we had been visiting was killed on the TransCanada highway. Her son Luke (not his real name), whom we had taken to the Indigenous Council on the Blood Reserve, was now about fifteen. When visiting, we could see he was full of sorrow. Though there was another Indigenous Bahá'í Council on Vancouver Island that summer of 1991 and we asked Luke to come with us, we didn't hear back from him. He was still grieving.

***

Untimely death

The pews at the little Morley church were completely filled. People stood at the back and the crowd spilled over outside. A palpable grief filled the air. One of Luke's grade school teachers from Exshaw broke down in sobs as she spoke from the pulpit about him. The sky outside was grey and overcast.

Deb Clement, our son Isaac, eleven, and daughter Zara, nine, sat beside me in the pew. We had known Luke for nearly ten years. At sixteen, he had been killed when a car driven by his brother-in-law overturned. This was one of the first times someone we knew well from the Reserve had died. Luke was grieving his mother's death deeply when we saw him not that long before.

All of a sudden the sun broke through the clouds and its rays fell upon us sitting in the pew. A few minutes later, toward the end of the service, the minister asked if anyone else would like to share some words about Luke. Deb nudged me to go up to the front. Nervous and shy, I felt unprepared. But I wondered if maybe Luke wanted me to say something. What could possibly be said to comfort, to explain such a loss? I stood up and spoke about our family's love for Luke, how he was like a brother to Isaac and Zara, how sad we all were. Then I offered a prayer for the children and youth of Morley.

At the end of the service, everyone lined up to file past the open coffin that contained Luke's body dressed in new clothes. We shook hands with all the relatives who stood in a semi-circle around the coffin and then filed out of the church. I saw Isaac stomp angrily away from the crowd, the grief tight in his shoulder blades. No sixteen-year-old should die in such a manner, I thought. Nor should any eleven-year-old have to experience the loss of a friend only a few years older than him.

After the funeral service, we went to the Wesley graveyard, which overlooks the 1A highway, the Bow River, and the first little church that had been built at Morley (The church was burned down in 2017). There are three graveyards on Morley, one for each band. The Wesley graveyard is set on this hill, in a large field that fills with wildflowers in the summer. Eagles and hawks soar overhead, deer often run through, wild horses circle its fences, kept out by a cattle guard.

Prayers were offered; then we joined with the others in waiting as the coffin was lowered into a large hole dug earlier. Then individuals took shovels in turn, piling dirt and rock over the coffin, and building a big heap over the grave. Someone pounded a large cross with Luke's name and date of birth and death into the ground. People placed the flowers and mementoes given to the family on the mound. In the Nakoda tradition, each person then picked up a handful of dirt, circled the mound clockwise, and dropped the dirt on to it before leaving.

We waited until most people were gone, then we stood by the newly dug grave and said the Bahá'í prayer for the dead. A couple of Nakoda women joined us and later asked how we knew Luke.

***

Reconnecting in 2013

In 2013, after massive floods in the Bow Valley have forced many Nakoda people into trailer camps for a few months, I meet Vivian Rider at the Bearspaw trailer camp. Vivian was one of the women who joined us at Luke's gravesite so many years before. I have not seen her in twenty-five years. We talk about many things, including Luke's death. We had greatly appreciated Vivian and her friend staying with us as we prayed. Today, Vivian is curious and asks about Bahá'í burial practices.

At the time of Luke's death, I asked his family if we could have a Bahá'í funeral for him. The Bahá'í funeral is very simple. The body is washed, wrapped in fine cloth, and placed in the coffin. There is no embalming. The body is buried within an hour travel distance from where the person passed away. Someone says a special prayer for the dead in the presence of everyone gathered. The family did not get back to me, so we didn't press them. In the ensuing years, I've realized that abiding by Bahá'í practice may take some time, even generations, until the people themselves absorb the teachings and begin observing them within their own cultural traditions.

Many more young people have died on the Reserve since Luke's death. Such tragic deaths have repeated themselves endlessly in First Nation communities across this land, a source of grief to countless families. The work of the Truth and Reconciliation Commission, in gathering testimony from survivors of residential schools and their descendants, has revealed a strong pattern of inter-generational trauma that has resulted from the deep wounds inflicted on those who attended the schools.

**

In the spring after Luke's death, I visited the family home. One of Luke's uncles came to the door and told me in a harsh tone that none of them wanted to be Bahá'ís anymore. Though it was a blow for me, after my efforts to maintain contact with the family, it was hardly surprising. Though the Faith had been in their family since the 1950s, no one had had opportunity to have much direct contact with the Bahá'í Writings. In the Bahá'í community, the institute process[80] had not yet become systematic. Though I visited the family with some consistency, that was the most I could say. Being from the dominant culture, there were many barriers.

Choked up, I told Luke's uncle they could remove themselves from the Bahá'í lists by writing to the National Centre. I don't know whether they ever did this. I left the home with a burdened heart and travelled north on the Reserve to visit another family. Passing the spot on the hill where the accident took place and Luke died, I prayed and asked him for help. Suddenly, an eagle swooped over the car. It seemed to be a sign from Luke, and from Bahá'u'lláh, to leave the family in the hands of God. We did meet up with the family or visit with some members occasionally in the years ahead, but we also made other friends. For me it was a real lesson in the Serenity Prayer. "God grant me the serenity to accept the things I cannot change, the courage to change the things I can, and the wisdom to know the difference."[81]

I now see this period of my Bahá'í service as being somewhat in a "missionary" mode, though Bahá'ís do not have missionaries. I knew the promises that 'Abdu'l-Bahá had made about the "original inhabitants of the Americas,"[82] and knew people had a right to hear the Bahá'í message. Because of the experience in the North when we couldn't follow up to help the new Indigenous Bahá'ís become deepened, I carried a deep sense of responsibility and felt a substantial commitment was necessary. Not knowing what to do and wanting to be consistent, I kept visiting. Not wanting to proselytize, I didn't "preach" about the Bahá'í Faith. While being convinced of the truth of the Faith, I didn't know how to adapt its presentation to the cultural and religious background of the people, as indicated in this quote from Shoghi Effendi.

Nor should any of the pioneers, at this early stage in the upbuilding of Bahá'í national communities, overlook the fundamental prerequisite for any successful teaching enterprise, which is to adapt the presentation of the fundamental principles of their Faith to the cultural and religious backgrounds, the ideologies, and the temperament of the diverse races and nations whom they are called upon to enlighten and attract.[83]

Now I see the family had little reason to trust me. They weren't interested in the Faith nor did we have activities to engage them, as we do today. No doubt they were fighting their own demons. Sometimes I had to force myself to go out to visit. I wouldn't do this now, but then my over-riding sense of responsibility kept me going.

My lack of knowledge of the history of settlement in Canada had not prepared me for the troubled social conditions I met. Being white, a woman and bringing a religion must have been looked upon with hesitation, even suspicion, especially given the fraught history of religions with the Indigenous people in Canada. A lady I met came to one of our annual picnics. She was annoyed when she found out that we belonged to a religion.

I found a humorous description of how a missionary might act in a novel by the late Indigenous author Richard Wagamese. In *Keeper 'n Me*, Wagamese uses humor, through the voice of Keeper, who explains how the Christian missionaries taught the people "that all (they) hadta do was believe in the Great Book and all the problems of the world would disappear." Keeper goes on: "Get on your knees an' pray, they said. So those Indyuns back then they got on their knees outta respect for their visitor's ways. Us we do that. And they prayed and they prayed and they prayed...When they looked up from all that prayin' they discovered all their land was gone." Wagamese's writing illustrates how impure motives so often tainted the connections between Indigenous people and settlers.[84]

Professor Jo-Ann Thom Episkenew makes the point that Keeper's criticism of the missionaries could offend many readers and to diffuse this, Keeper follows the above words by quickly apologizing and saying he was joking.

"Sorry. Don't mind me. Get goin' kinda always wanna throw in a funny."[85] Thom Episkenew says this allows the reader to save face. But she cautions that whether one likes it or not "to identify one's self as an Aboriginal person in Canada is to make a political statement. Contemporary Aboriginal writing reflects this reality in that almost all contemporary Canadian Aboriginal literature contains some kind of political agenda, usually one that corrects the inaccurate depictions of Aboriginal people in mainstream literature and works to advance social change."[86]

***

I learned that sometimes Indigenous people will agree to something they don't intend to do, just to please you. Eleanora McDermott, a Bahá'í originally from Piikani Reserve who lived in Calgary, and I made a plan to travel to a Bahá'í administrative meeting in Saskatoon in the mid-1980s. I asked a family from Morley if they'd like to go and they agreed. We were to meet in Airdrie and travel from there. Eleanora bought the biggest bucket of Kentucky Fried Chicken she could find and we waited in Airdrie. When it became apparent the Morley friends weren't going to show up, the two of us started out for Saskatoon. We ate that chicken morning, noon and night for a few days and shared lots of laughs about it.

***

November, 2015

It's over twenty-five years later and a group of us are on a retreat for youth workers and volunteers serving on the Stoney Nakoda First Nation. We've gathered in Kananaskis provincial park, in the Peter Lougheed Visitor Centre. We sit in a big room filled with sunlight, in front of a stone fireplace. Snow is piled up outside around the centre. Throughout the weekend, we play icebreaker games that make us laugh so hard we're brought to tears, review the past year's youth activities on Morley, envision goals for ourselves individually, as organizations, and collectively, all to empower Stoney Nakoda youth to reach their potential. Alyssa and Sarah of the Canada Bridges organization take us through different exercises using the sharing circle format.

When it's my turn to introduce myself, I share the story of Luke's death and its impact. Now, in 2015, under the Bearspaw Youth Centre director Cathy Arcega, there is a good-sized group of Nakoda youth volunteering to mentor younger youth. Activities have included a youth drop-in night, hip-hop and film-making camps, cultural camps, a Sioux Alliance summer camp with Nakoda people from other reserves, and much more. We Bahá'ís support whatever activities we can, offer children's classes, the junior youth spiritual empowerment program, a devotional and a Ruhi Book 1.[87] As I look around at the talent and dedication in the room and remember Luke, I see there is much momentum for change. It is truly breathtaking and I have a lot of hope.

CHAPTER NINE

The Healing Journey

Travelling along the TransCanada towards Alberta, Harry drives, my sister Coleen sits in the front seat beside him.

From my spot in the back of the car, my face flushed with anger and my usually reticent tongue let loose, I mutter, "He never stops talking. He doesn't make any sense. One day, he'll say this, another he'll change his mind and argue the other side. And he's so angry all the time. And always drinking."

Coleen's shoulders tense up.

"You know darn well he's always been a difficult man, no matter whether he's drinking or not," she says.

"I think alcohol makes it worse," I shoot back.

"Oh, you're so much like him," Coleen retorts. "Look, you're doing exactly what he does—arguing all the time. And judging everybody."

Her words sting. Like him? Oh, God forbid, no.

But her next words tear away the veil completely.

"But of course, he's an alcoholic," she says.

***

Coleen's outburst startled and shamed me, but in it I recognized the voice of truth. I *had* been judgmental just like Dad, standing back, listening to whoever is speaking, ready to pounce and totally destroy their argument. Just like Dad. How painful to see it all so clearly.

And that word, "alcoholic." At some level I had always known Dad was an alcoholic, but no one had ever voiced it before. I later learned that denial is a characteristic of alcoholism. Like the proverbial elephant in the living room, the disease extends its ugly tentacles by being neither named nor confronted. But what I didn't know yet was my own part in the complexity of the disease, even though I no longer drank alcohol. I didn't have any idea how deeply I had been affected and how much healing was to come.

***

I took a well-worn book down from the shelf. *Another Chance: Hope and Help for the Alcoholic Family* by Sharon Wegscheider-Cruse was published in 1981, but has been revised several times since then. Holding it, emotions flooded over me. I again felt the grief and sadness first felt when reading it. But then gratitude overrode everything. I realized how lucky I've been to receive help when it was most needed.

The book came to me around 1987 when Isaac was seven. Both strong-willed and similar to each other in personality, he and I were embroiled in daily power struggles and I sought counseling. It feels now like the hand of God in my life that the first counsellor I saw was trained in the rapidly emerging field of addictions recovery. Driving home after my first session, I felt raw, close to tears, almost blinded by the light of my growing awareness. The counsellor had explained how alcoholism affects the whole family. Using the analogy of the mobile, she said that when one piece of the mobile is out of line, all the other pieces adjust in whatever way they can to bring the system into some kind of balance. So all members, including the addict, take on unhealthy roles.

I was shocked to find that Wegscheider-Cruse seemed to be talking about my own family. I could fit myself, my mother and each of my siblings into one of the roles. How could the author know this so clearly? She wasn't a seer or psychic; these roles are typical and also limiting. It's possible neither my siblings nor I would fit these roles now. But we did then.

As the oldest of seven, my role was the hero, the child who, by my accomplishments, would "save" the family, help it to save face and redeem it. Alcoholism reinforced and magnified the overly-responsible role I had taken since childhood.

***

"You have to take a stand with your family," Jim Walton told me. We were at a Baháʼí gathering in Saskatoon in 1987. Jim was a Tlingit Baháʼí from Alaska who had developed an international cross-cultural alcohol recovery program, working primarily with Indigenous peoples.

I had recently gotten into an argument with my father when we visited at the farm and he was drinking. I left the room and threatened to leave immediately for our home in Alberta. But Mom begged me to stay. I think she was protecting Dad from the consequences of his actions. And she didn't want a breach in the family that might happen if I just up and left. So I did stay.

But in the months since the argument, I had been feeling I just couldn't go with the kids, who were still young, to the farm in the summer as we usually did and expose them to the drinking.

That morning, I had been feeling especially burdened, and during recital of the Long Obligatory Prayer[88] had a rare powerful sense of the presence of God. A sensation of strength and warmth passed over me. When I went downstairs in the hotel, I immediately ran into Jim and asked to speak with him about the drinking in my family.

"You have to take a stand," he repeated.

"I'll try, Jim," I told him.

"I don't want to hear 'try,'" Jim said. "I want to hear that you'll do it. Listen, is He really for you the King, the All-Knowing, the Wise?"

I was taken aback. Jim was referring to a powerful Baháʼí prayer called The Tablet of Ahmad,[89] which starts with the line, "He is the King, the All-Knowing, the Wise," referring to Baháʼu'lláh as the Manifestation of God.

Jim was questioning my faith in God. By this time, I had been a Baháʼí for twelve years and coasting. I thought I was probably a "pretty good little Baháʼí," active in the community, trying to follow the laws and live the Baháʼí life. But Jim was getting at whether I actually trusted in God. Trusted that if I took a stand with my family, things would turn out all right.

His question shook me. But he was right. I needed to commit.

"Will you do it?" he asked again firmly.

"Yes, I will," I said. As I left Jim and walked back into the main meeting room, I saw Jamshid Aidun, the father of my dear friend Laila Eiriksson. He had just lost his wife Gol in an unexpected tragic accident.

"You and the kids should come out to the farm this summer," he told me. The Aiduns had a small hobby farm outside Brandon, Manitoba, where Laila and her children would also be spending the summer. This was an instant confirmation of my decision not to take the kids to my parents' farm in British Columbia.

When I got back home, I worked with the addictions counsellor to compose a letter to my father, telling him I wouldn't be home that summer with the kids and why. The counsellor helped me own my feelings and worries in the letter rather than blaming my dad. Once the letter was ready, I decided to phone Dad and read it to him, then mail it. After procrastinating for several days, dreading the thought of confronting Dad with my true feelings, finally I phoned. He picked up, very unusual because normally my mother answered the phone. I read the letter to him, my voice shaking. He listened and didn't jump in right away. I finished the letter. Then he lashed out, calling me judgmental. At that point, I stopped the conversation and told him I couldn't listen any more. I mailed the letter later in the day.

That letter and phone call were among the hardest things I had done in my life. It did have an effect; shocked, Dad quit drinking for several weeks. He didn't seek treatment for alcoholism, though. As decided, we didn't go to the farm, and later in the summer, the kids and I went out to Brandon and enjoyed a lovely holiday with Jamshid, Laila and her children. Harry drove out to meet us and spend a few days.

Dad did go back to drinking, but he rarely drank to excess again while I was around. The next year, we got back to visiting Dad and Mom with the kids, and though Dad and I kept a guarded distance from each other, I didn't want to deprive him of the joy of knowing his grandchildren, nor them of knowing him and Mom.

***

"So he doesn't have any redeeming qualities?" asked the counsellor.

Several months after I had written the letter to Dad, I saw the counsellor again. Dad had started drinking again, and I spoke negatively about him to the counsellor. Through her question, she pointed out I was being judgmental. She was right, but her tone was aggressive. I got defensive and immediately resisted anything she was saying, telling her I wouldn't be coming back to counseling.

The exchange disturbed me very much. A few days later at a Bahá'í meeting, I told Ruth Eyford,[90] herself a counsellor, about the incident. She asked me a pointed question: when the counsellor spoke to me, how did it make me feel? I replied, "Humiliated, defeated, dominated." And what did that feeling remind me of? she asked. Immediately I recognized that it replicated the usual communication between Dad and me, especially when I was a little girl and he defeated me in every argument. Humiliated, I often broke down and cried. This feeling had echoed in my relations with strong dominant personalities over the years. I struggled in my communications with them.

The addictions counsellor also told me it was like my family was in a swamp. If I put my hands in to try to 'save' them, I would get sucked in myself. The most positive thing to do, she said, was to live my life the best way I knew, and perhaps it would influence them in some way.

I never went back to that counsellor, but the sessions with her gave me much knowledge and clues to a path of recovery, for which I remain grateful to this day. Ruth Eyford added another insight to my growing self-awareness. She remarked she had noticed a quality of dissatisfaction among children of alcoholics. I recognized that quality in myself and reflected on what would be the antidote to this bad habit. Realizing it would be gratitude, I decided to practice this virtue.

***

I ran to pick up the phone. My sister Coleen's voice was shaking and grave.

"Something's happened to Mike," she whispered.

"Oh my God, what's happened?"

"We're not sure, but he's been rushed to hospital. Mom and Dad and Tom are on their way there now. Apparently his former girlfriend couldn't wake him up this morning."

Michael Farley, "Mike," was Mom and Dad's oldest grandchild and my oldest nephew. My brother Tom and his first wife, Fran, had Mike and his brother when they were quite young. Their marriage broke down and eventually both Tom and Fran remarried. Mike, who was by now in high school, didn't fit in either of the new households and he went to live with my mother and father on the farm in Oliver, British Columbia, where he and his brother had spent many summers.

Mom and Dad loved Mike dearly though my father's sharp tongue was sometimes blistering. Mom had worked hard with Mike for him to finish high school. She felt this was one of the most important accomplishments of her life.

Sadly, despite all the love in my parents' home, it was an actively alcoholic household and Mike drank like most young people of his age. Recently he had told Mom he suffered from deep depressions, and he knew he had a problem with alcohol. He told her he planned to seek treatment.

It was hours before we heard the bitter truth. The hospital had pulled out all the stops to keep Mike alive, because he was a physically healthy and strong young man of twenty-five. But no matter what they had done, there was nothing on the brain scan. The doctor said he was making the decision to take Mike off life support, because there was no hope he could ever function again.

Though it was never fully determined what killed Mike, the likely cause was a combination of alcohol and a strong prescription drug, belonging to his former girlfriend. That lethal combination destroyed any hope of his brain recovering.

I was so angry I was afraid to talk with anyone. I took Mike's death, for a while, as a total personal failure. Other family members probably did, too. I was frustrated and furious at my family for never addressing the disease of alcoholism. Truth be told, I had become somewhat fanatic about the whole subject. It was easy for me to simply quit drinking when I became a Bahá'í, and for years I thought little about alcohol. But when I began to raise my own children and discover many of my co-dependent patterns, I started to look into it more closely and tried to share what I had learned with my mother and siblings.

I had been extraordinarily lucky to have the Bahá'í community as a support during the years of raising children, and Harry, though he liked to have a drink from time to time, honoured my wishes that we not have alcohol in our house while bringing up our children.

I had to go to the funeral, but I was afraid to go, afraid of my anger. I phoned my close friend Jean Hedley, and she listened and talked me through my grief. She even suggested I try to speak at the funeral. Heart heavy, standing beside the kitchen stove one night, I heard someone say, "Hey, Patty, I can fly." I knew it was Mike. I didn't claim it was exactly his human voice, but it was a voice or prompting from the spiritual world. The message, the tone, the use of my pet name in the family, "Patty," could only have come from Mike.

This very clear sign that Mike was okay where he was in the spiritual world, released from the struggles he had in this one, gave me strength. I decided to drive out to the funeral, as this would give me time to process my emotions. I prayed fervently during much of the ten-hour drive out to Oliver. Then my sisters and I plunged into baking and making food for the funeral reception. But my anger and frustration at my family lay under the surface like a pimple ready to burst. At one point, my brother Tom, Mike's dad, came to the house. I reacted to some comment he made about how Mike died.

"We all know *perfectly well* why Mike died," I burst out. Upset with people's denial of the disease, I had to leave the house. Driving south of Oliver to the next town and getting out at a park, I found a bench and sat down.

"I'm sorry, Mike," I burst out sobbing. "I couldn't do anything to stop this." I phoned back to my family. They had been been worried about me leaving in such a state. By the time I drove back, I was in better shape to apologize for my emotional outburst and to ask Tom if I might speak at Mike's funeral. He agreed.

The church was packed with young people, Mike's friends, shocked and distressed by his unexpected death. In a short talk, I told the story of Mike's voice coming to me in the kitchen and how comforting that was. Then I offered a short prayer for the departed by Bahá'u'lláh. Later, back at Mom and Dad's house, a young woman asked if I really heard Mike's voice. I replied that I believed he communicated, in his own unique way, to reassure us he was okay.

***

I ran outside into the chill September evening and flung open the front passenger door on Mom and Dad's van. Mom sat in the driver's seat, slumped over the wheel. Her shoulders were stooped and her face hidden for a moment. When she looked up at me, there were no tears, only despair and defeat. In my late forties, I had never seen those emotions on my mother's face before, even when Mike died. I felt her pain in the pit of my stomach. Within an instant, her face changed, rearranged itself into calm. She must have seen my stricken face and sought to comfort me.

"It's okay, Patty," she murmured.

A couple of decades later, I would still think about it with anger. "No, it's NOT okay. It wasn't then, and it isn't now. Why should she take on the whole burden and let Dad off the hook?" But that night Mom's words stopped me from pressing her further.

Our family had gathered in Golden at my sister's home for a town celebration. Dad had been drinking heavily and in the kitchen he lit into Mom with a vindictiveness he only used when he was drunk. Though he always argued, when he drank, the rhetoric escalated and any restraint he ordinarily exercised was lost. Mom responded in her quiet, dispassionate way. But this particular night, whatever he said was enough to push her to get up and leave the house.

Some of my siblings argued with Dad. I had long ago developed a habit of disengaging from the conversation when it got heated and sidling quietly out of the room. This time I followed my mother.

September nights in Golden held a strong hint of the cold that would soon touch the leaves of the aspen and burnish them with shades of gold. I sensed Mom wanted to be left alone and told her I loved her before getting out of the van. So often I had resented my mother's more stoic approach to life. Not that night. I stood there staring at the stars shimmering in the ink black sky above the trees surrounding my sister's house. I ached for my mother, was furious with my father, and felt helpless to do anything constructive.

***

Some wonderful confirmations happened during my recovery journey. A Bahá'í friend, Daphne Greene, said over lunch one day, "I think you're chronically depressed." This shocked me, but once again, it was the voice of truth. My wonderful family doctor had been encouraging me for several years to take medication for depression. But I had been reluctant, thinking I should be able to cope on my own. Daphne's words, at a sensitive time, penetrated deeply and I finally sought help. I began taking a very low dose of antidepressant medication over many years. The most significant effect was to help me stop negative thought processes that threw me into a descending cycle.

Another "blinding light" moment came when I read that depression is common in children of alcoholics. This told me depression is a physiological condition, not one I could use my mind to overcome completely, though changing thought processes is one effective strategy to deal with depression. I had always felt I didn't have a "right" to be depressed, being in a good marriage, having a strong faith, eating well, exercising, having access to Bahá'í prayers and Writings, being able to control my levels of stress, living without poverty, etc. Of course, the presence of depression had absolutely nothing to do with my free will. Even at the very low dose of antidepressant I began taking, the physiological effect was apparent.

A dear friend who had been counselling me suggested I develop a sense of humor about my life. It took a long time to even consider this suggestion. But one day, I decided to pray for a sense of humour. The Creator must have just been waiting for that prayer, and knew how badly I needed it, because "poof," I had one! I began to laugh more, make fun of myself and look for funny and joyful moments in life. I also came to greatly appreciate the humor that exists in Indigenous communities.

***

There are references in the Bahá'í writings to wine. Since Bahá'ís are prohibited from drinking alcohol, I wanted to know what wine means symbolically. 'Abdu'l-Bahá explains that this wine is the "wine of the Love of God," and that all other wine "hath depression as an after-effect."[91]

Bahá'u'lláh Himself explains that spiritual wine "intensifieth man's love for God, for His Chosen Ones and for His loved ones, and igniteth in the hearts the fire of God and love for Him, and glorification and praise of Him."[92]

***

Looking back at this long, ongoing process of healing from co-dependence,[93] one image brings a chuckle to my heart and a lightness to the whole situation. It came while talking with my friend Holly about how powerless I felt in the face of addiction, how it had taken hold of my family and my life, to say nothing of society.

She described the image of me she had in her mind. "It's like you're standing on the highway and a large semi-truck is barreling down towards you. And you're standing there, holding up your little stop sign."

I love that image, me holding up a little stop sign in the face of a wave of events and situations far beyond my control. This realization of powerlessness is one to which the Bahá'í Writings repeatedly attest. In the Short Obligatory Prayer, we recite, "I testify at this moment to my powerlessness and to Thy might."[94] The disease of alcoholism gave me a great need for control and an overdeveloped sense of responsibility for others. It's been a long process to let go, to trust, to become flexible, to go with the flow, to know that others are capable of handling their own lives, making their own decisions, making plans for their own community. It's a question of respect for the capacity of others. Intellectually I have that respect, but to actually feel it, when my whole youth was about taking responsibility, is a real challenge. Part of my journey has been learning not to take everything personally, to develop "detachment." By detachment, I mean taking the long view, keeping a vision of what's possible.

The journey to learn about and be in service with Indigenous peoples has paralleled my journey to healing from co-dependence. Taking too much responsibility for others in an unhealthy way needed to be transformed into strong patterns of co-existence, cooperation and collaboration. I had first encountered a community largely marginalized, robbed, their power taken from them to parent their own children, a community that had struggled with addictions, dependency and much tragedy. Many Indigenous individuals and communities have for a long time been in the process of seeking control over their own lives. The journey to decolonization and reconciliation is ongoing for both Indigenous and non-Indigenous people. But in the early years, I hadn't even thought about what "colonization" means.

***

An Indigenous Bahá'í friend, Riel Aubichon, who has done a lot of healing work from past trauma, said he felt there is a mysterious healing force that happens when we are serving the Faith and other people. I have pondered why this would be. But of course service means being less self-focused, more altruistic, looking for ways to contribute positively to the community. We develop our capacities while serving. A quote from Shoghi Effendi shows this link.

"The more we search for ourselves, the less likely we are to find ourselves; and the more we search for God, and to serve our fellow-men, the more profoundly will we become acquainted with ourselves, and the more inwardly assured. This is one of the great spiritual laws of life."[95]

Today in the Bahá'í community, we speak about individual transformation and community transformation as going hand in hand, inherently connected and mutually reinforcing. The youth have been counselled not to fall victim to "false choices," such as "whether one should study or serve, advance materially or contribute to the betterment of others, pursue work or become dedicated to service." The youth are encouraged that through service, "young people can learn to foster a life in which its various aspects complement each other...As they advance in their endeavours to contribute to the construction of a better world, their capacity to draw on the spiritual and social forces that make them builders of civilization grows manifoldly."[96]

CHAPTER TEN

Friendships and Learning

It was refreshing to meet Sheila Holloway who is Stoney Nakoda and lives on Morley. Sheila is down-to-earth, and we became true friends. To this day we take each other as sisters. Sheila's father, Frank, had become a Bahá'í before I met her; he had visited several of his daughters to teach them the Faith and had urged them to embrace it. I began to visit Sheila who was positive and kind. She had two older boys from an early relationship, and then with Ron Baptiste, a son, Tribune. Later Sheila and Ron had a daughter, Genevieve. I got to know Sheila's mother, Eliza, and sisters Margaret, Glenna and Donna, and brothers Farrell and Mark.

Through this family, I continued to see how tragedy strikes First Nation families. Sheila's second son, Brent, died in 1991 while walking on the TransCanada highway. Within a short time, in 1992, when in Saskatchewan with Zara doing research for the *Angus* book, I received a phone call from Harry that Sheila's oldest son, Edward (Tyvin), and a female friend, Twylla Ryder, had been killed in a motorcycle accident. We drove back quickly from Saskatchewan, stunned by the knowledge that my friend had lost her two eldest sons in a very short time. I made it to Sheila's house in the morning, just before the end of the wake, as the family prepared to take the body to the church for the funeral. Sheila asked me to say something. "We don't mind how long you talk," she said. I did speak but have no recollection of what was said.

Sheila was very pregnant at the time. Weeks after the funeral, she gave birth to her daughter, Genevieve. Visiting a day after this beautiful baby was born, I began to call her a pet name, "Rosebud."

Randall Brown had started the tradition of an annual summer picnic on Morley. A while after Edward's funeral, we planned the picnic, and I called to ask Sheila to come. She asked who was going to be there. I mentioned the names of some people and she said, "We don't really know them." I said, "But Sheila, Bahá'u'lláh came to bring us together." That was all, but Sheila and other members of her family showed up. It struck me how powerful Bahá'u'lláh's message of unity is. We sang and played games with the kids. Later I tried hard to find a place to have children's classes, even resorting to begging one lady to have them in her house. But she didn't get back to me.

Sheila's husband, Ron, is a very friendly person and a hard worker. In the past, he had a habit of binge drinking. Sometime after the death of her two boys, Sheila said to me, "I could drink too, but if I did, I would lose everything." She was painfully aware of the cost of drinking.

Sheila participated–sometimes with members of her extended family– with the Cochrane Bahá'í community in some Feasts and Holy Days and rode with us on one of our Labour Day floats. She attended a Náw-Rúz celebration where we sold desserts and raised money for the Eagle's Nest Family Shelter on Morley. Then she and I went to the shelter to make the presentation to the coordinator.

Sheila sometimes visited my home in Cochrane with her little girl and over the years came by with her children and then grandchildren, nearly every Halloween. At one point she felt pressure at being one of the few enrolled Stoney Nakoda Bahá'ís to take part in activities. It's hard to stick your neck out and be different in a community where tradition, both Indigenous and Christian, reigns strong. So one day when she was feeling that pressure, she phoned and said she didn't want to be Bahá'í anymore. She felt she had entered it without really knowing much about it and under some pressure from her father.

"Maybe one day I will learn more about it and if I'm in it, I'll really be in it," she said. Although she herself stepped back from the Faith, Sheila brought her son and daughter to Sylvan Lake Bahá'í Centre for a summer camp one year. She and Ron now have three granddaughters and have been raising two sons of a niece. Sometimes, she has joined us for a devotional on Morley.

Sheila and I shared these memories at a 2013 Christmas party in Morley. After I recalled some of the stories, she opened up.

"You know, when you first started coming around, I told my husband, 'tell them I'm not home,'" she laughed. "We used to take turns answering the door. Then it was my turn. You were out there with your two little kids. Their cheeks and noses were all red. It must have been winter." Feeling compelled to invite us in, Sheila started to talk with me and found it wasn't so bad. Despite the tentative beginnings, over many years we have remained friends.

More recently, Sheila said to me, "You go away, nothing will remain." It was a compelling reminder of how capacity must be built in local people, so when outsiders are unable to come, activities remain sustainable.

**

February, 1992

I hear about a round dance to be held at the old band hall on Morley. While round dances are a part of the Nakoda spiritual tradition, there hasn't been one on Morley for many years. Mark (Ricky) Poucette and his family are putting it up. When I get to the hall and walk in, there are already people seated on the benches around the room. I am the only non-Indigenous person. I see Sheila on the other side of the hall and make a beeline for her. I will always be grateful for her friendliness and acceptance. We sit as the drummers arrive and set up in the middle of the hall. Once the drumming starts and people get up to join hands and dance in a circle clockwise around the drummers, I participate, too. I love being part of the circle and once I catch on to the beat and footsteps, I'm hooked, getting up to dance most dances. This is finally some contact point with the culture that feels natural to me, an activity where I can be part of what's happening and feel one with the people.

**

A few days later, in the Cochrane IGA grocery store, I see an elder who had been at the round dance. I go up to her, introduce myself and mention the round dance. This is Beatrice Poucette, whom I will meet again many times over the years.

"Oh," she says, her eyes twinkling, "I was wondering who that white girl was!" We chat and she gives me her phone number.

During this time, our local Spiritual Assembly in Cochrane, which always supports service on Morley, has decided to try to create stronger bonds with the Reserve and wants me to inquire about hosting a round dance in town. I invite Beatrice to come to our house to talk about it. She, her son Mark and his wife, Francis, come to Cochrane. Over a turkey lunch, we consult about how we can arrange the event. There is often a give-away and big feast associated with a round dance, which may be sponsored by an extended family or organization on the reserve. We decide to have a somewhat modified round dance.

As they are leaving, Beatrice kindly says she takes me as a daughter, words that stay special and meaningful to me over the years. I begin to call her "Îna," mother.

***

The Spiritual Assembly rents the basement of the Cochrane community hall for the round dance and the Cochrane Bahá'í community prepares lots of food. The children's class led by Eleanor Munkholm decorates the hall. There is an Indigenous-design blanket over a table, the chairs are arranged in a circle. As gifts, we have copies of the Sam Bald Eagle Augustine tape (Sam was a Mi'kmaq Bahá'í elder from New Brunswick) and tobacco to offer the elders. We advertise on Morley and in Cochrane.

A couple of hours before the event is to begin, Sheila calls from Morley. She says the drummers from Morley aren't going to come, as somehow they object to having a round dance in Cochrane. She urges that we switch the venue to the band hall on the Reserve. I reply that all the plans are made and if no drummers show up, we'll play a round dance tape. I start out with trepidation for the community hall about half an hour early and already car-loads of Morley friends, and even some from Eden Valley Reserve south and west of High River, are waiting in the parking lot. And though the drummers from Morley don't show up, drummers from Tsuu T'ina Reserve just outside Calgary do come and drum.

Eddie Holloway, a respected elder from Morley, speaks at the round dance. He has lived on the Reserve all his life and says this is the first time he has attended a round dance in Cochrane. Johnny Lefthand, who has served for many years as a Bearspaw councillor on Eden Valley Reserve, has travelled to Cochrane with his wife Mary Jane and echoes his appreciation.[97] Elders Dick and Julia Amos, who later become Bahá'ís, attend, as well as members of the extended Holloway family and the Heavenfire family from Tsuu T'ina. Beatrice Poucette and members of her family are here. We serve a meal and make presentations to the speakers. We all dance, young and old, Indigenous and non-Indigenous alike. At the end we give out apples to everyone, a form of giveaway suggested by Beatrice's family.

***

As I look back, this was an audacious step for our Assembly, one that opened doors to friendships on the Reserve and cemented my relationship with Beatrice and her family. Later that year, I participated with the Poucette family in hosting a pow-wow to celebrate Beatrice's 75th birthday, held at the Goodstoney Rodeo Centre. Bahá'ís Allison and Earl Healy travelled from the Kainai Reserve to attend.

That year was a Holy Year for the Bahá'í community, the 100th anniversary of the passing of Bahá'u'lláh on May 29, 1892. In November, our son Isaac and I attended, along with many Alberta Bahá'ís, the World Congress in New York that commemorated the establishment of the Covenant. Bahá'u'lláh, in His Will and Testament, had appointed His eldest son 'Abdu'l-Bahá as the centre of the Faith to whom all Bahá'ís should turn after His passing. This Covenant, unique in religious history, has enabled the Faith to grow and develop with its unity intact since the passing of its Founder. Unlike previous religious dispensations, it has not fractured into divisions and sects.

The Healys arranged for a group of Maori Bahá'ís who attended the Congress to come to Morley to share their culture. Beatrice's daughter Annie and her family put up an annual birthday round dance on Christmas day for Annie's husband, Bill Wesley, whose birthday was on December 25.[98] The Maori group, wearing their traditional outfits, shared dances and songs from their culture in the old band hall, on an exceptionally cold winter night.

***

The Cochrane Spiritual Assembly sponsored a second round dance to celebrate Náw-Rúz, Bahá'í New Year, on March 21, the first day of spring, three years later in 1995. In preparing for the round dance, Beatrice gave me instructions how to set up the room for the drummers. The Lefthand Singers from Eden Valley drummed and we held a blanket dance to raise money to pay them an honorarium. The Bahá'í community at the time was hosting the Maxwell International Bahá'í School Youth Dance Workshop from Vancouver Island.[99] After the round dance, they performed their interpretive dances with themes of racial unity, equality of women and men, and the harmfulness of substance abuse. Over 175 people attended this Náw-Rúz event, which coincides each year with the United Nations Day for the Elimination of Racial Discrimination.

The next day, the Maxwell Workshop performed their dances at the Morley Community School. The feedback received was that "it was the best thing they had ever had at the school."

Though there had historically been friendships and working relationships between Nakoda ranchers and ranchers in the Cochrane area, as the town became more urbanized, the two communities remained separate. These efforts to build bridges between people from Cochrane and Morley were in some ways groundbreaking at the time.

***

For at least twenty years, Bahá'ís from off the reserve helped elect a Local Spiritual Assembly[100] on Morley. The Universal House of Justice temporarily, for a number of years, allowed Spiritual Assemblies around the world to be formed during the twelve days of the Riḍván Festival[101] rather than only on the first day. This was to accommodate forming Assemblies in areas that were difficult to reach. But in the mid-1990s the Universal House of Justice stipulated that all Spiritual Assemblies were to be elected on the first day of Riḍván, April 21. They indicated that the impulse for electing an Assembly needed to come from the local people themselves. For decades in Canada, Spiritual Assemblies had been formed on First Nation reserves, but usually assisted by believers from off-reserve coming in to help. So we had faithfully carried out this practice on Morley. In that early era, these Spiritual Assemblies rarely met.[102]

One year, when we went to the home of a Bahá'í to ask her to vote, she said she didn't consider herself a Bahá'í. As Randall Brown and I left her home, I felt badly, not wishing to let down the institutions of the Faith. We carried on to the home of Mary Beaver, the widow of early Bahá'í Judea Beaver. On the way, I said a prayer that begins with the words, "Oh, God, refresh and gladden my spirit."[103] Though it was a prayer to cheer and uplift one's heart, Randall told me with a chuckle that the way I prayed made it the saddest prayer he'd ever heard! Mary, who was blind, did vote, with our help, and it was her vote that elected the Assembly that year.

Once the Amos family[104] became involved with the Faith, we began to gradually train them about the Assembly and how to vote without reference to personalities or speaking with others about who to vote for. Members of the family counted the ballots and helped fill out the forms. Because they didn't have access to computers, I helped by sending out the notice of election each year.

The same year I met Beatrice and we had the first round dance in Cochrane, Sheila Holloway, who was still involved, agreed to have the election at her home. I sent out the notice of the election, and we received one mailed-in ballot from the Reserve, the only year anyone mailed in a ballot. Azar Bennett, a Bahá'í neighbour in Cochrane, planned to put together Persian kebab meat for a meal at Sheila's home. The morning of the election, I got a call from Sheila; she and her family were in California, so she couldn't have the election at her home! I panicked a little and decided to go out to the Reserve to see if I could find other members to vote.

Late that afternoon, just as I was about to leave for Morley, Beatrice Poucette drove up to my home with her daughter and asked if I would loan her money to play bingo. I had made a strong practice of not loaning money to people, based on past experiences of not being paid back and the loan becoming a barrier between me and the person who borrowed the money. I was in a pickle; this was my first test with Beatrice.

"I can't loan you money," I said, "but we've planned a supper, and we'd be happy to have you and your family come." I quickly checked with Azar, and she was fine with having the meal at her house. Then I checked the ballot we had received in the mail to see if it was a valid ballot. It was and that vote elected the Assembly that year! I am pretty sure that on Morley and on other reserves, one or two ballots elected Assemblies during those years. We had a wonderful meal with Beatrice and her family members. A number of them, including Beatrice, later became Bahá'ís.

***

When the Universal House of Justice said that all Assemblies needed to be elected on April 21, it signaled that Assembly elections should no longer be assisted by outsiders. I had a hard time letting go of the practice and we continued to help Morley elect its Assembly, through the Amos family, for a few more years. Then one year, I asked Allison Healy about it, and she advised me to give the papers to the family, explain the process, and leave it up to them. The Assembly was not elected then and has not been since. But I'm sure that one day the believers on Morley will happily arrange for their own Spiritual Assembly to be elected yearly.

***

Tom LaBelle was a veteran of the First World War. He was a Bahá'í, one among the first handful of Bahá'ís on the Reserve in the 1950s. He always welcomed a visit. He was a great storyteller and Randall Brown loved listening to him. But Tom never spoke much about the war, said Randall.

***

November 11, 1992

It's Remembrance Day, and Tom LaBelle's daughter, Yvonne Poucette, has asked me to speak about her father at the community service being held at the Morley United Church. I ask her some questions about Tom's life and plan a short talk. I'm nervous to speak in front of crowds. At the church service, my name isn't called. I pray hard and keep asking Bahá'u'lláh for help. After the service, Yvonne says I should speak at the community feast that afternoon at Nakoda Lodge. She takes it upon herself to give the chairperson of that event my name. This is a chief whom I feel doesn't like me, though we have actually never met personally. He has seen me at a number of community events.

At the feast, the speakers are invited up one by one; again my name isn't called. Continuing to pray, I'm resigned to not speaking. I get the feeling the chief doesn't want me to talk. But, all of a sudden, he gets called away for a family emergency in which someone has been killed. The next emcee invites me to speak.

When I speak, it's to share what Yvonne has told me about her father. Tom LaBelle was born in 1895 and died on January 1, 1990 at age 96. Tom served in the army in the First World War for three and a half years on the front line. He was wounded and had to have surgery. He was off the front line for a month, but when he recovered, he went right back to fight. A victim of a mustard gas attack that corroded his lungs, Tom suffered throughout his life with coughing. Remembrance Day was always big for him. He would attend the community service, then a community supper, and later, Yvonne would cook a turkey supper. His wife, Elsie LaBelle, passed away only 23 days after Tom, on January 24, 1990.

I share the Bahá'í message that there is one Creator, one God, in whom we all believe. Yvonne says her father especially believed the teaching that all people belong to one human family. When speaking of the beautiful diversity of the human family and the fact all our blood is the same colour, I notice a number of elderly Nakoda ladies nodding their heads in agreement. I share the special prophecy from 'Abdu'l-Bahá of the great role to be played by the original inhabitants of America in bringing about a united spiritualized world community. With Yvonne's permission, the talk ends by offering 'Abdu'l-Bahá's prayer that says, in part, "O thou kind Lord! Thou hast created all humanity from the same stock. Thou hast decreed that all shall belong to the same household....O God! Raise aloft the banner of the oneness of mankind. O God! Establish the Most Great Peace."[105]

Recently, while our study group discussed the concept of crisis and victory in religion and in our own lives,[106] I remembered this story. Though I was willing to let the opportunity go if it was not the will of God that I speak, it was surely by His power that His message was proclaimed, a message that clearly resonated with the Nakoda elders.

***

So many things happened over the years, it's hard to remember them all. I came across several old reports I had written in the early 1990s about the efforts on Morley. A common theme was our realization that for the Faith to grow strong roots on the Reserve, local people needed to rise in service. Here is one excerpt from a 1992 report, after Sheila Holloway's second son, Edward, had died.

> ...at National Convention this year...Louise Profeit-LeBlanc said that many Native people have low reading skills, but that most do have tape recorders and we should consider putting the Writings on tape, so they have access to the Sacred Word. It was not until the end of July, after Edward's death, that I felt the absolute urgency of this. I made a tape, dedicated to four youth on Morley who have passed away. It started with the Buffy Ste. Marie song, "My Heart Soars," and then went on with quotes about the soul, life after death, prayers for healing and so on...The tape seemed to meet a need. After Sheila said she liked it, I made about eleven more copies, which have gone to other Bahá'ís or family members who have lost people... Although people have not said too much, everybody had listened to it, and everyone seemed to have liked it and found it helpful.

***

Piikani

In the early 1990s, much activity happened at Piikani Reserve in southern Alberta. At the time there was a Bahá'í Centre on the Reserve, restored by the Bahá'í community from the old day school. Sometimes I travelled weekly with Beverley Knowlton to serve. Over periods of time, there were resident Bahá'ís at the Centre.[107] Among the activities were a winter school called "Chinook Winds," some of the first institute trainings and other regional gatherings. While many people from the Reserve became Baháʼís, there was still not enough systematic follow-up. Eventually the band council took over the building and used it for educational purposes. The following story comes from those days.

***

Snowy drifts nearly blocked the road, but we managed to drive through a few mounds of snow and stop at Peter's house. The walkway had been cleared. Our boots crunched on the packed snow as we climbed the porch steps. My companion, Gayle Strikes With a Gun, knocked once, then opened the door and we walked in.

"Hey guys, we're here. Merry Christmas," she called out.

Peter Strikes with a Gun, Gayle's brother, and his wife came from the back of the house and greeted Gayle with a hug. They both shook hands with me. We sat down. Peter's wife went to the kitchen and filled the kettle, then put it on the stove and turned on the element.

"Tea?" she asked.

Gayle looked at me. "Sure, thanks. We can't stay long, but tea would be nice."

On the coffee table in front of us were a big bowl of mandarin oranges, a second bowl of chocolates and candy canes, and a plate filled with sliced fruit cake. Peter's wife picked up two bowls and offered them to me.

"No, thanks," I said politely. We had just had lunch and I was quite full.

"You have to take some," Gayle whispered to me. "Otherwise, they'll feel you think you're too good to eat their food."

"Oh, my gosh," I gasped. "I had no idea." I reached for a mandarin orange and began to peel it.

Later after our visit, I realized how kind Gayle was to speak to me about this. We were on the Piikani Nation, a First Nation in southern Alberta. As a non-Indigenous woman, my presence in the Strikes with a Gun home was already somewhat unusual. Gayle saw that for me to refuse their hospitality would not create the bonds of unity that were our intention. I have carried her advice with me for many years and will always be grateful for the lesson she imparted. It was a gesture of true friendship to confront me honestly.

***

"You just need one friend," he said. The speaker was addressing how to learn cross-culturally, during a Bahá'í outreach on the Piikani First Nation in the 1990s. Having a friend of First Nation ancestry would help immeasurably, he said. This is the story of one such special friendship.

***

Learning through Friendship

"I really think you should write this book," my friend Beverley said. "There are so many stereotypes and racism out there. When people see an Indian drunk on the streets, do they ever wonder what might have happened in that person's life? Did they go to residential school? Did a tragedy happen to them?"

We were sitting at breakfast in the Nof Hotel in Haifa, Israel. Harry, Beverley Knowlton and I were on a Bahá'í pilgrimage to the World Centre of the Faith, in February 2012. It wasn't the first time we had travelled to Israel together. In 2003, Beverley accompanied Harry and me and our two children, Isaac and Zara, on the pilgrimage as well.

This pilgrimage was a bonus for us. A family on the Stoney Nakoda Reserve had expressed a strong desire to go on pilgrimage when they became Bahá'ís, so I applied for them and for our family, as well as Bev. Our pilgrimage date came up more quickly than expected and despite many efforts to help the Nakoda family to come, they backed out. Though they had the money to go, I think the prospect of overseas travel was scary for them and out of their comfort zone.

Through my friendship with Bev over many years, I had learned much about First Nations people. Her parents, Samson and Rosie Knowlton, embraced the Bahá'í Faith in 1959 on her home reserve of Piikani and were among the first Bahá'ís there. Beverley was then a young girl. Her father served on the band council.

Rúḥíyyih Khánum, the widow of Shoghi Effendi, visited Canada from her home in Israel a few years after her husband passed away in 1957. She wanted to visit Piikani, because the first elected Bahá'í Spiritual Assembly on an Indigenous reserve in Canada had been formed there in 1961. The meeting was to be at the Knowlton home in High Bush, near the Oldman River.

"You know, our house was really small, just two rooms," Bev told me. "I remember we took all the furniture out and my mother cleaned and cleaned before that visit."

The Indian elders and members of the band council who met with Rúḥíyyih Khánum treated her with great respect. They gave her a Blackfoot name, Natu-Okcist, "Blessed Mother." Young Beverley presented her with flowers.

The memory of that unique visit was precious to Rúḥíyyih Khánum, a tireless advocate for Indigenous people, who often spoke of it in her travels around the world. And it was very special to the Knowlton family. Many other Bahá'í visitors[108] also received a warm welcome in the Knowlton home. Later, when Bev was in high school during the activism of the 1960s and 70s, many young Aboriginal people were joining Indigenous youth groups.

"They were angry, so racist against white people because of the way we've been treated, so into Red Power.

"In my heart, I could never really agree with them. I was with them, but I had to be really quiet. I always thought of Dale (Lillico) and Joyce (McGuffie) (non-Indigenous Bahá'ís who lived on the Reserve). They were so much a part of our family."

At the same time, Bev was aware of the inequities and restrictions First Nations were suffering. Her father was a lifetime band councillor chosen by the elders, who worked for Indigenous rights.

"One of the things that really stood out with my father. He was on the band council, he consulted with James Gladstone, the first Indian Senator from Kainai Reserve. They were able to get some housing for the Reserve. And he really fought against legalizing alcohol on the Reserve."

When Bev's first husband died in a car accident in 1974, she had to get permission from the Indian agent to hire a lawyer to settle the couple's affairs. Bev has lived and worked in the city of Calgary for much of her adult life. She returned to work on Piikani as a social worker for a brief time in 2013. She was shocked to find that a strong level of control by the department of

Indian Affairs[109] still existed over the department she worked in, the legacy of colonialism not yet overcome.

Beverley, the youngest of ten siblings, didn't go to residential school. She told a story from her mother's experience at residential school that also showed the level of control and limits which were placed on young people. Rosie finished school early, (students only went to grade eight at the time). She was required to stay at the school for two more years until age eighteen to work, cleaning and serving meals to staff. Very intelligent, she became interested in medicine, reading everything she could. She told the Indian agent she wanted to be a nurse. His reply: "No, Indian women don't get educated. You are to stay on the rez, get married and have lots of babies." Later, Rosie pursued her interest by volunteering at the hospital at Brocket, but what loss of potential.

In my friendship with Beverley, I have noticed a quiet peacefulness and centredness much of the time. She seems to know how to listen to her inner voice and to set boundaries for herself.

Beverley loaned me a book called *Charcoal's World*, by Hugh Dempsey, Canadian historian and former chief curator at the Glenbow Museum in Calgary. The story had great significance to her because she grew up hearing legends of Charcoal, a powerful medicine man who was a member of several Indigenous societies on Kainai Reserve and a bundle holder. Charcoal had killed a man who was having an affair with his wife. He ran from the Northwest Mounted Police and evaded them for many weeks before finally being caught and hanged. It was rumoured Charcoal had hidden out not far from Bev's family home in High Bush.

The story took place during the late 1800s, after the treaties had been signed, when Indigenous people were first confined to reserves. Several books have been written about Charcoal, but Bev liked this one because it was well-researched and told the story from the Indigenous point of view. The book gave me a strong sense of the difficulty First Nations faced in adjusting from their former freedom to hunt and move over a large area, to attempting an imposed agricultural economy that wasn't working. The extinction of the buffalo, poor quality and meagre rations from the Indian agent, near starvation in some cases, cattle rustling and horse thieving characterized the time.

***

On our first pilgrimage together in 2003, Bev had a beautiful pair of beaded moccasins with white rabbit fur, crafted by a Sahtu (North Slavey) woman in the Northwest Territories where Bev was working at the time. When we went to the Shrine of Bahá'u'lláh to pray, she generously shared the moccasins with me, so that one time I wore them into the shrine; the next time she wore them. I loved those moccasins so much Bev sold them to me.

On our second pilgrimage together in 2012, Beverley had a new pair of moccasins and I had brought mine.

***

Visiting the Sacred Precincts

We approach the Shrine of Bahá'u'lláh down a long path of small white pebbles culled from the Sea of Galilee. At the entrance way, which is covered by a portico, we remove our shoes in preparation for entering. Bev and I each put on our beaded moccasins and approach the door. Inside, the floors, covered with thick Persian carpet, surround an inner garden. Ferns and other tropical greenery stretch towards the light streaming through the high windows near the roof. For a breathless moment we pause, then choose a place on the carpet to sit down. A profound silence reigns. We focus our eyes on an opening, a sort of portal across the room. Behind the opening, fresh bouquets of roses adorn the spot beneath which the earthly remains of Bahá'u'lláh lie. Birds sing outside. Utter peace fills my heart. We sit in silent communion for a long and sacred period.

Wearing the moccasins in the Shrine feels significant. We offer ardent prayers for the progress of the junior youth spiritual empowerment program just beginning on Morley. We find out later that while we pray on pilgrimage, several families attend a gathering on Morley with their children and shortly after, several junior youth join the program.

CHAPTER ELEVEN

Beginning to Dig into
History, Allison, Îna

Tatanga Mani, "Walking Buffalo," George McLean

Before starting to study Canada's history with its Indigenous peoples in earnest, I read two biographies, which gave insight into Stoney Nakoda culture and history. *Tatanga Mani: Walking Buffalo of the Stonies* was written by Grant MacEwan in 1969 and *The Song and the Silence, Sitting Wind: The Life of Stoney Indian Chief Frank Kaquitts* by Peter Jonker in 1988.

Tatanga Mani, Walking Buffalo, also known as George McLean, was born on March 20, 1871, to Wolf Ear and his wife, Leah Abraham, who died after childbirth. He was brought up by his two grandmothers. During the 1860s, Walking Buffalo's grandfather was chief of the Bearspaw band. Then it passed to Jacob Bearspaw, who signed Treaty 7. Under him, the younger Walking Buffalo became a minor chief. He later became a chief for fifteen years. Chiefs at the time were hereditary.

In Walking Buffalo's time, he received his education from the mouths of elders who recalled details of important stories and events in the lives of his tribesmen, such as triumphs in battles and hunting expeditions. The buffalo herds had disappeared before he was old enough to hunt himself, but he did take part in hunts. Walking Buffalo was six and a half years old at the signing of Treaty 7 at Blackfoot Crossing and retained vivid memories of it.

When Walking Buffalo started school, he met Reverend John McLean, a missionary to the Kainai tribe. McLean took an interest in Walking Buffalo, who was a fighter among the other kids and didn't like to attend school.

McLean got Walking Buffalo to take his own last name, took him as a son, and offered to help him get educated. "George McLean" then became Walking Buffalo's name. After finishing school in Morley, he spent two more years at school in Red Deer, where there was only one other Nakoda person, and a year at St. John's School in Winnipeg. On returning to the Reserve, Walking Buffalo was witness to the railroad coming through for the first time. The Nakoda, among many other tribes, were opposed to it; the coming of the railroad across their territory had not been a condition agreed to in the treaty. In November 1885, railroad crews from east and west met at Craigellachie near Malakwa, British Columbia, and hammered the last spike in the railway.

Walking Buffalo worked in Calgary for the local blacksmith, on the Reserve as a teacher, and as a police scout and guide. He struggled to know whether he should live in the city or on the Reserve. There was no human to whom he could turn for the answer, wrote MacEwan. "Instinctively, he went into the forest to be alone with his thoughts. It was like going to nature's cathedral for meditation. And the Great Spirit did not fail him. His voice was clear: 'You have been neglecting your devotions. You must gather your people to pray, and then you will discover what course you should follow.'"[110]

Walking Buffalo participated in a sundance and, on the last night, he heard a voice.

"You want to know where you should make a home for your children and grandchildren? I will tell you now. Make it with your own people where you can be a leader among them and be of service to them. Your children will be happier with the Stonies in these hills than on the streets of a city."[111]

Chief Jacob Bearspaw told Walking Buffalo that it would be up to him "to interpret the ways of the white man to the Indians and the ways of the Indian to the white man."[112] He made him a minor chief and councilor. Walking Buffalo, after a dream, chose buffalo horns for his famous headpiece. The buffalo symbolized strength and had long been considered a very special gift from the Great Spirit.[113]

Walking Buffalo's life fulfilled the chief's counsel to him. I was particularly struck by one instance of his staunch defense of Indian rights. The City of Calgary, which was growing larger, wanted to use the Bow River as a hydroelectric site. The Calgary Power and Transmission Company decided in 1906 to construct power sites on the Bow. They wanted to do so on Nakoda land, at Horse Shoe Falls close to the former townsite of Seebe and Bow Valley Provincial Park on Highway 1X. The Department of Indian Affairs drew up an agreement with the company and the Nakoda. Sometime later, the Calgary Power Company was formed and bought out the older company. R. B. Bennett, who was to serve as Prime Minister of Canada from 1930 to 1935, became president of the new company. He made plans to raise the water level at Lake Minnewanka near Banff, then build a dam at Kananaskis Falls, a few kilometres above Horse Shoe Falls. The Kananaskis project was to exceed the Horse Shoe Falls project. Though it was also on the Reserve, the Nakoda weren't consulted. Walking Buffalo confronted Bennett and asked what he intended to do about a settlement for the Nakoda.

"I don't have to answer you," Bennett snapped. "Natural resources belong to the crown, not to the Indians. We're dealing with the Canadian government."

"But you are on our reserve and are taking our land," Walking Buffalo rejoined.[114]

The Nakoda had only been paid ten dollars an acre for the Horse Shoe site and Walking Buffalo insisted they should be paid $100 an acre for the Kananaskis site as well as rental for the river. Two years passed without an agreement, and three band members, Jonas Benjamin, Dan Wildman and Walking Buffalo went to Ottawa. At another meeting with Bennett, they stood resolutely to their demand and the company was forced to accept their terms, signing an agreement in May, 1914. Later when Ghost Dam was constructed, the Nakoda had no trouble negotiating a settlement. MacEwan commented that Walking Buffalo and R. B. Bennett ultimately became friends.

> And Stonies, with strong convictions about conservation, approved of the expansion of hydroelectric power as a means of obtaining energy without depleting other resources which the Great Spirit had provided. As Walking Buffalo noted, water power from the Bow was a self-renewing resource, and the white man with an unfavourable record for exploitation could not exhaust it unless he went to the length of destroying the watershed above the streams.[115]

Walking Buffalo served as a chief until 1935. In his later years, he travelled widely with Moral Rearmament, an international non-denominational moral and spiritual movement started in 1938 by American minister Frank Buchman.[116] At eighty-eight years of age, in October 1959, Walking Buffalo took a world tour to speak on behalf of peace to nations and peoples who were arming themselves. The 18,000 mile trip included London, Denmark, Sweden, Lapland, Italy, Greece, Cyprus and Switzerland. In March 1960, he travelled to New Zealand to see the Maori people, as well as to Australia, South Africa, Rhodesia, Nyasaland, Uganda, Italy and Switzerland, another 42,000 miles. In this capacity, he strove to promote understanding between Indigenous and non-Indigenous people. He believed First Nations have much to offer the world community and explained his outlook on religion or spirituality.

> We saw the Great Spirit's work in almost everything: sun, moon, trees, wind, and mountains. Sometimes, we approached him through these things. Was that so bad? I think we have a true belief in the supreme being, a stronger faith than that of most of the whites who have called us pagans...Nature is the book of that great power which one man calls God and which we call the Great Spirit. But what difference does a name make?[117]

I found in Walking Buffalo's description of his people's spirituality reflections of passages from Bahá'u'lláh's writings about how nature reflects the attributes and will of the Creator.

"Nature in its essence is the embodiment of My Name, the Maker, the Creator. Its manifestations are diversified by varying causes, and in this diversity there are signs for men of discernment. Nature is God's Will and is its expression in and through the contingent world. It is a dispensation of Providence ordained by the Ordainer, the All-Wise."[118]

Walking Buffalo asserted that his people have been searching for truth for generations, and they continue to find it. He said that all races of people have conducted such searches. "Perhaps that explains why nearly all the world's religions have points in common, like charity, forgiveness and belief in a life after death…Who do they suppose inspired the Indian's religion?…Indians living close to nature and nature's ruler are not living in darkness."[119]

Walking Buffalo was deepened in tribal customs, ceremonies, legends and songs. He told MacEwan that ancient Indian mysticism should not be lost, that Indigenous people have much to offer to the world and can make a substantial contribution to Canadian culture.

> It may not have occurred to many white men that red, black, and yellow peoples might have some good ideas about satisfying the world's needs…We think whites would be better off to slow down and live closer to the soil and forests and growing things, instead of galloping around like stampeding buffaloes in cutbank country. If they would take some of our advice, they might find a contentment which they are not discovering right now in their mad rush for money and for the pleasures which they think it will buy. My Indians can still teach others about living in harmony with nature…[120]

Walking Buffalo believed Indigenous people should be encouraged to keep their individuality and said, "I hope my children will live in a world where people of all colours can sit and work together without having to conform completely to the majority's will."[121] Walking Buffalo died in December 1967.

***

Youtnah Peewin, "Sitting Wind," Frank Kaquitts

Fifty-four years after Walking Buffalo was born in 1871, Frank Kaquitts, the subject of *The Song and the Silence, Sitting Wind: The Life of Stoney Indian Chief Frank Kaquitts*, was born to Mary and John Morin, of Cree ancestry, in February 1925. Mary died and Frank went to Morley to live with his grandmother Moraha, Mary's mother, and her Stoney husband, Ben Kaquitts. Through this book, written in a warm storytelling fashion with rich details, I learned about Nakoda ways as well as the transition out of the old ways that faced the Nation.

As a baby, Frank had been very ill. A medicine man cured him and gave him the name Youtnah Peewin, Sitting Wind, predicting he would become a leader. He learned traditional ways, often going hunting for game with his grandparents. His grandmother especially loved the James River area off Highway 22 near Caroline. She loved "the challenge of living in harmony, nothing more complex than a slow inhaling and exhaling of earth and elements." While on the land with his grandparents and Ben's son Josiah, Sitting Wind learned survival, hunting and how to butcher meat. The book provides a description of the old ways, like utilizing the whole animal and harvesting wild vegetables and medicines.[122]

Then Sitting Wind spent time at the Stoney Indian Residential School, built under the direction of Reverend Staley at the Morley townsite in 1926.[123] Most kids knew no English at all when they entered grade one, but they were discouraged from speaking the Nakoda language. When Frank arrived at the age of five, his braids were cut and his beaded moccasins taken away. No one called him Youtnah Peewin anymore. By 1937, the school operated 1800 acres, had a herd of sixty beef cattle, twelve milk cows, fifteen horses, and some pigs and chickens.

As a young man, Sitting Wind joined the army in the Second World War. Though he took training, he didn't serve because of an accident in which his foot was gashed. He became a boxer and won medals. The Nakoda elders weren't in favour of the young people going to war. They worried this would be against Treaty promises. While in training together, Joe Poucette and Sitting Wind agreed that the "real purpose for fighting was to protect Stoney lands, to ensure that Germans would not bulldoze their way over Canada and take away the Indian lands."

"If one of us should die," Joe mused, "It will be first of all for Stoney people: so they can remain safe on their reserve, and gain more power to preserve Treaty rights."[124] Joe Poucette was killed in the war. The Nakoda Nation has honoured him with a statue on the hills on the north side of Highway 1A at the turnoff to the town site, and he is remembered each November 11th.

At age twenty-five, Sitting Wind married Kathleen Chiniquay, whom he called the prettiest girl on the reserve. Kathleen's father was Johnny Chiniquay, whose own father signed the treaty in 1877. Sitting Wind became a cowboy and a chicken dancer at the Banff Indian Days. He worked for the railroad; then, after meeting artists Peter and Catharine Whyte,[125] he started to paint and study at the Banff School of Fine Arts. In speaking with Catharine Whyte in 1957, Sitting Wind described the old days that were rapidly changing and the racism he often encountered.

> ...in the old days, when Treaty was made, our reserve was a safe place to which people could return after hunting and gathering treks. The mountains were like our backyard, where we would be busy for a season harvesting our food, and finally we would come home to the reserve as if it were a warm fireplace to tide us through cold winters. But it's completely different now. Today, our backyard is taken away: our source of food. And that's why our house is now a prison. Every time we step out through the door we are met with a heavy choking air of whitemen's laws and whitemen's disapproving scowls. That's how it's different today.[126]

Sitting Wind probably was referring to the pass system, which required band members, until the 1960s, to get permission from the Indian agent before leaving the reserve. Catharine asked how Sitting Wind continued to believe in the "whitemen's God." He was taken aback. His thoughts show his understanding of the oneness underlying religions, rather than their forms.

"Did it ever matter how God was addressed? Are not all gods the same in the end? As long as there is peace and understanding: sympathy, empathy, consideration. He merely wishes that whitemen would understand Indians, be patient, be considerate, be respectful of them as fellow human beings. Is that not what God represents?"[127.] Catharine strongly encouraged Sitting Wind to respect his traditional culture, not to be ashamed, nor to apologize for it, and that in many ways it was superior to the white man's culture.

In 1957, at age thirty-two, Sitting Wind was elected a band councillor. Then he was voted chief of the Bearspaw band in 1961. With others, he dealt with one of the biggest challenges on the reserve that endures to this day: few jobs. As well, hunting lands were running out. By February 1974, on his forty-ninth birthday, Sitting Wind had been elected grand chief of all three bands of the Nakoda people. This had never occurred before. Much debate had happened over the issue of unifying the three historically separate bands.[128] The Nation held a referendum in November 1973, which approved amalgamation of the three groups. Then Sitting Wind was elected grand chief by an overwhelming majority.

But almost immediately there was dissension among the bands who had been "at loggerheads virtually since the day they were herded together onto one undivided reserve almost 100 years ago."[129] Six weeks after the election, Sitting Wind went to Ottawa to get a letter from the then Indian Affairs minister, Jean Chretien, to say that having one chief would not diminish treaty rights. He met with several federal ministers and Prime Minister Pierre-Elliott Trudeau, and did succeed in getting the letter he had requested. But when he got home, there was a petition with 400 names asking to declare the election null and void. The majority of the council had, in his absence, already signed a resolution reverting back to the old three-chief system.

Before leaving for Ottawa, Johnny Chiniquay, his father-in-law, had warned Sitting Wind that "people can be unpredictable; can suddenly turn on you like a bull, with hostility, jealousy, maliciousness." He spoke of the traditional role of the chief.

"In the old days a chief was brave in battle and impartial in his favour to people under his authority. He was concerned especially for the weak, the disadvantaged, and poor. He was quick to encourage a peaceful settlement, and slow to become angry. But when provoked he showed no fear of adversaries."[130]

Sitting Wind's initiatives and enthusiasm were deflated, as the tribe went back to three chiefs, but he finished his term as chief of his band. He later served on the education committee and as a guidance counsellor assistant. And he starred as Sitting Bull in *Buffalo Bill: Wild West Show* with Geraldine Chaplin and Paul Newman,[131] though he was disquieted by the distortions of history in the movie.

Sitting Bull Visits Morley

I was surprised to learn that the great Sitting Bull, the most powerful Indian of his time, had visited Morley when the mother of Ben Kaquitts, Sitting Wind's grandfather, was a young girl. Ben shared that even the mention of Sitting Bull would "conjure up respect and awe in people's thoughts, because his bravery in battle had become known far and wide." The following story came down to Sitting Wind through his grandfather Ben.

A Stoney medicine man proclaimed that he had received an important message through a dream, that Sitting Bull was on his way to visit the Nakoda people within a matter of days. The people began immediately to make preparations, wondering how they should behave in the presence of such a powerful leader. They thought he might be a giant man who could frighten his enemies by staring at them coldly in the eyes.

The people eagerly awaited Sitting Bull's visit and to listen to his words. They erected their teepees at the west end of Morley Flats near the meeting place of the Bow and Kananaskis Rivers and camped for two days before Sitting Bull arrived. He was visiting Indigenous bands all over the prairies and foothills, to deliberate with the chiefs about settlers and dwindling game. On the third day, after the medicine man announced Sitting Bull was close at hand, the chief sent a scout to investigate. When he returned, the scout said the party was almost there, but there were only five people in it. And he remarked that Sitting Bull appeared to be a very small, unimposing man. As Sitting Bull approached, the medicine man went to greet him. Sitting down with the leaders, Sitting Bull prayed over the food.

> Being a Sioux, his language was similar to Stoney language. We could understand him easily. And he was not frighten-ing or mean, but simple, plain, and kind...(he) explained to everyone that Indians south of the border were being treated wretchedly by American soldiers, and were fighting for their lands and for their very survival. He warned us to beware of what was taking place, and to be alert. Even the chiefs and councilors were awed by the great strength of Sitting Bull's determination, compared to his small physical size.[132]

After visiting for half a day, Sitting Bull moved on, after receiving gifts of dry-meat and pemmican. Ben Kaquitts reflected that the Nakoda had learned it wasn't the size of a person but the size of his heart and of his courage that made him strong.

***

After I read *The Song and the Silence, Sitting Wind*, I met Frank and Kathleen Kaquitts when I dropped in at their home near the Kananaskis turnoff from the TransCanada highway. This was a few years before Frank died in 2004 at the age of seventy-eight. They welcomed me warmly. Frank told me about his painting. I had a hanging made by Indigenous people from South America, which I gave them. I visited another time with Ahmad Motlagh, a Persian Bahá'í. Now I've had the honour to meet their daughter Bernadette and several grandchildren.

In his introduction to *The Song and The Silence*, Frank Kaquitts wrote about his hopes for the book.

> I think many Canadians, if not most, have no understand-
> ing of what an Indian such as myself has to go through
> during a single lifetime...I saw in this (the writing of the
> book) an opportunity to show outsiders first hand what it
> is like to be an Indian, born on a reserve and trying to cope
> in today's world...I hope that every reader becomes more
> sympathetic and less judgmental of us Indians.

***

Regional Service

In 1994, I was invited to serve on the Regional Teaching and Administrative Committee for Alberta. This nine-member body became the elected Regional Bahá'í Council of Alberta within a few years, and I was to serve on that body until 2008, except for one year. Service on the Council was a wonderful opportunity to learn about the Faith and meet the Bahá'ís of Alberta. Serving together on the Council helped deepen my friendship with Allison Healy. Allison was born on the Blackfoot-speaking reserve at Siksika, but married Earl Healy from the Kainai Reserve where she has lived ever since.

Allison and I often travelled to meetings together, and she began to visit Morley more regularly. Since the Spiritual Assembly of Stoney Nakoda had been elected each year, but had not met, we determined in January 1994 to visit all its members and encourage them to meet. Allison came to Cochrane for ten days, and we went out each day to visit the Baháʼís. We didn't find the Assembly members at home, but we did visit people that Allison knew such as elders Dick and Julia Amos. When we visited them, we learned the family was linked, through Julia, to Jacob Bearspaw who signed Treaty 7 on behalf of the Bearspaw band in 1877. When Allison presented Dick and Julia with Baháʼuʼlláh's message of the oneness of humanity, they immediately accepted it. Julia Amos died within two weeks of enrolling as a Baháʼí. Both Dick and Julia had attended our first round dance in Cochrane a few years before this visit.

Dick lived for several more years and always welcomed us to his home. He had been active in rodeo and had many stories to tell. He especially liked to see Taban Behin, a youth from Cochrane who had begun serving on Morley. Dick still practiced the Indigenous way of going outside in the morning, facing the east and starting the day with prayer.

While we missed Julia's funeral and only learned of her death when we visited later, at the time of Dick's death in 1998, the family asked us to help by preparing a talk. Beverley Knowlton and I met with Richard and Dandy Amos, two of Dick's sons, who gave us information about his life. I wrote up a talk that included mention of Dick becoming a Baháʼí. When we returned to read the talk to them, I was nervous and took out the Baháʼí mention, but Richard remembered it and asked that it be put back in. I later enjoyed conversations about spiritual matters with Richard at Chiniki Restaurant, and we once shared Baháʼí prayers. Richard said they were like "new wine." He said his mom, Julia Amos, had felt the strong spirit of Baháʼuʼlláh's teachings and told him they should "tell this to the people."

***

Beatrice, "Îna"

During Allison's visit to Morley, we visited with Beatrice Poucette, whom I had initially met through the round dances. Allison's husband Earl was related to Beatrice, and they sometimes stayed with her during pow-wows on the Nakoda Nation. She welcomed us warmly to her home. During the visit, Allison presented the message of Baháʼuʼlláh to Beatrice, and she became a

Bahá'í. We learned Beatrice's father, Horace Holloway, was one of the early Bahá'ís on Morley, taught by Lily Ann and Arthur Irwin in the 1950s.

This connection deepened my relationship with Beatrice, and we sometimes travelled together to Bahá'í gatherings. We visited the Peigan Bahá'í Centre for a weekend where a pipe ceremony and honour dance were held for this respected elder. Beatrice and I travelled to the Sylvan Lake Bahá'í Centre for a pot-latch ceremony[133] for Mark Anderson, son of Ted and Joanie Anderson who had been Knights of Bahá'u'lláh to the Yukon.[134] Mark had died tragically and the Yukon Bahá'ís travelled to Alberta to honour the family. Beatrice also attended a meeting in Strathmore to elect delegates to the Bahá'í National Convention. She met Allison's mother there. Beatrice attended a number of picnics and other gatherings and told me she liked the Bahá'í pot-luck tradition where everyone brings a contribution.

Being close to Beatrice helped me meet many members of her family. We consider each other brothers and sisters. Beatrice stayed at our home in Cochrane a few times. One of my favorite stories of her is when I offered her some Earl Grey tea. She scrunched up her nose.

"You don't like the tea, Beatrice?" I asked.

"No, on Morley we drink Red Rose," she said emphatically.

Whenever I share this story on Morley, peals of laughter break out.

***

It was a few days before Christmas. My mother, Kitty, from British Columbia was coming to spend a few days with us before heading up to Edmonton to see my brother. I was visiting Beatrice on Morley and told her my mother was coming soon.

"When?" she asked.

"On December 23rd," I told her.

"Well, I'll come and see her on the 23rd," she told me.

The 23rd came and went and Beatrice didn't show up. But on the 24th, the doorbell rang, and Zalida, Beatrice's daughter, was there.

"I have Îna in the car," she said. We encouraged them to come in. Mom and Îna had a great visit together.

During a writing course, I penned the following character sketch inspired by Beatrice.

***

Beatrice, Îna, 2010

She sits staring out the wide living room window at the trees and snow-covered mountains. At age 93, she has well earned the leisure of watching for the subtle—or not so subtle—weather changes that life in the mountains brings. But she is not content with sitting in her wheelchair in the house all day long. When I enter the room, she quickly moves forward, turning the wheels of the chair and using her feet to propel it a little faster. She greets me with a kiss on the lips and shakes her head vigorously.

"I wanted to go to the round dance at Hobbema, but nobody took me," she says. Hobbema is a good three-hour drive from the Stoney Nakoda Reserve, where Beatrice Poucette is now the oldest member of the tribe.

"Maybe I'll go to bingo tonight!" she says, grinning.

Today, Beatrice is wearing a floral-patterned dress in vibrant colours: rose, blue and green the most dominant. Her headscarf matches the blue of the dress, and she's wearing a red cardigan. Her hair hangs in thin tightly-knit braids. She looks a lot better than the last time I was here. Then, her hair was in disarray, and she seemed embarrassed. There were no other adults around and several young kids ran around the house.

Beatrice was intensely active her whole life. Her weather-beaten face, deeply wrinkled, attests to years of ceaseless activity, raising a family, helping the renaissance of cultural activities on the Reserve, supporting the community through many happy and tragic passages.

The wrinkles on Beatrice's face grew out of kindness, as well as age. When she smiles, her face lights up. I've watched her greeting a myriad of people at round dances, pow-wows, funerals, weddings. She is cherished as an elder, for her humor, for her love. Behind her glasses, her eyes are piercing and full of curiosity. She wants to know what's going on at all times. When her hearing aids have new batteries, she doesn't miss a thing. When the batteries are dead, she is cut off and looks lost. There's a wonderful black and white picture in a living room cabinet of Beatrice and her grandmother sitting outside the church rectory where her grandmother worked as a cleaner. Even as a child, she had dignity.

Beatrice has kept a Stoney Nakoda tradition at the Calgary Stampede. The Stampede, "the biggest outdoor show on earth," which began in 1912, has always included the participation of Indigenous peoples. Beatrice camped at the Indian Village as a young girl. For many years now, she has been a teepee holder at the Stampede, though her extended family takes care of the many responsibilities involved, such as opening up the teepee for inspection and participating in the pow-wow, bannock making, hand games and teepee-raising contests. But Beatrice is often seen in front of her teepee in her wheel-chair, greeting guests from around the world, as well as the many friends she has from all over Indian Country. Prejudice isn't part of her vocabulary. She makes friends easily. Since we first met in 1992, our friendship has deepened and brought a wonderful richness to my life.

Beatrice's life has not been an easy one. As well as the socio-economic dis-advantages experienced by folks in Indigenous communities, she has suffered the loss of a son to a car accident and many years later, her oldest son to heart disease. A granddaughter died of a serious infection several years ago, leaving five children. Another granddaughter died in mysterious circumstances on a neighboring reserve. Beatrice herself was in a major automobile accident about fourteen years ago, when the van she was traveling in was struck by a drunk driver. Her knee was badly damaged. Until then, she was always one of the first to get up and dance at round dances.

Once near the end of her life, Allison and I visit Beatrice at her daughter's home. She has several bags of possessions with her and in one of them, I see a letter addressed to "Old Ena, Morley Alberta." There are many "old Enas (Îna)" on Morley, and I chuckle that the letter has found its way straight to Beatrice, so beloved by her community.[135]

***

During one of Allison's visits to Morley, we paid a visit to Wesley band chief, Ernest Wesley, and his wife, Belva. Allison and I requested permission to use the band hall on Sundays for children's classes and Chief Wesley gave us the go-ahead. Mahnaz Behin and I travelled out four Sundays in a row that winter to hold classes, but no-one showed up.

***

Jacqueline Left Hand Bull, a Lakota Bahá'í from the Rosebud Reservation in South Dakota, served as a member of the Continental Board of Counsellors. Jacqueline made several trips to Morley during the time she served as a Counsellor and was a source of great insight to me personally.[136] On one visit, Jacqueline met Frank Powderface, who had once been chief of the Chiniquay Band. We had a warm conversation outside of the Chiniki Restaurant.[137] Mr. Powderface told Jacqueline that the old people had chosen the land for the Nakoda Reserve. Jacqueline remarked with a smile that they certainly got more beautiful land than her own people did in South Dakota. The Nakoda, Dakota and Lakota are members of the Siouan or Assiniboine language group, though each has its own dialect.

Jacqueline met Beatrice Poucette's brother, elder Eddie Holloway, and his wife, Elsie, as well as his son "Snowball" (Clarence) during a visit to the Holloway home. Also teepee holders at the Calgary Stampede, the Holloways were strong in the Nakoda culture. Eddie and Earl Healy often organized events at Stampede Indian Village. At the first round dance in Cochrane, we had given Eddie a copy of the Sam Bald Eagle Augustine tape, which showed the close connections between Bahá'í and traditional Indigenous teachings, and he cherished it and listened to it constantly. Once his grandchildren broke the tape and he requested a replacement.

One year, during a commemoration of National Aboriginal Day on June 21 at Cochrane Ranche Provincial Park in Cochrane, Eddie and Elsie's son Henry Holloway, who was then serving as a chief from the Nakoda Nation, told the assembled crowd that the Big Hill, which towers above the town of Cochrane, was sacred historically to his people. He said that when the white people came, the Nakoda spoke about them in their language as "white human beings." I was struck by this beautiful expression of respect.

***

During the time I have had the privilege of serving among Indigenous people and even before, the Canadian Bahá'í community has participated in public discourse about Indigenous rights. In 1969, at the time when the White paper was put forward by the Pierre-Elliott Trudeau government and eventually dropped,[138] the Canadian Bahá'í community presented a brief on human rights to then-Minister of Indian Affairs, Jean Chretien. The brief emphasized that human rights are God-given rights, the importance of cultural identity and the need for a Canadian society founded on the principle of unity in diversity. Based on the brief, a pamphlet was developed, *The Right to an Identity*, which was used by the Baháʼí community to reach out with the central message of the right of each individual to his or her personal and cultural identity.[139]

The Baháʼí community further contributed to public discourse when the Royal Commission on Aboriginal Peoples (RCAP) conducted its hearings across Canada in the early 1990s. The following are excerpts from the 1993 Baháʼí submission to RCAP.

> Aboriginal cultures have been distinguished by a worldview best characterized as spiritual in nature. It is significant that Aboriginal leaders and members of Aboriginal communities at the grass roots refer so frequently to the Creator and to the human spirit when they approach the discussion of social problems. Failure to appreciate the gap between this approach to social reality and that of the dominant culture explains much of the misunderstanding and injustice between the Aboriginal peoples of this country and the dominant majority culture...

> The Aboriginal peoples have been among the most intensely affected victims of the dominant social forces operating in ignorance, or in systematic neglect, of spiritual principles fundamental to human happiness and the common weal...

> It has been the failure to apply spiritual principles and moral standards to the relationship between Canada's Aboriginal peoples and the population of the immigrants and their descendants that lies at the heart of the most disturbing problems now faced by our country. And moral standards take their authority from God, the Creator...

> Furthermore, the existence in Aboriginal communities of strong systems of religious belief and practice represent important resources for social development that must not

be overlooked. The survival among Aboriginal peoples of an evident religious inclination and spiritual aspiration must be supported and encouraged at official as well as informal levels in whatever programs and policies are recommended by the Commission.[140]

The Canadian Bahá'í community also made a submission to the Truth and Reconciliation Commission of Canada in September 2013. This submission is presented in full in Appendix I.

Chapter Twelve

Building Bridges, the Amos family

Women's Conferences, Sharing Circles

Parallel to our efforts to form relationships on Morley, the Bahá'í Community of Cochrane initiated an event in the town, which still takes place annually. In 1995, the Fourth World Conference on Women was held in Beijing, China. The National Spiritual Assembly of the Bahá'ís of Canada asked local Bahá'í communities to outreach to see if other organizations were interested in collaborating on follow-up to the conference. Judie Bopp and I approached Holly Strand, director of Community Services in Cochrane (now Family and Community Support Services), who endorsed the idea. The first step was a sharing evening about Beijing; later that fall, the first Women's Conference, called "Beyond Beijing: Women Moving Forward," took place, with keynote speakers Maureen McTeer, Norah Husband, Joyce Irvine and Judie and Michael Bopp. The positive response to the conference led to an ongoing committee, eventually named Tapestry of Women.

I served on the committee for five years. The members were dedicated to building relationships with the women of Stoney Nakoda, and we were lucky to enlist the participation of Belva Wesley and Tina Fox of Morley on the organizing committee for several years. The highlight for us was the 1997 conference held at the Western Heritage Centre[141] called "Singing the Same Song: Women Celebrating Women." Speakers included well-known Canadian singer Ann Mortifee, Tina Fox and Joyce Irvine. A good number of women from Morley attended. After the keynote talk, participants gathered in small circles to tell stories from their lives. My friend and fellow committee member Chris Pike, reminiscing about the activity, remembered being moved by the openness of the Nakoda women in sharing their sometimes harrowing and painful stories with other women.

A women's sharing circle grew out of the conference and met several times both on Morley and in Cochrane. I remember one circle in particular, held at a home on Morley, where at one point we were all talking about soap operas and laughing and kidding. At that moment, I felt we weren't Nakoda women or women of European descent any more, we were just women enjoying each other's company.

During another circle, a Nakoda woman shared the story of her mother, who ran away from the residential school on Morley in the dead of winter. She and her friend had found pieces of cardboard, which they wrapped around themselves to protect against the freezing weather. When they finally made it home, the family rushed around to warm them up. These opportunities to listen and learn about the experiences of our neighbours, so different from our own, were precious indeed.

At the same time these efforts were going on, there were rashes of suicides on the reserve, most often among the youth. On at least three different occasions, I heard about multiple deaths over a short period of time. Eleanor Munkholm, a Bahá'í who taught elementary school at Morley for over ten years, once attended a camp to remember the victims and pray for the youth. She offered to say the very powerful "Long Healing Prayer"[142] by Bahá'u'lláh and this was accepted. We also said that prayer on another occasion at the home of Warren and Mary Anna Harbeck at Ghost Lake, for conditions on Morley to improve.[143]

Tina Fox once told me she kept a notebook where she recorded names of young people who had died, and she had over 100 names. This was back in the nineties. She shared these with a suicide inquiry called for by Provincial Court Judge John Reilly in the mid-nineties. Reilly also called for a Crown investigation into social conditions and allegations of political corruption on the reserve.[144] Reilly has written two books about this harrowing time in Nakoda history.[145] I met another lady who had married into the Stoney Nakoda tribe who told me she had kept a "pain journal" of examples of racism her family had experienced, many of which happened in nearby non-Indigenous communities.

The women's conference committee was privileged to be part of nominating Tina Fox for a Women of Distinction award presented by the YWCA. Tina was the first member of Nakoda Nation to pursue post-secondary education. She served on the Tribal Council for many years, and was instrumental in getting a shelter built for victims of family violence, a new health centre and other initiatives. She later trained as a counsellor and now works at Nakoda Elementary School. For all her achievements and for her courage in standing up and supporting the Crown investigation into conditions on Morley, in 1998 the YWCA gave her the Lifetime Achievement award in a beautiful ceremony at the Jack Singer Concert Hall in Calgary. Sadly, Tina herself later lost a beloved daughter and two well-loved grandsons to tragic deaths.

**

Amos Family

In August 1994, the Cochrane Bahá'í community had a small outreach project for about ten days on Morley. We had invited Mr. Ahmad Motlagh, an elderly Persian believer who had served as an Auxiliary Board member in India in his younger years, and in Canada served for several years as a custodian of the Bahá'í Centre on the Piikani Reserve. Mr. Motlagh was an experienced "direct" teacher, able to speak to people openly about Bahá'u'lláh and the Bahá'í teachings.

During the project, we met daily at the home of Zabi and Mahnaz Behin, prayed, deepened and then reached out on Morley. We used the Ruhi materials, quite new to us, to prepare. I was struck when the tutor recited by heart the first quote of Ruhi Book 1: "The betterment of the world can be accomplished through pure and goodly deeds, through commendable and seemly conduct."[146] This call to selfless service seemed especially significant.

During the project, the friends visited on the Reserve each day. Partway through the week, Ralph Smith[147] showed up unexpectedly. Ralph had operated a service station on the TransCanada highway at Morley for several years, but had been living in British Columbia for some time. He accompanied us to Morley and, through him, we met the family of Wilfred and Caroline Amos. Wilfred was the son of Dick and Julia Amos mentioned previously.

They were warm and welcoming to us because they had known Ralph for many years. Some of the Amos daughters had worked for him, and Ralph and his wife had lived in a home on the Reserve close to theirs.

The sunny day we met them, the Amoses had a teepee set up in their backyard and we visited outside. Wilfred and Caroline and three of their daughters, Victoria, Evelina and Cornelia, became Bahá'ís. I've always remembered Caroline saying that day, "You know, we're really good people. We don't drink, and we always teach our children to pray." Those few profound words, how many families anywhere can say them? Caroline also mentioned that the old people on the reserve had told them to keep their language.

Wilfred and Caroline were truly kind and loving and always welcomed us to their home. Wilfred had developed a virus around six years of age that caused him to lose his hearing and ability to speak, though he spoke and heard normally as a younger child. These impediments did not hinder him from communicating, however. He used a form of sign language that his family also used with him. But most of all, Wilfred spoke with his heart. His eyes lit up when we visited, he'd give us a hug, and we always knew he was happy we were there.

***

A funny incident happened to me during the teaching project. Mr. Motlagh wanted to go to the Reserve on Saturday morning to visit someone he had met during the week. He said the house was a log one at the townsite. When we got there, we couldn't find the person he knew, though we did go to a couple of houses made of logs. I was already a bit nervous. I hadn't ever been to Morley on a Saturday morning before; we might be disturbing people, I thought. As we were leaving the townsite, I saw a well-built log house on the hill and decided to go there. As we approached, I realized it was the building that housed the tribal police. Just then, a stocky tribal policeman came out of the building. Nervous, I started to back the car up, not looking where I was going. Suddenly Mr. Motlagh said, "I think you may have done something to your car." I hadn't felt anything. But I got out of the car and saw I'd run into a telephone pole, crunching in the fender.

The tribal policeman looked at us for a long while. Then he walked slowly down to us, shaking his head. "The pole was in plain view!" he exclaimed.

Then he shook his head and muttered, "Stupid woman driver." He didn't give me a ticket so we pulled away. As we drove, Mr. Motlagh said to me, "Your husband is going to be so mad at the Bahá'í Faith." I replied, "Mr. Motlagh, he isn't going to be mad at the Bahá'í Faith, he's going to be mad at me!"

As it turned out, Harry wasn't mad and said that, in the overall scheme of things, we had a lot more important things to worry about. When I told this story to Jacqueline Left Hand Bull, she laughed and gave me some good advice. "Pat, you should just travel out there as though you're a part of the community."

I took Jacqueline's advice and began to feel more relaxed and more at home. A short time later at the Stoney Nakoda pow-wow, I saw the same tribal policeman. I went up to him and asked if he remembered me. His grimace told me he did!

***

We began visiting the Amos family regularly. The Ruhi Book 3 materials for children's education were available and we began children's classes with Dacster and Lorenzo Chiniquay, Wilfred Jr. Amos, Jovon Beaver, Kengal, Stetson and Clovis Amos, and sometimes with other cousins. We didn't go on a weekly basis–that developed years later–but we did manage once or twice a month. Taban Behin, who started going to Morley when she was just twelve, was my partner, and the children really loved her. Sometimes she went with her older sister Nava or with her parents, Zabi and Mahnaz. Nava and Taban always played with the children, who came to relish their visits. They were also good at inventing games and crafts.

The children caught on quickly to the spiritual education lessons provided by the Ruhi Institute. Through this experience, I saw the value of a set curriculum to which other activities, including cultural, could be supplemented. The lessons were user-friendly for the teacher and based on spiritual virtues such as humility, courage, love, kindness and truthfulness. We added some action songs to the ones based on Bahá'í themes, songs like "Hokey-Pokey," "Head and Shoulders, Knees and Toes," "Love is something if you give it away."

Though I had never considered myself a children's class teacher and did struggle with classroom management, this was one of the most positive experiences of my Bahá'í life. I loved how responsive the kids were to our coming, how loving they were, and how easily they grasped spiritual concepts.

***

Lorenzo was the child with the stutter in our children's class. His eyes shone with light and eagerness, his warm smile showed his happiness we had come. But he always stayed on the sidelines, a hint of anxiety in his luminous eyes. He never joined in the songs and discussions.

Each lesson, based on a spiritual attribute, has games to back up the theme. The day we focused on "possessing a pure heart," I took small sticks and tied them with a large scarf around one of Jovon's arms. Jovon, Lorenzo's cousin, had to pick up a glass of water and drink from it. Since his elbow couldn't bend, the task was impossible. Lorenzo was the first to understand. He quickly seized the glass of water himself and lifted it to Jovon's lips. He "got" the lesson in a flash. At that moment, I realized not being able to speak easily in no way impaired Lorenzo's spiritual perception and his pure heart. With encouragement, he gradually spoke more. Then one summer, he overcame his shyness and took part with his cousins in a summer camp at Sylvan Lake Bahá'í Centre, a few hours from home. He took the leap and stepped out of his comfort zone.

***

The Amoses moved to a new home on their property. Ted Glabush, our Auxiliary Board member for propagation at the time, was doing finishing carpentry on the Reserve and worked on the Amos's home. When they found out he was a Bahá'í, they were very excited to meet more members of their worldwide Bahá'í family. Over the years, they met several more Bahá'ís, whom we took to visit at their home. This included Jacqueline Left Hand Bull; Ruby Gubatayo, an Aboriginal elder living in Alaska who loved to travel in Alberta; Mark Wedge, a member of the National Spiritual Assembly of the Bahá'ís of Canada, who shared a legend from his Tlingit/Tagish heritage with the family; Kevin Locke, a world-renowned Lakota flute player and educator who used hoop dancing to express spiritual principles. On one of

Kevin's trips to Calgary, we arranged for him to speak to children at Morley Community School about the principles behind his hoop dances.

The family met more Bahá'ís when, for several summers, they were sponsored by individuals, communities and institutions to go to a children's or junior youth camp at Sylvan Lake Bahá'í Centre. Debbie Stachnik and Stacey Aidun, as co-directors of the camp, were responsive to making the experience positive, as many of the children were initially shy. Sheila Holloway's son Tribune also went one summer. He had been traumatized by the deaths of his two older brothers. He rarely joined group activities but circled around the classroom setting. Debbie and Stacey's sensitivity helped make it a positive experience for him, as well as for his younger sister. The camp provided spiritual instruction, sports and a wide range of arts, as well as opportunities to serve. Caroline and Wilfred Sr. and other family members drove to Sylvan Lake to see the children perform at the end of their camp sessions.

***

Dacster Chiniquay was the most eager youth from the extended Amos family. He often organized others when we planned service projects or performance evenings. The Amoses had transformed an old vacant nearby house on their property by building a small stage and outfitting it with stereo equipment. Most of the kids did lip-sync and some played guitar. While Bahá'í Shabnam Tashakour[148] worked for The Four Worlds Centre for Development Learning[149] with the Wesley Band, she and her husband, ballet dancer Travis Birch, worked with the Amos youth on step dancing and other dances derived from the Maxwell youth dance workshop. Travis also took the youth into Calgary to a facility owned by Alberta Ballet, so they could practice their dances in a studio outfitted with a proper floor and mirrors. Pillars of Peace, an Alberta dance workshop similar to the Maxwell workshop, also came to the Amos's little cabin and worked with the youth.

All of this activity was especially attractive to Dacster, who competed in a couple of national music competitions for Indigenous youth. In the early years, he sometimes talked with me about his life and how he was writing about it and what he hoped to do in the future. One summer, I went out several times to sit with Dacster while he read to me, to help him improve his reading ability.

When we first visited the Amoses, very few of the children were going to school. They said it was because of the bullying they experienced. Zabi Behin was so concerned about this that he brought out pencils and paper and taught them some writing at the same time as encouraging them to go to school. In time, almost all the children went to school.

The Amos youth came to some off-reserve Bahá'í gatherings where they shared their talents. From time to time, they talked about getting a youth program going with the Bearspaw band or renting a hall so youth could perform their lip-syncs. The dark shadow of the Reserve fell on them when someone torched the little house where they had held so many gatherings and jam sessions. The family had also held a traditional autumn memorial feast for their departed loved ones at that house and a Bahá'í Nineteen Day Feast. Later, Dacster set up stereo equipment in another old house near their family home. We did a weekend workshop in that house tutored by Daniel and Helen Kohm from Calgary with several youth: Dacster, Wilfred Jr, Clovis and Jackson Salter, and Kiemya and Shawyun Refahi from Airdrie. They completed chapter one of Ruhi Book 1. Not long after that, someone stole the stereo equipment from the house.

Along with study, we encouraged the youth to serve. We spent one long day cleaning up the yard for their grandparents. We also spent a weekend on a training for children's class teachers. Shannon Samari[150] helped and they did wonderful crafts. However, it wasn't enough of an impulse for them to take up doing the classes on their own. We began to realize that much more accompaniment was needed for people to have confidence to arise on their own.

We completed a couple of chapters of Ruhi Book 1 with the adults and older youth, and, for a period of time, Bahá'ís from Airdrie, Fariba Refahi and Janette Behrouzi, taught children's classes, with interesting science-based activities.

***

Drumheller Celebration and a Lesson Learned

We've finished the first book of the junior youth series, *Breezes of Confirmation*, and we want to celebrate. So we've planned a trip. We're going to the Royal Tyrrell Museum in Drumheller, a world-class showcase of dinosaur remains, about three hours away. Though the Amoses have all been born and raised in southern Alberta, none of them have ever been to Drumheller. Shannon Samari and her two boys, Denzel and Cayman, and Taban Behin and I are accompanying them.

Though it's a beautiful day, a small incident mars it for me and makes me aware of the dangers of my stress levels getting too high. When Shannon and her boys and I arrive at the Amoses this morning, most of the family aren't ready. Shannon is a little impatient, and I find myself, as frequently happens, caught between two worlds—of the dominant society with its attention to punctuality and the First Nations society going with the flow. I know that travel is frequently a challenge for some Indigenous families, who struggle with proper transportation (as the Amoses have always done), and different events disrupting large extended families. We from outside the Reserve are still making many of the efforts—getting there on time, providing the rides and most of the food. It's definitely not yet an "equal" relationship of reciprocity.

When we finally get going and are on our way to Airdrie, I'm feeling super-stressed, responsible for the whole day, and rather angry about the whole thing. As we approach Airdrie on a back road, there is a train across the tracks in the distance. I don't know what possesses me, but I decide to pass a couple of cars on the two-lane road. I pass Taban, and she looks over at me with a questioning smile. I pass someone else and then see a car heading straight for us in the left lane, a car I haven't noticed before. Mrs. Amos lets out a quick "Pat!" as I just manage to pull my vehicle over into my own lane, before the car speeds by. I can't believe I've taken such a risk with a carful of adults and children.

When we stop five minutes later in Airdrie, I feel shocked to have done something so uncharacteristic for me, and which could have been disastrous if we'd been in an accident. I've lost my good judgment because of stress, feeling so responsible for getting the event happening, just wanting to "get it done," rather than letting go and letting it happen. This is a huge wake-up call. Gradually I learn to listen more closely to my inner voice, instead of overriding it, and to take breaks from service, if necessary.

In the end, we have a wonderful day. It's beautiful, hot and sunny. We stop for a break in Airdrie, then a picnic at Beiseker, and take marvellous photos of everyone in front of the museum and at Horseshoe Canyon. At the museum, Dacster and Taban push Caroline and Wilfred Sr. around in wheelchairs. On the way back, we stop again at Beiseker for another picnic.

***

One of Mr. Amos's favorite activities was a yearly picnic in the summer, which we held on Morley for years. Randall Brown started it in the 1980s, and it came to be a treasured event for the Amoses. Mr. Amos loved to choose the location. One year, we held the picnic on their own property, a beautiful area bordering the Kananaskis River. Others, we went to several locations in Kananaskis country south on Highway 40. When Gregston, one of Evelina's sons, was a toddler, he stepped into deep water at our picnic site and it was a quick reaction on Evelina's part to grab him out. This incident became a bit of a family legend, and the family called the lake "Shogheh's spanakeh," "Gregston's spa." Shogheh is Gregston's Nakoda name meaning "chubby."

The picnic was held a few times in Bow Valley Provincial Park, at Dead Man's Flats, and several times at Stoney Indian Park. One year, Shannon Samari and Brenda de Vries camped out with their children at the Amos home. The next day, others came, and we celebrated the Nineteen Day Feast in their backyard. One year, we travelled all the way to Bragg Creek, then south into the Elbow Falls area of Kananaskis right down to Forgetmenot Pond. Zabi Behin had gone ahead and staked out a campsite. We were late gathering people up and it started to rain hard. I stopped in Bragg Creek for dry firewood. By the time we reached the designated place, Zabi and a couple of other people had already left because of the rain. But other Bahá'ís from Airdrie and a bunch of us from Cochrane and Morley arrived. I was so happy to have the dry firewood so we could roast wieners. The rain stopped, the sun came out, and we managed to have a lovely picnic. Evelina brought a huge birthday cake for one of her boys and shared it all around.

***

The Amos family long remembered the warm hospitality of Jim and Bonnie Nesbitt, who had been caretakers for several years at Sylvan Lake Bahá'í Centre. The Nesbitts invited the Amos family to visit them and stay overnight at their home in Okotoks. We drove together, and Mr. Amos showed me a shortcut through Tsuu T'ina Reserve. Jim and Bonnie, with the help of the Okotoks Bahá'ís, served us pizza and the next morning we had breakfast and a devotional gathering together. When Jim died in 2004, Wilfred and Caroline attended his funeral. Jim had reached out to friends on Eden Valley Reserve and was especially close to Johnny Lefthand who had accepted the truth of Bahá'u'lláh's teachings. Johnny's wife, Mary Jane, remembered Jim's ability to reach out with gifts of tobacco and food, which endeared him to people.

***

Evelina was the backbone of the Amos family for many years. She lived with her parents and sons, Craig and Gregston. As the daughter living at home (her sister Cornelia worked at the time painting houses for the band), she was responsible for keeping the house clean and in general for looking after everything, as her parents were aging. When the youth of the extended Amos family got to the age of fifteen or sixteen, they started to make some of the choices their peers were making, such as taking common-law husbands or wives, and getting into alcohol and drugs. The wanton vandalism of their little cabin where they used to perform music, and theft of the stereo equipment had been discouraging. When the youth started straying, Evelina stayed up night after night waiting for them to get home and constantly tried to counsel them. Taban Behin also tried to counsel them. Things were falling apart with the youth. Evelina was extremely distressed. One day I was there and could tell she was upset and angry. We drove to the Tim Horton's in Canmore and talked a lot. Upset about the whole situation, she wanted out. Within a few months, she had met someone and moved out of the main house. She started a new family with Keon Crawler and now has stepsons and two more little boys. They live north at Big Horn Reserve. Dacster also wanted more in his life, and moved to Toronto for eight years where he worked for Indigenous organizations. Most of the youth eventually settled down with their own families. Cornelia became the backbone of the family and lived with her parents.

***

Within a few short years, the Amos family experienced the loss of their oldest son Fred, a former rodeo champion, who died tragically in March 2013; Wilfred Amos Sr., who passed away from illness in October 2013; and Caroline Amos, who also died from illness in June 2014. Ralph Smith, who had always been close to the family, attended Mr. Amos's funeral and within a few months, he too had passed away.

In August 2015, the family helped organize a memorial picnic at Deadman's Flats to honor the Bahá'ís in the family who had died, as well as Beatrice Poucette, one of their relatives. Everyone brought food to share and we had prayers and stories about these friends. Craig Amos had composed a beautiful drum song for his grandparents, which he sang for everyone.

***

Yet more tragedy was visited on the Amos family in January 2016. While most of the youth managed to get out of the cycle of addiction, Wilfred Junior, who had been in our early children's classes and went to several summer camps, got caught. In the end, after some years of addiction, he was a victim of manslaughter.

At the time of his death, he was still deeply grieving the early death of Fred and his mother and father, Caroline and Wilfred Sr. Junior was a father of two young children, in an off- and-on-again unhealthy relationship with their mother. Junior made efforts to get counselling, though he never got into treatment. Often just getting transportation to appointments was difficult. He tried to stay sober for his children during their last Christmas together. During his last summer, he stayed for a time on the Big Horn Reserve with Evelina and her family. He went hunting and shot an elk. After they dried the meat, the family was able to sell it to get badly-needed cash for groceries.

Though we hear so many stories about deplorable conditions in Indigenous communities, Junior was not a statistic. He was a kind and gentle young man who spoke his language fluently. He had worked for some time as a chef.

His death cut short a life that should have been full of promise, the kind of life every youth in our land should have. While the deterioration of society, at the family, community and institutional level is proceeding rapidly, as the Guardian of the Faith said it would,[151] through Junior's life, and that of others, I have seen how, to date, Canada's Indigenous communities have suffered disproportionately from conditions of injustice and oppression. The harsh reality of life on most reserves or poor neighborhoods where many First Nations live today is a long way from the lives of most average Bahá'ís, myself included.[152]

***

May, 2016

Dacster Chiniquay and I are sitting in the restaurant at the Stoney Nakoda Resort and Casino in Morley a few months after Junior's death. He has taken time to heal from the deaths of his grandparents, Wilfred Sr and Caroline, and his two uncles Fred and Wilfred Junior. He has recently received the good news of his acceptance into an Indigenous program at the Banff Centre. I ask Dacster about the experience of his family with the Bahá'í Faith.

"My grandparents showed we can still keep our culture and still be open to new things. Because I have seen a lot of religions that kind of wipe out our way of living.

"With Bahá'u'lláh, we can be who we are. No judgment was there...And we had exposure to international people, and I learned about different cultures...

"It is important that the Faith allows Indigenous people to keep their traditions. I was impressed by that." Dacster tells me spirit is still very important to his people. Prayer is important, as is Indigenous and non-Indigenous people learning together, he believes.

Dacster speaks highly of the purity of his grandparents. His grandmother Caroline had gone to residential school, but did not want to talk about it with her family. The family of his grandfather, Wilfred, had hidden him away, so he didn't have to go to residential school. Dacster's grandparents gave them a very traditional upbringing, speaking the Nakoda language. The children from the extended Amos family had participated in Bahá'í children's classes and junior youth activities, which helped them to write and read English, in addition to speaking their native tongue. Dacster feels young people today, such as his younger cousins, may be losing the Nakoda language with the increased use of technology.

When his grandparents opened their doors to the Faith, "it made me what I am today," says Dacster. "It made me believe in my own goals and future. People valued my opinion."

Dacster's grandparents witnessed dark times in their lives, as they adapted to changes on the reserve. But they kept joy in their lives.

"If they managed to heal and be joyful, then we can do that in this generation. I see things a lot brighter," Dacster says.

"The Bahá'í Faith brings joy from a different angle; the culture brings joy too. It makes it lighter."

***

Writing, Travelling

Over the years we had been developing friendships on Morley, I was working on the *Angus* book. By the time it was finished in 2000, the whole process had taken over eleven years. The actual writing had taken about two years; the rest had been spent interviewing people, researching, and getting over my feelings of inadequacy. I sent an initial manuscript out to readers and, based on their feedback, began to weed out repetitious material and shape the writing into a chronology and themes. When editing began–always the most exciting part of writing for me–I literally ran to my computer every day, finally feeling things were flowing.

The manuscript went for review to the National Spiritual Assembly of the Bahá'ís of Canada. This review is done to ensure a work is in conformity with the Bahá'í teachings, is accurate and dignified in presentation.[153] I began to wonder about publishing and began to read a book about self-publishing. There was a check-list of questions a writer should ask themselves when considering self-publishing. To my surprise, I could check off positively almost every item. The most attractive reasons to do this were speed of publication and to have control of the final product. Having spent so long on the book,

I just wanted to get it out there. I borrowed money from Mom and our son Isaac to publish.

Needing to register a company to publish, we named it Springtide Publishing, inspired by this quote from the Bahá'í Writings:

> Gradually whatsoever is latent in the innermost of this Holy Cycle shall appear and be made manifest, for now is but the beginning of its growth and the dayspring of the revelation of its Signs. Ere the close of this Century and of this Age, it shall be made clear and manifest how wondrous was that Springtide and how heavenly was that Gift! [154]

The hope portrayed in this quote had always inspired me and seemed fitting for a book about Angus Cowan, who believed so strongly in the potential of Indigenous people. Still anxious, knowing the book covered sensitive issues, and not wanting to offend anyone, I consulted with my mentor Jacqueline Left Hand Bull who had already read the manuscript and made many valuable suggestions to improve it. She suggested another reviewer, Patricia Locke, of Dakota, Lakota and Anishinabe origins, who was serving on the National Spiritual Assembly of the Bahá'ís of the United States. She lightly warned me that Patricia had been an activist and that her opinion was just one opinion to weigh. Of course that made me even more nervous but determined to make sure that before letting the manuscript go, it be appropriate. When Patricia did contact me after reading it, she spoke highly of Angus's noble character and his service to Indigenous people. She had only a few minor suggestions for editing and also kindly agreed to write an endorsement for the back cover. I finally could let the book go.

The printing was scheduled for late fall 1999 and during that time I had an opportunity, through my sister Coleen, to write a book about one of the major employers in my hometown of Golden, Evans Forest Products (now Louisiana Pacific Building Products). An American entrepreneur, Georges St. Laurent, had come to Golden in the 1990s and turned the fortunes of the failing company around, so that it remained viable and able to provide many jobs. Georges wanted a book written about that challenging time.

The terms were excellent; they paid me a contract fee and covered all the costs associated with doing the interviews, getting photographs, hiring a graphic designer and printing the book. And they wanted the book done in four months. Whoa! For someone who had taken years to complete my first book, this was going to be a challenge. However, in those few months, I worked to the deadline, doing forty interviews, developing a manuscript, and collaborating back and forth with St. Laurent and some company officials.

The book, called *Eagles of the West: The Evans Story*, was published by Springtide Publishing in early 2000, right around the time when the *Angus* book was ready. When the *Angus* books arrived on a pallet, Zara and I carried the boxes of books to the basement without even opening one. Finally, we opened a box and saw the book cover Stan Phillips had designed.

"It's beautiful, Mom," Zara whispered. What a moment, to hold that first book in my hand!

***

The initial responses to the *Angus* book were overwhelmingly positive. I breathed a sigh of relief and began to make plans to travel. That summer of 2000, Allison Healy and I made a trip across the Prairies to share the *Angus* book and to visit the many communities where Angus had lived and served the Faith. The trip was organized with the help of Bahá'í institutions and many individuals. We started in the Cutknife/Battleford area of Saskatchewan and visited several reserves, including Little Pine, Sweetgrass, Red Pheasant and Mosquito. Allison knew many people from the pow-wow circuit and the Calgary Stampede and everywhere we were welcomed. People would often ask, "How *do* you know each other?" We'd laugh and say we'd known each other (at that time) for twenty years. Allison opened many doors that I couldn't have gone through without her friendship. We stayed in Fort Qu'Appelle and visited Day Star, Pasqua, Muscowpetung and Piapot reserves.

We visited Kawacatoose (formerly Poorman Reserve), where at one time, while Angus was involved, nearly every family had become Bahá'í. We visited the cabin, still standing, where Old Ed Poorman, the chief of the Reserve, had given Angus his parchment Treaty from the signing of Treaty 4 in 1874 and his pipe. This highly significant gesture, showing his understanding of the value of Bahá'u'lláh's message to his people, is described in the book. We met community members, presented a book to the library and participated in a wagon ride and wiener roast with the Headstart program.

A couple of months before our trip, there had been a national meeting in Montréal to help us understand more about the Ruhi Institute,[155] and we encouraged everyone along our way to participate. Allison conducted a study circle with the friends on Kawacatoose. Among the many people we met, we said prayers with those who had recently lost loved ones and were grieving, attended the funeral of a young woman, and heard about racism in towns and schools from a family whose son had recently been beaten up by a large crowd of non-Native kids. We drove as far east as Kenora, Ontario, with stops in Brandon, Winnipeg, Shoal Lake First Nation and Washagamis First Nation. While we were in Winnipeg, a community meeting was held in a large old brick building. Allison told me the building reminded her of residential school.

When we got back to Alberta, I took another trip to share the *Angus* book through the East Kootenays with musician Caroline Mackay and her daughters Jasmine and Siobhan. The Baháʼí community was small and scattered, yet had managed to organize several concerts and book signings for us. Then Allison and I again set off on a trip to Northern British Columbia. We visited Baháʼí communities and some friends and relatives in Williams Lake, where I had been born, as well as Quesnel, Prince George, Burns Lake, Smithers, Prince Rupert and all the way to New Aiyansh in Nisgaʼa Territory. The Nisgaʼa Final Agreement had come into effect that year, after a quarter century of negotiations. It was British Columbia's first modern treaty, which guarantees the Nisgaʼa people's right of self-determination and includes self-government provisions. Baháʼí Dr. Tania Nordli and her family worked at New Aiyansh at the time and through her we met many people and attended a traditional feast. We also went as far as Fort St. John and Dawson Creek and visited friends on the Moberly Lake First Nation.

***

After having spent much of the 1990s researching and writing, it was time to get some steady paid work. I got part-time work proofreading and copyediting at the local newspaper and was hired as an editor/researcher for a well-known cookbook author. In March 2002, I became acting secretary of the Baháʼí Council of Alberta and later was elected secretary. I carried out this service for five and a half years.

Pat's Irish grandparents, Michael Walsh and Hannah Sheehan.

Pat's Croatian grandparents, Yvonne and Mike Mesich.

Joe and Kitty Walsh, Pat's parents, 1961, Vancouver.

From left, Coleen, Pat, Mom, Tom, at Williams Lake, circa 1955.

From left, Tanya, Karen, Tom, Mark, Pat, Carmen, Coleen, circa 1963.

Pat's university graduation 1970.

With my orange Volkswagen.

The Rioux family. Back from left, Huguette, Jean-Guy, Christian. Middle row, Francis, Madeleine, Louis-Philippe, Hélène. Front: Marielle.

Wedding of Harry and Pat, December 1971.

Maddie Wingett, Pat's Bahá'í teacher.

Sarah Lynk and Fran Maclean, Halifax.

Mom, Zara, Dad, Isaac and Harry, Airdrie circa 1983.

Early Morley picnic. Back row, Ursula Beaver, Deb Clement, Pat, Virgil Lefthand,
Leland Beaver. Front, Zara and Isaac.

Sheila Holloway, Genevieve Holloway, Allison Healy.

Maori Baháʼís visit Morley, old Band Hall, Christmas 1992.

Round Dance in Cochrane at Náw-Rúz, early 1990s. From right, Johnny Lefthand, Tom Heavenfire, Eddie Holloway, unknown, Mark Poucette, Newton Poucette.

Pat and Beatrice Poucette, at Rafter Six Ranch 1990s.

Julia and Dick Amos, early 1990s.

Eddie Holloway, Elsie Holloway, Jacqueline Left Hand Bull, 1990s.

Allison and Earl Healy.

Tina Fox, Nakoda elder, recipient of YWCA Lifetime Achievement Award.

The "Amos clan". Back row, Dacster Chiniquay, Clovis Amos, Evelina Amos, Wilfred Jr. Amos, Craig Amos. Second Row, Garrick Amos, Victoria Amos, Junior Amos, Kengal Amos with Garrina Amos, Caroline Amos, Wilfred Amos Sr., Stetson Amos. Front row, Gregston Amos, Cornelia Amos, Taban Behin.

Amos youth with a friend from Alexis First Nation
at Sylvan Lake summer Bahá'í camp.

Tania Nordli, Sylvan Lake Bahá'í camp facilitator,
with Wilfred Sr. and Caroline Amos, Evelina Amos.

Travis Birch, centre, teaching youth dance moves at "Amos Hall".

Our trip to the badlands at Drumheller. Back row from left, Caroline and Wilfred Amos, Evelina and Craig Amos, Dacster Chiniquay, Cornelia Amos, Taban Behin, Shannon (Samari) Bell. Front row, Pat, Gregston Amos, Lane Twoyoungmen, Brennan Amos, Denzel and Cayman Samari.

CHAPTER THIRTEEN

Turning Point

During the years I had the privilege of service on the Bahá'í Council of Alberta, the Bahá'í world itself had reached a critical turning point. At the beginning of the Four Year Plan (1996-2000), the Universal House of Justice indicated that the "next four years will represent an extraordinary period in the history of our Faith, a turning point of epochal magnitude."[156]

The progress in the community included the development of human resources for service through a network of training institutes in all countries. In time, the curriculum of the Ruhi Institute, which had been developed among Indigenous people in Colombia, was adopted by all training institutes throughout the world. This meant a Bahá'í could travel anywhere in the world to offer service and find virtually the same materials being used, albeit in the hundreds of languages of the world. It also meant a great step forward in meeting the challenge of adequate consolidation and deepening of new believers. The Universal House of Justice, at Riḍván 2004, said the training institute had proved itself to be an "engine of growth."[157]

Courses are constantly developed and tested widely through the Ruhi Institute. They are based on the Word of God with service as a central principle. Courses train teachers of children's classes, animators of junior youth groups, and tutors of study circles, and cover themes from the individual's spiritual development, to the building of vibrant communities.

The Universal House of Justice also guided the Bahá'í communities of each nation to divide their countries into "clusters," based on existing patterns of interaction and communication. In the clusters, such as my own of Rockyview-Bighorn, smaller communities, rural areas, and isolated friends learn to work with each other, while a larger city might be divided into a number of workable sectors.

Through the many changes, the Bahá'í community has been guided to adopt a learning mode, coming together in many social spaces to study, consult, act and reflect, constantly adjusting action as it learns. It has also become much more "outward-looking," seeking to serve with others, not drawing artificial lines between itself and others. Its core activities are open to all as community building activities.

***

Regional Conferences

In 2009, a series of historic conferences was held around the world, called for by the Universal House of Justice and designed to bring all Bahá'ís, whether they had been directly involved or not, up to date on the "framework of action," which the Universal House of Justice said had crystallized. Later, in a letter dated April 19, 2013, the Universal House of Justice clearly explained the "framework of action" as a process that leads to both individual and social transformation.

> This framework promotes the transformation of the individual in conjunction with social transformation, as two inseparable processes. Specifically, the courses of the institute are intended to set the individual on a path in which qualities and attitudes, skills and abilities, are gradually acquired through service—service intended to quell the insistent self, helping to lift the individual out of its confines and placing him or her in a dynamic process of community building.

The same letter speaks about the community.

> They are members of a purposeful community, global in scope, pursuing a bold spiritual mission—working to establish a pattern of activity and administrative structures suited to a humanity entering its age of maturity.[158]

There were two large regional conferences held in Canada, in Vancouver and Toronto, to consult about the framework, and I attended the Vancouver conference. Several months later, areas for intensive programs of growth were named in Alberta, and our Rockyview-Bighorn cluster was one of them. The Bahá'í Council of Alberta indicated that it saw service among the residents of the Stoney Nakoda Nation as a wonderful area for learning.

Those of us who had served on Morley knew of the spirituality of the people. Yet at first I resisted the idea. Having felt somehow responsible for the growth of the Faith on Morley for many years, I felt burdened by this request. However, I soon overcame my resistance, since the Council assured the assistance of Calgary Bahá'ís. Eventually a great change in the nature and consistency of our service on Morley took place. Here is some of our learning during this intense period:

That October, we held a launch in Cochrane for the intensive program of growth in the cluster. Zabi Behin had approached youth Leva Eghbali to serve with her mother, Humeyra, on the Reserve and they soon began to accompany me to Morley. We had a ten-day teaching project when Bahá'ís from Calgary came out to assist. We had training on the first weekend, then prayers and deepening each day before visiting on Morley. The Area Teaching Committee arranged for a prayer chain throughout the campaign and sent out a report each evening to the friends. Friends signed up for a ten-day roster of meals. We followed later with several similar, though shorter, projects, which also included some outreach in Cochrane. During this cycle, five friends from Morley, including four members of Beatrice Poucette's extended family, declared their faith. We made many efforts to follow up by starting Ruhi Books 1 and 3. Mahnaz and Zabi Behin, assisted by Nonie Rideout of Banff, held children's classes, which included the grandchildren of Annie and Bill Wesley who had lost their mother, Cynthia, a few months before.

During this time, Beatrice Poucette was staying in the Bearspaw-Chiniki Elder's Lodge on Morley. Though Beatrice was a member of the Wesley Band, she was able to stay there for some time. We began to visit her and gradually got to know some of the staff, including Patsy Ryder and Dianne Ridsdale. Sheila Holloway was also working at the lodge. Beatrice was always happy to have a visit. During our first project, we asked permission to have a celebration for the Birth of the Báb Holy Day. With twenty-two participants, including the elders resident in the lodge, we had prayers, music, a spiritual program and refreshments.

Those reaching out to Morley began a rhythm of three-month cycles, punctuated with reflection on our actions. During our second cycle in January 2010, we held a devotional gathering at the Elder's Lodge with good participation and lots of children and junior youth. Teams went out every day for home visits. As I reviewed all the emails from these cycles I saw how many visits were made and the many attempts made to have Ruhi study circles, start children's classes and set up junior youth groups. Mahnaz and Zabi Behin, Mitra Shakibanejad, Leva Eghbali and Nonie Rideout went out nearly every week for children's classes. We had difficulty maintaining the classes, partly because of absentee children, partly because the Behins left for service in the South Pacific and the classes were not continued. We also didn't have a steady central place to have classes. When Behins returned, they tried to get the classes going again but found they weren't sustainable. That year we also had our Náw-Rúz celebration at the lodge. During these activities Allison Healy visited and helped us. Prayer chains and remembering the ongoing sacrifices of the Bahá'ís in Írán,[159] were part of our cycles.

I had known the family of Jennie and Gerald Clarke for many years. Their children had attended Cochrane schools and our Cochrane youth had participated with their son Chris Clarke in a drama. When Allison and I visited the Clarke's home, Jennie said her parents from the Rain family had been among the early Bahá'ís on Paul Band Reserve west of Edmonton, but she knew little about the Faith. One day, she asked us to share some of the teachings with her. Another daughter, Ashley (Shannon), had worked with a Bahá'í at a restaurant in Cochrane many years before. One day while visiting the family with Deloria Bighorn, Gerald Clarke told us about his background, which includes Nakoda, Salish, Kootenay, Irish and Scottish ancestry.

That summer of 2010, after the picnic that was held at Forgetmenot Pond,[160] I stopped by the Clarke home to say hello. I found Jennie Clarke visibly distraught. Her adopted son, Tarrence Cecil, nicknamed "Krokus," had recently been killed in an accident on the highway. The whole family, including all her grandchildren, was suffering. I wondered if having spiritual education classes at their home might help, and Jennie said this would be good for the children, to take their minds off the accident. For the next few years, we went about every two weeks to the Clarke home. Leva and Humeyra were wonderful with the children. Leva began to work with the junior youth age and invited her friend Sama Imamverdi to help.

Deloria Bighorn visited our area that fall. With her, we attended a wake on Morley for Mac Chiniquay, an elder and the husband of Georgie Chiniquay, whom Allison and I had visited several times during the past year. The Chiniquays were teepee holders at the Calgary Stampede. The next day, thirteen people came to a gathering at the Bearspaw-Chiniki Elder's Lodge where Deloria spoke on the theme of women's development. That week, Leva organized for some of the Clarke young people of junior youth age, Shanessa, Liam and Jaelyn, to attend a junior youth camp in Calgary, and Deloria spent time with them there.

On November 13, 2010, the Area Teaching Committee wrote to the friends in the cluster, sharing its observation that "we have assumed the posture of learning that the House of Justice referred to in its various messages." Around this time, Mina Moayed, who had recently moved to Cochrane, began helping on Morley, particularly with the food. Allison and I also made strong efforts to begin a Ruhi Book 1 with adults on Morley, but it did not continue after the first session.

***

Summer Camp

The Bahá'í Council had asked us to plan a summer project in 2010, but it actually happened in summer 2011. Allison and I had been visiting Mrs. Chiniquay and asked if we could have a children's camp in her lovely back yard. She agreed and we also arranged a backup place in case the weather was bad. We visited Patsy Ryder, then caretaker of the Chiniki-Bearspaw Elder's Lodge, and learned that the lodge had been closed as a seniors' facility so staff could get more training. Patsy was the only staff remaining. She consented to having the camp there if needed and was also interested in having her grandchildren attend. Deloria Bighorn visited again and helped extend more invitations.

The morning of the camp, it was pouring rain. Allison visited Mrs. Chiniquay with Alice and Jerry Bathke, friends from my first pilgrimage in 1978, then caretakers of the Native American Bahá'í Institute (NABI) in Arizona, who were in Alberta to attend an Indigenous gathering at Sylvan Lake Bahá'í Centre. We changed the location to the lodge, and later that week, Allison brought Mrs. Chiniquay to meet the children.

We had a great response to the three-day camp, with thirty-three people there on the last day. Though we had originally planned full days, we found we had to shorten the days, as we simply didn't have the manpower. The lodge was also not completely safe, as it is built on a hill with some steep drops. The Airdrie community prepared food for the whole three days and Mina took charge of the kitchen at Morley.[161]

We consulted with Patsy Ryder's family, who helped us set up a barbecue lunch on the last day. They got the children to choose rocks and place them in a circle. We opened with a Nakoda and a Bahá'í prayer and an elder explained the significance of rocks to the Nakoda culture. They built a fire and the older youth helped young ones with cooking hot dogs. This was an excellent example of collaborating with the Nakoda people to organize. The camp concluded with a sharing circle for participants.

***

Becoming more systematic

Following the summer camp, Patsy gave us permission to use the lodge on a weekly basis. Sama's parents, Mehran Imamverdi and Shamim Alavi, and her brother and sister, Amin and Neda, began to participate as did youth Naim Bakhshayesh-Rad. We planned several six-week cycles of children's classes. And we began to hold regular reflection meetings with the "Morley team." I sent this email on Oct. 27, 2011, to the team: "As most of you know, we had our first junior youth group and children's classes last week, with seventeen children coming. The spirit was good and we hope the numbers will even increase! Building up to the first class, five trips for home visits were made, to inform the friends of the classes and encourage the parents to come to register them. We will have to keep working on this and developing our relationships with the families."

There were more junior youth camps in Calgary and ongoing Morley team meetings. In January 2012, we planned an Ayyám-i-Há[162] party at the Lodge. Harry, Beverley Knowlton and I were going to be on pilgrimage during that time and Farzin and Mitra Shakibanejad were in Haifa for service. While there, we prayed fervently for the activities on Morley.

Just before the party, Shanessa Clarke arranged an outreach for the youth at the school, where they explained the junior youth spiritual empowerment program.[163] As a result, many junior youth came to the party with their families and began attending the junior youth group. The report from the Area Teaching Committee described the event: "We had a wonderful Ayyám-i-Há gathering on Sunday. Local junior youth and children were decorating and inflating a mountain of balloons as most of us arrived...We were treated to a program of music, prayers, and a charming children's drama before a hearty hot lunch. Our appreciation also goes out to Fariba Refahi and Mahnaz Behin (and their Bahá'í food contributors) for the bountiful lunch enjoyed by at least sixty people."

The youth began to be in the vanguard and the role of adults became one of support. That spring (end of April 2012), we had an example of crisis and victory when we arrived one Sunday for children's classes and the lodge was locked. Patsy Ryder had been let go as caretaker and there was no key for the building. We didn't know what to do. Alvin Young, the grandfather of some of the junior youth, pulled up with them, and Leva told him the situation. He phoned the Chiniki chief Bruce Labelle and spoke with him. The chief talked to his administrator, and we were assured of a key. The next day, Allison Healy and Leva went to the administration building and, by the end of the week, we had our own key. It was a clear instance of someone from the community taking responsibility and defending the program. We have all become close to the extended Young family.

***

During our ongoing reflection, Auxiliary Board member Neda Etemad helped us deepen on the importance of the team having unity of vision. We learned how to consult, work in a group, and that unity is more important than being right. We deepened on Section thirty of Ruhi Book 6 about including culture in our activities.

In preparation for a summer of service in 2012 for Leva, Sama and Naim, Counsellor Dan Scott visited Calgary in June 2012 and came out to Morley with Deloria, Neda and Allison. They participated in the classes and then the team had a short reflection. Deloria spoke about how the junior youth becoming children's class teachers could restore the parenting skills lost in the time of residential schools.

We began to learn that centuries will elapse before the full transformation towards the worldwide civilization of peace and prosperity for all people, as promised in Bahá'u'lláh's writings, will be established. Dan Scott reminded us of this reality by referring to the Riḍván 2010 message, which states: "There are no shortcuts, no formulas. Only as effort is made to draw on insights from His Revelation, to tap into the accumulating knowledge of the human race, to apply His teachings intelligently to the life of humanity, and to consult on the questions that arise will the necessary learning occur and capacity be developed."[164]

Dan said that, given this reality, all we can hope is to contribute a little to this vast process and to build with excellence. Otherwise we will get anxious. His words greatly reassured me. He said we need to think about the next steps to take and to be highly systematic. This is urgent because the condition of the world is dire. The processes we are engaged in will bring a new culture, where everyone goes to the Writings, reads, reflects, gains insight, applies it in their own lives and to their communities, and patterns of thinking begin to change.

That spring, Leva, Sama and Naim reached out on Morley to the cadets, to a youth coordinator and to the school and asked to be able to use the Elder's Lodge full-time to work with junior youth in the summer. Because of security concerns, they couldn't stay at the lodge overnight; however, they travelled out three days a week in the summer to have junior youth groups. The children's class teachers and support people who had been assisting all year consulted and decided not to have the Sunday children's classes in the summer, but to step back, let the process unfold organically and be willing to help if needs arose. We committed to praying daily for the success of the program.

At the end of the summer, the youth reported the project had broken new ground, with six junior youth coming regularly. They finished *Breezes of Confirmation* and started the book *Glimmerings of Hope*. The junior youth related to the books and the issues they raise because of social conditions in their own community. The junior youth did service at the food bank and planted seedlings in the flower boxes at the Elder's Lodge. Once the word got out that things were happening at the lodge, some children came along with the junior youth. There were up to eleven children at any one time. The youth taught the children, with some help from Airdrie and Cochrane adults. They got to know people working at the Lodge and a Christian group that was translating the Bible.

The following year, 2012-2013, we held a junior youth group and children's classes every Sunday, the first time we ever held weekly classes. The junior youth group sometimes met more often to finish the book they were studying. In October, they visited the Calgary Zoo. Preparation for that visit included discussing animal rights and the interdependence of nature and humanity. They also visited the university and the junior youth expressed great excitement about the possibility of attending. Some of the junior youth from those days went on to enroll in university in Calgary. At a reflection that October, the animators reported that the junior youth were bonding, and often called or texted the animators several times a week. One had spoken about God for the first time.

Concurrently, in the children's classes, though attendance was not quite as consistent as for the junior youth, parents sometimes dropped in to the lodge, expressing concern about their children and life on the Reserve. Among those was Kengal Amos who had participated in children's classes herself many years before, and now dropped in with her children.

***

Clarifying our intentions

When our team met in January 2013, Shamim Alavi had made up a chart to show that we had contact with sixteen children. We wished to get the parents more involved and planned a mid-January reflection meeting/sharing circle for parents, to ask about their vision for their youth and children. We decided to do home visits to invite the parents.

Allison Healy came up for a visit, and we visited the day care as workers from there had dropped grandchildren off at the lodge during the summer project. Then we went to see Beatrice Poucette, who was at her daughter Annie Wesley's house. Beatrice's health was poor, and she needed oxygen, though she didn't want to take it. But she did recognize us. We said prayers for her there and the Long Healing Prayer the next morning. She was later admitted to hospital and was placed, for some time, in a senior's facility in Calgary, where we later visited her.

During this visit, we had lunch with Deb Clement, with whom I had visited Morley in the 1980s. Now living in High River, Deb was working in social work for a few months on Morley. We also went to Sheila Holloway's home to invite her. At one point, Sheila asked, "Why are you still coming?" (after all these years). Allison explained that it's our duty to share, and we come because of our love for the Creator and for the people.

At the same time as we were making these visits, other Bahá'ís were visiting more families. As it turned out, only two adults from Morley came to the reflection/sharing circle. Deb Clement joined us as well. We shared about the efforts we were making on Morley to work with the children and junior youth. Later I received an email note from one of the adults that questioned our motives. She said it seemed like we were trying to make the Bahá'í community bigger by proselytizing. This upset me, because in the many years I've been connecting with Stoney Nakoda people, I've never pressured anyone into accepting the Faith or its teachings. But this minor "crisis" became a key to new learning. Realizing we Bahá'ís need to honestly and clearly state our intentions, I replied. Here is part of my email to her to explain our motivation.

> It was very nice of you to send me an honest and open response. In offering to show you the book, *Reflections on the Life of the Spirit*, it was only because you seemed to have some interesting questions on the life of the soul (e.g. about reincarnation) and I thought some of the Bahá'í Writings might be of interest to you.
>
> Bahá'ís are forbidden by our religion to proselytize. What we do is encourage independent investigation of the truth and offer the Bahá'í teachings as one would offer a gift to

a king. We accept whatever the person's response is. It is the right of every person to make their own choices and we never exert any pressure.

Our offering of the service to youth and children is with completely pure motive. We are trying to help build up capacity within the children themselves, for the future generations. Whether or not people become Bahá'ís is not the point. Should they choose to, that is wonderful, but they can use the teachings we have for the progress of themselves and their people without ever feeling they need to become Bahá'ís. We want to walk with people and learn together. This is the purpose of our activities.

The lady's response to my email was extremely positive.

***

The Institute Process As a Way to Work for Individual and Collective Transformation

Paul Hanley writes in his ground-breaking book, *Eleven*, about how a projected huge growth in world population by the end of this century will force everyone to change. He describes the Ruhi institute process as a viable way to work locally for individual and collective transformation, whether or not people are Bahá'ís. The Ruhi-inspired training institutes are administered by Bahá'í institutions but "participants are not required to be Bahá'ís or, for that matter, to subscribe to any religion. In fact, most institute participants are typically not Bahá'ís. The process is freely available: anyone who can recognize in its methods and instruments potent means for movement towards a better society is welcome to participate."[165]

Hanley describes how Ruhi has embedded within it a participatory study-action-reflection process.

> ...Ruhi is a process model. It is not exported or imported as a kind of *fait accompli*, to be superimposed on local

communities. It is an organic, grassroots process of cultural transformation and community building that local people can learn from and apply according to their needs and capacities. They then contribute to its further development by sharing what they have learned. Learning from local experience is accumulated at the regional, national, and global level and reflected back to communities to assist further study, action and reflection.[166]

As mentioned previously, the Ruhi Institute evolved out of work with Indigenous populations in Colombia. While many people had joined the Bahá'í community there, more than ten years of experience promoting the teachings had shown that "merely transferring knowledge—no matter how progressive and attractive that knowledge may be—is not an effective means of helping people or communities transform."[167] These challenges led the Colombian Bahá'ís to an intensive period of reflecting on their purpose and goals.

"What really is the purpose of their religion? Was its objective merely to gain converts to a different religious 'brand'? To build a congregation of followers who attend religious events? Or was its object to affect a transformation in individuals and society so that the just, equitable, and peaceful world anticipated by all world religions could finally be achieved?"[168]

The Ruhi Institute courses are based on the Word of God for today and also include wisdom and stories gleaned from earlier religions.[169] It is envisioned branch classes will be developed, by local people, to include spiritual wisdom, history and stories from their own people.

As Hanley points out, the Ruhi change model is not easy. It requires "a compelling vision and tremendous capacity for self-sacrifice, including countless hours of volunteer time...initiating change is difficult, particularly at the initial stages when few people in a community are aware of the inherent potential of the process."[170]

***

Youth Conferences

In 2013, the junior youth participated in more service projects, such as picking up garbage around the Trading Post convenience store, a volunteer effort greatly appreciated by its owners. They also spent a day cleaning the Elder's Lodge. Initial contact was also made with the Bearspaw Youth Centre to see if activities could be held there. Allison made another visit. Then dear elder Beatrice Poucette passed away on June 29, 2013, at the age of ninety-five.

In February, the Universal House of Justice wrote to the Bahá'ís of the world announcing a series of ninety-five youth conferences worldwide, (which was expanded to 114 because of interest) and extended an invitation to "every youth who recognizes in the methods and instruments of the Plan potent means for movement towards a better society."[171] We were excited about the potential for youth to attend from Morley.

Around this time, I was invited to Myrna Kootenay's fiftieth birthday party. I had first met Myrna through one of the Cochrane women's conferences and had gotten to know her four children over the years. I wondered if any of them might wish to attend the conference and prayed to be able to invite someone. At the party, I spoke to Camron Kootenay, but he and his wife, Jovi, would be on the pow-wow circuit in the summer, as would many other youth from Morley. He suggested speaking to his brother Daryl, who had recently returned from a year serving abroad with Canada World Youth. Having never met Daryl and nervous to approach him, I stalled. When we were just about to leave the party, he was speaking at length with someone. I didn't want to interrupt and waited, then thought maybe I should just leave it. But then I apologized for breaking in and asked for Daryl's email to send him information about a youth conference. Daryl showed immediate interest and I quickly told him about it.

Daryl ended up making the decision to forgo the August long weekend pow-wow and joined the more than 100 youth from Alberta heading by bus to the conference at the University of British Columbia in Vancouver. He participated actively, drummed during a devotional for the whole conference, which got all the youth up round dancing, and enjoyed the diversity of the participants. When Deloria Bighorn visited in September, Harry and I hosted a dinner for the Kootenay family and their relatives and the youth serving on Morley to reinforce our bonds of friendship. The Kootenay family has actively supported our service on Morley. When Leva and Sama began a year of service on Morley in October 2013, Myrna made a connection for them with the director of the Bearspaw Youth Centre, Cathy Arcega.

Year of Service

From fall 2013 to fall 2014, Leva and Sama moved to Cochrane in order to offer more intensive service than had previously been possible. Leva took a break from attending university and pursued some courses online while Sama, who had just graduated from high school, took the year off. The Cochrane Bahá'í community is small and no family could offer accommodation, so I worried where they might stay. I had taken a yoga course that spring and met Naeodi Downey. We had tea one day and she mentioned, quite out of the blue, that she had a suite she was trying to rent. I immediately asked to see it. It was a fully-furnished walk-out suite in a beautiful neighborhood near the Bow River. The Bahá'í Council approved the rent and Leva and Sama moved in October 1. What a wonderful confirmation, as the vacancy rate in Cochrane is low and rentals tend to be pricey.

Leva and Sama began by going to Morley Community School offering to volunteer. The principal, Wes Malo, supported their efforts to engage with the youth during their breaks and lunch hours. Leva and Sama helped the youth form a "Spirit Committee" at the school to provide extra-curricular activities, such as decorating the school, sports, bake sales, dances and talent shows. They helped organize the school's library, which was in disarray after being used for donated clothing during the 2013 floods in the Bow Valley.

Whenever I visited the school with Leva and Sama, I noticed some youth sought them out for talks. Often these youth were going through personal issues, such as bullying or depression, and needed a kind listening ear. Leva and Sama's openness, friendliness and enthusiasm greatly attracted them. Leva and Sama took every opportunity to engage with the Nakoda community, including supporting a weekly youth hang-out night at the Bearspaw Youth Centre, attending cultural camps, hip-hop camps, round dances, pow-wows, sweats, Christmas parties, graduations, film nights, learning some of the Nakoda language, and any other activity happening. They assisted with *A New Warrior for Peace*, a film about bullying and drugs.

Cathy Arcega, program manager for the Youth Empowerment Strategy for the Bearspaw Band, supported Leva and Sama and provided space for them to begin reaching out to youth with the youth conference materials. These materials, studied by youth all over the world that year, included sections on the importance of the period of youth; the two-fold moral purpose for each individual to both develop their own capacities and contribute to social progress. It also covered the special age of junior youth (age twelve to fifteen years). Other topics included fostering mutual support and assistance, community building and contributing to the advancement of civilization.[172] Leva, Sama and Naim studied the materials with a few youth from Morley.

In December, Leva and Sama hosted a cluster reflection meeting at their suite, attended by four youth from Morley, who participated in the consultation and shared what the Spirit Committee at the school was doing. Cathy Arcega also examined the junior youth spiritual empowerment program materials and gave Leva and Sama the go-ahead to work with some junior youth who came to the Bearspaw Youth Centre. Naim faithfully took over the group for eight months.[173]

We volunteered at a children's Christmas party at the youth centre in December, then during the Christmas break, the youth held their first two-day training on Morley to take six youth through the junior youth book, *Glimmerings of Hope*, giving them a taste of the kind of material they would use as animators. The youth were touched by "Kibomi's story" and could relate to the issues facing this youth in a war-torn African country. Five of those youth began a Ruhi Book 1. At the same time, another five youth completed *Glimmerings* with Sama and Naim. The hope was that later, a number of them would recruit junior youth and begin their own groups, accompanied by the team. They would study Ruhi Book 5 (animator training) simultaneously. We asked for prayers from the Holy Land.

I was very excited about the developments as the youth showed a depth of understanding of the materials. In that first training, one youth commented on how much this line from Bahá'u'lláh's prayer had touched him.

"In the darksome night of despair, my eye turneth expectant and full of hope to the morn of Thy boundless favor and at the hour of dawn my drooping soul is refreshed and strengthened in remembrance of Thy beauty and perfection."[174] The youth incorporated the arts into their training, and part of this prayer was used on a wall plaque. The team also built reflection into each training.

As with much of our work, we experienced crisis and victory. We hoped to do more training right away, but that winter Leva injured her knee. During her recovery time, I accompanied Sama to the school each day where we volunteered in the library, an opportunity for me to get to know some of the staff and the youth. It was hard to recapture the training momentum once Leva got back.

Harry and I began hosting weekly suppers for the Morley team. We enjoyed eating together and much laughter. We often had prayers and reflection, which clarified many issues. For example, while deepening on "Frontiers of Learning,"[175] we learned that we could start training animators by taking them through Book 1 and Book 5. It wasn't necessary to go immediately through the sequence of courses, although the goal is for each person to eventually proceed through the whole sequence. We also clarified that it was the Regional Bahá'í Council itself that would provide overall direction to the service on Morley.

Many people had been displaced from their homes during the 2013 flooding and a series of trailer camps, one for each of the three bands, was built on Morley while repairs were done. When the camps opened, we met people in all three camps and had children's classes in two of them. The staff welcomed us, as did the children. Sama, Gage Beaver, Erin Young and River Baptiste planned classes and carried them out. After a year, the tribe found the trailer camps cost too much and shut most of these facilities down.

That year, Leva, Sama and Naim helped the youth put on a talent show. The following year, it happened again, and was based on the theme of "true beauty." They worked closely with the youth, in conjunction with the school music programs, and the quality of the performances took a leap. They ranged from traditional Indigenous dancing, to hip-hop, to rapping, to lip-syncing. It was wonderful to see the potential of the youth for the arts and their enthusiasm once they were encouraged.

A highlight that summer was when several youth from Morley attended a youth conference at the University of Calgary that replicated the regional youth conferences of the previous year. The youth studied the conference materials and made plans for service in their local areas. The Morley team was asked to help decorate the main venue. Leva and Sama, with help from Chantelle Carlston, painted beautiful banners, blue with prairie gold wheat and a cross signifying the four directions. The banners were also used at the school talent show and a Morley youth conference the following years.

The Morley youth[176] excelled at expressing through the arts what they had learned at the conference and performed for the whole audience, doing raps and hip-hop dancing, helped by Karim Rushdy, using the quote "Shut your eyes to estrangement, then fix your eyes upon unity."[177] In another skit with unity and collaboration as the theme, the youth jingle danced in a circle. Their performances were uplifting, engaged the audience, and demonstrated the principle of mutual support.

Over the next year, Leva and Sama returned to full time studies at university. But the team managed to have weekly gatherings on Morley, and two intensive Book 1 Ruhi trainings, one at Leva's home and one at Deadman's Flats.

In summer 2015, several youth took a road trip to Saskatoon to see the development of the junior youth program there and to participate in parts of Books 1 and 5. Later that summer, Tyson Bearspaw attended a third youth conference held in Calgary and also animated junior youth at the Alberta summer school at Wabamum Lake.

That year, with Leva and Sama's encouragement, Tyson enrolled in university in Calgary, staying with Drew Erickson and his roommates. He came faithfully once a week to Morley with Leva and Sama to animate the junior youth group.

***

For many years, when I wanted to contact a friend on Morley, it was difficult. Often phones were out of service or people had changed their numbers to prevent prank calling. So I needed to take a trip out and sometimes wouldn't find them at home. Now with the age of cell phones and smart phones, it has become much easier to connect with people, especially the youth. The youth use text, Facebook, and other apps with great ease, and have even taught me to use them.

Once I confided in someone that I just couldn't keep up with the youth. She looked me straight in the eye and said, "Pat, you can't keep up with the youth!" The energy and enthusiasm of youth are something to be cherished and I've been learning to do small services to support, with gratitude that I'm still involved.

***

November 2014

The sun shines brightly as we head west on Highway 1A towards Morley. On this last warm day before a sudden weather change and snowstorm, the brown November hills seem to anticipate they will soon be blanketed white. A chinook cloud hangs low, stretched across the cobalt sky, its billowing whiteness punctured by foreboding black patches.

Leva, Sama, Naim and I have just finished lunch at a cafe in Cochrane and are heading out to say prayers at the grave of Beatrice Poucette in the Wesley graveyard. Leva's cell phone rings. The youth we are going to visit with after the prayers and then take to his job in Cochrane—I'll call him Brett—wonders when we're coming. He and his friends are thinking of taking off to a local lake. Leva checks quickly with us, then says we'll come to get him right away. He can join us for the prayers.

We take the Morley turnoff, drive over to the TransCanada, then travel to the far west end of the reserve, near Seebe junction. We get on to a dirt road. Brett had told us to turn at the red pylon and we drive down the road to a house that isn't Brett's home, but a "party house," he tells us later. Leva phones him again. After a few minutes, Brett comes out of the house, a drink in his hand. Our friend is obviously intoxicated, slurring his words, but glad to see us. He calls his friends out of the house to meet us, two young women and a young man.

In the past, I would have made the visit as short as possible and found a way to leave without our friend. Having alcoholism in my background, I seem to be able to smell booze a block away, and even being in a place where people are drinking excessively makes me nervous. I'm never sure whether the conversation will turn vile, or whether those drinking will even remember it, or if something chaotic will happen. All my "control issues" come into play. I have learned to quietly leave parties early.

But I've also learned to trust the instincts of the Bahá'í youth who are leading the way in forming friendships. And they had committed to spending the day with Brett. They make no reference to his drinking, joke and carry on conversations with his friends. Finally it's time to leave. Brett goes back in the house with his friends, and we wait for what seems a long time in the car. I keep thinking we should just drive away, but don't voice it. Finally Brett comes out and we start back towards the Morley townsite. He's playing music on his phone and rapping. Leva, Sama and Naim ad-lib lyrics with him. Naim even beat-boxes.

Though Brett is not from the Wesley band, he tells us he recently went to the Wesley graveyard when his brother's best friend died. The young man's mother died too, soon after losing her only child. This year there has been a string of deaths on the reserve, some of them suicides.

We find Beatrice Poucette's grave and say prayers. I especially want to ask her to help the youth of Morley progress to their potential. Then we find the adjoining graves of the young man and his mother. Brett tells us a little about the two deaths. Then he says he isn't going to spend time with his own best friend. He's keeping him at a distance.

"Because my brother lost his best friend, my sister lost her best friend, my mother lost her best friend, my grandpa lost his best friend. I just need to stay away from him."

Brett's decision—to stay away from his best friend because he has seen that getting close to someone probably means losing them—breaks my heart. I wonder whether Brett might not have shared that story if his ordinary defenses weren't numbed by drink.

Quietly Leva says that maybe these are the times we need to surround our friends. And that is exactly what she, Naim and Sama do for the rest of the day, surround Brett with their friendship.

Each of us wanders through the graveyard with our own thoughts for a few minutes. Then we get back into the car and drive to Cochrane. The youth still have a couple of hours to drink coffee with Brett before driving him to work.

CHAPTER FOURTEEN

Exploring Irish Roots

Parallel to serving with Indigenous people, beginning in 2003, Harry and I made five trips to Ireland over eleven years. Like many Canadians whose families have immigrated to this country, whether recently or generations ago, I felt somewhat "rootless." But as a young woman, I hadn't been interested in knowing about either my father's Irish or my mother's Croatian culture.

We didn't travel to Ireland while we lived in Germany in the early 1970s, though we did travel to Croatia. For me a dark cloud hovered over the Irish side of my ancestry because of alcoholism and mental illness. What I experienced and learned from the Ireland trips has contributed to my spiritual growth, embrace of my own cultural heritage and, significantly for this book, an understanding of the connection between the history and culture of the Irish and the First Nations.

I've had a deep allegiance to land since earliest childhood, rooted in the places we've lived in Canada. Not surprising then, that my soul responded so strongly to Ireland's haunting beauty. There is an astonishing variety of landscape for such a small island and the famed "forty shades of green" of the fields, mountain sides and groves of trees. Most spaces in Ireland are laden with remnants of its ancient history, from megalithic tombs, to Celtic dolmans and Ogham stones, to the remains of early Christian monasteries, to peasant homes with thatched roofs, to sites associated with the centuries long Irish quest for freedom from oppression. I've often felt you could not plumb the depths of Ireland's offerings in a whole lifetime.

Because the "Irish connection" began with my father, this is the place to start.

***

We sit in the Williams Lake front room with its deep rose-shaded wall and my father holds me tight. He coos the Irish lullaby, "Too ra loo ra loo ral." I start to cry. I love that lullaby, but cry every time he sings it. I'm a tiny girl, pre-school age, and this is one of my first memories. There is such intimacy in these times with my father, which I crave. But I still cry, never knowing why. Is there grief, melancholy, in his tone? Is he remembering his own mother singing to him?

***

Dad wasn't born in Ireland but in Canada, on the prairies. His parents, Michael Walsh and Hannah Sheehan, had emigrated from County Cork, Ireland in the second decade of the twentieth century because land was so scarce in Ireland. My grandfather's older brother would inherit the family farm, so my grandfather had no choice but to leave. My grandparents were also first cousins, and such unions were greatly frowned upon in Catholic Ireland.

My dad was a generation removed from his Irish roots, but their imprint on him was indelible. This quote in *Native Wisdom for White Minds* by Anne Wilson Schaef resonated deeply for me.

"His race lives in him; he thinks as they thought, their loyalties are his; his memory goes back to their beginnings; their long experience is his counsellor."[178]

My travels to Ireland became a catalyst to accept the complexities, pain and richness of the inheritance from my dad.

***

I might never have visited Ireland if it weren't for Maeve Binchy, an extremely popular Irish writer who dealt warmly and humorously with the complexities of Irish family life. Reading her novels made me want to visit Ireland. Funnily enough, when we did go, I didn't recognize the Ireland in her novels, which I had probably romanticized.

On our first trip to Ireland in February 2003, Harry, Zara and I got off the plane in Dublin at night. The previous week in Israel, where we had been on a Bahá'í pilgrimage, the temperature had reached plus twenty Centigrade.

Now the snow came down in large wet flakes and stuck to the sidewalks. We took a cab to our bed and breakfast in downtown Dublin. We were starving and once we had settled in, walked up a few blocks to main O'Connell Street. We found most restaurants closed. In a tiny sandwich shop, the staff rushed around cleaning up. The doors weren't locked so we walked in. Glancing at our chilled hungry faces, the two young women seemed to make a mutual wordless decision: *Feed these poor tourists, even though our day's nearly done and we want to leave for home.* Those white bread sandwiches, which we never ate back home, tasted wonderful, made, as they seemed to be, with kindness.

***

I felt raw on that first trip, stripped of my moorings to the life I had always known in Canada. My dad, who had died less than two years before, was always at the back of my mind. A day or two into the trip, we saw an old man in a fish and chip shop. I wrote a version of this poem.

Reflections in Dublin, Feb. 2, 2003

Old man, hunched over fish and chips dinner,
Eats slowly, system rejecting real food.
Pulls out his change, stacks it on table in neat little rows.
Duffle bag beside him, all his worldly possessions.
Stares vacantly into space
Gash on forehead belies many a bar room fight
Many an argument waged simply for the sport of it
Fueled by cheap whiskey
Recycling past real and perceived injustices.
His visage haunts me.
Is my good fortune now due to the
Hardships and loneliness endured by my Irish grandparents in a new land?
Could this have been my father's life
Were it not for my mother's stability?
Could this have been my life
If I hadn't left alcohol behind?

The damp intense cold chilled our bones. Only after I began to wear a thick pure wool sweater of Zara's did I get comfortable. Rain poured down the grey day we left Dublin by car. After travelling through the Wicklow mountains south of the city, we headed west towards Galway. Around dusk, Harry was frazzled; this was his first day driving in the left lane, and he just wanted to find a place to stay. We began stopping at every bed and breakfast sign we saw. They were all closed for the winter season. We started to get desperate. Finally we turned at one sign and drove up a long driveway to a large farmhouse. A cheerful, ruddy-faced woman answered our ring.

"Oh my dears," she exclaimed. "You must be so cold. Come in, come in. You are very welcome." We came to love that greeting, often heard in Ireland.

She ushered us into a parlour with a small gas fireplace (we found many B & Bs did not have central heating, but heated one room at a time). Within a few minutes, she brought us tea and biscuits. We basked in the warmth and her kindness. Then she took us upstairs to a large bedroom. Both beds had electric blankets, which she had already turned on, and thick comforters. The rest of the room was frosty and the tiles on the bathroom floor icy. We quickly crawled under the blankets and didn't bother with supper that night. Zara, then 21, looked at her watch. There we were in bed at 8 p.m.! Not exactly a night on the town for a young woman.

The next morning, our hostess fed us a full Irish breakfast of cereal, juice, bacon rashers, eggs, toast and tomato, before sending us off. We encountered this warm hospitality frequently in Ireland and a concern that we be comfortable and well-fed.

***

We met my father's relatives on our first trip, including his cousin Maura Walsh and her family, and his second cousin May Buckley. We saw the farm at Grenagh, County Cork, where my grandfather Michael Walsh grew up, and a house belonging to my grandmother Hannah Sheehan's relatives. We enjoyed their generous and warm hospitality. Saulteaux Bahá'í Tom Anaquod[179] had once told me that the Irish are the most tribal of the European peoples. I found evidences of this throughout our visits. While we were staying with Maura and her husband, Ned, she told us she had two funerals to go to that day.

"We don't really know them, but we go to all the funerals," she said. I smiled inside because of observing for many years that tribal peoples in North America, including the Stoney Nakoda, do the same. In this way, the whole community supports the grieving relatives.

On another trip, when we visited the Aran Islands off the western coast of Ireland, our guide told us that when someone dies, family members dig the graves themselves. They hold a three-day wake during which the body is never left alone, and people share stories about the person's life. When the time for the funeral comes, they carry the body to the church and later to the graveyard. How strikingly similar to Stoney Nakoda people.

Beyond their own people, my Irish relatives had developed a world vision. One of Maura and Ned's daughters had adopted a baby who had been in a Russian orphanage. While we visited, he seemed quiet and passive for a toddler. Maura anticipated this would change as he gradually acclimatized to his new surroundings and received more stimulation. Another relative hosted children from Chernobyl, Ukraine each year, to give them a break from the polluted environment in which they lived.

***

August 16, 2014

The narrow road winds past two small lakes in the Doolough Valley in County Mayo, Ireland. Doolough means "black lake" and is pronounced "doo-lock." There are no human dwellings; verdant mountains and water reflect a constantly changing sky. Today, as we make our way north from the tiny village of Delphi, moments of sunlight heighten shades of lemon and moss-green in the rough grass and deepen the lakes' slate blue.

This landscape, pristine and hauntingly beautiful, contains a sorrowful history. I knew nothing of that history when we passed through on our first trip to Ireland in winter 2003, yet the landscape imprinted itself on my memory. Back then, driving through the valley, we caught on camera the Mweelrea Mountains shrouded in low-lying snowy cloud. We stopped briefly at a monument with a simple rough-hewn Celtic cross. Its words hit me hard: "...to commemorate the hungry poor who walked here in 1849 and walk the Third World today." Another side of the monument marked a 1991 famine walk attended here by Archbishop Desmond Tutu and stated, "soon afterwards we walked the road to freedom in South Africa."

At the time, I was touched by how the Irish, the memory of their own intense famine suffering never far from national consciousness, showed such a deep sensitivity to the pain of others in the world. But I did not know then what had actually happened in the Doolough Valley.[180]

Though we have been back to Ireland several times since 2003, we have not returned to the Doolough Valley. This year I feel compelled to go again. Though the weather is lovely on our way north in the valley, rain pours down incessantly as we drive back south past the stark memorial. I now know what took place here and why a visit to the valley stirs such deep emotions. We have learned that because of its huge impact on Irish history, the Great Famine, 1845-1851, is usually capitalized. During the Famine, two million people died or were forced to emigrate from Ireland. During this time, there were bountiful harvests of grain and dairy products, but while people starved, Ireland was forced to export its food to Britain and overseas.

In March 1849, in the midst of the Famine, a group of 600 starving people showed up in the small town of Louisburg at the north end of the Doolough Valley. Recipients of a program of relief for people who didn't work in workhouses and owned less than a quarter acre of land, they need to be "inspected," ostensibly for whether they actually needed relief. Without explanation, they were told that they had to report to Delphi, some fifteen kilometres away at the south end of the valley, if they wanted to continue to receive the benefits. Walking through the night, these weak, emaciated people made their way through the cold, narrow mountain pass. On arrival, they had to wait outside the lavish home of their landlord, the Marquis of Sligo, while the famine relief inspectors dined. Then when they pleaded their case, the landlord refused help. So the group began the long freezing journey back, through a springtime hailstorm with high winds that swept the valley. The next day, frozen bodies lay along the road and in the lake. Those found were buried without coffins, markers or ceremony.

The number of people who died in the Doolough tragedy will probably never be accurately known, as reports ranged wildly from twenty to 400. But I feel the intensity of this incident, one of many similar tragedies in Ireland, is deeply etched into the landscape. Each year, people from around the world participate in a famine walk along this valley to commemorate the Doolough victims and others who suffer famine.

∗∗∗

The Long March

In 2013, I was organizing books on Indigenous history and cultures at the Morley Community School library, when *The Long March*, a children's book, caught my eye.[181]

Curious about the title, I pulled it out. I was familiar with a similar term, the "Long Walk," which described the forced 1864 journey, because of government policy, of some 8500 Dine (Navajo) people almost 300 miles from their homelands in northeastern Arizona and northwestern New Mexico to Bosque Redondo, a barren piece of land in eastern New Mexico. About 200 Navajo died of cold and starvation during the trip, and more died when they reached their destination. Four years later, they were finally allowed to return to their homeland, Dinetah.

I had also heard the term "Trail of Tears," which paints a picture of the pain and suffering of several Native American tribes, including Cherokee, Creek, Seminole, Chickasaw and Choctaw nations, when they were dislocated from their ancestral homelands in the southeastern United States (modern-day Mississippi, Florida, Alabama and Louisiana). The Indian Removal Act of 1830 required the tribes to move to Indian Territory in what is now eastern Oklahoma. These removals saw many Native Americans suffer from exposure, disease, starvation, and death. By 1837, 46,000 Native Americans had been resettled, which opened up twenty-five million acres for predominantly white settlement in their former homelands.

In *The Long March*, Irish author Marie-Louise Fitzpatrick discovered a true story connecting the Choctaw Indians of Oklahoma to the Great Irish Famine. I was intrigued. Only sixteen years before the events in the book, the Choctaw Indians had their Trail of Tears, marching to Oklahoma during one of the coldest winters on record. Many tribal members lost their lives. Nonetheless, in 1847, when the community heard about the Irish potato famine, they gathered together whatever money they could from their meagre resources and sent $170 to the starving Irish community. This amount, representing great sacrifice, is about $5000 in today's currency.[182]

In *The Long March*, Fitzpatrick created the story of a young Choctaw man who struggled to find enough forgiveness in his heart to contribute to the relief fund. He knew the Irish were among the Europeans who had exploited Native Americans. The words of his grandmother, however, overcame his resistance. "We have walked the trail of tears. The Irish people walk it now. We can help them as we could not help ourselves. Our help will be like an arrow shot through time. It will land many winters from now to wait as a blessing for our unborn generations...."

Indeed, the people of Ireland have never forgotten the kindness shown by the Choctaw Indians. In 1995, Irish President Mary Robinson visited the Choctaw Nation in Oklahoma to personally thank them, on behalf of all Irish people, for their gift. She said the gesture was made, though Ireland was "thousands of miles away, in no way linked to the Choctaw Nation until then, the only link being a common humanity, a common sense of another people suffering as the Choctaw Nation had suffered when being removed from their tribal land..."[183]

Members of the Choctaw Nation have frequently traveled to Ireland to participate in the annual commemorative Famine Walk in the Doolough Valley. Gary Whitedeer, an elder of the Oklahoma Choctaw who wrote the Foreword to *The Long March*, explained to the Irish President that "taking part in that walk and remembering the past between the Choctaw Nation and Irish people and relinking our peoples, is completing the circle." Recently, residents of County Cork erected a beautiful sculpture called "Kindred Spirits," by sculptor Alex Pentek, to memorialize the generosity of the Choctaw.[184]

I heard this story again, when I attended the Bahá'í summer school in Kilkenny, Ireland in August 2014. Paul Hanrahan is a Bahá'í who is part of Action Lesotho, a small NGO helping grandmothers in Lesotho rear their grandchildren whose parents have died from AIDS. During a visit to a Lesotho tapestry factory, Hanrahan told the grandmothers about the Irish famine, the burial of people in mass graves, the food that was going out to the United Kingdom, and how many people died or had to emigrate. Then he told them about the gift of the Choctaw Indians to the Irish people.

"I told them we were helped then, now we help you, you will help others." Hanrahan said that, at these words, the grandmothers all got up and cheered and danced around.

"They said that, until then, they didn't know why we were coming," said Hanrahan.

This made me think of the time I heard Jacqueline Left Hand Bull comment that Bahá'ís should not make "social work" visits to the Indigenous people. For me, her remark meant we go as equals, as people who want to walk together. And if we are in the position to give a leg up, those who are helped will in their turn help others. In this way, no one sees themselves as "victims" or "saviors."

Reading *The Long March* helped me discover another link between my Irish heritage and the Indigenous people of North America.

***

Learning about the Irish has given me insight into the importance both First Nations and the Irish place on culture, and why they cling so strongly to it. Suheil Bushrui, in his book *The Wisdom of the Irish*, gives a succinct summary of Irish history in these words:

> The history of Ireland is intensely turbulent: almost seven hundred years of British rule; eight major armed rebellions; a Jacobite war; the persecution of Catholics and dissenters, denying them basic human rights and dispossessing them of land and property—amounting, indeed, to nothing less than systematic exploitation; wide-scale evictions; a major disaster known as the Great Famine or Great Hunger (1845-8); a de facto partition of Ireland..., a bloody Civil War (1922-3); and finally wide-scale emigration of the young, the able and the productive who left their country to seek a better life elsewhere, but mainly in North America.[185]

Bushrui says that in the midst of such suffering, "the Irish entertained hope against all hope, and in the face of misery, deprivation, hunger and destitution, they remained resolute in search of their identity."[186]

Learning about the long, complex, and often violent Irish fight for freedom from centuries of English domination helped to explain my father's—and my own—resistance against imposition of power, ideas or ideologies by one people on another. Indigenous peoples, for their part, have resisted domination and assimilation through the 500 years since contact with Europeans.

Author Anne Wilson Schaef, who has Native American as well as Irish ancestry, reflected on the common struggle for justice of these two peoples.

> I remember deciding, on my first trip "back home" to Ireland, I would travel around and get a "feel" for the homeland of my ancestors. What I experienced was a surprise to me. I felt a fierce sense of love of freedom and justice coming right up out of the earth of my ancestors. There was no energy of conquest or of imposing ourselves on others. There was simply an unspoken legacy of freedom and justice. I realized that my Irishness had given me two of the most important principles that have guided my life.[187]

Schaef linked the struggle of the Indigenous peoples and the Irish very specifically.

"How fiercely the Irish hold to the concept of freedom, and how vocal they are about the attempts to destroy their culture. Tribal people the world over identify with such attempts to have their culture destroyed."[188]

A revival of the language took place in Ireland in the late 19th century that brought back teaching Gaelic in schools and its use on signs throughout the country. It is spoken in daily life in some regions like the "Gaeltacht" areas of western Ireland. As with the Stoney Nakoda language, efforts are being made to ensure the survival of the language, which is under siege in an environment and business climate dominated by English.

***

Parallels with the Irish and Indigenous people include the terrible suffering of children in residential schools. In 2009, a 3000-page report of the

Commission to Inquire Into Child Abuse revealed the widespread abuse of children in Ireland who had out-of-home care.

"In most instances the reported abuse occurred while witnesses were in the care of the State. They reported being physically, sexually and emotionally abused and neglected by religious and lay adults who had responsibility for their care, and by others in the absence of adequate care and supervision."[189] Reading the report, I found striking parallels with the evidence uncovered by the Truth and Reconciliation Commission of Canada.

***

Ireland was once a land of some eight million people. As a result of the Great Famine, two million died or were forced to emigrate, followed by generations of Irish emigrating for better possibilities, particularly to the United States (there are an estimated 34.7 million Americans with Irish ancestry), Canada, Australia and New Zealand. Today's combined population for both Northern Ireland and the Republic of Ireland is about 6.4 million.

In the Famine, most people emigrated from Cobh in southern Ireland, then called Queenstown. The *Titanic* made its last stop there in 1912, before it hit an iceberg three days later. And the survivors of the ship *Lusitania*, torpedoed by a German submarine off the coast of Kinsale, Ireland in 1915, were brought to Cobh. We visited the old railway station in Cobh, which has been converted into an evocative interactive Heritage Centre. We entered a darkened room and immediately felt we were on the ship that surrounded us. We heard the howl of wind in the riggings and the pounding of ocean on the hull of the wooden ship. We felt the hunger of the people on these "coffin ships," as they were known because of the numbers who died on them. We imagined the hope they clung to, that the new life they travelled toward in America or Australia would be better than the one they were leaving. I was especially moved by a video that re-enacted a gathering to bid farewell to a family member setting out for the new world. In the somber scene, a young woman played the harp and a deep sense of sadness pervaded the room. The family seemed to sense they might never set their eyes on the traveller again.

My grandparents lived a couple of generations after the Famine. They didn't come directly to Canada, but lived in England for a year before emigrating. When we visited Cobh, I imagined the poignancy of their leave-taking.

***

Because Harry, who is not a Bahá'í, likes to drink an occasional Guinness, and because good food and the best Irish music can be found in pubs, we visited quite a few during our five visits. Most of the time, I could get a good cappuccino and I fell in love with Irish music. The pub and drinking culture has been greatly romanticized in Ireland, in advertising and in tourist literature. For many it has become the place where the community comes together.

Though about one-fifth of Irish don't drink alcohol at all, I became aware that over half of all Irish drinkers are problem drinkers and that alcoholism affects one in ten people in Ireland. Binge drinking is endemic. Young people age 25 to 35 tend to have a high level of education, but this age group surprisingly also has the highest incidence of cirrhosis of the liver. In an incisive 2012 article called "Breaking the Code of Silence: The Irish and Drink," the late Dr. Garrett O'Connor, an addiction psychiatrist, recovering alcoholic, and former director of the Betty Ford Institute, traces heavy drinking in Ireland back to the 1600s when "to dull the chronic pain of hunger and humiliation, the peasantry drank home-distilled poitín, made from potatoes or grain..."[190]

In a discussion at the Bahá'í summer school in Kilkenny in 2014, we realized that, besides their salutary aspects, our cultures can have us trapped. The speaker said that if you don't drink in Ireland, you are outside the group and can be very isolated. It made me wonder what aspects of all our cultures are actually stopping our progress as peoples, what aspects have us trapped. The speaker concluded that a complete moral transformation is needed.

***

The greatest attraction for me in Ireland was the strong evidence everywhere of its spiritual legacy. From our first trip in 2003, we explored places that reflected that history, from Druid stone circles to Christian monasteries to the grave site of George Townshend, one of the first Bahá'ís of Ireland. And I came to the conclusion that the most important link between my Irish ancestry and Indigenous people is spirituality. Mr. Townshend believed that the genius of the Irish is, in fact, "the temperamental mysticism of the native race."[191] I believe this may well be the genius of the Indigenous people who have clung strongly to their belief in the Creator and their cultural ways through centuries of oppression.

***

We drove down a country lane overshadowed by trees. Ahead of us was a lineup of cars virtually at a standstill. I got out and walked past them. In front was a farmer herding his sheep. The drivers looked impatient, but there was definitely no room to pass while the farmer was moving his sheep to another pasture.

And so we waited, drinking in the beauty of the day and the warm quiet breeze. When we could move again, we came to the site of the Drombeg Stone Circle in West Cork, tucked away on a rocky ridge, surrounded by a patchwork of green fields. In the distance we could see the sea. We had seen many stone circles in Ireland, as there were hundreds. But this one was stunning in its size and the majesty of its surroundings. It had been carbon dated to around 945 to 830 BC. Restored some years ago, it was aligned to the winter solstice. There were thirteen massive stones in a circle, out of the original seventeen. It was a mystery how people could move them.

Drombeg Stone Circle is known as the Druid's Altar. Druids were priests in the old Celtic religion, before Jesus Christ. It felt like a place of prayer, though what stone circles were used for isn't known for certain. Most believe they were sacred places and used for rituals. They may also have been used to calculate the seasons or some may have been tombs. In 1950, excavations found the cremated bones of a young teenager buried near the centre of the circle at Drombeg.

Near the circle is a big cooking pit with a hearth where hot stones were taken from the fire and dropped into the water trough and seventy gallons of water boiled in about fifteen minutes. This story sounds uncannily like a story I've heard about the origin of the word, "Stoney." The Stoney Nakoda refer to themselves in their own language as "Nakoda," meaning *friend, ally*. But the name "Stoney" was given them by white explorers, because they added fire-heated rocks to boil broth in bowls made of hide.[192]

Drombeg was an eerie place. By the time we were ready to leave, fog had rolled in from the sea and mists had gathered around the large stones, adding to the aura of mystery.

***

We stepped off the boat after a roiling sea voyage from Ballinskelligs and looked straight up.

"I'm not going up there," muttered one of our journey-mates as she stared at the 600 steep steps going up to the monastic site. We were at Skellig Michael, one of the wonders of the world and a UNESCO World Heritage Site. The towering sea crag rose straight up out of the Atlantic Ocean, almost twelve kilometres out from the western shore of County Kerry, Ireland.

"Those steps would never pass a safety inspection in Canada," I thought. There were no guard rails, nothing to hang on to during the 150-metre path up. We were lucky to have gotten there. About two days out of seven, boats can't land because the waters are so rough. Three of my sisters, a couple of years after our visit, had to be satisfied with circling the island in their boat.

So our mate stayed near the safety of the landing dock as we clambered up Skellig Michael. This was the dramatic home to an ascetic group of early Christian Coptic monks for some seven hundred years, from the sixth to the twelfth or thirteenth centuries when they left for the mainland. In the "saddle" of the rock, a flat area, they built oratories for worship and "beehive" cells of rocks and earth to live in. These still survive, along with a south-facing vegetable garden plot and cistern for collecting water, a testament to the skilful labour of the monks. Little is known about their life, but records show Vikings raided them twice. A legend has it that the monks taught the Christian faith to one of the raiders, Olaf Tryggvesson, who became Norway's first Christian ruler.

What drew the monks to this windblown, isolated, mystical place, I wondered, as I gingerly picked my way down the precipice, back to the landing. It must have been desolate in winter, even dangerous, with high winds off the ocean. But the monks had been here during one of the most creative times in Irish spiritual history. I had first learned about this from George Townshend's 1930 essay, "The Genius of Ireland." In striking language, he wrote about the role of Ireland during the centuries when Europe was reeling during the fall of the Roman Empire.

> Once, and only once, and for One only has Ireland taken the
> part of a leader among the peoples of Europe. Save for this

one historical achievement, she has stood outside the main currents of development in the West, and has mingled little in European affairs. During the sixth, seventh and eighth centuries, and later, she played an illustrious part in the propagation of Christianity in Europe, and won for herself the undying title of the Island of Saints and Scholars.[193]

Thomas Cahill, in his 1995 book, *How the Irish Saved Civilization*, describes how Christianity in Ireland began with St. Patrick. I learned his name at birth was Patricus; he was a young man of Roman background who was brought as a shepherd-slave to Ireland. After several years, he escaped to Europe, and eventually made his way back to his parents in Britain. After having visions of the Irish, he went to Gaul (today's France) to train at a monastery, before returning as a missionary bishop to Ireland in 432 AD. According to Cahill, Patrick was earthy and warm, cheerful, good humoured and generous, and he had a lifetime commitment and steadfast loyalty to the Irish. He had to find a way of connecting his message to the deepest concerns of the Irish and their way of seeing the world.

Like many Indigenous people, the Irish had a "sense of the world as holy, as the Book of God—as a healing mystery, fraught with divine messages," wrote Cahill. In Ireland, "mystical attitudes toward the world were taken for granted..."[194]

While the Irish did embrace the new faith in droves, they "very much remained Irishmen and Irishwomen. Indeed the survival of an Irish psychological identity is one of the marvels of the Irish story," writes Cahill.[195] Ireland is unique in religious history, because it is the only land where Christianity was introduced without bloodshed. The Irish also made it their own, rather than a Romanized version of the faith.

During Patrick's thirty-year mission to the Irish, the Irish slave trade came to a halt, as did other forms of human sacrifice, and war significantly diminished. Patrick died in 461. The Irish Christians became the first Irish literates. While books were being destroyed on the European continent, as Teutonic barbarian hordes were over-running Europe and destroying the fruits of classical civilization, in one generation the Irish mastered Latin, Greek and some Hebrew; devised an Irish grammar and recorded their native oral literature; and copied the great books from the continent. They created and perfected the art of illuminated manuscripts, usually made of dried sheepskin parchment or calfskin velum. Employing spirals, intricate knotwork, ancient religious and historical figures, animals, birds and fish, the manuscripts were true works of art. The most famous Irish manuscript still in existence is the Book of Kells, on display at Trinity College in Dublin.

Though undoubtedly Christianity in Ireland has a much darker side to its later history, Cahill, like Townshend, maintained that the early Irish Christians helped the faith survive, in its early years, even on the European continent, preserved Latin and Greek and the richness of European civilizations, and illuminated beautiful passages from the Gospel.

***

In our first winter trip of 2003, we visited George Townshend's grave at Enniskerry, a small town in the Wicklow Mountains south of Dublin. His grave has the words, "I saw a new heaven and a new earth," a reference to promises in the Bible.[196] Townshend had spent several years in America, had returned to Ireland and become a Church of Ireland (Protestant) clergyman, when he received some pamphlets about the Bahá'í Faith from an American friend. He immediately recognized the truth of its teachings. In December 1920, he wrote his recognition to the head of the Faith, then 'Abdu'l-Bahá, who replied that every word of Townshend's letter "indicated the progress and upliftment of thy spirit and conscience." He also expressed the hope that "thy church will come under the Heavenly Jerusalem."[197]

It was this wish of 'Abdu'l-Bahá that kept Townshend in the church for twenty-eight more years, always yearning and striving to bring his fellow Christians to a recognition that their prophecies had been fulfilled with the coming of Bahá'u'lláh. During this time, he rose to the station of Archdeacon of Clonfert and Canon of St. Patrick's Cathedral in Dublin. A scholar of deep knowledge, he wrote many books eloquently exploring the relationship of Christ and Bahá'u'lláh. Though he was widely respected and loved, his efforts fell on deaf ears within the church and, at an advanced age, he withdrew from the church to dedicate his efforts fully to the Bahá'í Faith, thereby also giving up the salary and comforts to which as a clergyman he had been entitled.

Townshend lived in an isolated village called Ahascragh in County Galway and was completely alone as a Bahá'í in Ireland for many years. Though isolated, the beauty of the countryside in western Ireland gave Townshend time and inspiration in his literary work. A gifted writer, he assisted Shoghi Effendi in translations of Baháʼí scripture, but never met him personally. His gentleness and humility belied his greatness of character. Shoghi Effendi appointed him a Hand of the Cause of God,[198] and wrote on his death in 1957 that he was one of three "luminaries" shedding light on the Irish, English and Scottish Baháʼí communities.

Part of what so affected me in Mr. Townshend's life was how alone he was and how seemingly unresponsive the Irish people of the time were to the great message he had embraced and worked tirelessly to share.

With such a rich spiritual legacy from its earliest history, George Townshend eloquently asked if Ireland could repeat today the great contribution to civilization it had made in the past.

> To consider in how marked a degree this precious gift of spirituality has been theirs in the past: to look back at their history and see how the religious genius of the people has over centuries made Ireland a lamp of Faith in a darkened world, directing its light both East and West, to realise that still there burns deep in the heart of the people that ancient fire: to hear to-day in our midst the voice of poets beginning to raise again the strain so long unheard, and chant in the ears of a forgetful world the praise of eternal beauty and eternal truth: thus to watch, to listen, and to reflect is to be filled with hope that Ireland may not be slow to catch the vision of the New Day, of the coming of the Kingdom of God, and that she may do for mankind now such service as she did for the world long ago in the hour of its darkness and its need.[199]

***

After a few trips to Ireland, resentment of my father had disappeared, to be replaced by understanding and gratitude for such a rich cultural legacy. When we returned from our second trip to Ireland, I strongly wished to visit my Irish grandparents' graves. I didn't even know where they were, but found out from a cousin that they are buried in the Catholic cemetery in St. Albert, north of Edmonton. I took flowers and, in my prayers, thanked them for their sacrifice and struggle, acknowledging that I stood on the shoulders of ancestors on both sides of my biological family.

Chapter Fifteen

Investigating the Truth Part One

After I had explored my cultural roots, I felt the need to know a more accurate history of Canada with respect to its Indigenous people and started this in earnest after getting back from pilgrimage in 2012, over 30 years after I had met Indigenous people as an adult.

***

I nervously sat in the circle, wondering what would happen next. Roger, an elder from Kainai Reserve, began to share his memories of being taken away from his family at the age of five, to the St. Paul Anglican residential school on the Reserve.

"The first thing, they stripped us of the clothes we were wearing, threw us in the shower, and cut our hair. Most of us had braids; we all got the same short haircut. They said we might have lice."

Roger continued: "I heard at another residential school in Saskatchewan they didn't explain why they were cutting everyone's hair. For one young boy, he only knew that, in his culture, you cut your hair when a beloved relative dies. So he thought his mother had died."

Roger was speaking during a preparatory workshop in June 2013, for the final national meeting of the Truth and Reconciliation Commission (TRC), which would take place in March 2014 in Edmonton. The meeting, co-sponsored by a number of churches and by the TRC itself, took place in Indus, a tiny hamlet southeast of Calgary. I attended with my friend Allison Healy, at the request of the Spiritual Assembly of the Bahá'ís of Calgary.

Each child got a number, said Roger. I imagined scenes eerily familiar to the photos we had seen at the Holocaust Museum in Jerusalem the year before.

"That first night and for many more nights, I woke in the dark to hear children crying 'Mama' and 'Dadda,'" Roger went on.

The food for the children was of extremely poor quality while, at the same time, the teachers and clergy ate well.

"We saw the roasts they were eating and the butter. Only the best," said one survivor.

Because of the bad nutrition, staff gave children cod liver oil. One survivor remembered the staff used the same spoon to give the medicine to all the kids. At a time when tuberculosis was rampant in the schools, this showed unconscionable negligence. Of all the things I heard, this made me the angriest.

After Roger spoke, he asked us to go around the circle and share one new thing we had learned about residential schools. The most painful moment came when Roger's wife broke down and left the circle, saying she couldn't participate. We learned that, only two weeks before, their twenty-four-year-old youngest son died. I couldn't imagine how much courage it took for her to come to the meeting. The young man had committed suicide. No doubt lingered in my heart that this loss had a direct connection to the intergenerational trauma of the residential schools.

On the way home, I drove to our daughter's house in Calgary. I had been looking after our grandson Cedar, a toddler, a couple of days a week. I felt drained, but I desperately wanted to see him. How wrenching it would be to see Cedar taken away and put in a school where I wouldn't see him for months, even years, where I couldn't show him my love and affection, couldn't tell him family stories, couldn't teach him lessons I have gleaned from life. The immensity of the loss to Indigenous people over many generations boggled my mind.

On the second morning, we heard more about the work of the TRC in recording the stories of survivors and in educating non-Indigenous Canadians. Though gently presented, the weekend exposed the magnitude of the repercussions from this deep wound in Canadian history.

At noon I walked out into the sunshine, my shoulders slumped over, a weight in the pit of my stomach. I called Zara.

"What's the matter? You sound awful," she asked anxiously.

I tightened my grip on the phone.

"No one should ever have to go through what these kids went through," I muttered. I asked to see Cedar again on my way home.

Allison, herself a First Nation survivor of a residential school, cried during the weekend. The churches were there and actively involved in the truth and reconciliation work. What should we be doing as Bahá'ís? she asked. I pledged then not to let this opportunity for awareness and education slip away. We called the secretary of the Alberta Bahá'í Council and asked for a meeting for Allison and I to share what we had experienced and to make recommendations for educating the Alberta Bahá'í community. We also later met with the Spiritual Assembly of Calgary.

When I went back into the main hall to examine the displays about St. Paul residential school, Roger came over to talk with me. He seemed to sense my anguish. He shared stories and answered my questions. His kindness and humility, despite his own unimaginable suffering, revived my flailing spirit and strengthened my resolve.

A couple of weeks before the workshop, I dreamt that I ran away from the pain in the meeting. Roger's sensitivity helped me to stay. I committed myself to becoming an ally and friend in the healing between our peoples.

***

Duane Mark and I sit together in the library of the Morley Community School. Duane, who is the cultural specialist at the school, quietly answers the question I've posed.

"I don't really understand why I didn't educate myself more about First Nations history, given how many years I've been involved with the Aboriginal community," I say. "It's only now that I've decided to really educate myself. I've been reading for a couple of years. And I am someone who has been *involved* with First Nations. There are so many others who have not."

Duane's reply is succinct. "I think it's because people think they will feel a lot of guilt and shame and they just don't want to feel it. So they just avoid the subject."

Duane's reply illumines the resistance and defensiveness I have felt regarding learning about Canadian history. I know in the past I didn't want to feel the burden of our shared history, I didn't want to feel responsible for the injustices that exist to this day. I felt I had committed myself to First Nations because of the promises in the Bahá'í Writings and that was enough.

But I've been troubled with many of the online comments that appeared during the Idle No More Movement that began in Canada in December 2012.[200] Some comments are so ignorant, so racist, I'm ashamed for my fellow Canadians. I read another, follow-up article in *The Globe and Mail* about Idle No More, by Drew Hayden Taylor[201] and of the sixty-five comments, at least two-thirds are negative and of the same ilk as those two years before.

How have we gotten into this terrible abyss, this deep separation between our peoples? The ignorance is astonishing: comments that Indigenous people receive everything free, that all they get is on the backs of "us taxpayers." Why don't they just get a job and work like everyone else? Why don't they just "get over it?"

The prevalence of such divisive discourse has forced many news organizations, such as the Canadian Broadcasting Corporation, the *Victoria Times Colonist*, the *Toronto Star* and the *Toronto Sun* to close online comments for Indigenous issues.[202]

An incident that occurred in Nanaimo, British Columbia in 2013 illustrates both underlying tensions and constructive response. A letter to the editor containing racist comments about Indigenous people was published in the *Nanaimo Daily News* in March 2013.[203] After the letter appeared, more than 300 people protested outside the newspaper offices, including members of the local Snuneymuxw First Nation, the mayor of Nanaimo, local community groups and citizens. More than 1,000 joined a Facebook page protesting the Nanaimo paper's editorial judgment. While the newspaper removed the letter from its website and said it should not have been published, it also defended the writer's right to free speech.[204]

In response to the letter, local, provincial and national First Nations leaders, local community groups, members of the university community and city hall came together in a series of public dialogues. Dr. Roshan Danesh,[205] who facilitated a large gathering of 300—400 people that lasted many hours, said the message and theme of the whole evening, among everyone, "was about love. That this challenge about reconciliation is about learning to love one another. It's not about learning to tolerate one another or just live side by side. It's not about just learning to accept our differences. It's about learning to love." A statement made that night said: "At its core, reconciliation demands a new mindset and orientation to ourselves, each other and the relationships we forge between us. It is rooted in the firm recognition that we must form bonds of unity amongst us that recognize, respect and build upon our diversity. Reconciliation demands that we move far beyond merely learning to tolerate one another but rather cultivate true altruistic love in our hearts and minds for each other."[206]

***

I received literally no education about First Nations during my school years, nor did I take any Indigenous history courses at university. In general what I know comes from my own experience serving among First Nations and reading a few books. But until recently, I hadn't delved into the overall history of the relations between Indigenous people and settler Canadians. But there are so many troubling questions that can only be answered by at least a cursory knowledge of Canadian history.

In the process of learning, I often called to mind a Bahá'í quote that I found: "...a massive dose of truth must be administered to heal...."[207] As in addiction—where to find any kind of healing, we must become completely honest with ourselves—I felt a deep need for understanding why we are where we are in Canada, no matter if the truth lead to me feeling guilty, defensive or ashamed. Interestingly, I have not ended up feeling these emotions as much as grief and sorrow for what Indigenous people have suffered and more committed to fostering friendships and reconciliation.

I'm a slow reader and there are literally thousands of books written by Indigenous and non-Indigenous authors about every aspect of history, culture and the relationships between our peoples. I didn't start out with a reading list, but read some older and more current books. In struggling to discern how to share the learning, I realized each individual will find their own way to educate themselves, some through formal courses, others through reading, others through their professional work with Indigenous people, still others through friendships, voluntary efforts in various organizations devoted to reconciliation, or youth development and sports. My hope is to share my learning journey and encourage and stimulate others to do theirs. The historical issues that have led us to where we are today are complicated and as varied as the local peoples themselves. What I describe is merely an overview and risks being over-simplistic, because such a brief space cannot do justice to the complexities of many issues. For anyone who has really studied them, it will only be "Native Studies 101." But we all need to know at least a bare minimum.

After three years of researching, I felt completely burdened by the learning, well aware of having barely scratched the surface and totally inadequate to share it. But about this time, *Honouring the Truth, Reconciling for the Future: Summary of the Final Report of the Truth and Reconciliation Commission* (HTRF) became available. In reading the document and the accompanying one, *The Survivors Speak,* I realized that the TRC had succinctly written about the history and outstanding challenges that face Canada in the quest for true justice for Indigenous people and reconciliation between them and the rest of Canada. I did not have to reinvent the wheel; rather, I could strongly urge my readers to study these documents.[208] In what I have written, the choices of subjects and the emphases are strictly my own.

***

In Search of April Raintree

Finding Indigenous literature a helpful way to become better informed, the first book I re-read was *In Search of April Raintree,* by Beatrice Culleton Mosionier, a harrowing fictional story of two Métis sisters who were brought up in separate foster homes and the effects of racism on their lives. I had read the book many years before on the advice of a friend; this second edition included ten critical essays following the story. *In Search of April Raintree* was one of the first books to portray the anguish of life for Indigenous children removed from their homes and living with sometimes racist foster parents and in an unsupportive society. April, whose skin is lighter than that of her younger sister, Cheryl, tries to live life fully in a white society, marrying into a rich white family tainted with prejudice. Through the sisters' connection with each other, though they don't live together, April tries to give Cheryl pride in their parents and in their heritage. Cheryl's later realization of their parents' alcoholism is crushing to her. When April is raped by a group of white men, who mistake her for Cheryl, both her world and Cheryl's begin to fall apart. The result is tragic. Though Culleton Mosionier finishes the book on a positive note, this book opened my eyes to the realities of life for many Indigenous women. Gritty and depressing, it dealt with racism, alcoholism, foster care, various kinds of abuse, rape, prostitution and suicide.

For many Canadians, this may have been the first novel they read about Indigenous women, though there have been others written about these subjects since Culleton Mosionier's ground-breaking work. Though I might try to tell myself that the story is an isolated one, I know in my heart it isn't. Recently I read *Birdie* by Tracey Lindberg, a gripping contemporary novel that explores themes of sexual abuse and missing and murdered Indigenous women.[209]

As I write in 2017, there is an ongoing national inquiry into missing and murdered Aboriginal women in Canada, and by the RCMP's statistics, there were at least 1,017 Aboriginal women and girls murdered from 1980-2012. This is a homicide rate roughly 4.5 times higher than that of all other women in Canada.[210]

Professor Jo-Ann Thom Episkenew observed that reading books such as these that deal with actual experiences lived by our fellow citizens is "traumatic" for both Indigenous and Euro-Canadian students.

> Steeped in the mythology that Canada was settled, for the most part, by peaceful negotiation and that Canadians are, as a whole, polite, considerate, and a trifle boring, my white students—and I think many white readers—are startled to see themselves through Métis eyes and to hear their behaviour analyzed from a Métis point of view...In both *Halfbreed* and *In Search of April Raintree*, white readers learn that racism in this country is not just the practice of a few isolated individuals; it is a significant part of Canadian culture.[211]

I was struck by one online comment about *In Search of April Raintree*.

"It's a sad book to read but every woman in Canada should read it, because it happens all the time."

***

The Inconvenient Indian

I now read alternative histories to the ones taught when I went to high school in the 1960s. In my generation, we focused solely on European history, the exploration of Canada, and the defining battle between what were called "the two founding nations" of Canada, the English and French, on the Plains of Abraham. Indeed it seems that a great deal of our national history must be rewritten. I have talked with young people who today learn about Indigenous history, including residential schools, during their high school years. But this process is just at the beginning. The TRC has worked with all provinces and territories to ensure this history is included in all curriculum, both in the school system and at the university level.

I highly recommend *The Inconvenient Indian*, a contemporary work by Thomas King, for anyone who wishes to get an overview of both Canadian and American Indigenous/non-Indigenous relationships and history. King imparts difficult information with a substantial dose of humour while working to give an accurate view of history. He describes his struggle with most history written by the dominant society.

"I simply have difficulty with how we choose which stories become the pulse of history and which do not," King writes.[212] He gives as an example the 1876 Battle of the Little Bighorn in which former successful Civil War commander George Armstrong Custer headed a battle against Lakota and Northern Cheyenne people lead by Crazy Horse and Sitting Bull. The arrogant Custer suffered a defeat with the loss of 258 soldiers, seven civilians and three Arikara scouts. Though it was a huge Native American victory and the worst U.S. Army defeat in the Indian wars, in the retelling of the story, we've created a myth, says King.

"…we've told the story of Custer's defeat so many times, in so many ways, that his moment on the plains of Montana has become a metaphor for heroic but ill-advised and failed endeavours."[213] King points out that we always talk about "Custer's Last Stand" and Custer as the defiant hero. This myth plays itself out in many fairs and public re-enactments, while we know next to nothing about the principal Indigenous heroes in the battle. King believes most Indigenous history has been forgotten, and, when it is remembered, it's a series of entertainments, "an imaginative cobbling together of fears and loathings, romances and reverences, facts and fantasies into a cycle of creative performances, in Technicolor and 3-D, with accompanying soft drinks, candy, and popcorn.

"In the end who really needs the whole of Native history when we can watch the movie?" he asks sardonically.[214]

In the history I learned in high school, there was no mention of such heroic figures as Sitting Bull, Crazy Horse, Gabriel Dumont, and Little Crow, though the history is readily available should we choose to explore it.

***

In *The Inconvenient Indian*, King defines terms such as "Status" or "Legal" Indians, explains treaties, notes there are over 600 recognized Aboriginal nations in Canada and 550 in the United States, and that in Canada there are fifty-two distinct Indigenous languages. He describes the Removal Act of 1830 in the United States, which saw the majority of tribes east of the Mississippi moved out of their homelands to Oklahoma by 1840.[215]

King gives examples of tribes being relocated from their lands for hydro-electric projects in both Canada and the United States. Most dams built on Indian lands destroyed Aboriginal hunting and fishing and flooded villages and sacred sites.[216] An example was the Pick-Sloan Plan in 1933 for flood control on the Missouri River. A system of dams and reservoirs was built on the land of over twenty-four tribes. None of the tribes were consulted about the project. The Army Corps of Engineers ignored the treaties, acquired land through eminent domain (the right of a government or its agent to expropriate private property for public use, with payment of compensation) and built the dams, which forced 1000 families to relocate and flooded 155,000 acres of Indian farmland. None of the non-Indian towns were flooded.[217] A similar situation occurred in Stoney Nakoda territory, discussed later in this chapter.

There are several contemporary examples of land use disputes involving Indigenous land in both Canada and the United States, which have elicited widespread protests. These include the Dakota Access Pipeline, the Liquified Natural Gas (LNG) projects in northern British Columbia, and the Site C dam, a project for a large-scale earth fill hydroelectric dam on the Peace River in north-eastern British Columbia.

King provides numerous stories in *The Inconvenient Indian* that illustrate the tenacity of Indigenous nations in struggling for their rights and in particular for their land. As an example, in 1868, the U.S. government signed the Treaty of Fort Laramie with the Lakota, guaranteeing them the exclusive use of the Black Hills that were sacred to them. Nine years later, after gold had been discovered, non-Indigenous people flooded into the Black Hills. That same year, 1877, Washington unilaterally confiscated the Black Hills and turned the land over to White miners and settlers.[218] The Sioux worked for generations to claim back the hills and almost a hundred years later, in 1980, in the lawsuit *United States v Sioux Nation of Indians*, the Supreme Court ruled that the Black Hills had been illegally taken and they should be paid back $106 million. The Lakota refused the settlement.

"Money was never an issue," wrote King. "They wanted the Hills back."[219] To this day, the Lakota have not given up their claim to the Hills. King describes the importance of land to the Aboriginal people.

"Land. If you understand nothing else about the history of Indians in North America, you need to understand that the question that really matters is the question of land," he writes.

"Land has always been a defining element of Aboriginal culture. Land contains the languages, the stories, and the histories of a people. It provides water, air, shelter, and food. Land participates in the ceremonies and the songs. And land is home. Not in an abstract way."

King says Blackfoot friends from Kainai Reserve in Alberta have more than once told him Ninastiko or Chief Mountain is a special place for them and that when they can see it, they know they are home.[220]

The story that hit me most describes the origins of the Oka crisis that occurred in Canada in 1990. King traces the story back to the early 18th century when France gave Mohawk land to the Sulpician Missionary Society. The Mohawks had protested and asked for the land back for over two centuries. In 1959, the town of Oka built a nine-hole golf course right next to the band's cemetery. The Mohawks launched a legal protest but the golf course went ahead. In 1977, the Mohawk filed an official land claim, but in 1986 it was rejected. In 1989, the mayor of Oka announced the golf course would be expanded to eighteen holes and luxury condominiums built. King writes that for this expansion, the town planned to move on the Mohawk, taking more of their land and leveling a forest known among the Mohawk as "the Pines." They would build new fairways and condominiums on top of the band cemetery.[221] On March 10, 1990, the Mohawk began occupying the Pines. Months later, a confrontation became a shooting war, and Corporal Marcel Lemay died and Mohawk elder Joe Armstrong suffered a fatal heart attack. The crisis began in earnest after that and endured a total of seventy-eight days. The Sûreté du Québec was joined by the RCMP, 2,500 members of the Canadian military, and jets, tanks and armoured vehicles.

King describes in detail how the confrontation, which cost over $200 million, could have been avoided. Québec's Minister of Indian Affairs at the time, John Ciaccia, had realized the potential for trouble months before and had urged the federal government to buy the disputed land from Oka and give it to the Kanesatake Mohawk.

"Of course, the Kanesatake Mohawk already had Aboriginal title to the land, had had title to the land long before France gave it to the Sulpicians, but Ciaccia's idea was, given the circumstances, a reasonable compromise." But politicians at all levels stalled and did nothing.

Ironically, in 1997, seven years after the Oka crisis was finally over, the Department of Indian Affairs and Northern Development quietly purchased the disputed land for $5.2 million and "gave" it to the Mohawk for their use.[222]

I watched and highly recommend the film by Alanis Obomsawin, *Kanehsatake: 270 Years of Resistance*, which shows how the conflict escalated from peaceable beginnings to armed conflict.[223] The Oka crisis highlighted long-standing issues in Canada and in 1996, the federal government appointed the Royal Commission on Aboriginal Peoples (RCAP), the most wide-ranging study of Aboriginal peoples ever done, which provided a baseline history of Aboriginal and non-Aboriginal relations since first contact.

One final example of the many stories in King's book of the Aboriginal struggle for justice concerns the Taos people of New Mexico. Carson National Forest park in the northern part of the state covers 1.5 million acres and contains Wheeler Peak, the highest mountain in New Mexico. To create the park, Theodore Roosevelt's administration confiscated 50,000 acres of Pueblo Indian land without a treaty or payment. The area included the Ba Whyea, or Blue Lake, a remote mountain lake sacred to the Taos people.

King writes: "Oral tradition has it that the Taos tribe was created out of the waters of the lake, and the area around the lake has always been part of the tribe's ceremonial life."[224]

In the early 20th century, the Forest Service ran a trail up to the lake, stocked it with trout, and built a cabin near the lake for forest rangers. The Taos protested the seizure of the lake and land and the opening of it to public recreation. The Land Board awarded almost $300,000 to the Taos but they countered, offering to waive any cash compensation in exchange for a clear and exclusive title to Blue Lake and the land around it. But the Forest Service objected.

Again, in 1933, the commissioner of the Bureau of Indian Affairs helped the Taos get a statute passed for a fifty-year permit to allow them year-round exclusive use of the lake and the area around it. But the Forest Service stalled. Seven years later, the Service allowed a permit to the Taos to use the lake for three days in August each year.

Finally, in 1951, the Indian Claims Commission affirmed that Blue Lake had been taken illegally, but the Commission had no power to return the land. But the Taos hadn't changed their minds. Taos elder Juan de Jesus Romero summed it up nicely.

"If our land is not returned to us, if it is turned over to the government for its use, then it is the end of Indian life. Our people will scatter as the people of other nations have scattered. It is our religion that holds us together."

King writes, "He might have gone on to say that Taos religion was in the land and the land in the religion, but for him, that would have been stating the obvious."[225]

Finally after sixty-four years of fighting, in 1970 President Nixon signed Bill 471 into law. This gave the Taos people trust title to 48,000 acres of their land, including Blue Lake and 1,640 acres surrounding the lake.

The examples Thomas King provides in his book taught me a lot about the injustices underlying much settling of North America. I needed to know more.

***

I examined some basic concepts about the history of Canada after hearing a keynote talk by lawyer Louise Mandell[226] at the 2012 Conference of the Association for Baháʼí Studies in Montréal. Dr. Mandell was part of a legal team assisting the Union of British Columbia Indian chiefs and its president, George Manuel, fight to ensure Indigenous participation in the patriation of the Canadian Constitution from Great Britain in the early 1980s. When the Constitution was patriated in 1982, as a result of strenuous efforts on the part of Aboriginal groups and activists across the land, the rights of Aboriginal peoples were enshrined in the Constitution Act through Section 35.[227]

Mandell was also counsel on the famous Delgamuukw case that spanned the 1980s and 1990s. She was on the legal team for the Gitksan and Wet'suwet'en Nations in northwestern British Columbia, arguing they have Aboriginal title over territories they've inhabited for thousands of years, title that continues to exist. The ownership is recorded in their oral histories and ceremonies. This concerned land in the area where my Croatian grandparents had homesteaded.

On the opposing side, the Crown argued that 19th century colonial law extinguished Aboriginal title and that oral tradition could not be relied on as evidence in court. In the landmark 1997 ruling, the Supreme Court of Canada affirmed the existence and constitutionally protected status of Aboriginal title, and judged Aboriginal oral traditions to be admissible as evidence.

Following Mandell's talk, I wanted to examine many historical realities of which I had been ignorant. These included the origins of Indigenous populations, the discovery of America, *terra nullius* and the Doctrine of Discovery, early contact, the Royal Proclamation of 1763 and Treaty of Niagara, treaties, colonialism and residential schools.

***

Origins

Today much research is going on into the origins of the Indigenous populations of the Americas. Estimates of the beginning date of human habitation in North America range up to 40,000 years ago. Indigenous scholar Olive

Dickason has reported that by about 11,000 years ago, "humans were inhabiting the length and breadth of the Americas, with the greatest concentration of population being along the Pacific coast of the two continents...About 5,000—8,000 years ago, when climate, sea levels and land stabilized into configurations that approximate those of today, humans crossed a population and cultural threshold, if one is to judge by the increase in numbers and complexity of archaeological sites."[228]

According to the Report of the Royal Commission of Aboriginal Peoples (RCAP), the population of the Indigenous peoples in North America at the time of initial sustained contact with Europeans was 500,000, though some believe this to be a conservative estimate. Dickason reported that greater populations existed where resources were easily accessible, such as on the Northwest Coast with its abundance of fish and in what is today southern Ontario, where farming was practiced by Iroquois tribes. Other Aboriginal groups were hunters and gatherers, such as on the northwest plains where nomadic tribes survived on the communal bison hunt, and where there is strong evidence of buffalo drives and jumps. Dickason commented on the high degree of cooperation and organization required for these forms of hunting, with self-reliance, loyalty and mutual support as critical elements of tribal survival over thousands of years.

The 4,000-page RCAP report, released in 1996, documents extensive research done on every aspect of Aboriginal life. It affirms that before contact with Europeans, Aboriginal nations were fully independent and organized into societies, occupying the land as their ancestors had done for centuries before them. There is growing research into these early civilizations.[229]

***

"The Discovery of America"

While evidence shows that America was populated for vast centuries before Europeans arrived, history did not even get straight which Europeans first came to this part of the world. It's now well-known and documented that Christopher Columbus was not the first European to "discover" America on behalf of the Spanish empire, when he landed in the Bahamas archipelago, on an island he named San Salvador, in 1492. Rather, Viking Leif Eriksson is generally regarded as the first European to set foot on the shores of North America, nearly five centuries before Christopher Columbus. Believed to have been born in Iceland around 970 AD, one theory states that Eriksson was travelling from Norway to Greenland when his ship went off course and arrived on the North American continent.[230]

The exact identity of the area Eriksson called "Vinland" is uncertain, but in 1963, archaeologists found ruins of a Viking-type settlement at L'Anse aux Meadows in northern Newfoundland, which correspond to his description of Vinland. More than 2,000 Viking objects have been recovered from the site, which has been declared a UNESCO World Heritage Site. The settlement dates to approximately 1000 AD.[231]

In Iceland today, it's commonly believed Christopher Columbus had actually visited Iceland's Snaefellsnes Peninsula in 1477 to learn about earlier Viking trips to the New World before he took his own voyages. Though Leif Eriksson did not remain in the region, and in fact never returned to it, there is evidence other Vikings did reach North America.[232]

***

terra nullius and The Doctrine of Discovery

Two concepts about which there has been no information or much misinformation in our history books are "*terra nullius*" and the "Doctrine of Discovery." These two concepts prevailed at the time of the first contact of Europeans with the American continent. RCAP explains that *terra nullius* is a Latin term referring to empty, barren and uninhabited land. Until recently, the history of North America was about discoverers, explorers, soldiers and settlers from Europe who arrived to a new world of wilderness, forest and lakes. The Indigenous people were portrayed as bands of nomadic hunters, few in number, and their lands as virtually empty—*terra nullius*. These lands were a "wilderness to be settled and turned to more productive pursuits by the superior civilization of the new arrivals. In the same way, Indian people have been depicted as savage and untutored, wretched creatures in need of the civilizing influences of the new arrivals from Europe."

RCAP states that this "unflattering, self-serving and ultimately racist view" coincided with the desire of British and colonial officials to acquire Indian lands for settlement with the minimum of legal or diplomatic formalities. RCAP goes on to state that we now know this idea was simplistic and one-sided and that Indian nations were organized into societies of varying degrees of sophistication.

"Many practised and taught agricultural techniques to the new arrivals and had established intricate systems of political and commercial alliances among themselves. The forests were not trackless; they were traversed by well-known trails created for trade and other social purposes well before the arrival of Europeans." So too, writes RCAP, rivers and lakes served as highways and natural boundaries between tribal nations. Many tribes were relatively large in population and had spawned smaller off-shoot tribes precisely because of population pressures.

"In short, there is an increasing body of evidence that Indian nations were far more subtle, sophisticated and numerous than the self-consciously 'civilized' Europeans were prepared to acknowledge."[233]

***

The Doctrine of Discovery is explained in *Honouring the Truth, Reconciling for the Future: Summary of the Final Report of the Truth and Reconciliation Commission* (HTRF). Prior to Christopher Columbus's voyages to the Americas, the Catholic papacy was granting Catholic kingdoms the right to colonize lands they "discovered."

"In 1493, Pope Alexander VI issued the first of four orders, referred to as 'papal bulls' (a term that takes its name from the Latin word for the mould used to seal the document), that granted most of North and South America to Spain, the kingdom that had sponsored Columbus's voyage of the preceding year." These orders helped shape the "Doctrine of Discovery," the political and legal arguments used to justify the colonization of the Americas in the sixteenth century. In return, the Spanish were expected to convert the Indigenous peoples of the Americas to Christianity.[234]

While rulers of other European countries didn't accept that the Pope could give away sovereignty over half the world, they didn't reject the Doctrine of Discovery either. They changed it to suit their own needs. The English, for example, "argued that a claim to 'discovered lands' was valid if the 'discoverer' was able to take possession of them."[235]

RCAP commented that when faced with the reality that people already inhabited the lands, European commentators popularized the notion that Indigenous peoples were merely in possession of such lands, "since they could not possibly have the civilized and Christian attributes that would enable them to assert sovereign ownership to them. Over time these ethnocentric notions gained currency and were given legitimacy by certain court decisions."[236]

The papal bulls were used to justify processes that were to come: conquest, colonization and exploitation. There is a movement today within the Catholic Church to have the Pope rescind the centuries-old papal bulls that provide the basis for the Doctrine of Discovery.[237]

***

Early Contact

According to RCAP, the early history of contact between the Indigenous peoples and Europeans was characterized less by "European pretensions and open conflict with Aboriginal peoples than by a mixture of mutual curiosity, halting efforts at friendship and some considerable apprehension."[238] While some Aboriginal groups retreated, others did enter into trading relationships with the new arrivals right away. Aboriginal peoples knew the land and how to survive in it and were more populous.

"These factors contributed to early patterns of co-operation and helped to overcome the colonial attitudes and pretensions the first European arrivals may originally have possessed."[239] The report notes that the existence of relatively strong, organized and politically active and astute Aboriginal nations were the reason the Europeans recognized, at first in their relationships, and later in law, "the capacity of Aboriginal nations not only to govern their own affairs and to possess their own lands, but also to conclude treaties with them of a type similar to those the European nations were accustomed to making with each other."[240]

The report strikes a cautionary note, however: "... by highlighting areas of co-operation, recognition and mutual benefit, it is not our intention to minimize the hardship, the diseases and the sheer racial and religious prejudice that were also characteristic of the initial period of contact."[241] While the newcomers suffered greatly from illness and exposure, the help of Indigenous people with food, medicines and survival techniques no doubt prevented even worse suffering for them.

"Much more devastating, though, was the impact of imported diseases on the Aboriginal population, whose numbers are estimated to have declined by at least 50 per cent, if not more, in the first three hundred years of sustained contact."[242] While the population of Indigenous people before contact with Europeans has been estimated to be between 500,000 and over two million, with disease, a census estimate of the size of the Aboriginal population in Canada in 1871 places the number at 102,000.[243]

***

The Royal Proclamation of 1763

The complex history of relations between the British colonies and Aboriginal peoples is important to understand, to discover the roots of misunderstandings that continue even to this day. In the summer of 1763, after the Treaty of Paris ended the Seven Year's war, New France was ceded to the British Crown.[244] At the same time, in the American interior, a widespread war led by the Odawa chief Pontiac was erupting over unresolved grievances. This showed the need for a comprehensive and enforceable Indian policy. In response, the British government adopted the somewhat unusual measure of issuing a royal proclamation, declaring in resounding terms the basic tenets of British policy toward the Indian nations.

The ensuing proclamation, known as the Royal Proclamation of 1763, was based on two key principles, according to RCAP. The first principle recognized the autonomous status of Indian peoples, organized in nations or clans, with their own leaders, and envisaged the establishment of treaty relations. A second principle acknowledged that Aboriginal nations were entitled to the territories in their possession unless, or until, they ceded them away.[245]

The Truth and Reconciliation's final report (HTRF) underlines the continuing importance of this proclamation. On October 7, 1763, King George

III issued the Royal Proclamation by which the British Crown first recognized the legal and constitutional rights of Aboriginal peoples in Canada. The Proclamation declared that all lands west of the established colonies belonged to Aboriginal peoples and that only the Crown could legally acquire these lands by negotiating Treaties.

"At a time when Aboriginal peoples still held considerable power and conflicts with settlers were increasing, British officials sought to establish a distinct geographical area that would remain under the jurisdiction of Indigenous nations until Treaties were negotiated..."

The Royal Proclamation was ratified by over 2,000 Indigenous leaders who gathered at Niagara in the summer of 1764. The Treaty negotiations were conducted in accordance with Indigenous law and diplomatic protocol.[246]

HTRF states that both the Royal Proclamation of 1763 and the Treaty of Niagara of 1764, "established the legal and political foundation of Canada and the principles of Treaty making based on mutual recognition and respect."[247] Anishinabe legal scholar John Borrows notes that twenty-two First Nations, composed of 2,000 people, camped for two months at Niagara. The signing of the treaty in these circumstances meant Canada was founded by the intermingling of British and Indigenous law, according to Borrows.[248]

Because the provisions of historic treaties have been violated so often, and to reset the relationships between Indigenous people and Canada, the TRC recommends a new proclamation to reaffirm the long-standing, but often disregarded, commitments between Canada and Indigenous peoples. The proclamation would include an official disavowal of *terra nullius* and the Doctrine of Discovery and a commitment to the full implementation of the United Nations Declaration on Indigenous Peoples.[249]

"The principles enunciated in the new Royal Proclamation will serve as the foundation for an action-oriented Covenant of Reconciliation, which points the way forward toward an era of mutual respect and equal opportunity."[250]

***

Confederation

The Aboriginal peoples were the first partners of both the English and French newcomers who arrived on this land. However, in 1867, at the forming of the Confederation of Canada, the partnership did not include them at all. RCAP states that the Confederation, while momentous for the non-Indigenous society, had little positive significance for Indigenous people, who were completely excluded as active participants.

"They and their rights and privileges seem to have disappeared almost completely from the consciousness of Canadians, except for the provision in section 91(24) of the *Constitution Act, 1867* making 'Indians, and Lands reserved for the Indians' a federal responsibility, an object of future federal legislation." Through the *Indian Act* and related legislation, section 91(24) gave the authority for federal government intervention in the internal affairs of Indian societies, as it attempted to promote the eventual break-up of Aboriginal societies and the assimilation of Aboriginal people into mainstream, non-Indigenous society.[251]

There had been many pre-Confederation treaties[252] and economic relationships between Indigenous people and settlers, especially based on the fur trade. But particularly after Confederation, Canada began to need more tracts of land to house large numbers of incoming settlers, soldiers, administrators and others. With the colonial expansion, RCAP states that "the impact on indigenous populations was profound."

> Perhaps the most appropriate term to describe that impact is 'displacement'. Aboriginal peoples were displaced physically — they were denied access to their traditional territories and in many cases actually forced to move to new locations selected for them by colonial authorities. They were also displaced socially and culturally, subject to intensive missionary activity and the establishment of schools — which undermined their ability to pass on traditional values to their children, imposed male-oriented Victorian values, and attacked traditional activities such as significant dances and other ceremonies. In North America they were also displaced politically, forced by colonial laws to abandon or at

least disguise traditional governing structures and processes in favour of colonial-style municipal institutions.[253]

The earlier period, which had seen a formal nation-to-nation relationship of rough equality between Indigenous nations and newcomers, changed with Confederation. The newly-elected first Prime Minister of Canada, John A. Macdonald, bluntly announced to Parliament that it would be Canada's goal "to do away with the tribal system and assimilate the Indian people in all respects with the inhabitants of the Dominion."[254]

***

The Indian Act

The Indian Act of 1876, in giving the federal government broad responsibility for all aspects of Aboriginal lives, became a central instrument for their colonization. Amendments made particularly, but not only, during the time Duncan Campbell Scott was superintendent of Indian Affairs, sought to further and further control Indigenous lives, becoming a tool of breaking up families, dispossessing peoples of land, violating their human rights and committing cultural genocide.[255] Below is a condensed version of certain amendments to the act that shows the tight control taken by the government over Indigenous lives.

An 1881 amendment prohibited the sale of agricultural produce by Indians in the prairie provinces, to keep them from competing with white farmers. In 1885, an amendment prohibited religious ceremonies and dances, such as the potlatch and thirst or sundance. An amendment passed in 1905 allowed the removal of Aboriginal people from reserves that were too close to white towns of more than 8,000 residents. A 1911 amendment allowed municipalities and companies to expropriate portions of reserves, without the permission of the band, for roads, railways, and other public works.

Legislation was passed to prevent Indian bands from hiring their own legal counsel; they had to use lawyers picked by the Department. The Indian Act was amended in 1927 to stop anyone from raising or receiving funds to pursue legal claims without the minister's consent.

Until 1968, status Indians could be enfranchised (i.e. status taken away and replaced with Canadian citizenship) in order to get a university degree, serve in the military, be a clergyman or lawyer, drink alcohol, or to marry, if they were women, non-Native or non-Status men.

Two provisions added in 1927 forbade Indigenous people from forming political organizations and from speaking their Aboriginal languages. They were also unable to vote in federal elections until 1960.[256] And one of the worst violations of human rights possible came with an amendment, in 1920, to allow the government to compel any Indigenous child to attend residential school.[257]

For a long period of time, Indians couldn't leave the reserves without getting a pass from the Indian agent. This provision was implemented after the Riel Rebellion in 1885, though it was never legislated by Parliament and was a violation of treaty provisions. Research has shown that Hayter Reed, who served as deputy superintendent general of Indian Affairs from 1893 until 1897, knew the pass system wasn't legal (even the Northwest Mounted Police had protested it wasn't law) and tried to keep it secret as long as possible. This system gave Indian agents much power over people. Permits or passes were found dating as late as 1969.[258]

In much of British Columbia and certain other parts of Canada, land questions had never been settled. In 1916, the McKenna-McBride Royal Commission was formed, with a mandate to resolve questions of Indian reserves in British Columbia where no treaties had been signed. The federal and provincial governments passed legislation removing extensive tracts of valuable land from many reserves in BC, without approval of Indigenous governments, and until recently without compensation.[259]

In 1914, Duncan Campbell Scott, who had been recently appointed as Deputy Superintendent General of Indian Affairs, added harsher measures to the Indian Act, including an amendment requiring Indians to get official permission before appearing in Aboriginal dress in any dance, show, exhibition, stampede or pageant. Having long enjoyed an annual visit to the Indian Village at the Calgary Stampede, I was surprised to learn how the First Nation tribes almost didn't become part of it.

During the first Stampede in 1912, Guy Weadick, American cowboy, entrepreneur and mover and shaker behind the Stampede, wanted the southern Alberta Indigenous nations to be part of it. However, officials at the Department of Indian Affairs didn't want the tribes to participate. Some prominent Albertans, including Senator James Lougheed and R.B. Bennett, a future prime minister,[260] exerted pressure on the minister of Indian Affairs to overrule his department and allow the tribes to leave their reserves and go to Calgary. Two thousand Indians took part that year.

For several years after 1912, there was little Indigenous participation in the Stampede. But when Guy Weadick returned from Wyoming in 1919, he applied to Scott to include Indians in the Victory Stampede that year. Scott refused, but Weadick invited the Indians to come anyway. Weadick felt their participation was necessary to make the event a complete success and, in the opening parade, Chief Yellow Horse of the Blackfoot rode beside Weadick and many other First Nations rode as well.

In 1923 when the Stampede became an annual event, organizers again asked Scott if the Indians could take part, and he refused. However, the new minister of Indian Affairs, Charles Stewart, a former premier of Alberta, overruled his deputy, Scott. From then on, to this day, Indigenous people have played a strong role in the Stampede. Author Mark Abley believes that the Indigenous peoples' resistance came as an unpleasant surprise to the department that expected compliance and had grown used to passivity.

"What's important about...the early Calgary Stampedes, is that the Aboriginal people chose to take part, even though they were breaking the law. True, their participation depended on the support of powerful members of society who were willing to defy Indian Affairs. But this support would have meant nothing if the Aboriginal people themselves had given up."[261]

While problems with the Indian Act endure to this day, and there is frequent talk about abolishing it, in 1969 when the (Pierre) Trudeau government brought in the "White Paper" on Indian Policy, that called for the repeal of the Indian Act, and that would wind up the Department of Indian Affairs and lead to the eventual extinguishment of the Treaties, almost every Indian organization came out against it.

"Whatever the problems were with the Indian Act and with the Department of Indian Affairs, Native people were sure that giving up their land and their treaty rights was not the answer," wrote Thomas King.[262] The White Paper was abandoned two years later.[263]

***

Cedar and Crowfoot's grave, August 2013

I strap my fourteen-month-old grandson, Cedar, into his car seat, kissing his blond curls and hoping he'll soon fall asleep. For a few weeks, I'm looking after him until a child care spot opens in September. Used to falling asleep at his mother's breast, he doesn't nap easily. So nearly every day we set out on a car trip to neighbouring villages. Today we are off through prairie land east of Calgary to the Blackfoot Crossing Historical Park at Cluny on the far east end of Siksika Reserve.

As we drive, I notice in the rear-view mirror that his eyes are drooping, and he is soon asleep. Good. We've taken a secondary highway east. The undulating green fields of grain are beginning to ripen in anticipation of a bountiful harvest. The spring was wet, so wet that massive flooding struck southern Alberta, including Siksika Nation. I have heard all homes in certain sections of the reserve are flooded out. There are still pools of water in some ditches we pass. We drive through the reserve and notice many cars around the recreation centre, which has been turned into an emergency shelter. Almost 800 people are displaced from their homes by the waters that over-flowed the banks of the Bow River.[264]

We join the TransCanada, travel for several kilometres, then turn south to the interpretive centre. It's built into a bluff high above the Bow River, so the building hasn't been affected by the flood. Its unique architecture is based on Blackfoot culture and incorporates such elements as teepees, an eagle feather fan, a buffalo jump and sundance arbour within its design. Today, a problem with electricity means there is no light or sound for the exhibits. So after a short tour of the building, Cedar and I get back into the car and carry on to several nearby historic sites.

I'm just beginning to read about Treaty 7, signed in 1877 with the Canadian government and people of the Tsuu T'ina Nation (Sarcee), the Nakoda Nation (Bearspaw, Chiniquay and Wesley bands) and the three tribes of the Blackfoot Confederacy, Siksika, Piikani, and Kainai. At the monument to Treaty 7 on the brow overlooking the Bow River, I gaze across the water to the grassy area called Blackfoot Crossing. Over a ten-day period in September

1877, all the tribes above set up teepees, camped, and signed the Treaty. This was the last of the treaties to be made in Canada in the 1800s; the next treaty would not be signed for another twenty years. Later, I will discover how the First Nations who were present interpreted the Treaty very differently than did the government representatives.

While we're at the monument, a member of Siksika Nation drives up to inquire why we're there. He says that all the homes in the river valley below where we stand had to be vacated because of the flood and that no one will be allowed to live in the low-lying area again. He is doing security because there has been looting. He encourages me to visit Chief Crowfoot's grave, as well as his last camping site, all located on this brow overlooking Blackfoot Crossing.

The Blackfoot Crossing area was a traditional wintering grounds, river-crossing, and gathering place for the Blackfoot Confederacy over the centuries. Chief Crowfoot, who was born into the Blood tribe but became a chief of Siksika, insisted that the treaty be signed at Blackfoot Crossing, rather than at Fort Macleod, which had previously been arranged. Crowfoot, playing a pivotal role at the negotiations, spoke for the 5,000 people gathered for the treaty signing and, at the conclusion, asked the government to be charitable and that the police protect the Blackfoot. The signing of Treaty 7 opened up 50,000 square miles to development, settlement of newcomers, and the building and completion of the transcontinental railroad.

Called the "Father of his people," Crowfoot had welcomed the Northwest Mounted Police coming west to stop the whiskey trade. He led his people through the changes facing them from the extinction of the buffalo, hunger and the encroachment of settlement. He later became disillusioned with the Department of Indian Affairs and the Indian agents on the Reserve. But he honoured the conditions of the treaty by not joining forces with Louis Riel and Big Bear, who sent a delegation asking him to join their fight against the Canadian government when they were seeking recognition and land.[265]

It's a gloriously sunny day, and I can smell sage and wild roses as Cedar and I get out of the car at the Crowfoot cemetery. We walk through the gate and down a long narrow pathway bordered on two sides by white fencing. Crowfoot's grave (he died in 1890) has a cross on it and is surrounded by a wrought iron fence. Cedar poses happily in front of the grave. I wish for my grandson that he will grow up knowing the truthful story of Canada and with respect for the sacrifice and dignity shown by figures like Crowfoot in that history.

Here is Crowfoot's speech at the signing of the treaty:

> While I speak, be kind and patient. I have to speak for my people who are numerous, and who rely on me to follow that course which in the future will tend to their good. The plains are large and wide, and we are children of the plains. It is our home, and the buffalo has been our food always. You must look upon us as your children now, and be indulgent to us. If the police had not come to this country where would we all be now? Bad men and bad whiskey were killing us so fast that very few would have been left today. The police have protected us as feathers of a bird protect it from the frosts of winter.

> It always happens that far away people hear exaggerated stories of one another. The news grows as it travels until it becomes from a little thing to a big lie. Often I hear things about the white man...I do not believe them till I find the truth. Why should you kill us or we kill you? Let our white friends have compassion, and we will have compassion. I have two hearts my friends; one is like stone, the other is kind and tender. Treat us badly, and my heart is like stone. Treat us kindly, and my heart is the heart of a child.[266]

Treaties

The Truth and Reconciliation Commission has explained why the Royal Proclamation and the Treaties continue to be relevant today.

"It is important for all Canadians to understand that without Treaties, Canada would have no legitimacy as a nation. Treaties between Indigenous nations and the Crown established the legal and constitutional foundation of this country."[267] RCAP stresses that while many Canadians and their governments may look on the treaties, both pre- and post-Confederation, as "ancient history," as inconvenient, irrelevant, and "obsolete relics of the early days of this country," the fact remains "that Canada has inherited the treaties that were made and is the beneficiary of the lands and resources secured by those treaties and still enjoyed today by Canada's citizens."[268]

There is much talk in the news today about treaty rights and how all Canadians are treaty people. *The True Spirit and Original Intent of Treaty 7* was helpful for me to understand more about the treaty signed in southern Alberta. This book examines testimony of over eighty elders from the First Nations in southern Alberta who had signed Treaty 7 at Blackfoot Crossing in September, 1877. The motivation for sharing these stories was to educate both the members of the First Nations tribes and the descendants of the newcomer society.

In their own younger days, these elders had heard stories from tribal members who had been present at the signing. The stories passed down by the Aboriginal elders show a remarkable similarity. To a person, they said the treaties were never considered a land surrender, but rather a "broad process of peacemaking or of forging new relationships."[269]

"On one of the most crucial issues, whether the treaty was a surrender or an agreement to share the land, the two sides have disagreed fundamentally. The First Nations were unanimous in their understanding that the treaty signified that they were willing to share the land with the newcomers, not that they had agreed to sell or to 'cede, release and surrender' it."[270]

In his Preface, then Chief Roy Whitney stated that elders from all Treaty 7 nations were in accord that what was agreed to was a peace treaty between themselves and the Canadian government.

"The First Nations agreed to share the land with Canadian newcomers in return for the Crown's promises, which entailed annuity payments, education, medical care, ammunition, assistance in farming and ranching, and assurance that we would be free to continue to hunt as we always had." Whitney said all the First Nations elders said that their people did not give up the land.

"... in fact concepts such as 'surrender' and 'cede' had been untranslatable to them. What is clear from the elders' testimony is that our people would allow newcomers to farm and to use the topsoil of the land. Our elders from each of the nations were adamant that there was no discussion of surrendering the land."[271]

The True Spirit and Original Intent of Treaty 7 gives background to the circumstances in which Treaty 7 was signed. It was the seventh of eleven numbered treaties.[272] In the years leading up to Treaty 7, conditions were changing swiftly in the west. Alliances of peace had been formed between Plains First Nations themselves. An example in Southern Alberta was the peace alliance in 1870-71 formed between the Cree and Blackfoot after a gruesome battle at the Belly River near Lethbridge, with tremendous loss for the Cree.

The Cypress Hills Massacre had also occurred in 1873.[273] The massacre had precipitated the 1874 arrival of the Northwest Mounted Police (NWMP) in the west. This police force had been planned by Prime Minister John A. Macdonald. Fort Whoop-Up near Lethbridge in southern Alberta, built by Fort Benton whiskey traders Healey and Hamilton in 1869, had become a crime centre and was playing havoc with First Nations lives.

Historian Grant MacEwan, in *Tatanga Mani: Walking Buffalo of the Stonies*, said whiskey traders watered down the booze and spiced it with contaminants like chewing tobacco, red pepper, ginger, tea, painkiller or red ink to stretch it. Some Indians died of convulsions as a result of drinking the deadly concoction. MacEwan described how traders took advantage of the effect of alcohol on First Nations. Sometimes a buffalo hide would be traded for a tinful of whiskey; for ten gallons, a trader might get up to 250 buffalo robes, a bale of mink furs, a few horses and a large store of pemmican.[274] At this time, too, there was widespread hunger because of the almost total disappearance of the buffalo. In response to these conditions, James Macleod, the leader of the NWMP, established Fort Macleod in 1874.

***

At the Blackfoot Crossing encampment for the treaty signing in 1877, there were 1,000 lodges. Present were chiefs from all five tribes, headmen, medicine men and spiritual leaders, the governor general the Marquis of Lorne, government commissioners David Laird and James Macleod, the chief factor for the Hudson's Bay Company, missionaries, NWMP officers, and translators.

There were many translation problems at the treaty signing. No single person could speak all of the languages.[275] Reverend John McDougall who accompanied the Nakoda, spoke some Cree, but not the Nakoda language, so he was unable to communicate what was being agreed to directly to the three Nakoda bands. Elders of the Kainai, Piikani and Siksika tribes recalled that Jerry Potts, a mixed blood guide, couldn't understand legal and formal English, and though he translated into Blackfoot dialects, it was a seriously inadequate translation. There is also evidence Potts had been drinking at Blackfoot Crossing and quit translating partway through.[276]

During the ten days of the encampment, the assembled First Nations discussed each term of the treaty among chiefs, headmen, medicine men and spiritual leaders, with prayers and ceremonial songs.

"It is within this cultural and spiritual context that our forefathers arrived at their understanding of the meaning of the sacred treaty," wrote Chief Whitney.[277]

While the chiefs had a specific agenda to cease war among themselves, control the encroachment of newcomers, protect the buffalo, control American traders and protect their way of life, the Treaty commissioners had a much different agenda: "to extinguish all Indian title to land and to facilitate settlement of the Northwest by placing Indians on reserves."

> When one compares the two perspectives as well as the different understandings of the narrative that took place, it is apparent that although each side had voiced its concerns, neither had heard the other. Every once in a while, one finds in history books evidence of this major misunderstanding.

> …Our elders have carried, in their hearts and spirit, their story through some five generations since the treaty. Hope among our people is truly a great gift, and our elders say that now is the time to tell the story. Now is the time that people will listen. For a long time people had no ears.[278]

Nakoda elder and former chief of the Bearspaw band Bill Mclean,[279] said that "…the White people's side, the government people, had a pre-written document containing only their concept of what the treaty entails. They told the Indian chiefs, 'This is our terms of the treaty and this is what will be in the treaty agreement.' But in those days there was nobody at all from the Natives' side to translate or understand exactly the legal jargon in the treaty document."[280] Mclean said the concept of the treaty and what was actually meant was never conveyed to both sides. He added, "The only time each individual tribe was asked anything was when they were asked to select land."[281]

The late Nakoda elder Lazarus Wesley shared this: "What they (the Nakoda) understood was the concept of the government to only turn the topsoil and to plant seeds. They accepted that because they had tasted bread and knew how it goes well with other food. They didn't give away their land just for that either. The government was just allowed to use the land for growing things, not given (it)." Wesley said this story has been handed down from the people, not from documents. According to Wesley, the government said it wouldn't impose regulations on the wild game or hunting it. Nothing was mentioned about "cutting up the land here and there into recreational areas and provincial parks, etc."[282] Lazarus Wesley's words also indicate that mineral rights were never surrendered.

Today, Treaty 7 is again being examined through the Making Treaty 7 Cultural Society, dedicated to educating the public about the ongoing significance of Treaty 7. The theatrical presentation featuring over twenty First Nations and non-Aboriginal performers, musicians, dancers and poets, looks into the history and legacy of this founding event of modern southern Alberta. It has played to sold-out audiences for several years and is being creatively developed each year.[283]

***

Pursuit of Justice

As I continued to study, I was struck by the long history of resistance to assimilation and the fight of most tribes for basic human rights. How deep a conviction it would take to work ardently for rights for years and years, even for generations. These struggles are examples in real life of the Bahá'í principles of justice and protection of cultural diversity by people who, through so much suffering, have never given up belief in their own identity and culture.

Bahá'u'lláh writes that "The best beloved of all things in My sight is Justice."[284] While He teaches that the remedy for the healing of all the world is the unity of its peoples, His teachings are clear that unity cannot be achieved without justice. "The purpose of justice is the appearance of unity among men."[285]

An example of this struggle for justice is the Nakoda pursuit, over seventy years, for more land for their people. At the signing of Treaty 7 at Blackfoot Crossing in September 1877, three chiefs represented the three separate bands of Nakoda: Jacob Goodstoney for the Wesley band;[286] John Chiniquay for the Chiniquay Band; Jacob Bearspaw for the Bearspaw Band. The traditional lands used by these three bands, as described by elder George Ear, were "Wesley...people migrated north to the North Saskatchewan River (this is in the Kootenay Plains-Big Horn area)...Bearspaw moved down to Chief Mountain area (the territory is along the foothills of the Rocky Mountains from near Morley south to the border with the United States)...Chiniki stayed along the Bow River."[287]

As mentioned, translation at the Treaty 7 negotiations was completely inadequate. John McDougall, Methodist missionary to the Nakoda people, who was with them at the negotiations, spoke Cree but not Stoney. At the end of the treaty signing, these three chiefs each believed they had secured their traditional lands for their reserves. But when the lands were surveyed for the reserve a couple of years later, the only land surveyed was at Morleyville, near today's Morley townsite, traditional land for the Chiniquay band. In his book, *These Mountains Are Our Sacred Places*, the late Chief John Snow noted that both the Wesley and Bearspaw chiefs were out on their traditional hunting grounds at the time of the survey, and only Chief Chiniquay was in Morleyville. The surveyor believed the chief was representing the entire tribe. Snow also believed that John McDougall had an over-riding influence on what happened.

"We now know and realize that John McDougall had a personal interest in having one large reserve established at Morleyville; the church was there, his home and farm buildings were there, the hay fields were nearby and a small area was under cultivation. It was apparently his feeling that the church could not continue effectively Christianizing my people if we did not all settle on one reserve."[288]

McDougall's role is controversial for other reasons. He had also, in 1874, accepted a commission to go among the southern Alberta tribes to explain the treaty process and encourage them to participate. He was given money to use as gifts to convince people to welcome the Northwest Mounted Police and he also was to talk about white settlement. In this way, at the same time he was advocating for the Nakoda, he was also an agent of the government.[289]

The years following the signing of the Treaty and the disappearance of the buffalo were extremely difficult for many First Nation tribes. The Stoney Nakoda were more fortunate because, while they had taken part in the buffalo hunt in the past, they were not as dependent as other tribes upon it and had hunted and trapped along the Rocky Mountains for generations. So despite not having reserve lands both north and south of Morleyville, a pattern began in which most of the tribe wintered at Morleyville and then returned to their respective hunting grounds for the rest of the year.[290] But some Wesley (also known as Jacob's Band) families continued to live north of Morleyville on the Kootenay Plains seventy-five miles west of Rocky Mountain House and some Bearspaw members lived south of the townsite, near the Highwood Pass. The attempts at Morleyville to turn members of the tribe into an agricultural society mostly failed because of the poor land. Though some tribe members planted crops and raised cattle, most retained their traditional hunting life.

By 1888, however, Nakoda hunters were finding it difficult to provide enough food for their families. The Rocky Mountain Park (now Banff National Park) had been created two years before and this restricted areas open for hunting. While the traditional territory of the Nakoda had extended south of the Alberta-Montana border, it now became more difficult to cross the border. Members of the Chiniquay band had been hunting in the head-waters of the Bow River, in British Columbia, and had come in conflict with the Kootenays and Shuswaps. A meeting was held in Golden in 1893, and eventually the tribes accepted the Great Divide (between British Columbia and Alberta) as the demarcation between their hunting grounds.

Snow wrote: "The wide expanse of territory traditionally travelled by the Stoneys in hunting and camping was gradually being whittled down."[291]

During the Riel Rebellion in 1885, Nakoda chiefs who had smoked the pipe with the Queen's representatives at the signing of the treaty eight years before, decided they would not break the promise they had made regardless of their disappointment at the treaty provisions not being fulfilled. They did not join the insurrection. But the public outcry around the Rebellion led to more restricted conditions, such as the pass system, for Indigenous people. This meant they could not travel for pow-wows, sundances and other social activities without a pass. Snow wrote there was an outright breaking of treaty promises in 1893, when the government brought in a policy banning game hunting in the national park.[292] Rations were cut back and the Nakoda were finding it harder to eke out a living.

In 1889, the Stoney Tribal Council petitioned Indian Affairs to enlarge the Reserve in order to support herds for ranching. Because of the poor conditions, in 1894 Peter Wesley moved back north to Kootenay Plains along the banks of the North Saskatchewan River with about 100 members (one-third) of Jacob's Band. This was their ancestral territory. A great hunter, Wesley was highly respected, and given a second Indian name, Ta-otha, Moosekiller, or "the one who provides."

Because of red tape with different government departments, the question of additional land for the Nakoda was not dealt with and was again raised in 1901. John Snow takes several chapters to describe the long and arduous process of getting more land for Jacob's Band. Again in 1909, ninety-nine Wesley band members (Jacob's band was now called Wesley band after Peter Wesley) petitioned Indian Affairs for a reserve in the Kootenay Plains. There were further petitions, many delays, obstacles put in their path, and disagreements between various levels of government. It took more than seventy years after the signing of Treaty 7 for the people whose traditional hunting grounds were on the Kootenay Plains to receive land in the vicinity. (An additional complication was that the area in question did not fall within the Treaty 7 boundaries, but rather within Treaty 6 boundaries.)

In 1948, the Government of Canada finally established the special Big Horn Reserve 144A. The Reserve was not on the Kootenay Plains, but at the confluence of the Bighorn and North Saskatchewan Rivers. The size of the Reserve was much smaller than requested; the Nakoda agreed to the Reserve based on the understanding they would receive more land later. They also protested construction of the Bighorn Dam that created Abraham Lake and covered much traditional Nakoda hunting land, but were unable to stop it.

Around 1946, the government provided land for members of the Bearspaw Band who had traditionally hunted to the south of Morley, along the Highwood and Pekisko Rivers. This land, too, had been requested at the treaty signing. The government purchased a ranch on the Highwood River and converted it to special reserve status in 1948. The 5,000 acre reserve is known as Eden Valley.[293]

This is just one story of tenacity in a long fight for justice. These stories abound in Indian Country.

***

Owning the History: *A Geography of Blood*

Author Candace Savage has told a story that I believe is an excellent example of how non-Indigenous people can begin to "own" correct history of Canada. In her award-winning book, *Geography of Blood: Unearthing Memory From a Prairie Landscape,* Savage examines the history of the Cypress Hills in southwestern Saskatchewan. She and her partner had moved to Eastend, a small town of 600 people east of the Hills, about fifty-five kilometres north of the Montana border. Savage writes movingly of her reaction to uncovering the blood-soaked history of the area. When she started researching the origin of the many stone circles found near the town, she discovered the shameful legacy of the colonial and settlement era.

"All I had wanted to know was who had made the stone circles, and yet here I am instead, surrounded by desperation and the nameless bodies of the dead. Yet if these memories are part of my inheritance as a prairie person, I am determined to accept them as my own. I will let them settle around me quietly, layer after layer, loss upon loss."[294] Savage's determination to tell the truth leads to her meticulous research. I feel certain, as she does, that the history she uncovered is not isolated; that there are hundreds of equally tragic stories that happened across Canada during the colonial age.

Savage discovered the long history of the Indigenous presence in her new home. While the majority of the abandoned campsites and stone circles she found date from the last 2,000 years, some may date back much further, to the retreat of the glaciers.

"Ten thousand years of hunting and gathering, of births and deaths, of hard work and repose. Ten thousand years of continuity, adaptation, and survival. Although the physical traces the people left were often subtle, their perennially renewed presence on the landscape was a monument in itself and put my four generations of proud belonging into a humbling new perspective."[295]

***

One scene in the book hit me hard. On their first trip to Eastend, Savage and her partner visited the busy Jack's Café for breakfast. Savage was struck by a mural painted by an earlier owner of the café, which extended around all four sides of the café. The first part was of prairie landscape, grazed by herds of buffalo. Then First Nations people herded buffalo over a cliff and pitched their teepees in a valley. But after that, the only inhabitants of the long mural were the early settlers in covered wagons, led by the Northwest Mounted Police. Then homesteaders broke sod, a train steamed into the station. All this was followed by modern combines, the technology of the 20th century and, in the distance, oil wells and the skyline of Calgary. There was no longer any evidence of First Nations.

What struck me so much about this image was how common it is in our country and the history most of us grew up with. First Nations were often portrayed as a dying people, stuck in the past. In fact, *The Imaginary Indian*, written by Daniel Francis, is devoted to the images in our minds that we projected upon First Nations people, from the romantic warrior to the dying man on a horse. Savage makes the point that "history" in our country most often begins with the settlement of European newcomers. "It was as if the settlement experience marked the beginning of time."[296]

"Fine and dandy, except of course, that's not really what happened. The indigenous civilizations of the Great Plains did not die out in the nineteenth century, whether the 'frontier' had ended or not. They were present when the settlers arrived, and they are fiercely alive right now. So why have the keepers of Western history...been so obsessed with defining the end of the old, indigenous West?"[297]

***

Savage chronicles the accelerating disappearance of the buffalo. In the Eastend area, at Chimney Coulee, Isaac Cowie had established a Hudson's

Bay Company outpost in 1871 and acquired buffalo meat to make pemmican. That winter, he had so much meat he didn't have enough carts to pack it all out and many carcasses rotted.[298]

Montana-based Moses Solomon and Abe Farwell were selling the buffalo hides for leather to make belts to power the machines and factories of eastern cities. Around 1871, hide hunters were buying up to 200,000 hides a day, producing a huge slaughter. The slaughter continued, and within a decade, the Great Plains, which were once home to more than thirty million buffalo, had only 200 survivors in about six shattered groups.[299]

Allowing the disappearance of the buffalo was at least partly a policy in Canada. The government knew that its loss would force the Indigenous people on to reserves.[300] In 1875 in the United States, Lieutenant General Philip Sheridan, who would become the commanding general of the U.S. Army, asked Congress to authorize the slaughter of the remaining herds. Mark Abley writes that "he saw their extinction as a weapon to force the Plains Indians into submission. As long as buffalo herds roamed the West, Indians would pose a threat to settlement."[301]

As the buffalo died out, life became much harder for the Indigenous people. A tragic story played out in the Cypress Hills, northwest of Eastend, in 1873. A band of starving Nakoda (a branch of the Sioux related to the Stoney Nakoda) settled in the Hills, at the confluence of Whitemud Coulee and Battle Creek where they could hunt game. On May 31, 1873, Farwell and Solomon, the American traders out of Fort Benton, were selling goods there. A couple of wolfers (wolf hunters) rode up and everyone started drinking. The next day, word went out that a horse had been stolen. The horse was discovered, but the wolfers rushed out with repeating rifles to fire in the Nakoda camp. Reports of the massacre stated that anywhere from fifteen to eighty Nakodas died, including the chief. Women were taken captive and raped, then released next day. The Nakodas who were left headed for Chimney Coulee and were taken in by Métis.[302]

Word reached eastern Canada of the massacre. John A. Macdonald already had plans to have a paramilitary service to be called the Northwest Mounted Police to establish law and order on the plains, and the massacre precipitated the move westward of the police force. Only three of the accused were charged, and none were convicted. In 1875, Fort Walsh, an outpost for the Northwest Mounted Police, was built in the Cypress Hills.

***

Savage emphasizes that the "grand narrative" of prairie settlement is not just the "up-by-the bootstraps" stories of the newcomers. The story of those who were here first has been ignored for too long.

"To really acknowledge what happened, we also have to write in the tens of thousands of displaced people, refugees in their home and native lands, who were launched on a journey of desolation."[303] She writes about the effects of this dislocation on our relationships even to this day.

"If the goal of the reserve system had been to get Aboriginal people out of the settlers' way and keep the two groups apart, the authorities have clearly succeeded beyond all expectation. Almost a century and a half after the signing of the treaties, we still live for the most part in weirdly separate worlds, with decades of mistrust, sharp as razor wire, in between us."[304]

Savage writes that forcing people on to reserves had "signaled the beginning of a traumatic period of authoritarian misrule." This period was characterized by hunger, outlawing important ceremonies, "virtual imprisonment" with the pass system, withholding agricultural technology "on the pretext that Indians needed to start with hand tools and work their way up, through the ages and stages of human development", and the confinement of Aboriginal children in "residential-school hells."[305]

Chapter Sixteen

Investigating the Truth Part Two

Residential Schools

My first brief awareness of residential schools came in Yellowknife when we lived there in the late 1970s, but at that time, few stories had emerged of the kinds of abuse subsequently uncovered across Canada. When we moved to Alberta, we visited Heritage Park in Calgary, and there I saw for the first time photos of children in a residential school classroom. Those photos, of which there are thousands, are haunting. The children sit immobile, with identical haircuts and uniforms, unsmiling and often vacant-eyed. What is reflected is contrary to everything we know today about healthy child development, no matter the culture: the importance of parent-child bonding, individual attention, stimulation, loving care and nurturing. The schools wiped out the unique ways First Nations had traditionally educated their young, through oral storytelling, observation, experience and accompaniment.

When I interviewed Indigenous Bahá'í Millie Stonechild for the *Angus* book, she mentioned that for three generations in her family, children had been sent to residential schools. She belonged to the first generation raising its own children again. She had not learned to parent. Visiting Angus and Bobbie Cowan's home in Regina and Brandon was a wonderful opportunity for her to see how a healthy family lived, she told me.[306]

***

Honouring The Truth, Reconciling For the Future (HTRF), the Final Summary Report of the TRC, was released in June 2015.[307] According to the report, there were 139 government- and church-operated residential schools in Canada attended over a 160-year period by 150,000 First Nations, Métis and Inuit children.[308] According to the TRC, First Nations never asked for residential schools as part of the treaty process, and neither did the government suggest that such schools would be established. The education provisions varied in different treaties but promised to pay for schools on reserves or teachers.[309]

The residential schools were based on British industrial schools for poor children, and some were modelled on the first federally funded off-reservation Native American industrial boarding school at Carlisle, Pennsylvania, established in 1879. The summary report describes how such residential schools had been used all over the world by imperial powers.

"The history of the schools can be best understood in the context of this relationship between the growth of global, European-based empires and the Christian churches. Starting in the sixteenth century, European states gained control of Indigenous peoples' lands throughout the world."

During this era of mass migration, millions of Europeans arrived as colonial settlers in most parts of the world. The European-led slave trade transported millions of Africans; traders from India and China spread throughout the Red Sea and Indian Ocean and brought indentured servants with them who were treated similarly to slaves.

"The activities of explorers, farmers, prospectors, trading companies, or missionaries often set the stage for expansionary wars, the negotiation and the breaking of Treaties, attempts at cultural assimilation, and the exploitation and marginalization of the original inhabitants of the colonized lands." The residential school system was set in place to separate Indigenous children from their parents in places as far flung as Africa and Siberia.[310]

The racial tone of the federal government's efforts to provide education came through strongly only a few years after Canada formed as a country in 1867. In 1883, the first prime minister of Canada, Sir John A. Macdonald, who simultaneously served as superintendent of the Department of Indian Affairs for eight years, spoke to the House of Commons to explain the need for residential schools: "When the school is on the reserve, the child lives with his parents who are savages; he is surrounded by savages, and though he may learn to read and write, his habits and training and mode of thought are Indian. He is simply a savage who can read and write."[311]

The history of residential schools is now wide open to everyone after years of effort by survivors of the schools in Canada. In 2006, the Indian Residential Schools Settlement Agreement (IRSSA) was reached and the following year was approved by the courts. The IRSSA has five main components: a Common Experience Payment; an Independent Assessment Process; support for the Aboriginal Healing Foundation; support for residential school commemoration; and the establishment of a Truth and Reconciliation Commission of Canada.[312]

I met Indigenous scholar Bob Watts Jr.[313] while collaborating with his late mother, Evelyn Loft Watts, in writing the story of her parents and Bob's grandparents, Jim and Melba Loft. The Lofts were the first Indigenous Bahá'í family of Canada.[314] Bob is an adjunct professor and fellow in the School of Policy Studies, Queen's University, in Kingston, Ontario. Bob has said when he introduces residential school history to his students, they are at first sad, then very angry that they were not taught before about residential schools by their high schools, parents or churches.

Watts talked about the conspiracy of silence surrounding residential schools during the 2012 Vancouver Human Rights lecture, which he delivered at the University of British Columbia.[315] The silence was both within the Aboriginal community and in the whole of Canadian society. Watts said a straight line can be drawn between most pathologies in Indigenous communities today and residential schools. The work of the TRC was to bring the truth of what happened in the schools to light, so it will never be forgotten and cannot happen again.

Watts noted that Duncan Campbell Scott, the principal architect of the residential school system, lost his own daughter, who died at a Swiss boarding school. Scott suffered a deep depression at the loss of his only child and was inconsolable. Watts puzzled over how Scott didn't seem sensitive to similar losses of Indigenous parents.

"What is amazing to me is that he didn't have the ability to look at the Aboriginal people in this country, whose children were dying in huge numbers in residential schools, and sometimes sent home sick and then dying at home. Sometimes dying at school and their families not knowing about it for years.

"Were Aboriginal people viewed to be less human?" Watts asked.

I have frequently asked myself the same sort of question, when I hear about the many accidents, suicides and premature deaths on reserves in Canada. Are some lives expendable? Our knowledge of each other and caring about each other's lives greatly needs to grow.

The TRC Final Report underlines the consequences of our continuing ignorance of the legacy of the schools and of historical conflicts. It states that this ignorance has serious consequences for the Indigenous peoples of this land and for the country as a whole, and leads to poor public policy decisions.

> In the public realm, it reinforces racist attitudes and fuels civic distrust between Aboriginal peoples and other Canadians. Too many Canadians still do not know the history of Aboriginal peoples' contributions to Canada, or understand that by virtue of the historical and modern Treaties negotiated by our government, we are all Treaty people. History plays an important role in reconciliation; to build for the future, Canadians must look to, and learn from, the past.[316]

The last federally administered residential school in Canada closed in 1996, a mere two decades ago. At the time of the IRSSA, there were still 80,000 survivors alive. A common experience payment was made to every survivor of the schools. This, said Bob Watts, was needed to recognize harms done at the school, "for having your spirit stolen, for having your heart broken, for having your family taken from you."

An additional process called the Independent Assessment Process (IAP) allowed survivors of physical and sexual abuse to file claims. By early January 2015, 37,951 claims under the IAP had been made, by nearly half of the living survivors.

Not only were the children deprived of the love and affection they should receive, the residential schools were a deliberate assault on Aboriginal culture, spiritual beliefs and languages, as the survivors' stories heartbreakingly show.

Only a handful of stories from survivors are included here, from scores in the TRC reports.

Agnes Moses said that her time in residential schools in northern Canada left her wanting "to be white so bad" and with a shame about her own mother.

"The worst thing I ever did was I was ashamed of my mother, that honourable woman, because she couldn't speak English, she never went to school, and we used to go home to her on Saturdays, and they told us that we couldn't talk Gwich'in to her and, and she couldn't, like couldn't communicate. And my sister was the one that had the nerve to tell her.

"We can't talk Loucheux [Gwich'in] to you, they told us not to."[317]

The schools tried to destroy any evidence of culture. On her arrival at the Presbyterian school in Kenora, Lorna Morgan was wearing "these nice little beaded moccasins that my grandma had made me to wear for school, and I was very proud of them." She said they were taken from her and thrown in the garbage.[318]

At most schools, nutrition was extremely poor, which left all children vulnerable to disease. Many children were starving all the time and resorted to stealing food or eating rotten food from the garbage at grocery stores. Victoria McIntosh said she was harshly disciplined—her face shoved in the porridge, her body thrown against the wall, and beaten for refusing to eat porridge with worms in it at the Fort Alexander school.[319]

While some teachers and staff showed affection and kindness to the children in their care, most schools felt loveless, and children ended up hardening their hearts. Rick Gilbert remembered the Williams Lake, British Columbia school.

"...that was one thing about this school was that when you got hurt or got beat up or something, and you started crying, nobody comforted you. You just sat in the corner and cried and cried till you got tired of crying then you got up and carried on with life."[320]

Nick Sibbeston, who was placed in the Fort Providence school in the Northwest Territories at age five, recalled it as a place where children hid their emotions.

"In residential school you quickly learn that you should not cry. If you cry you're teased, you're shamed out, you're even punished."[321]

Jack Anawak recalled his time at Chesterfield Inlet in the 1950s, in what is now Nunavut, that "there was no love, there was no feelings, it was just supervisory."[322]

Lydia Ross, who attended the Cross Lake school in Manitoba, said, "If you cried, if you got hurt and cried, there was no, nobody to, nobody to comfort, comfort you, nobody to put their arms."[323] Lydia once looked out the school window and saw her parents, whom she missed terribly. But she wasn't allowed to visit with them.

The staff's lack of compassion affected the way students treated each other, and their trust. Victoria McIntosh said that life at the Fort Alexander, Manitoba, school taught her not to trust anyone.

"You learn not to cry anymore. You just get harder. And yeah, you learn to shut down."[324]

Survivors also testified that student bullying was common and often not dealt with, contributing to the atmosphere of fear and violence in the schools. The TRC believes the betrayal by fellow students has contributed significantly to the schools' long-term legacy of continuing division and distrust within Aboriginal communities.[325]

Living conditions in the schools, particularly bad quality food, poorly maintained buildings and fire hazards, left the children vulnerable to disease and accidents. The TRC believes the number of students who died at Canada's residential schools will probably never be known in full. Unmarked graves are still being found. The TRC has established a National Residential School Student Death Register, the first effort in Canadian history to properly record the number of students who died in residential schools.

***

Dr. Peter Bryce

Alarm bells were set off early about conditions in the schools. The story of Dr. Peter Bryce shows an individual of the era willing to stick his neck out to protest the poor conditions. Dr. Bryce was the chief medical officer of Indian Affairs. His 1906 annual report observed that the Indian population of Canada had a mortality rate of more than double that of the whole population, and in some provinces, more than three times.[326] Tuberculosis was the prevalent cause of death. Dr. Bryce made a tour of the schools in the West in 1907. Tuberculosis was rampant. He described overcrowding, lack of ventilation, filth, unsanitary conditions, and staff who minimized dangers of infection. *Saturday Night* magazine got hold of a copy of his report and wrote that it exposed a situation "disgraceful to the country." They said Indian boys and girls were "dying like flies."[327]

Dr. Bryce recommended in 1909 that residential schools be turned into sanatoria and placed under his administration and that schools become day schools. But rather than follow his recommendations, in 1910 the government negotiated a contract between Indian Affairs and the churches that increased grants to the schools and imposed a set of standards for diet and ventilation. The contract also required that students not be admitted unless a physician verified their good health. The contract did lead to improvements in the short term, but inflation eroded the benefit of the increase in grants. As well, grants were repeatedly cut during the Great Depression of the 1930s.

"The underfunding created by the cuts guaranteed that students would be poorly fed, clothed, and housed. As a result, children were highly susceptible to tuberculosis."[328]

Dr. Bryce had estimated that at beginning of the 20th century, tuberculosis was killing Aboriginal people at a rate nineteen times higher than non-Aboriginals.[329] When Duncan Campbell Scott took over as Deputy Superintendent-General in 1913, he cut back on expenses and told Dr. Bryce his annual medical reports were no longer required.[330] In 1922, Dr. Bryce published a booklet called *A National Crime* that named Scott and personally blamed him for the miserable condition of the schools. Even after this, the residential school system expanded.[331]

While the historical reputation of Duncan Campbell Scott has suffered a fatal blow, that of Dr. Peter Bryce has not. The Canadian Pediatric Society has instituted a P. H. Bryce award for someone whose work in public health has bettered the lives of Aboriginal children and youth.[332]

Duncan Campbell Scott

I learned more about Duncan Campbell Scott when I read a 2013 book, *Conversations with a Dead Man: The Legacy of Duncan Campbell Scott*, by Mark Abley. Commissioned to write a book about the controversial Scott, Abley searched for a way to utilize extensive research into his life and the times in which he lived. He took a fascinating creative non-fiction approach, by developing a series of imaginary conversations between himself and Duncan Campbell Scott, based on the facts of Scott's life. The conversations go deeply into Scott's justification for the residential schools and assimilation of Indigenous people.

Starting in 1879, Scott worked for fifty-two years in the federal civil service, starting off as junior copy clerk. He mastered bookkeeping and became the chief accountant for the Department of Indian Affairs. In 1913, he was promoted to head the whole department and served as Deputy Superintendent-General of Indian Affairs until he retired in 1932. Many of the most pernicious policies of the residential schools were put in place during his tenure.[333]

The inflammatory quote, "kill the Indian in the child," has often been attributed to Scott. However, Abley discovered Scott had never used these words. They are traced back to a high ranking officer in the U.S. Army, Richard Henry Pratt, who became superintendent of the Carlisle Industrial School mentioned at the beginning of the chapter. Pratt had said, "All the Indian there is in the race should be dead. Kill the Indian in him, and save the man."[334]

However, while speaking before a committee of the Canadian House of Commons looking at proposed amendments to the Indian Act in 1920, Scott did make the following statement, strongly promoting assimilation:

"I want to get rid of the Indian problem...That is my whole point. Our objective is to continue until there is not a single Indian in Canada that has not been absorbed into the body politic, and there is no Indian question, and no Indian department, and that is the whole object of this Bill."[335]

During his tenure as head of Indian Affairs, Scott made a number of amendments to the Indian Act that further attempted to extinguish

Aboriginal culture, and to keep Indigenous people completely under government control (see Chapter Fifteen). Attendance at residential schools became mandatory.

I've often asked myself whether I would have had enlightened ideas if living at the time of Duncan Campbell Scott and residential schools. This was the time of social Darwinism and the concept of "survival of the fittest." Darwin was one of the main sources of racial doctrine. He wrote, "At some future period not very distant as measured by centuries, the civilized races of man will almost certainly exterminate and replace throughout the world the savage races."[336]

Indigenous scholar E. Richard Atleo (Umeek), in his book, *Principles of Tsawalk*, analyzes how Darwin was used against Indigenous peoples. The Darwinian theory of evolution and its interpretations "created, for colonizers, a view of differences between people that was and is characterized by superiority and inferiority."[337]

Author John Ralston Saul adds that natural selection was somehow a reason for colonial wars. "Evolutionary biology became an excuse for any kind of organized racism. The preservation of favoured races in the struggle for life was an explanation for empire."[338]

While we recognize today that the measures Scott took were racist and assimilative, Scott was not alone in his thinking, writes Abley.

"This was the mainstream. This was what North Americans saw, heard, read. This was what Northern Americans thought. The distinction between savagery and civilization had the weight of science behind it. Race was not a discredited concept; race was an inescapable concept. Racism was not even a word at the time, although society was shot through with it."[339]

Abley gives other examples of racist attitudes of Scott's time, against the Irish and Chinese, that would also be denounced at once today, and states that racism was stitched deep into the fabric of Western society.[340]

Duncan Campbell Scott's reputation, particularly as a well-known poet, survived for many years. While his poetry treated the subject of First Nations with respect, it also portrayed, in romantic tones, his view, shared by many others of the time, that the Indian race was dying. Scott's downfall in the public eye began in 1986 when E. Brian Titley wrote *A Narrow Vision: Duncan Campbell Scott and the Administration of Indian Affairs in Canada.*[341]

***

November, 2013

The rock is small and polished, pinkish purple with hints of brown, smooth, oblong. Silky to the touch, it feels like a talisman or worry bead.

I receive this rock when I attend, for the second time, a meeting of the Truth and Reconciliation Commission. The TRC is receiving testimony about Canada's shameful history of residential schools that Indigenous children were forced to attend over a 100-year period. I have made a personal commitment to learn all I can about this period of our history, of which I, along with much of dominant Canadian society, am woefully ignorant.

As I enroll for the hearing, a registrar invites me to take a rock.

"They have been smudged and prayed over by Indigenous elders," she says. Smudging is considered a sacred process in which sage, cedar or sweetgrass is burned, and the smoke is blown over individuals or objects in order to purify and help prayers ascend to the Creator. I am attracted by this small beautiful rock and hold it in my hand for the whole day.

As a non-Indigenous person, I feel my presence, along with many others, at the hearing is to bear witness to the suffering that my own government, in collusion with the churches, visited upon generations of Indigenous people in our land. This learning is for my own edification, but I also feel a responsibility to share the new knowledge with others.

The rock feels like a gift of the TRC, which has thoughtfully planned the process with everyone in mind. They have already heard 6,000 separate testimonies from residential school survivors across Canada (and would hear 7,000 by the end of the Commission's mandate). For the survivors of the schools who will testify publicly, there is individual support before, during and after their testimony. People who do not wish to speak in public can give their testimony privately.

For we who are witnessing the testimonies, trained staff keep a watchful eye on the audience and come to offer help if listeners become emotional and overwhelmed. The planners, who themselves often suffered grievously from abuse, have designed this challenging process for everyone with kindness and tact.

Before Commission members speak, a special opening ceremony takes place. In a Grand Entry, the Treaty 7 flag is brought in accompanied by drummers and the three members of the TRC, Justice Murray Sinclair, Chief Wilton Littlechild and Dr. Marie Wilson. Powerful honor songs and prayers are offered. Chair Sinclair speaks kindly to everyone, outlining the scope of the Commission. He states that it is not a legal body and requests survivors not to state the names of their abusers, as this may jeopardize any legal proceedings underway through other processes.

In the morning, we hear three harrowing testimonies. An elderly lady speaks of the sexual abuse she suffered at the hands of a female school employee and her lifelong struggle to feel good about herself. A male elder tells the Commission that after speaking his own language, he was taken to an abandoned building near the school and brutally raped. Another man speaks angrily of the hatred he developed after being abused.

"It was the only thing I learned at school. I decided to join the military because all I wanted to do was kill...Only my partner finally, with her love, helped to soften my heart."

As the survivors courageously share their stories, I hold the rock, my fingertips rubbing it, turning it around, pushing it back and forth across the palm of my hand. This releases pent-up energy. As I listen, I begin to ponder my motives for being here. As Bahá'ís, we were not involved in running the residential schools. Promoting the opposite of the expressed purpose of the schools to destroy culture and assimilate children into the mainstream, the Bahá'í Faith works for unity in diversity and the protection of cultural diversity. Am I being a voyeur, or trying to assuage my guilt and feel better about myself and the Canadian legacy by listening to these testimonies?

Paulette Regan, in *Unsettling the Settler Within: Indian Residential Schools, Truth Telling, and Reconciliation in Canada*, cautions against an approach that is sympathetic or empathetic, yet does nothing.[342] For much of the time that I have wanted to forge close relationships with First Nation individuals and families, the residential school legacy has been the shadow in the background. Now I finally understand the not-surprising suspicion Indigenous individuals have of the dominant culture, why it takes so long to gain trust, how important consistency and "walking the talk" are. Though I hear the testimonies, I will never completely understand what it was like to go through such experiences. There is so much to learn, like how to stand up for justice, however limited my means for doing so may be.

After lunch we hear more testimonies, a few from descendants of residential school survivors who have suffered "intergenerational trauma."

"My mother was a walking boarding school," says one man as he describes the physical and verbal abuse he suffered as a child. Another speaker, a daughter of survivors, after being apprehended by social services and placed in a foster home, was sexually abused. She tried to run away with her brother. Decades later, she took the foster parent to court and won a settlement. Today this woman, a social worker, helps children who have undergone trauma.

Another daughter of a survivor tells the Commission her father wrote his memories of boarding school, but did not find a publisher before he died. Justice Sinclair tells her the TRC would be happy to receive the memoirs and would assure them a home. All testimonies are recorded and will be held in the National Centre for Truth and Reconciliation at the University of Manitoba that will preserve the history for generations to come.[343]

At the end of the day, Commissioner Wilton Littlechild summarizes what has been shared. The speakers have consistently described feeling lonely, a different unique kind of loneliness experienced at the schools. They have talked about their tears. "If it was not for tears I would be dead," said one. One survivor spoke of finding himself, as an adult, in a sweat lodge ceremony and realizing he had a sacred right to heal. Another told about bullying among the students for food. Still another observed how the schools separated boys and girls, and siblings from each other. Siblings ended up being strangers to each other. One person shared that, once they got out of the schools, the only time the siblings could really talk to each other was while they drank.

After truth must come reconciliation and Commissioner Littlechild focuses on elements of reconciliation that the survivors have mentioned: forgiveness of self and others, culture and ceremony, family, prayer. "We are wealthy, we are rich in culture," one survivor said. Several people had quit drinking as a significant step in their healing. Others insisted accurate history must be taught in all schools in Canada.

Today I hold on to the rock and realize there is beauty in the harsh stories I've heard. My rock will always remind me of the survival of Indigenous people despite brutal attempts to annihilate their cultures, languages and spirituality.

Legacy of the Schools and History

The final summary report of the TRC outlines in detail the aftermath, not only of the residential schools, but of the centuries-long unjust relationship between Indigenous and non-Indigenous Canadians. This legacy, say the HTRF authors, is now reflected in the significant educational, income, health, and social disparities between Aboriginal people and other Canadians, in the intense racism some people harbour against Aboriginal people and in the systemic and other forms of discrimination Aboriginal people regularly experience in this country.

During the decades when the residential schools were winding down, the "Sixties Scoop" happened, the wide-scale national apprehension of Aboriginal children by child-welfare agencies. Authorities removed thousands of Aboriginal children from their families and communities and placed them in non-Aboriginal homes without taking steps to preserve their culture and identity. The parents of these children were most often residential school survivors. The TRC believes this practice simply continued ways of assimilation.[344]

The report makes ninety-four calls to action to address the gaps. These include equalizing different levels of funding for Aboriginal students attending schools on reserves with those attending off reserves. They include addressing health issues, such as high rates of suicide, diabetes, infant mortality and child poverty. Other recommendations deal with education, healing and justice among many.

The authors of the Final Report believe the disproportionate numbers of Aboriginal people who are imprisoned and victimized can be explained in part as a result of the way Aboriginal children were treated in residential schools, where they were denied an environment of positive parenting, worthy community leaders, and a positive sense of identity and self-worth.[345] They describe what many contemporary Indigenous children and young adults have to live with every day as the legacy of residential schools. They deal with high rates of addictions, fetal alcohol disorder, mental health issues, family violence, incarceration of parents, and the intrusion of child-welfare authorities, all of which place them at greater risk of involvement with crime.[346]

The TRC has documented the critically endangered status of most Aboriginal languages and made recommendations. I didn't understand the impact of losing one's language until recently. Sabrina Williams, an intergenerational survivor from British Columbia, expressed that loss to the TRC and the need to reclaim the languages.

> I didn't realize until taking this language class how much we have lost—all the things that are attached to language: it's family connections, it's oral history, it's traditions, it's ways of being, it's ways of knowing, it's medicine, it's song, it's dance, it's memory. It's everything, including the land.... And unless we inspire our kids to love our culture, to love our language ... our languages are continually going to be eroded over time. So, that is daunting. Yeah. So, to me that's part of what reconciliation looks like.[347]

The TRC believes reconciliation is in the best interests of our whole country; one reason is for Canada to remove a "stain from its past and be able to maintain its claim to be a leader in the protection of human rights among the nations of the world." As Canadians, we can't take pride in the country's treatment of its Indigenous peoples and "for that reason, all Canadians have a critical role to play in advancing reconciliation in ways that honour and revitalize the nation-to-nation Treaty relationship."[348]

There are signs everywhere that Canadians are waking up to these realities. What is needed is courage and will. Justice Murray Sinclair stated at the unveiling of the final report of the TRC in Ottawa in December 2015, that he was hopeful that "a period of change is beginning that, if sustained by the will of the people, will forever realign the shared history of Indigenous and non-Indigenous peoples."[349]

***

Colonialism

Coming to awareness of how colonial powers wrested most of the land from Aboriginal people in the process of nation-building was, to say the least, "unsettling." It took me a while to understand the concept of colonialism. I first began to think about how it applies to Canada after attending the Emily Carr exhibit at the Glenbow Museum in Calgary in 2008. I purchased a book about Carr by Susan Crean called *The Laughing One.* Crean takes a long look at the revered legacy of the famous Canadian painter and writer and the times in which she lived. She argues that Carr, though she had more contact with First Nations than most people of her time, treated "Native" subjects more than almost any contemporary artist, and had one close Squamish friend–Sophie Frank[350]–in fact still had a colonial approach in her lack of real consultation with First Nations before exploiting their heritage as subject matter for her drawings, paintings and writings.[351]

"...while displaying uncommon interest in and respect for Native peoples and their cultures, she had nevertheless absorbed the prevailing concept of Aboriginal societies as 'primitive' in comparison to the achievement of White culture," wrote Crean.[352]

I had come across the word "colonialism" at least twice before Crean's strong treatment of the subject. In 2006, Harry, Zara and I had visited the United Nations building on a stop-over in New York on our way to Ireland. We took a tour, where we saw the rooms for the UN General Assembly, the Security Council and UNESCO. The guide pointed out another chamber for the Trusteeship Council. This was a venue for the discussion of decolonization that was no longer used, she said, because there were few colonies left worldwide.[353]

There is strong evidence that colonialism still affects many marginalized peoples, though most countries are no longer officially "colonies." Confederation in 1867 supposedly meant Canada was no longer a colony, but First Nations in particular are still suffering the effects of it.

I also read a master's thesis, "As ye have faith, so shall your powers and blessings be"[354] by Chelsea Horton, who is not a member of the Bahá'í Faith and who has done much of her academic research on the relationship of Indigenous peoples to the Faith. Horton used the term "colonial" several times. She had interviewed many Indigenous Bahá'ís in British Columbia for her thesis, and they had voiced a concern with the way the Bahá'í community operated; not how it should operate, according to the principles of the Faith, but how, at least at that time, it operated in practice. Horton took up the theme again in her PhD thesis, "All is One: Becoming Indigenous and Bahai in Global North America" in 2013[355] and again, some Indigenous Bahá'ís voiced this concern.

Reflecting on what "colonial" means, I found that the root word, "colony," is defined by the Canadian Oxford Dictionary as "a group of people who settle in a new territory (whether or not already inhabited) and form a community connected with a mother country." On the other hand, those who are already there live a different reality. José R. Martínez-Cobo, Special Rapporteur on Discrimination against Indigenous Populations, provided a working definition:

> Indigenous communities, peoples and nations are those which having a historical continuity with pre-invasion and pre-colonial societies that developed on their territories, consider themselves distinct from other sectors of societies now prevailing in those territories, or parts of them. They form at present non-dominant sectors of society and are determined to preserve, develop, and transmit to future generations their ancestral territories, and their ethnic identity, as the basis of their continued existence as peoples, in accordance with their own cultural patterns, social institutions and legal systems.[356]

As previously discussed, during early contact, Indigenous peoples in the Americas did not see the relationships they entered into as colonial, but rather as reciprocal relationships. They welcomed the newcomers, helped them survive what were to the new arrivals harsh conditions, and then later entered into economic, trading relationships. However, relationships began to change. I found a trenchant analysis of colonialism and its effects in *Century of Light*, a statement commissioned by the Universal House of Justice in 2001.

> These masses of humankind, despoiled and scorned—but representing most of the earth's inhabitants—were seen not

as protagonists but essentially as objects of the new century's much vaunted civilizing process. Despite benefits conferred on a minority among them, the colonial peoples existed chiefly to be acted upon—to be used, trained, exploited, Christianized, civilized, mobilized—as the shifting agendas of Western powers dictated. These agendas may have been harsh or mild in execution, enlightened or selfish, evangelical or exploitative, but were shaped by materialistic forces that determined both their means and most of their ends. To a large extent, religious and political pieties of various kinds masked both ends and means from the publics in Western lands, who were thus able to derive moral satisfaction from the blessings their nations were assumed to be conferring on less worthy peoples, while themselves enjoying the material fruits of this benevolence.[357]

The TRC further speaks about the direct link of colonial attitudes and residential schools and states that the colonial process relied for its justification "on the sheer presumption of taking a specific set of European beliefs and values and proclaiming them to be universal values that could be imposed upon the peoples of the world." This universalizing of European values, extended to North America, "served as the prime justification and rationale for the imposition of a residential school system on the Indigenous peoples of Canada."[358]

I asked myself why we Bahá'ís, with such strong writings about the oneness of humanity and the importance of diversity, could exhibit attitudes that could be termed "colonial." The major reason I came up with is that we are ignorant of the history of our land and unconsciously replicate common attitudes and behaviours that may be perceived as colonial. In our communities, I wonder if subconscious colonial attitudes may lead to conditions such as domination in consultation, dismissal of ideas from the minority, neglect of issues facing the minority or lack of appreciation of diverse cultural expressions of faith.

As Bahá'ís, we may wonder how we can relate to the complicated issues that arise and how, as citizens, we can help overcome such an overwhelming legacy. In addition to the many Bahá'í references on the oneness of humanity and eliminating prejudices of all kinds, as well as the current framework for action,[359] I found comfort in the work of Victoria Freeman, author of *Distant Relations: How My Ancestors Colonized North America.* Freeman uncovered the history of her own relatives who were implicated in the nitty-gritty business of colonialism, of dispossessing Indigenous people in New England and Ontario.

Freeman believes guilt and fear paralyze, and often non-Indigenous people don't go near Indigenous issues because they are afraid of what they will feel as they learn the truth. While uncovering her family history, Freeman had to work through her defensiveness. But in the end, what she felt was grief, rather than guilt, at the history. And she believes it is appropriate to grieve; this is something we can all share and opens our hearts to feel "even a smidgen of the pain of what has happened which Indigenous people have had to live with."[360]

Freeman believes non-Indigenous people don't live on this land with integrity. Colonialism was the work of millions of people, it is a whole system, one that isolated and separated us as peoples. We have all been affected by it. To decolonize, we need to rebuild relationships on every level. Freeman suggests that non-Indigenous people educate themselves, find opportunities to be in relationships with Indigenous people and to hear their point of view. If we do this work, it is for ourselves we do it as well.

> I believe it is possible to move beyond this ugly and often violent history, to be a society that is founded not on mere "tolerance," but on respect, a society that lives up to its word. But I know we can't move forward until we look the past in the eye, until we understand ourselves more deeply, acknowledging and exploring even the darker aspects of our history—not to damn our forebears, but with hope for a more humane world.[361]

Reclaiming Indigenous Voice and Vision is a series of academic essays about colonization and decolonization. The writers, Indigenous and others, had been impacted, thought deeply, and had a clear idea of how we need to move towards true equality, beginning with Indigenous people themselves, with the revitalization of language and cultures and the redress of past wrongs. I benefited greatly from reading these perspectives.

Dr. Leroy Little Bear is a member of the Kainai tribe of the Blackfoot Confederacy, former director of the Native American program at Harvard University, and professor emeritus of Native studies at the University of Lethbridge. He writes about a clash of worldviews that occurs with colonialism, which "tries to maintain a singular social order by means of force and law, suppressing the diversity of human worldviews."[362] Little Bear writes of the philosophy of the Plains Indians, which sees all things as "animate, imbued with spirit, and in constant motion."[363] Interrelationships are of paramount importance in this holistic and cyclical view of the world, which contrasts with the worldview of Western Europeans, which is "linear and singular, static, and objective."[364] Yet, with contact between cultures, Little Bear emphasizes that neither have pure worldviews completely Indigenous or Eurocentric, and worldviews are constantly in flux.

Erica-Irene Daes, who is of Greek origin, is an academic, diplomat, and United Nations expert best known for her almost twenty years work with the United Nations Working Group on Indigenous Populations (1984–2001), promoting the cause of the world's Indigenous peoples. During this time, she authored many United Nations reports on Indigenous rights issues and was a driving force behind the United Nations Declaration on the Rights of Indigenous Peoples. Dr. Daes believes that nearly every people have been oppressed at one or more times in their histories. All forms of oppression "involve a denial of the individual spirit and its quest for self-expression. Colonialism, slavery, intolerance, discrimination, and war—all these cruel experiences share a common element: the utter denial of the victims' relevance." She believes our spiritual side leads us to desire freedom, to express ourselves, be recognized, have a name and destiny, and that oppression destroys this inborn spiritual faith in our value.[365]

One of the most destructive experiences of colonized peoples is intellectual and spiritual loneliness, says Dr. Daes. "From this loneliness comes a lack of self-confidence, a fear of action, and a tendency to believe that the ravages and pain of colonization are somehow deserved. Thus, the victims of colonization begin, in certain cases, to blame themselves for all the pain that they have suffered."[366] Dr. Daes believes the antidote to internalized oppression is travel, rebuilding old alliances and kinships across borders, and discovering like-minded peoples in other parts of the globe.

Dr. Daes also believes much damage is done to the colonizer; they too have to heal.

She writes that aggression returns to haunt oppressive nations "in a cycle of internal mistrust, domination, and violence. In the course of mobilizing their power to dominate others, they suffer their own spiritual deaths." Daes maintains that colonization is a shared experience and both oppressors and oppressed need healing to stop the cycles of external aggression and self-destruction.[367]

Canada adopted the United Nations Declaration of the Rights of Indigenous Peoples, though later than most countries, on November 12, 2010. This declaration has the distinction of being the only Declaration within the United Nations that was drafted with the rights-holders themselves, the Indigenous peoples of the world.[368]

***

The Benevolent Peacemaker

One of the most challenging books I read was *Unsettling the Settler Within* by Paulette Regan, director of research for the Truth and Reconciliation Commission, who holds a PhD from the Indigenous Governance Program at the University of Victoria. Regan, herself a non-Aboriginal, calls on non-Aboriginals to do the hard work of decolonizing our mindsets and becoming informed of accurate history of our country so we can effectively contribute to reconciliation. The content left me with my chin on the floor for weeks, particularly a chapter Regan devotes to deconstructing the Canadian myth of the "benevolent peacemaker." She believes the myth is deeply embedded in dominant Canadian society's beliefs about our history and that deconstruction needs to be done primarily to get Canadians to face the truth of our colonial history.

While Canadians have often been fond of viewing our early history as more peaceful than that of the "Indian wars" in the United States and have had a "smug self-satisfaction" about our history,[369] research shows this view is simply not true. While in the early days of European settlement, the Indigenous people were military and trade allies, after Confederation, as the treaty-making process moved west, the relationship changed to one much less of equals, but one that saw Indigenous people become wards of the state, seen as a moral and economic burden. The government was more concerned with "administration of a fiscally responsible Indian policy rather than a commitment to nation-to-nation treaty making."[370]

Regan writes that by 1874, the government was aware of the looming crisis with the buffalo. She quotes writer Sidney L. Harring as suggesting that, while some members of Parliament believed the dominion had responsibility and a treaty obligation to preserve the buffalo, "the dominion government deliberately failed to take action because it was understood that the buffalo hunt was central to the social orders of the Plains tribes; the government knew that destroying the buffalo would force the Indians to reserves."[371]

Some First Nation tribes, for a long time, refused to sign treaties. An example was Cree chief Big Bear and his followers. Rations were withheld from them until they agreed to sign a treaty. Regan quotes Sarah Carter as concluding that "study of the post-treaty years challenges comfortable assumptions about Canada's benevolent and wise Indian policy, as the history is one of broken treaty promises, fraud, and the use of coercive measures, enforced with the aid of the police and later troops."[372]

Settlement of the frontier, contrary to our proud and self-laudatory view, was characterized by violence and the devastating effects of starvation and disease on Indigenous populations. These effects are graphically outlined in the book *Clearing the Plains* by James Daschuk.

Duncan Campbell Scott, according to Regan, "played a significant role in creating the peacemaker myth in political circles and in the public mind." Not only was he for years the director of the Department of Indian Affairs, Scott was also a well-known poet and author.

"...he reiterated the widely accepted belief that Indians were perilous yet childlike savages in need of strong guidance from government officials and missionary teachers to curb their war-like tendencies." He conveyed "the mixed feelings and attitudes of a settler society that was uneasy about its relationship with Indigenous people..."[373]

Regan explains that this myth also crystallized in the public mind from people like treaty commissioners Alexander Morris and David Laird during the western prairie settlement period. Their vision of a "wise, paternal, and just government" that would fulfill treaty obligations and elevate Indians towards civilization was widely shared. It became "analogous with settler responsibility for solving the Indian problem."[374]

However, treaties were increasingly ignored by the government as a way to fulfill its obligations; rather, the government focused on the Indian Act and developing Indian policy. By the middle of the 19th century, Indigenous people were treated not as partners, but as dependent, childlike wards of the state.[375]

Regan argues that challenging this myth is so important today because, as members of the dominant society, we have not yet acknowledged that we are "the primary beneficiaries of colonial policies that marginalized Indigenous people in their own lands..."[376] Regan believes non-Indigenous Canadians must be willing to make substantive changes to the status quo. Apologies aren't enough. The changes must come not only in the pocketbooks, but in the hearts, souls and conscience.

While Canada can be justly proud of its peacemaking service on the world stage, Canadian intellectual John Ralston Saul believes that these peacemaking skills of consensus building and inclusivity based on consultation and negotiation actually have Indigenous, rather than European, roots.[377] They don't just start with Lester B. Pearson in the 1950s but were influenced by Indigenous diplomatic approaches to peaceful relations among diverse peoples. So Canada's peacekeeping in its original form comes very close to a First Nations model, which incorporates more complex ideas of belonging and identity. Ralston Saul writes:

> ...one of our unwritten realities is that the country is built upon a triangular foundation—Aboriginal, francophone, anglophone. The ease with which Canada embraces diversity today has been made possible by our non-monolithic foundation. And that foundation worked to the extent it did largely because of the more complex ideas of belonging and identity in Aboriginal societies...Without that underlying complexity we would have found ourselves in the European nightmare—the delusional myth of *one blood, one race, one people*. And so if you undermine the complexity of our foundation, you undermine diversity as the Canadian model.[378]

***

Paulette Regan challenges the frequent resistance of Canadians to learning about our history by stating that, as Canadian citizens, we are ultimately responsible for the past and present actions of our government. She believes we can learn from the past even if we can't change it and "can better understand how a problematic mentality of benevolent paternalism became a rationale and justification for acquiring Indigenous lands and resources, and drove the creation of prescriptive education policies that ran counter to the treaty relationship."[379]

Regan challenges the idea that residential school survivors should just "get over it" by stating emphatically that "asking victims to bury a traumatic past for the 'greater good' of achieving reconciliation does not address the root of the problem—colonialism."[380] She believes that settlers need to enter a space of not knowing, of becoming "unsettled."

"...my own deepest learning has always come when I was in unfamiliar territory culturally, intellectually, and emotionally. It seems to me that this space of not knowing has power that may hold a key to decolonization for settlers."[381]

Regan also believes that those who have benefited from colonialism "bear a responsibility to address the inequities and injustices from which they have profited."[382] John Ralston Saul, in *The Comeback*, also cautions us against slipping back into "passive forms of sympathy."[383] Many of our systems of government have been based on Victorian ideas of charity, rather than justice. Paternalism comes when the poor "are seen as passive people in need of control by others for their own good."[384] We may need to check ourselves for these attitudes that have surrounded us for so long.

Saul points out that Indigenous people have made a remarkable comeback from a very low point. They now have the highest growth rates in population, and are one of the largest cultural groups in Canada. At any one time more than 30,000 Indigenous people are enrolled in universities and colleges.

"What is happening today," says Saul, "is not about guilt or sympathy or failure. It is not about a romantic view of the past. Nor about old ways versus new ways. Nor about propping up people who can't make it on their own.

"What we face is a simple matter of rights—of citizens' rights that are still being denied to indigenous peoples."[385]

An acknowledgement of the importance of honoring treaties has led the Supreme Court of Canada, over the last four decades, to rule repeatedly in favour of the Aboriginal position and against that of Ottawa, the provinces and the private sector. Saul comments on the creativity of many recent Supreme Court decisions.

"Each time the Supreme Court rules on an Aboriginal question, it seems to feel obliged to engage in original thinking. Why? Because it comes up against the originality of the Canadian reality, in which indigenous ways of thinking can be as important as the imported European methods."[386]

I am including a few paragraphs from a 2004 case of the Haida Nation versus British Columbia (Minister of Forests), which went to the Supreme Court of Canada, to give an example from the Court as to what must be the changing attitudes at all levels of our society.[387]

> The government's duty to consult with Aboriginal peoples and accommodate their interests is grounded in the honour of the Crown. The honour of the Crown is always at stake in its dealings with Aboriginal peoples...It is not a mere incantation, but rather a core precept that finds its application in concrete practices. (paragraph 16)

> The historical roots of the principle of the honour of the Crown suggest that it must be understood generously in order to reflect the underlying realities from which it stems. In all its dealings with Aboriginal peoples, from the assertion of sovereignty to the resolution of claims and the implementation of treaties, the Crown must act honourably. Nothing less is required if we are to achieve "the reconciliation of the pre-existence of aboriginal societies with the sovereignty of the Crown"...(paragraph 17)

> The honour of the Crown also infuses the processes of treaty making and treaty interpretation. In making and applying treaties, the Crown must act with honour and integrity, avoiding even the appearance of "sharp dealing"...(paragraph 21)

Treaties serve to reconcile pre-existing Aboriginal sovereignty with assumed Crown sovereignty, and to define Aboriginal rights guaranteed by s. 35 of the Constitution Act, 1982. Section 35 represents a promise of rights recognition, and "[i]t is always assumed that the Crown intends to fulfil its promises"...

This promise is realized and sovereignty claims reconciled through the process of honourable negotiation. It is a corollary of s. 35 that the Crown act honourably in defining the rights it guarantees and in reconciling them with other rights and interests. This, in turn, implies a duty to consult and, if appropriate, accommodate. (paragraph 20)[388]

New ways of thinking, new patterns of relationship, are needed, and through their professions, Bahá'ís may well have opportunities to help these changes happen more quickly. As he ruled in the Delgamuukw case in 1997,[389] Chief Justice Antonio Lamer called for negotiations to reconcile the pre-existence of Aboriginal societies with the sovereignty of the Crown. Then he looked to a future of reconciliation when he said, "Let us face it, we are all here to stay."[390]

***

Justice

As both Indigenous and non-Indigenous Bahá'ís, we have been given much guidance about how to apply the teachings of Bahá'u'lláh to the urgent needs of the world. In recent years, we have been continuously encouraged to become more involved in society. The Universal House of Justice stressed that isolating ourselves will not bring Bahá'u'lláh's healing remedy to the world, and that many more people are needed to do so. It writes, in its message of December 28, 2010:

What should be apparent is that, if the Administrative Order is to serve as a pattern for future society, then the community within which it is developing must not only acquire capacity to address increasingly complex material and spiritual requirements but also become larger and larger in size. How could it be otherwise. A small community, whose members are united by their shared beliefs, characterized by their high ideals, proficient in managing their affairs and tending to their needs, and perhaps engaged in several humanitarian projects—a community such as this, prospering but at a comfortable distance from the reality experienced by the masses of humanity, can never hope to serve as a pattern for restructuring the whole of society. That the worldwide Bahá'í community has managed to avert the dangers of complacency is a source of abiding joy to us.[391]

The Universal House of Justice also called on the Bahá'í youth to understand the real condition of humanity, including the injustice that now prevails.

The world that Bahá'í youth are inheriting is one in which the distribution of educational, economic and other basic opportunities is grossly unjust. Bahá'í youth must not be daunted by such barriers. Their challenge is to understand the real condition of humanity and to forge among themselves enduring spiritual bonds that free them not only from racial and national divisions but also from those created by social and material conditions, and that will fit them to carry forward the great trust reposed in them.[392]

Being more involved will mean becoming aware of the suffering so many have felt. A quote included in Sue Monk Kidd's powerful novel about slavery and abolition, *The Invention of Wings*, touched me very much. The words are from author and professor Julius Lester.

"History is not just facts and events. History is also a pain in the heart and we repeat history until we are able to make another's pain in the heart our own."[393]

In *Creating a New Mind*, Paul Lample offers a description of a Bahá'í approach to the quest for truth and justice, which avoids strife, contention and an adversarial process.

To work for justice does not entail parroting support for popular issues or the causes of the moment. Justice is not an excuse for the promotion of self-interest. It is not obtained by righteous indignation and loud demands made from a distance on behalf of the oppressed when one is cushioned by the comforts of privileged circumstances. It is promoted, instead, by patience and long-suffering, through persistent action and loving education. One endures injustice in the process of building justice. Bahá'u'lláh's life is eloquent testimony to this truth. "Because He bore injustice, justice hath appeared on earth, and because He accepted abasement, the majesty of God hath shone forth amidst mankind."

A community of individuals who uphold truth and champion justice faces challenges, hardship, and even persecution with composure and equanimity as it labors to establish Bahá'u'lláh's system of justice for all humanity.[394]

CHAPTER SEVENTEEN

Reconciliation

"Reconciliation turns on this concept: I want to be your friend and I want you to be mine. And if we are friends then I will have your back when you need it and you'll have mine." Justice Murray Sinclair.[395]

"When we speak of reconciliation we are referring to the movement towards peace and unity, and the individual and collective transformation that is required in order to achieve that goal. Reconciliation involves a process that contributes to the achievement of progressively greater degrees of unity and trust. Fundamentally, reconciliation is a spiritual process. It is the process of realizing the essential oneness of humanity in all dimensions of human life." Submission of the Bahá'í Community of Canada to the Truth and Reconciliation Commission, September 20, 2013.[396]

The TRC defines *reconciliation* as an ongoing process of transformation, in order to establish and maintain respectful relationships between peoples and nations.[397] The TRC believes reconciliation is in the interests of both Indigenous and non-Indigenous Canadians, must become a way of life in Canada, and that it will take time to repair damaged trust and relationships in Aboriginal communities and between Aboriginal and non-Aboriginal peoples.[398] In this chapter are various perspectives on reconciliation.

A comment that struck me in the TRC documents was from survivor Evelyn Brockwood at the Manitoba National Event in 2010, who spoke about why it's important to ensure there is adequate time for healing to occur in the truth and reconciliation process.

> When this came out at the beginning, I believe it was 1990, about residential schools, people coming out with their stories, and ... I thought the term, the words they were using, were truth, healing and reconciliation. But somehow it seems like we are going from truth telling to reconciliation, to reconcile with our white brothers and sisters. My brothers and sisters, we have a lot of work to do in the middle. We should really lift up the word healing.... Go slow, we are going too fast, too fast.... We have many tears to shed before we even get to the word reconciliation.[399]

The Guardian of the Bahá'í Faith Shoghi Effendi spoke about the need to be patient, and for those who want to form strong relationships, to master their "impatience of any lack of responsiveness on the part of a people who have received, for so long a period, such grievous and slow-healing wounds."[400] What is so heartwarming to me is that many Indigenous people have kept the door open for true friendships and partnerships. The TRC underlines this, saying that Indigenous people have always remembered the original relationship of mutual support, respect and assistance they had with early Canadians. These were confirmed by the Royal Proclamation of 1763 and the treaties that were "negotiated in good faith by their leaders. That memory, confirmed by historical analysis and passed down through Indigenous oral histories, has sustained Aboriginal peoples in their long political struggle to live with dignity as self-determining peoples with their own cultures, laws, and connections to the land."[401]

Surveying the news these days, I can see that many organizations, from governments to universities, non-profits, schools, cities and towns, have taken the TRC's recommendations to heart and are finding ways to contribute to reconciliation.[402] The TRC envisions a real contribution youth can make to this process. During the seven national events, over 15,000 high school youth took part in educational days.[403] Indigenous and non-Indigenous youth told the TRC they want to know the truth about the history and legacy of residential schools as well as all other aspects of the relationship between Aboriginal and non-Aboriginal peoples.

The TRC says that in order to develop self-respect, young Indigenous people need to know who they are and where they come from and take pride in their roots. They need to know answers to basic questions such as "Who are my people? What is our history? How are we unique? Where do I belong? Where is my homeland? What is my language and how does it connect me to my nation's spiritual beliefs, cultural practices, and ways of being in the world?" They need to know why things are the way they are today, which requires understanding the history of colonization, including the residential school system, and how it has affected their families, their communities, their people, and themselves.

Non-Indigenous children and youth equally need to understand how they have been shaped "by a version of Canadian history that has marginalized Aboriginal peoples' history and experience. They need to know how notions of European superiority and Aboriginal inferiority have tainted mainstream society's ideas about, and attitudes towards, Aboriginal peoples in ways that have been profoundly disrespectful and damaging."[404]

The TRC in its reports has frequently emphasized that survivors should be seen as more than victims. Through their suffering, they have demonstrated wisdom, courage, vision, strength and endurance.[405] Through their testimonies they have given a gift to Canada.

At the Ottawa gathering, survivor Victoria Grant-Boucher shared:

> I'm telling my story ... for the education of the Canadian general public ... [so that they] can understand what stolen identity is, you know, how it affects people, how it affects an individual, how it affects family, how it affects community.... I think the non-Aboriginal person, Canadian, has to understand that a First Nations person has a culture.... And I think that we, as Aboriginal people, have so much to share if you just let us regain that knowledge.... And I also take to heart what Elders talk about ... we have to heal ourselves. We have to heal each other. And for Canada to heal, they have to allow us to heal before we can contribute. That's what reconciliation means to me.[406]

The TRC believes that religious diversity courses should be mandatory in schools, and include a segment on Indigenous beliefs and practices.[407] At the TRC national events, there was emphasis on seven core values needed for reconciliation, known by many Indigenous peoples as the "Seven Sacred Teachings": respect, courage, love, truth, humility, honesty and wisdom, values that appear in all world religions.

The TRC also believes that reconciliation with the natural world is needed, because if human beings "resolve problems between themselves but continue to destroy the natural world, then reconciliation remains incomplete. This is a perspective that we as Commissioners have repeatedly heard: that reconciliation will never occur unless we are also reconciled with the earth."[408]

***

Speaking My Truth

A book published by the Aboriginal Healing Foundation, *Speaking My Truth: Reflections on Reconciliation and Residential Schools*, has been a wonderful way for me to grapple with what contributing to reconciliation might mean for a member of the settler society in Canada and a Bahá'í. Contributions to the book come from a wide variety of Aboriginal and non-Aboriginal sources, and were selected by broadcaster Shelagh Rogers, Mike DeGagné, Jonathan Dewar and Glen Lowry. The book, free and available in an electronic version,[409] could be used as source materials for study groups, book clubs, seminars or individual learning.

In her Foreword, Shelagh Rogers challenges readers not to be afraid of what they will feel as they learn. She, like Paulette Regan, believes we must be willing to feel unsettled and uncomfortable.

> You may feel shame if your relatives were among the colo-
> nizers. I have felt this shame. I had to witness before more
> than one thousand people, at the Northern Gathering of
> the Truth and Reconciliation Commission of Canada. The
> day set aside for me to talk about what I'd seen, heard, and
> learned was July 1st— Canada Day. I felt deeply ashamed of
> my country and the policies that lead to residential schools.
> But an Ojibway elder told me that this feeling was the begin-
> ning of real learning, as rational understanding makes way

for the heart to take it in. The real shame, he said, would be to feel no shame.[410]

Rogers believes the "longest journey is from the head to the heart" and asks Canadians to open their hearts "so that we may help carry the pain that Indigenous peoples in Canada, for centuries, have been carrying alone." She believes non-Indigenous people will not be fully at home here as Canadians until we acknowledge Canada's colonial past and present. When that is recognized and accepted, "we will have a chance to live on this land with some feeling of wholeness and integrity." Rogers writes that the tentacles of colonialism reach into the present, and reconciliation will involve taking apart a whole system of colonialism and entrenched relationships, personal, political, and philosophical.

"It isn't going to be easy, but it's our only chance. And the very soul of Canada is at stake."[411]

Garnet Angeconeb, a residential school survivor, believes that the overall impact of colonization and assimilation is "the disempowerment of people. That is why, today, we are still plagued by issues of poverty, racism, missing women, and other horrifying impacts of that broader policy…." Angeconeb speaks of our need to mend historical misunderstandings, for example about treaties, and accept the truth about Canada before moving on.

"When you're ashamed of your own history, you deny…What it all boils down to is respect. Denial is damaging and disrespectful, not healing. Our new relationships have to be built on respect."[412]

David Macdonald, a former MP and United Church minister, shared that his life experiences getting to know Mi'kmaq people on Prince Edward Island lead him to truly understand how personal relationships can alter "deeply entrenched attitudes that inhibit trust, respect, and goodwill among people with very different cultures and life experiences." He shared that a First Nations person had once said to him, "You should know that Aboriginal relations are fundamentally personal."[413]

***

Another selection from *Speaking My Truth*, "Returning to Harmony" by the late well-known Ojibwe writer Richard Wagamese, impacted me greatly and clearly describes intergenerational trauma. The child of residential school survivors who turned to alcohol to numb their pain, Wagamese writes of the harrowing trauma he suffered and his healing journey. When Wagamese was almost three, the adults in the family left his two brothers, sister and himself alone in a bush camp when they went to a town sixty miles away to drink. It was February and blowing bitterly. The firewood and food ran out. Wagamese's sister and brother hauled the two littlest ones across the bay on a sled piled with furs in a raging snowstorm. When they reached a little town, they huddled outside a train station until a policeman found them. He took them to the Children's Aid Society. Wagamese did not see his extended family again for twenty-one years. He lived in two foster homes and an abusive adoptive home that he fled for life on the streets. At the age of twenty-five, he reunited with his family and culture. Later he became an award-winning writer, and dedicated energy to reconciliation.

Wagamese believed the Canadian public also needs to hear stories about the Aboriginal people who have left hurt behind, about their capacity "for forgiveness, for self-examination, for compassion, and for our yearning for peace because they speak to our resiliency as a people."

> It's a big word, *reconciliation*. Quite simply, it means to create harmony. You create harmony with truth and you build truth out of humility. That is spiritual. That is truth. That is Indian. Within us, as nations of Aboriginal people and as individual members of those nations, we have an incredible capacity for survival, endurance, and forgiveness. In the reconciliation with ourselves first, we find the ability to create harmony with others, and that is where it has to start—in the fertile soil of our own hearts, minds, and spirits.[414]

***

Kukdookah, Terri Brown

I attended sessions on reconciliation at the final national hearing of the TRC held in Edmonton from March 27-30, 2014. While grappling with the meaning of the word and its implications, I had seen an interview with Justice Tom Berger on the Aboriginal People's Television Network (APTN) before attending the TRC hearing. Justice Berger, now eighty, had argued and won many ground-breaking legal battles on Aboriginal treaty rights in Canada and had authored the Mackenzie Valley Pipeline Inquiry in the 1970s.[415] The young interviewer's last question concerned reconciliation and what Justice Berger thought about it.

"It's the story of our country," Justice Berger replied. He stated emphatically that the divisions—and the relationships—between Aboriginal peoples and the rest of Canada, as well as the French-speaking peoples of Québec and the rest of Canada, are two major issues that Canada, as a nation, must come to grips with.

At the Edmonton national TRC hearing, Commissioner Justice Murray Sinclair said everyone can do something to contribute to reconciliation, whatever community we are from. On a panel called "Reconciliation and Collective Memory in a Divided Society," the contribution of Kukdookah (Kukdookah means "a woman paddling a canoe in the deepest waters"), Terri Brown, of the Tahltan First Nation in northern British Columbia, most touched my heart.

"Reconciliation is such a slippery word," said Brown, who served as a member of the Indian Residential School Survivor Committee (IRSSC), an advisory body to the TRC.

"It doesn't identify me or you. Put 'us' in that word."

Brown began to tell the story of her own life. She was born in 1954 in Telegraph Creek to a large family who lived in the bush. At the time, no white people were allowed on the reserve. Her birth was a difficult one, and the midwives from the community got in touch with a white man they knew who had training in first aid, who managed to get on to the reserve and help deliver her. Three out of the eight children, including Terri, attended residential school.

Later, she became a strong leader and advocate of justice for Aboriginal peoples. Among other accomplishments, she served as president of the Native

Women's Association of Canada, which founded the "Sisters in Spirit" campaign to document the stories of disappeared Aboriginal women in Canada. She brought up her children as a single parent and often had to be away for work. To survive, Brown became hyper-vigilant and very task-oriented.

"I couldn't do anything in a relaxed way. It had to be perfect. Like making a bed had to be perfect, like it had to be in residential school."

But until she was asked to serve on the IRSSC, Brown never actually faced what had happened at residential school nor had she ever talked about it with her children.

"Most survivors didn't tell their kids what had happened to them," she said. "I didn't even tell myself."

When the survivors committee first met, they began to share their stories with each other. When Brown began to speak of what she had held in for years, it poured out. On the ten-person committee, horrific stories abounded. Brown has now studied the Jewish Holocaust and she believes what happened to the children in residential schools "is that horrific."

"The birth of a baby is the most important thing in a family's life," she said. "Why did they do that (take the children away)?"

Today, Brown finds herself close to reaching forgiveness for what happened to her people, attributing this to her work on the TRC. She spoke glowingly of her love for her granddaughter and how that relationship itself brings her reconciliation. The spirituality and teachings she learned from her people saved her, she believes, cautioning that everything we do in our home teaches our children, even what we do on an "off" day.

All the survivors have hope, Brown said. It is that hope, and the efforts each of us can make, no matter in what form, that will advance reconciliation.

"We can change what is happening today. We can't change the past," she said. "I wish us to walk together. There has been enough fighting and hating."

As a grandmother myself, Brown's words resonated strongly with me. I sought her out after the session to tell her how much what she shared had touched my heart.

***

Re-telling Reconciliation

"Re-Telling Reconciliation" was the name of a talk Bahá'í lawyer Roshan Danesh[416] gave in August 2014 at the Association for Bahá'í Studies conference in Toronto. It helped clarify my thinking and gave a Bahá'í perspective on what I encountered in my research on reconciliation. Danesh admitted, to my surprise, that though he came from a family that provided him access to the best schools in Ottawa, he had grown up knowing nothing about Indigenous history, as I had in British Columbia. Danesh argued Bahá'ís have a responsibility to know accurate Canadian history. We must address the challenge of reconciliation, because our fundamental values and beliefs in the oneness of humanity necessitate our work of bringing together vastly different traditions, ways of life and people to create a unity that respects diversity. This is, in essence, what reconciliation is. He also pointed out that no fundamental issue in Canada dealing with economic or environmental matters can now be addressed without addressing reconciliation with Aboriginal peoples and the rest of Canada. For Bahá'ís, it means making a choice between justice and injustice, as expressed in this quote from 'Abdu'l-Bahá:

> Justice is not limited, it is a universal quality. Its operation must be carried out in all classes, from the highest to the lowest. Justice must be sacred, and the rights of all the people must be considered. Desire for others only that which you desire for yourselves. Then shall we rejoice in the Sun of Justice, which shines from the Horizon of God.

> Each man has been placed in a post of honour, which he must not desert. A humble workman who commits an injustice is as much to blame as a renowned tyrant. Thus we all have our choice between justice and injustice.[417]

Danesh said that when Mr. and Mrs. Ali and Violette Nakhjavani[418] came to Vancouver to speak with Indigenous believers in 2007, Mr. Nakhjavani–despite his vast knowledge from serving on the Universal House of Justice for decades–consulted with local Indigenous people ahead of time about what he could offer. At the end, he approached an invited guest, Michael Leach, hereditary chief of the Stl'atl'imx people in Lillooet British Columbia, embraced him and said, "Help us." Danesh believes most of Canada's historical approach to Aboriginal people, and even sometimes our Bahá'í approach has been, "Let us help you."

These two approaches are vastly different. One stems from a colonial attitude, implicit in which is the belief that we are somehow superior, and we can help others save themselves by becoming more like us. Danesh said this attitude has resulted in such destructive effects as the Doctrine of Discovery and *terra nullius* or empty land.[419] Danesh believes both these attitudes have affected our thinking within and outside of the Bahá'í community. We are ignorant of honest history and passive in face of it, claiming it is too difficult, too complicated, too hard. We may think "history will take its course; European ways will triumph." Unfortunately, Canadians, particularly Indigenous Canadians, live daily with the effects of our shared history, said Danesh. He added that for Bahá'ís, justice is a prerequisite for unity. To create a unified world community, which is the purpose of Bahá'u'lláh's teachings, all people need to be protagonists, and make their own contributions, not be passive recipients of the actions of others.

Danesh went on to examine the *Tablets of the Divine Plan*[420] from a different perspective. He said that at the historic time they were being written, most Bahá'ís were either Persian or American. 'Abdu'l-Bahá singled out for a special promise the original inhabitants of the Americas, who had been the most oppressed, ignored and unseen, and thus showed that those who had been brought low in the world had the potential of a great spiritual destiny. Danesh said this was a challenge to ideas in the Persian culture that certain people were to be elevated because of lineage and kinship, or the notion in American culture that material wealth should elevate people. 'Abdu'l-Bahá was challenging our mindsets and our instinct to distinguish between people on false criteria, commented Danesh.

***

Amatu'l-Bahá Rúḥíyyih <u>Kh</u>ánum

The wife of Shoghi Effendi, Hand of the Cause of God Rúḥíyyih <u>Kh</u>ánum, visited Indigenous people all over North and South America and in 1969, wrote a thirty-page letter to the Indigenous friends.[421] In analyzing the letter, Danesh said Rúḥíyyih Khánum's approach was not "let us help you." She recognized that the Americas were the homeland of the Indigenous peoples, not the "new world" of the Europeans. She praised the cities, technologies and accomplishments of the Indigenous people. She rejected the notions of assimilation and denial and replaced them with affirmation and recognition. She went on to say:

"You must never feel that you are an inferior people, a people without knowledge. My friends, each of us has five fingers on his hand. We know that we need each one of our fingers. There are red men, black men, white men, brown men and yellow men (as we call them in our language) in this world; they are like the fingers of the hand, each one needed, each one a part of the same hand."[422]

Rúḥíyyih Khánum stated that each of the central figures of the Baháʼí Faith called to Indigenous people to join with non-Indigenous in becoming agents together to help effect change and progress. Indigenous peoples' coming to the Faith will enrich them and the whole Baháʼí community, as in this quote:

"Shoghi Effendi is also most anxious for the Message to reach the aboriginal inhabitants of the Americas. These people....should receive from the Baháʼís a special measure of love, and every effort be made to teach them. Their enrollment in the Faith will enrich them and us, and demonstrate our principle of the Oneness of Man far better than words or the wide conversion of the ruling races ever can."[423]

Rúḥíyyih Khánum spoke about the future potential of humanity when the Indigenous peoples take the lead in the forefront of the Baháʼí Cause and society. In its own learning about how to reflect principles of justice and unity, the Baháʼí community needs Indigenous people to become Baháʼís, she said. The community is not to be made up of people who are alike but people who are different. Without Indigenous people, we are incomplete, as Canada is incomplete. As for the attitudes of the non-Indigenous teachers, she quoted Shoghi Effendi's advice:

"We should meet them as equals, well-wishers, people who admire and respect their ancient descent, and who feel that they will be interested, as we are, in a living religion and not in the dead forms of present-day churches."[424]

Rúḥíyyih Khánum went on to say that Indigenous people must be in the forefront of teaching Indigenous people and be the protagonists of the spiritual maturation of humanity. Non-Indigenous people don't know the Indigenous languages and often can't adjust to difficult circumstances. In acknowledging that reaching Indigenous people will require suffering and sacrifice, she reminded her readers of the self-denial of Bahá'u'lláh Himself.

> It will no doubt comfort and interest you to know that Bahá'u'lláh, although He came of a wealthy family of great chiefs, walked in the wilderness for many months, slept on the ground, lived on a handful of food and patiently endured both extreme heat and extreme cold. He had the fortitude of the Redman and not the weakness of the white man. So friends, you must follow in Bahá'u'lláh's own footsteps and walk out to teach your own people His glad tidings in this new day we are living in.[425]

Danesh concluded that in the Bahá'í Faith reconciliation is not a choice or action out of guilt, but a requirement for advancing civilization. The perfection of humanity will only come about when all peoples are contributing their gifts and ways of thinking.

***

CHAPTER EIGHTEEN

The Blending of Hearts

Reconciliation between peoples is essentially a spiritual process, Shoghi Effendi wrote to Marion Jack, who devoted over twenty years of her life to service in Bulgaria, including during the darkest times of World War II. He wrote about the "blending of hearts."

> The blending of hearts is the foundation-stone of the Bahá'í social order. It is at once its stronghold and its inherent motivating force. Through it no obstacle can withstand the triumph of the constructive forces of the world. And by its means national and racial prejudices of all sorts melt away and make, thereby, the establishment of an international order not a dream but a living reality.
>
> It is this fundamental truth, that the basis of world unity is essentially spiritual, that makes the strength of the Bahá'í Faith. And it is because our statesmen and leaders have failed to accept such a truth that they find themselves so helpless in the face of the dark forces that are so vehemently assailing the world.[426]

This theme—that true reconciliation means caring about one another—was reflected in talks given by Shaw A-in-chut Atleo and Douglas White in late 2015, in the months before the final report of the Truth and Reconciliation Commission was released. Atleo, former grand chief of the Assembly of First Nations, and White, former chief and now councillor of the Snuneymuxw First Nation, both have histories of fighting legal battles for their people–Atleo for fishing rights, and White for more land base for his people. Yet they spoke about going much further than legal battles to create genuine relationships based on respect and recognition, and they each left a door wide open for Canadians to walk through to forge these deeper bonds.

Atleo[427] gave the inaugural Indigenous Speaker Series address on November 26, 2015, at Vancouver Island University in Nanaimo. He called it "Daring Greatly Together: Reimagining Canada."[428]

Atleo spoke personally and passionately about a process of "rumbling and reckoning" he believes Canadians need to go through together as peoples. In this, we have to face the hard truth of the past. Atleo believes Canada has "disowned its own story." One of the results is that "many of us have not felt part of the fabric of this country." He spoke about a condition of indifference and denial in Canada, remembering hundreds of "Indian 101" talks he had over the years with non-Indigenous people, to answer questions from them like, "Who are you?" and "Where do you come from?" He said that, in most cases, the individual would turn away at the end, saying, "Well, that's not really that important."

"I remember how heartbreaking it felt, how difficult it felt," said Atleo. "You'd put yourself out there, over and over again. And if you had one person say, 'okay, I'm going to find a way to walk with you,' man, you grabbed on to that."

But Atleo believes these conditions in Canada are changing. "We are now moving into conversations that so many of us have been thirsting for for so long." Atleo said the process of "rumbling and reckoning" will be unsettling, and will not be easy; we will need to risk ourselves and be bold. It will require vulnerability and trust. Douglas White, who chaired the meeting, added that reconciliation will require "significant introspection on all parts and significant new ways of talking to each other." Atleo said we need to acknowledge the anger people may express about how painful it has been to be an Indigenous person in this country. If Canadians get angry at this knowledge, they can channel it so future generations will not be holding on to anger, he said. I've personally felt a lot of anger while researching Canadian history.

Atleo attended the apology for residential schools by Prime Minister Stephen Harper in the House of Commons in summer 2008, with his late Granny Elsie, then eighty-seven years old. She turned to him and said, with a tone of optimism, "Grandson, they are just beginning to see us." I've wondered about this statement several times. What would it be like to feel invisible in your own country?

Atleo described a dream his Grandmother had of a dark heavy book. The only way to turn the page on the book was if we all work together, she said. Atleo related that Granny Elsie was a great believer in the role of education and felt the Indigenous fight for rights will happen there, rather than through fists. While plans are underway in most provinces and territories for accurate Indigenous history at every grade level, institutional arrangements must also change, such as indigenizing the academy, said Atleo. Vancouver Island University, at which Atleo's father had begun the first Indigenous studies course, is now one of the first two universities in Canada to accept elders as full faculty members. At many universities, there are now Indigenous studies degrees from the bachelor to doctorate level. At several universities, so far, it will be mandatory for all students to take at least one Indigenous studies course from a wide variety offered over a number of disciplines.[429]

Atleo referred to the number of ground-breaking court decisions–some 170 as of November 2015–won in recent years by Indigenous peoples. First Nations now have the power and responsibility to help shape developments like our energy future, and industry needs to learn to work as partners with First Nations, he stated.

What was reassuring to me in Atleo's talk was his conviction that, working together, we can build a country that will be a leader in the world. He acknowledged that Canada is populated with people who have come with their own stories of trauma. Atleo said the way forward won't be easy, as addressing the underlying issues may trigger "massive emotions and trauma that we have experienced as a country." He believes we have inherited this history together and we should see its complexity as abundance.

Atleo proudly told the story of Ahousaht First Nation members who, because they knew their traditional territory, played an important rescue role when a whale-watching boat capsized off the Vancouver Island town of Tofino on October 25, 2015, killing six people. Five boats of people from Ahousaht who were fishing immediately responded to a flare that went out and helped in the rescue before the Coast Guard arrived.[430]

Atleo expressed his conviction that Canadians can heal the past.

We need each other. We matter to one another...I have always believed in my heart that if Canadians were supported to understand the truths about what had happened to Indigenous people...I believe that Canada and the people within Canada are by and large good and great and that we would get to a place where if we exchanged these senses of feelings about our own histories, that we could forge a new and better path together.

***

Douglas White[431] believes that reconciliation is the most important outstanding defining issue facing Canada at this time, necessary for Canada to grapple with in order to be a great nation. In a September 2015 talk at a Bahá'í Indigenous gathering at Harper Mountain near Kamloops, British Columbia, White stated he believes we are now at a remarkable moment in Canada for a number of reasons. These include generations of advocacy by Indigenous people working hard for their rights.

Generation upon generation of people standing up in the most dignified beautiful way to talk about who they are and where they come from, what their values are, what do they cherish most in life, what are their most sacred teachings and how does that all inform them about how they are meant to be in this world, how they are meant to understand themselves, their relationships to their families, to their children, to their grandparents and to each other, to other people in the world.[432]

White shared the story of a long legal battle in the 1960s, during the time his grandfather was the Snuneymuxw chief, when one of his cousins, the late Clifford White, and David Bob were charged for hunting deer out of season. They were hunting in accordance with their own laws and traditions, but not the provincial game act. At the court case in 1963, Clifford White stated that the pre-Confederation treaty his people had signed in 1854 (there were fourteen treaties called the Douglas treaties, signed between 1850-1854), recognized the people's right to carry on hunting in accordance with their own traditions. During the case, an elder shared the strong oral history of the treaty signed over 100 years before.

While their lawyers abandoned White and Bob, new lawyers including Thomas Berger[433] took up the case, that went all the way to the Supreme Court of Canada. The court decision supported the treaties and White and Bob's right to hunt. This was the first major litigation in the modern era, where now hundreds of cases have gone to court.

White pointed out that a shift took place from the respect and recognition shown at the time of the original treaties, by non-Indigenous people to Indigenous people, to a turning away, particularly after Confederation. It was as though the treaties were seen as a divorce or a conclusion or a finality.

"It's not about creating a relationship, it's about *ending* one. And so there is that negative storyline unfolding." This was a tragic shift, said White, leading to lots of misery, patterns of conflict, and Indigenous people being dispossessed of their relationship with their territories.

It was a shift to a "denial that any of this even matters, shocking because of that ugly idea that we don't matter to each other, that it's not necessary for us to build strong understandings and relations together."

White, a lawyer himself, has much experience fighting for rights. But the process becomes hyper-adversarial, he said, and this is not the way he wishes change to come about. "In my experience, getting something meaningfully done for our peoples is a real fight. It brings you to the brink of indignity, that fighting."

White, who has been thinking deeply about how society changes fundamentally, believes great moments change the hearts, minds and souls of people to where the world becomes a different place. The social and political context in which we now live is opening space for change. The TRC final report and ninety-four recommendations, along with various court decisions such as the Tsilhqot'in Nation decision,[434] are changing legal, economic and political frameworks.

White feels we can turn to the Bahá'í teachings as a source of knowledge. He believes what holds reconciliation together is the idea of love, and there can be no reconciliation without love and justice. Both Indigenous and Bahá'í people are rooted in this idea of unity and love and justice as being at the core of the foundation of human relations, he said.

White referenced a work, *Love Power and Justice* by William Hatcher,[435] which distinguishes between tolerance, conditional love and altruistic love. Tolerance is acceptance without concern, conditional love is concern without acceptance, but altruistic love means we matter to each other. This understanding was a major breakthrough for White.

> I want my children to be loved by other peoples in this country. I want them to love the people in this country. I want their hearts and minds to be turned to each other on a constant basis. Where they are always concerned about how to be of service and what needs to be done. To uphold the dignity of others. To look after others. To be concerned and wrapped up in each other's lives. That's the stuff that I want. Justice is an important component of that.[436]

***

When 'Abdu'l-Bahá visited Canada in 1912, he made astounding statements about the future of Canada.

"...the future of the Dominion of Canada, however, is very great, and the events connected with it infinitely glorious. It shall become the object of the glance of providence, and shall show forth the bounties of the All-Glorious."

"Again I repeat that the future of Canada, whether from a material or a spiritual standpoint, is very great. Day by day civilization and freedom shall increase. The clouds of the Kingdom will water the seeds of guidance which have been sown there."[437]

I have asked myself whether 'Abdu'l-Bahá's prophecy connects directly with our country's challenge to heal the deep-seated wounds that affect the relationships between Indigenous and non-Indigenous peoples. Perhaps as we work together towards reconciliation with good hearts, we will be contributing to this great vision of our future as a nation.

Trip to Skellig Michael, Ireland, 2006. Zara and Pat.

Trip to Drombeg Stone Circle, Ireland 2008.

Elder Beatrice Poucette ("Îna") and Pat's Mom Kitty Walsh.

Children's and Junior Youth camp, Summer 2011.
(photo courtesy Mehran Imamverdi.)

Doing crafts at camp. (M. Imamverdi photo).

Cooking hot dogs at camp. (M. Imamverdi photo).

Group photo of children's and junior youth camp. (M. Imamverdi photo).

Beverley Knowlton at approach to Shrine of Bahá'u'lláh, Pilgrimage 2012.

Leeora Simeon painting during study of *Glimmerings of Hope*, 2013.

Supper and visit with National Spiritual Assembly member Deloria Bighorn, 2013. From left back row, Toshia Kootenay, Lionel Crow, Allison Healy, Myrna Kootenay, Deloria Bighorn, Jovi Kootenay, Daryl Kootenay. Front row, Sama Imamverdi, Leva Eghbali, Drew Erickson, Naim Bakhshayesh-Rad, Camron Kootenay.

Participants at Youth Conference at University of Calgary 2014. From left,
DeAngelo Cecil, Shawyun Refahi, Naim Bakhshayesh-Rad, Chantelle Carlston,
Leva Eghbali, Sama Imamverdi, Adam Julian, Garrina Amos, Dacster Chiniquay.

Chilling at Book One, Tyson Bearspaw, Sama Imamverdi, Sally Twoyoungmen,
Leva Eghbali, Manda Hunter.

Grandson Cedar at Chief Crowfoot's grave, Siksika Nation, 2013.

Studying Book One at Bearspaw Youth Centre. Bodee Beaver, Humeyra Samii,
Tyson Bearspaw, Gage Beaver, Sama Imamverdi, Sally Twoyoungmen, Pat.

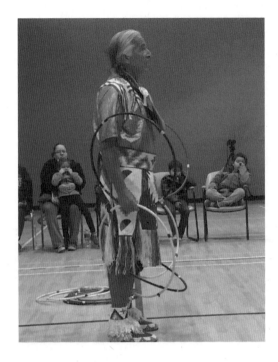

Kevin Locke visit to Morley cadets, March 2016.

Elders' supper and visit with Counsellor Borna Noureddin, April 2016. Front row, Florene and Gilbert Francis. Middle row, Sama, Pat, Patsy Ryder, Diana Melting Tallow, Shamim Alavi. Back row, Vernon Young, Allison Healy, Bill Maclean, Gage Beaver, Tyson Bearspaw, Borna Noureddin.

Retreat with Stoney Nakoda Youth Collaborative. Back row, Tara Beaver, Vernon Young, Joey Mackinaw, Leva, Alton Kaine Rider, Emily and Ashraf Rushdy. Front row, Pat, Cathy Arcega, Sama, Sarah Kinnie, Alyssa Lindsay.

First Youth Conference at Morley, October 2016.

Book One Intensive, January 2017.

Children's class displaying art. From left, Kassius Young, Dante Young, Kylen Young, Clayvin Young, 2017.

Junior Youth group baking. From left, Nisa Lambrecht, Dovey Simeon, Jenna
Snow, Sydney Clarke, Monir Imamverdi, 2017.

CHAPTER NINETEEN

Making the Links

"The oneness of the kingdom of humanity will supplant the banner of conquest, and all communities of the earth will gather under its protection."[438]

Members of each Indigenous nation, as they learn about Bahá'u'lláh, will find parallels with His teachings and their own cultural heritage. I spoke with my dear friends Allison Healy and Beverley Knowlton, both members of the Blackfoot Confederacy (Allison originally from Siksika, but married into Kainai Nation, and Beverley from Piikani Nation), to find out how each had found the parallels between their culture and the teachings of Bahá'u'lláh.

They first mentioned the practice of dawn prayers in Indigenous communities. Traditionally, elders prayed first thing in the morning, starting by facing east. Then they prayed in all directions, for all people of the world. Beverley remembered her great-grandmother got up early and went to the creek to pray and feed the birds. Bahá'ís also are urged to pray at dawn.

"Supplicate to God, pray to Him and invoke Him at midnight and at dawn."[439]

Both friends said elders had told them that in the future all the races of people will come together.

"After I became a Bahá'í I used to think about it. The elders already knew the colours would come together," said Beverley.

Indigenous cultural practices such as fasting before and during sundances and vision quests, and sweats for physical and spiritual healing, find parallels in the Bahá'í practice of fasting. For Allison, a residential school survivor who had been restricted from speaking her language or practicing any aspect of her culture, going to a sweat for the first time was transformational. She had gone to support her husband, Earl, in his sobriety.

"I found myself in the sweat, and I felt wholeness. I learned about my identity and started to take part in our traditional ways, like dancing," said Allison. Both she and Earl became traditional dancers well-known in Indian country, as well as teepee holders at the Calgary Stampede. Allison was confirmed in exploring her cultural identity and felt a rebirth when she read Bahá'u'lláh's teaching that each person should know themselves. "...man should know his own self and recognize that which leadeth unto loftiness or lowliness, glory or abasement, wealth or poverty."[440]

Both Allison and Beverley still speak their native tongue, reflecting another teaching of Bahá'u'lláh that encourages each person to learn their own native tongue, in addition to one other language, a universal language that will be chosen by the nations of the world. Such a universal language will facilitate building unity, understanding and progress towards the oneness of humanity.

For Indigenous people, children are a sacred trust. Beverley and Allison found this teaching affirmed by 'Abdu'l-Bahá in such words as "The education of children is one of the most great services. All these children are mine. If they are educated and illumined, it is as though my own children were so characterized...."[441] The spiritual teachings of their Blackfoot culture say the parent should pray right away when the child is born, so that when it grows up it will have respect for elders and parents. Likewise, the Bahá'í teachings counsel respect for parents. In traditional Blackfoot culture, there was respect for women; women and men worked together, each fulfilling important duties. This reflects the Bahá'í principle of gender equality. Allison and Beverley mentioned the importance of sharing food with neighbours, a practice reflected in the traditional hunts and carried on to this day, as well as feasts to honour the departed.

Bahá'u'lláh speaks about the importance of investigating truth for ourselves; no one should force religious belief on another person for any reason, such as tradition, or family and community loyalty. He speaks about justice and how it is related to this independent search.

"The best beloved of all things in My sight is Justice...By its aid thou shalt see with thine own eyes and not through the eyes of others, and shalt know of thine own knowledge and not through the knowledge of thy neighbor."[442]

When Allison signed an enrollment card after two years of learning with Bahá'í teachers, she saw it as making her very first choice for herself. In residential school, she had been conditioned to automatic obedience and ritual, not independent thought and choice. Allison attributes being able to remain steadfast over many years, despite some initial opposition from her family and inevitable life tests, to having really good first Bahá'í teachers. Joyce McGuffie and Eva Statz came to her home on the Reserve over a period of two years. At first they taught about the life of Jesus, using film strips, then they told her the story of Bahá'u'lláh.

Eventually Allison's teachers moved away, and she was left responsible to continue visiting people on the Reserve who had become Bahá'ís. She found that for many years she was seen as clergy, because people had been conditioned to clergy. There is no clergy in the Faith and all individuals are urged to read sacred scripture for themselves.

Allison's first teachers also taught her about tests and difficulties. When Allison met Melba Loft, the first Canadian Indigenous believer in Bahá'u'lláh, Melba said she had overcome her own personal troubles by reading the Bahá'í Writings, a practice she strongly recommended.[443]

Remembering the lifelong sufferings of Bahá'u'lláh has also frequently helped Allison through periods of struggle.

I had firsthand experience of seeing Allison's steadfastness when she and I were visiting Morley together. Someone gave us directions to the house of a friend we wanted to visit. Though we had seen dogs running wild on the reserve many times, neither of us had expressed any fear of dogs. As we drove up to the house, we saw a dog in the yard. A car was running, so we thought the people would be coming out soon. We waited. When they didn't come out, Allison got out of the car and approached the house. The dog growled, turned and attacked her. I was still in the car and started pressing hard on the horn. The people came running out of the house, and one chased the dog away with a broom.

The dog had ripped Allison's clothes and his claws had torn into her leg. When she had tried to push him off, he tore at her hand. Once the dog was gone, we quickly drove into Cochrane. At the third clinic, the only one to accept us without an appointment, the nurse continuously washed the wounds with water; the doctor suggested going to the emergency at Canmore Hospital, because the wounds were too deep for them to deal with.

The doctor on call in Canmore fortunately had experience with similar cases and said stitching would likely cause infection in the hand wound, because it was too deep. He carefully pulled back the skin to its proper place, dressed the wound, and said we would need to return every day that week to get the dressing changed. He also attended to the leg wound.

Allison was our house guest that week and each day took the trip to Canmore. The owner of the dog was terribly upset and came to visit. The dog had been her son's and brought up in the bush and she herself had always been afraid of it. The dog had been taken immediately to the Cochrane Humane Society and kept for several days' testing before being put down. The owner felt horrible, but Allison reassured her.

Allison's daughters came to drive her home. When she went to get the wound checked, her family doctor warned Allison not to go back to Morley. But intrepid soul that she is, Allison returned to Morley not long after her wounds had healed. We had learned one painful lesson. We are now always careful to check out the dogs when we approach any home. We honk the horn and wait until the owner comes out if there are dogs, a practice of the Nakoda themselves. I had never been comfortable culturally honking the horn, but I am now! We also joke that Allison shed her blood for the folks on Stoney Nakoda!

***

Finding the way into my faith

While the Stoney Nakoda people will make their own connections between their ancestral ways and Bahá'u'lláh's teachings, an important benefit for me of learning about another culture was to understand more deeply the Faith I had embraced. My dear friend Taban Behin, who grew up in a Persian family that has been Bahá'í for several generations, told me she studied Buddhism as a youth and this gave her another "way in" to the Bahá'í teachings. Similarly, learning about the spiritual teachings of my Indigenous friends has illuminated my understanding of many spiritual concepts.

Bahá'í teachings on the soul and life after death are profoundly comforting to me. So many people today deny eternal life, but I have never found this in

Stoney Nakoda people; in fact, I have never met an Indigenous person who has not believed in the existence of the Creator. In the wakes and funerals, ceremonies, pow-wows, round dances, feasts, sweats, sundances, birthdays and other gatherings I have attended, prayer and acknowledgement of the future life is always an integral part. People shared ideas similar to those I had found in the Bahá'í Writings.

"All things proceed from God and unto Him they return. He is the source of all things and in Him all things are ended."[444]

At wakes and funerals, people often shared a belief in a reunion with their departed ancestors after the death of the physical body. This belief too is strong in the Bahá'í Writings.

> And know thou for a certainty that in the divine worlds the spiritual beloved ones will recognize one another, and seek union with each other, but a spiritual union. Likewise a love that one may have entertained for anyone will not be forgotten in the world of the Kingdom, nor wilt thou forget there the life that thou hadst in the material world.[445]

The Stoney Nakoda people live in such a beautiful part of the world, whether it be at Morley, Big Horn or Eden Valley. I have felt so blessed to share in that beauty over the years. Bahá'u'lláh deeply loved nature and was deprived of its beauty during much of His life as a prisoner. He is known to have said, "The country is the world of the soul, the city is the world of bodies."[446]

One of my most treasured passages from Bahá'u'lláh's Writings speaks of how nature reflects to us the attributes of the Creator. I often think of it while making the beautiful drive to Morley. Here is a small part of the passage.

> By Thy glory! Every time I lift up mine eyes unto Thy heaven, I call to mind Thy highness and Thy loftiness, and Thine incomparable glory and greatness; and every time I turn my gaze to Thine earth, I am made to recognize the evidences of Thy power and the tokens of Thy bounty. And when I behold the sea, I find that it speaketh to me of Thy majesty, and of the potency of Thy might, and of Thy sovereignty and Thy grandeur. And at whatever time I

contemplate the mountains, I am led to discover the ensigns of Thy victory and the standards of Thine omnipotence.[447]

***

Kindness to all

Now must the lovers of God arise to carry out these instructions of His: let them be kindly fathers to the children of the human race, and compassionate brothers to the youth, and self-denying offspring to those bent with years. The meaning of this is that ye must show forth tenderness and love to every human being, even to your enemies, and welcome them all with unalloyed friendship, good cheer, and loving kindness.[448]

The exhortations to be loving and caring to each human being are abundant in the Bahá'í Writings. In my observation and experience with the Stoney Nakoda people, I've seen in action many of these teachings. I penned my experience of attending the funeral of elder Eddie Holloway Sr. after his passing in November 2012. It wasn't the first funeral I'd been to; I've attended many funerals over the years, some of them tragic, others celebratory. I have felt grief, regret, sorrow, even anger, at some of them. But Eddie's funeral gave me a chance to savour the best in Nakoda culture and the deep sense of community that I had been getting to know, little bit by little bit.

***

Funeral of Eddie Holloway

Eddie Holloway, Sr., whose Nakoda name was ija To, Blue Mountain, was a respected elder deeply attached to his culture, who had lived to the ripe old age of ninety-one. Active at the Calgary Stampede Indian village for years, he helped the village showcase the cultures of the Treaty 7 First Nations. He could always be found at sundances, pow-wows, round dances and cultural camps for youth. I had met Eddie through his older sister Beatrice Poucette, had taken visitors to meet him and his wife, Elsie, and attended an autumn feast at their home in memory of their departed son Clarence, "Snowball."

Once, when unsure about proper protocol, I asked Eddie if it would be all right for me to wear a shawl and dance during inter-tribal dances at the Stoney Nakoda pow-wow. As a non-Indigenous person, I wondered if it might offend or be seen as an attempt to appropriate the culture, yet I felt drawn to join in the spirit that seemed so evident in the dancing. Eddie replied warmly, "It's a celebration. Enjoy." I relaxed right away, his kindness helping me join in the marvellous celebration of unity and diversity that the pow-wow offers.

On another occasion, I attended a sundance on the reserve, in a large field sheltered by trees from the nearby highway. This was the first time I'd been invited to a sundance, one of the most sacred ceremonies for the Nakoda. Unlike the pow-wow, it is more rare for non-Indigenous people to be invited. My friend Deb Clement stressed that I should respond to the invitation.

The hot June sun beat down, and the smell of fresh sage wafted, as I walked timidly across the grounds, wondering what to do. Then I saw Eddie and approached him, offering the tobacco I had brought along on Deb's advice. His face lit up when he accepted it, and he motioned for me to approach the sundance lodge and observe the dancers from a distance. In each encounter with Eddie, I felt acceptance, no matter my skin colour.

The morning of Eddie's funeral, I rushed out of my Cochrane house at ten in the morning because the funeral was due to start at Morley at eleven. I didn't want to be late because I knew the gymnasium in the arena would fill up, just as it had for the funeral of Eddie's wife more than two years before. We had just had the second big snowstorm of the season, bringing a large dump of snow and temperatures near minus fifteen Celsius. Morley is about a twenty-minute drive from Cochrane, but I didn't want to end up standing outside, so I gave myself lots of time. The 1A highway to Morley has just two lanes, and from just before the summer village of Ghost Lake, the road doesn't have shoulders. Though the road had been cleared, it was slippery. I enjoyed what met my eye; before me, the snow-covered peaks of the Rocky Mountains jutted up against a clear azure blue sky.

When I got to the arena around 10:30 a.m., I had to laugh at myself. A plow was removing snow in the large parking lot and only one other vehicle had arrived. I should have known better, I thought. Most events I had attended on the Reserve didn't start on time. People always joked about "Indian time." But the odd event did start on time, enough to throw me off the idea that I should plan to get there an hour or two later than the assigned time.

Pulling over near the back of the parking lot and leaving the car running, I checked the funeral home website on my phone to make sure the time for the funeral hadn't changed. No, there it was, due to start at eleven. I felt silly, but settled in for the wait. Coming early gave me a chance to observe all the comings and goings. Gradually a few cars showed up. Most people stayed warm in their cars, but in time, a few started to make their way to the gym. Elders walked in, sometimes using walkers. They were always assisted by someone, usually a younger relative. Several wore bright multicoloured coats in a geometric design, reflective of the Plains Indian culture of the Nakoda. The elderly ladies wore bright printed scarves over their hair and carried blankets to place on the hard seats. Youth clad in black hoodies and jeans hung out around the gym doors. My friend Zalida Poucette,[449] Beatrice's daughter and Eddie's niece, pulled up beside me with her two sons, Bubba and Cavan, and granddaughter Chanel. After we chit-chatted for a while, she said she was going home, at least a twenty-minute drive from the gym. She'd drive slowly, she said, because of the icy roads, and by the time she got back, the funeral would just be starting. And she was right, it didn't start until after noon.

I finally went into the gymnasium and sat at the back with Dianne Ridsdale and elder Margaret Hunter. To care for Margaret, Dianne was picking her up every night to stay over at her house, and then taking her back home in the morning. I wondered how many in my culture would do this for aging relatives.

In front of the stage hung a large cloth in a geometric design and, to its left, a tapestry on canvas, a likeness of Eddie and Elsie, his wife of seventy years, standing outside their teepee. The teepee had been raised every year since 1969 at the Stampede Indian Village, forty-three years.[450]

When Elsie had died two years earlier, Eddie was lost. Already in poor health, he clearly missed her terribly. I had seen him at a musical exchange between Morley and Cochrane, and his sparkle was gone. His family banded together and found a spot for him in a seniors facility in Cochrane where he stayed until he passed away.

People of all ages began to stream into the gym: babies in moss bags snug in their parents' arms, kids in their best clothing, pre-teens, young adults, men and women of all ages. Many greeted each other with the customary handshake or a hug. Observing the warmth, I thought about the similarities with my Irish relatives who attend all the funerals and wakes in their community.

The speakers filed in and sat on the stage. Members of the family rushed in with flowers from the wake and equipment for the video show. I popped outside to find Yvonne, the eldest Holloway daughter, to give her some baking. I hadn't been able to get out to the wake because of the weather. As is the custom, the wake had been held at the Holloway family home throughout two days and nights. During that time and after the funeral, the family fed all the guests. Dianne told me that during the funeral, people were at the house busily preparing food for a feast after the burial.

The hearse had made its way towards the townsite, east on Chiniki Lake Road to Highway 1, then north on Morley Road. When it reached the arena, drummers lined up ready to drum the coffin into the gymnasium. It was still bitterly cold. I quickly spoke with Yvonne and went back to my seat. The drumming began and everyone in the gym stood up. The power of the drumming and high-pitched singing touched my heart and soul as the coffin was brought in, the large extended Holloway family walking slowly behind it.

Bill Wesley, a traditional Nakoda, and the husband of Eddie's niece Annie, emceed the funeral. Much of the service was in the Nakoda language, but in the courteous manner of the Nakoda, most speakers gave at least part of their message in English for the benefit of guests who had come from off-reserve or Nakoda who don't speak the language. The funeral home representative spoke of Eddie's help to him in understanding the culture over the years, so funerals could be held in the proper manner. He presented a Pendleton blanket to the family.[451] A volunteer from the Calgary Stampede spoke of Eddie's kindness in teaching him about Nakoda culture to be sure everything was done appropriately at the Indian Village.

Two of the three Reserve chiefs and a representative of the third spoke, a mark of respect for Eddie, mentioning his spiritual qualities of kindness, respect, courage, and his contributions to preserving culture. Between each speaker, the drummers beat out traditional music and everyone stood. Then we viewed a video of Eddie's life.

After the program, a wide circle of family and relatives formed around the coffin. People who had been waiting outside and in the hall formed a lineup and went around the circle, shaking each person's hand and stopping at the coffin to have a last brief look at one who had lived a long and fruitful life. Drummers sang continuously, tears sprang to many eyes. The lineup of people, similar to the one at Elsie's funeral, seemed to be never-ending. People signed the guest book and visited along the way. I saw friends and enjoyed watching people visit with each other. At the end, the family spent more time around the coffin, until they were ready to let go. By the time I had gotten through the line, and by the time the family was prepared to go to the graveyard, it was already four in the afternoon. Likely more than 1,000 people filed past the coffin.

Moved by the strong community feeling and support for the grieving family, the respect shown elders, the blending of all the ages from infant to elder, and the powerful traditional drumming, I realized what an honour it was to be present.

***

Relationship of ancestral Indigenous teachings and the Bahá'í Faith

Kevin Locke, Lakota flute player, hoop dancer, educator and world cultural ambassador, visited Morley as a young man to attend a series of ecumenical councils held in the 1970s.[452] North American Indigenous cultures had been under assault for decades by both church and government, and the ecumenical councils played a big role in helping revive them, Locke said on a 2016 visit to Morley. He shared his personal journey of connecting his Lakota beliefs with the Bahá'í Faith in a *One Country* magazine article, referring to teachings brought by White Buffalo Calf Woman (Ptehíŋčala Ska Wiŋ), considered a Holy Soul by the Lakota.

As he (Kevin Locke) explored the history and tenets of the Faith, which teaches that there is only one God and that all of the world's religions, including many indigenous ones, are expressions of the same ancient and eternal faith, he decided that many of the prophecies of the White Buffalo Calf Woman had been fulfilled. "The central prayer of the Lakota is to be sheltered under the 'Tree of Life,' and the teachings about the great 'Hoop of Life' are that the many hoops of creation, or, peoples of the world are interconnected and destined to come together," he said, pointing out that one of the titles of Bahá'u'lláh, the Founder of the Bahá'í Faith, is the "Tree of Life."

"I realized that the teachings of the Woman (White Buffalo Calf Woman) were part of a great process of divine revelation that all peoples have taken part of, and that it has reached its culmination in the Bahá'í Faith," he said. "I also realized that what the Bahá'í Faith teaches does not detract from or in any way negate my own traditional religion. Many people ask me, 'How does the Bahá'í Faith tie in with your Indian spiritual traditions?' Because there is an assumption that people get from their experience with Christianity, at least as practiced here, that you have to renounce your former practices when you join a new religion.

"But the Bahá'í Writings say that all people have received a portion of the divine bounty, and that this bounty is all from the same source," he said. "In other words, the truly valid and beautiful spiritual traditions are from one source and they all have prophetic traditions that point to the same point of unity and to the same glorious future for humanity, which is the unfoldment of an all-embracing world civilization. So there is no need to deny or negate or invalidate each other's spiritual heritage."[453]

***

Donald Francis Addison Ph.D. and Christopher Buck Ph.D. explored the concept of Messengers of God to Indigenous people in North America when they examined a tablet to Amír Khan, a Persian inventor and importer, in which 'Abdu'l-Bahá states, in speaking about the earliest inhabitants of America, "Undoubtedly in those regions, the Call of God must have been raised in ancient times, but it hath been forgotten now."[454]

This Bahá'í belief, that all peoples have received divine guidance, is spoken of by the Universal House of Justice, which refers to the "profound spiritual truths which are to be found in...their (Indigenous peoples') pre-Christian religions..."[455] The Universal House of Justice wrote about other holy figures besides the ones widely known.

"...there are also other prophetic figures who are under the shadow of the Manifestation, and personages, such as sages, seers, and divine men of learning, who because of their wisdom and guidance, profoundly influence the lives of people in certain parts of the world."[456]

Dr. Addison, who is an elder in the Choctaw community, has written an article about some of these spiritual leaders and their beliefs.

> Many Native American spiritual leaders over the centuries foretold this phenomenon we are privileged to see today. White Buffalo Calf Woman, a Lakota, spoke of a great spiritual renewal. Other American Indian prophets expressed a dream that Indian and non-Indian would someday come together in unity. Deganawidah, Peacemaker of the Iroquois Confederacy, long ago promised he would "return",[457] and other great messengers left similar prophecies that a great teacher would come, as the Navajos believe, from the East.
>
> Bahá'u'lláh, the prophet-founder of the Bahá'í Faith, did come from the East and Native Americans are increasingly joining his faith, because they believe Bahá'u'lláh has fulfilled these prophecies. The Hopi, for example, foresaw a time when the Indian and the Euro-American would join together in unity. Bahá'u'lláh proclaimed this, saying, "Ye are the flowers of one garden and the leaves of one tree." ...

The Bahá'í prayers revealed by Bahá'u'lláh for believers to use do not preclude using prayers of other religions, including those of indigenous religions in American Indian languages. Bahá'ís believe in the same God as Native Americans, Christians, Jews, Muslims and the other world religions...

Many folks ask about the sad things that happened to Indians over the last 600 years. Those things really did happen, so let us learn from those experiences and teach our children to look at all peoples as members of the same family, enjoying the beauty of all our cultures and languages. The Bahá'í Faith gives me this hope.

What the Bahá'ís express about unity can also be summed up in probably the most famous American Indian expression one can find around the country today: *"Mitakuye Oyasin."* Though it is Lakota, this phrase is used by Indians from many different backgrounds; it means "all my relations" or "all my relatives." In other words, we are all related in one family. So we must put hatred and prejudice behind us because one must not hurt one's own relatives. *Mitakuye Oyasin!*[458]

In the co-authored article cited above, Dr. Addison remarked that, unlike the spread of Christianity within Indian country, "the Bahá'í Faith has never been associated with a fortification of colonial occupation, Euro-American assimilation, or forced conversions of Native Americans."[459]

A number of statements from the TRC documents mirror the ideas expressed above. In its final report, the TRC stated, "No one should be told who is, or how to worship, their Creator. That is an individual choice and, for Indigenous peoples, it is also a collective right. However, First Nations, Inuit, and Métis people need to be assured that they do indeed have the freedom to choose and that their choice will be respected..."[460]

The United Nations Declaration on the Rights of Indigenous Peoples Article 12 states:

Indigenous peoples have the right to manifest, practice, develop and teach their spiritual and religious traditions, customs and ceremonies; the right to maintain, protect, and have access in privacy to their religious and cultural sites; the right to the use and control of their ceremonial objects; and the right to the repatriation of their human remains.[461]

Helping people build capacity by sharing the healing message of Bahá'u'lláh's Revelation is not a forceful process nor does it ask people to replace what they formerly believed.

Further Prerequisites for this service

Those hoping to serve with Indigenous people will wish to ponder on the spiritual qualities needed.

O CHILDREN OF MEN! Know ye not why We created you all from the same dust? That no one should exalt himself over the other.[462]

The Master has likened the Indians in your countries to the early Arabian Nomads at the time of the appearance of Muhammad. Within a short period of time they became the outstanding examples of education, of culture and of civilization for the entire world. The Master feels that similar wonders will occur today if the Indians are properly taught and if the power of the Spirit properly enters into their living.[463]

In *The Advent of Divine Justice*, Shoghi Effendi described the spiritual prerequisites for success in any service the Bahá'ís attempt to carry out. They include rectitude of conduct, a chaste and holy life, and complete freedom from racial prejudice.[464] He called racial prejudice the "most challenging issue" facing the Bahá'í community. While he was primarily referring at the time to the relationships between African American and white believers, I've often thought the qualities the Guardian said are needed by the Bahá'ís also apply to relations between Indigenous and non-Indigenous Bahá'ís and are a fruitful source for meditation for those who wish to contribute in this important field. He spoke about the "tremendous effort" needed by both races "if their outlook, their manners, and conduct are to reflect, in this darkened age, the spirit and teachings of the Faith of Bahá'u'lláh." Shoghi Effendi called for the white race

> to abandon once for all their usually inherent and at times subconscious sense of superiority, to correct their tendency towards revealing a patronizing attitude towards the members of the other race, to persuade them through their intimate, spontaneous and informal association with them of the genuineness of their friendship and the sincerity of their intentions, and to master their impatience of any lack of responsiveness on the part of a people who have received, for so long a period, such grievous and slow-healing wounds.

Shoghi Effendi went on to appeal to the black race to "show by every means in their power the warmth of their response, their readiness to forget the past, and their ability to wipe out every trace of suspicion that may still linger in their hearts and minds." He cautioned the Bahá'ís that they should not wait for the solution of the problem to take place outside of the Faith. He then called them to the spiritual qualities that will be needed:

> Let neither think that anything short of genuine love, extreme patience, true humility, consummate tact, sound initiative, mature wisdom, and deliberate, persistent, and prayerful effort, can succeed in blotting out the stain which this patent evil has left on the fair name of their common country....[465]

In the materials prepared for the worldwide youth conferences held from July to October 2013, a whole section was devoted to "fostering mutual support and assistance." In discussing the true friendships that must be established between the youth as they serve together, one friend said, "I think when people become true friends, and are constantly encouraging each other, even what may at first seem impossible becomes achievable. Then service becomes pure joy, and the circle of friends grows."[466] Building relationships is always important, but within Indigenous communities, many have told me, and I have discovered, it is paramount to any progress. It calls to mind 'Abdu'l-Bahá's exhortation to us: "Concern yourselves with one another. Help along one another's projects and plans. Grieve over one another. Let none in the whole country go in need. Befriend one another until ye become as a single body, one and all ..."[467]

***

In September 2014, I attended a Bahá'í Indigenous gathering at Harper Mountain, near Kamloops, British Columbia. Kamao Cappo and his wife, Cora, came to the gathering from Muscowpetung Reserve in Saskatchewan. Kamao had spoken earlier that year at the Bahá'í National Convention in Toronto, and the substance of his talk at Harper was the same. He said that many of the Bahá'ís, and I believe he meant both Indigenous and non-Indigenous, had experienced "failure" in attempting to teach the Faith to First Nations. He said that the old methods had been ineffective for the most part, and in some cases had actually built an immunity to the Faith. But he said that building relationships was essential, friendship was the basis for everything. He said that those First Nations who had stayed steadfast in the Cause were the result of the sincerity of the early teachers. His words struck and comforted me.

At Harper, Kamao added another element to his talk. We had been studying the *Tablets of the Divine Plan* that day, and had referred to the astounding promise of 'Abdu'l-Bahá about the "original inhabitants" of the Americas. He commented that for such promises to be fulfilled, enormous effort would be needed. I breathed a great sigh of relief. Of course, this pearl of great price, this gem, could not be fulfilled without a great deal of patient effort. This special prophecy of the Master is in the hands of the Creator, the Manifestation of God and the institutions working to serve communities, but primarily it is in the hands of local Indigenous people. Those of us attracted to this field of service, both Indigenous and others, are called to prepare and educate ourselves, to become strong in many ways, and to persevere.

***

Some reflections on protection of cultural diversity

"The Cause does not wish to suppress national characteristics. It abhors too much uniformity, and stands for the principle of unity in diversity, which principle we believe can alone provide a solution for the unification of mankind."[468]

Advice about working with other cultures and how each culture can make its own contribution to world civilization can be found in Section 30 of Ruhi Book 6. The section clarifies that the purpose is "to bring them to the Message of Bahá'u'lláh; you are not there to impose on them your own tastes." While interaction between cultures will occur naturally, a problem can arise "when one group considers its culture so superior that it decides to aggressively propagate it and erase all others. When teaching among a population whose culture is different from our own, we have to be aware of this danger and recognize the fact that every people can move directly to Bahá'u'lláh; they do not first need to adopt our culture."

This has implications for how Bahá'u'lláh's teachings will be implemented in a local population.

> The diverse peoples of the world may be seen as points scattered on the outer surface of a sphere with Bahá'u'lláh at its center, at its core. There are forces in the world that are trying to pull all the points towards one pole, bringing them together in what is claimed to be a universal culture. But, when this happens, the points only move from one place on the surface of the sphere to another, and their distance from the center, their distance from Bahá'u'lláh, does not change. On the other hand, if each one of these points, if each one of these peoples, is allowed to move along its own direct path towards Bahá'u'lláh, they will naturally come closer to one another. Their cultures will change and be enriched as they each make contributions to the emergence of a world civilization.[469]

***

At the time of the 2006 Canadian census, more than half of people identifying themselves as members of at least one of Canada's Aboriginal groups (First Nations, Métis or Inuit) resided in urban areas. Over 200,000 lived in five cities: Winnipeg, Edmonton, Vancouver, Calgary and Toronto.[470] Shoghi Effendi particularly spoke about cities as places to make relationships with Indigenous peoples.

> He adds one suggestion (he does not know if it is practicable or not): Can contact not be made with Indians who have become more or less absorbed into the life of the white element of the country and live in or visit the big cities? There, people, finding the Bahá'ís sincerely lacking in either prejudice—or that even worse attitude, condescension— might not only take interest in our teachings, but also help us to reach their people in the proper way.
>
> It is a great mistake to believe that because people are illiterate or live primitive lives, they are lacking in either intelligence or sensibility. On the contrary, they may well look on us, with the evils of our civilization, with its moral corruption, its ruinous wars, its hypocrisy and conceit, as people who merit watching with both suspicion and contempt. We should meet them as equals, well-wishers, people who admire and respect their ancient descent, and who feel that they will be interested as we are in a living religion and not in the dead forms of present-day churches.[471]

Persian Bahá'ís

Many Bahá'ís of Iranian ancestry have made North America their home. The Persian Bahá'ís (Persia was the traditional name of Írán), with their history of sacrifice and suffering, have a great deal to offer to the reconciliation and teaching work among Indigenous peoples, I believe.

The history of the persecution of the Bahá'ís of Iran, which has endured for over 170 years since the Faith began in that country, is the story of another people who have been oppressed simply because of their beliefs. Similar to the Indigenous people who have been unwilling to barter away their spiritual beliefs despite massive attempts to assimilate them, the Persian Baháʼís have been unwilling to betray their beliefs in the Revelation of Baháʼuʼlláh, even in some cases giving up their lives rather than renounce their faith.

While members of the Iranian Baháʼí community have been targeted since the beginning of the Faith, the oppression has once again intensified since the Iranian Revolution in 1979.

Baháʼís, who are Iran's largest non-Muslim religious minority, are routinely arrested, detained and imprisoned. They are barred from holding government jobs, and their shops and other enterprises are frequently closed or discriminated against by officials at all levels. Young Baháʼís are prevented from attending university, and volunteer Baháʼí educators who have sought to fill that gap have been arrested and imprisoned. Added to that have been attempts to incite hatred against the Baháʼís in the official news media, which has led to violent attacks on individuals and properties, including vandalizing or destroying Baháʼí cemeteries.

At the same time all this has been going on, the Baháʼís have attempted to make constructive contributions to their society.

"Iranian Bahaʼis deeply love their homeland, despite all the suffering they have endured. Regardless of the restrictions imposed on them, they fulfil their spiritual and social responsibilities. Through participation in constructive discourse with neighbours, co-workers, friends and acquaintances, they nonetheless continue to contribute to the advancement of their nation and its people."[472] Like many Indigenous people, the Iranian Baháʼís have striven to achieve justice through legal means open to them and the international community has helped raise awareness of the violation of their human rights.

The Universal House of Justice, in encouraging the Baháʼís to overflow with a universal love for each other and for all humanity, pointed to the resilience displayed by the Persian believers in circumstances of the utmost oppression.

"Look within your own ranks, at your dear Baháʼí brothers and sisters in Iran. Do they not exemplify fortitude born of the love of God and the desire to serve Him? Does not their capacity to transcend the cruelest and most bitter persecution bespeak the capacity of millions upon millions of oppressed people of the world to arise and take a decisive part in building the Kingdom of God on earth?"[473]

Another quote from the Universal House of Justice acknowledges the deep suffering that so many peoples have endured.

> Our world is passing through the darkest period in the entire history of civilization, in which unnumbered millions of people suffer grievous wrongs that drive them to the edge of despair. It is one of the mysteries of the spiritual realm that the destinies of those who have great contributions to make should entail suffering of the kind your letter so movingly describes. What we do know, beyond any possibility of doubt, is that these black clouds will lift, that the spiritual potentialities of those who are now undergoing such severe testing will find fulfillment and that the whole world will benefit.[474] .

Indigenous people may have much to share with the Persian community, even well into the future. Shamim Alavi, Sama's mom, shared with me a pilgrim note[475] from her grandfather with an astounding promise—that in the future, Indigenous Bahá'í youth would teach the Faith in the place of its birth, Írán.

***

In its final report, the TRC acknowledges that many newcomers to Canada have endured trauma and oppression and suggests that for them, "finding common ground as Treaty people involves learning about the history of Aboriginal peoples and finding ways to build stronger relationships of solidarity with them. The Commission believes there is an urgent need for more dialogue between Aboriginal peoples and new Canadians."[476]

Honorary witness to the TRC, Mayor Gregor Robertson of Vancouver, said that Canada had welcomed many people from families, clans and cultures that had been wiped out and had to leave their own homes and countries.

"We were forced off our territories, and somehow we've managed to make a home here. That's largely because of those First Nations ancestors who welcomed us ... who made it possible for refugees, for people of broken cultures all over the world to settle here, to stay here, even though our predecessors and our ancestors turned it right around and terrible things have happened."[477]

Reflections on PTSD

I lay on the bed, quietly sharing a memory from childhood. My room-mate, with whom I was sharing the hotel room for a night, said, "Well, that's your PTSD (Post-Traumatic Stress Disorder) coming through."

My jaw dropped and I nearly fell off the bed. "Is it that obvious?" I asked. First of all, I had never thought of myself as having PTSD. And to think it was so "obvious" was shocking. I felt I had worked long and hard on my "issues." My friend assured me it wasn't *that* obvious, but that, as a counsellor, she is very sensitive about such matters and picks them up. I guess I knew deep down that traces of trauma still remain, like when bouts of anxiety and nervousness crop up, or it's difficult to limit taking on commitments.

So it was no surprise when I read how PTSD has affected whole cultures and how much effort and time will be needed to journey to wellness. I read more about this in Linda Covey's Master's thesis on Dine (Navajo) becoming Bahá'í. Linda, of Native American heritage herself, believes Native Americans as a whole population—and by extension the Indigenous peoples of Canada—suffer from PTSD.

> It has long been my contention that American Indians, as a body of people, suffer from post-traumatic stress disorder (PTSD) as a result of five hundred years of invasion and constant attempts at assimilation. Five hundred years is a mere blink of the eye in the timeline of a people. Historical examples are replete that show whole societies of people continue to struggle, resist, and suffer for centuries after conquest has come to an end. PTSD manifests itself in American Indian culture through high rates of alcoholism, domestic violence, child abuse, suicides, broken families, and the loss of dignity, culture, traditions, and languages—in short, a crisis of loss. PTSD is most often identified in individuals following the aftermath of wars, natural disasters, and other traumatic, uncontrollable events that deeply

impact the individual psyche. In the case of Native America, the shared trauma of conquest and assimilation has continued for decades after the last Indian war (1918) was fought less than a hundred years ago—still recent in their collective consciousness.

Imagine a whole continent of people whose way of life had vanished, whose ability to control or gain their most basic needs was precarious, whose sacred sites were disrespected and destroyed by their conquerors, and who had little to no control over the future of their children and grandchildren—then one can catch a glimpse of the depth of PTSD in the American Indian community... no trauma has been greater, more difficult to recover from, or more destructive than the on-reservation and off-reservation boarding school systems.[478]

U.S. studies have shown greater prevalence of post-traumatic stress disorder among African, Hispanic, Native and Pacific Island Americans in comparison to their white counterparts.[479] Much research is now being done into intergenerational trauma that has resulted from residential schools. My friend Reggie Newkirk[480] sent me an article that made direct connections between intergenerational trauma experienced by the Irish and by the Oglala Lakota Sioux.[481]

As children see an earlier generation's experience of trauma manifest in anger, depression and alcohol/drug abuse, each successive generation of new parents "can (inadvertently) 're-traumatize' their children," leading to multigenerational trauma, according to the article. However, studies show that strong identification with traditional culture can act as a "positive and protective factor against trauma." And there is growing evidence that combining western therapy and cultural practices can increase mental health healing. One Lakota study with parents and youth, using the extended family network and traditional Lakota practices and ceremonies such as the sweat lodge, drumming, talking circles, language development and womanhood and manhood ceremonies, lead to impressive results in family functioning.[482] A lesson the worldwide Bahá'í community is learning with the junior youth spiritual empowerment program is that being of service to one's community can also be protective.

***

Learning about vicarious traumatization and self-care, 2015

In its message of December 29, 2015, the Universal House of Justice states that through its activities, the Bahá'í community is "being drawn further into the life of society."[483] As this happens, there may be times we become overwhelmed. This is one such personal story.

I am speaking with a young woman at a youth drop-in. She says she's feeling super stressed. I probe a little, and she discloses she was sexually abused by a relative at a young age. This still affects her with bouts of anxiety. I urge her to seek counselling. Later that week, in another setting, a long-time friend discloses she was a victim of incest when she was younger.

Then a friend asks me to accompany her to visit a family I know well, for whom she hopes to arrange counselling. Though I have wanted to find ways to become closer to people on the reserve, learning of some of these deep struggles hits me hard. Not sure I can handle situations for which I have no professional counselling training, I begin to lose sleep.

At my annual check-up, I explain what's happening and ask my doctor for more sleeping pills. I normally get about six pills every year for times I cannot wind down from over-stimulation at big meetings. I only take half a pill at a time and sometimes the six pills last two years. But this year, I'm running out. I ask for double.

"I can prescribe the pills for you, and I will," says my doctor. "But it's a slippery slope. Would you consider getting mental health counselling?"

I'm a bit shocked but agree, recognizing my need for help. The young counsellor I go to listens very carefully to my story; he confirms that stress levels affect how well we sleep. Then he acknowledges that I have many things to be stressed about. He asks if I have ever heard the term "compassion fatigue," also known as vicarious traumatization. I haven't, but the term resonates. On his advice, I attend a seminar on the subject at Mount Royal University. I later find this definition: "Compassion Fatigue is a state experienced by those helping people or animals in distress; it is an extreme state of tension and preoccupation with the suffering of those being helped to the degree that it can create a secondary traumatic stress for the helper."[484]

I learn that, sometimes, it's possible to care too much or feel too responsible, and that destructive behaviours can then surface, such as apathy, isolation, bottled up emotions and substance abuse. The counsellor also helps me to see the difference between "commitment to" a friendship, and feeling "responsible for" that person. This is excellent learning for me. It helps in my journey to decolonization by affirming that individuals have capacities to change and that they will do so of their own free will. In the case of the young woman who had been abused, I share resources with her that she can access and trust that when she is ready, she will do so. I also attend a two-day workshop for volunteers who serve in the community, which gives knowledge of the many professional resources available and how to discern when help is needed urgently. Most of all I learn the importance of self-care, of setting boundaries. The facilitator stresses that friendship, caring and listening are among the most important assets we have as volunteers.

***

CHAPTER TWENTY

Taking Ownership

Man is not intended to see through the eyes of another, hear through another's ears nor comprehend with another's brain. Each human creature has individual endowment, power and responsibility in the creative plan of God.[485]

...pioneers from a foreign land can never take the place of native believers who must always constitute the bedrock of any future development of the Faith in their country.[486]

Shoghi Effendi makes clear the indispensability of Indigenous believers assuming the lead in taking the Faith to their own people, and this has been confirmed in guidance from the Universal House of Justice regarding the institute process. I have asked myself what it means to take ownership and why counter forces have been so strong.

Each of us, whether Indigenous or not, is called to move from passivity to active participation. The Universal House of Justice has explained why passivity is rampant, indicating that it is "is bred by the forces of society today. A desire to be entertained is nurtured from childhood, with increasing efficiency, cultivating generations willing to be led by whoever proves skilful at appealing to superficial emotions."[487]

I learned a lot through conversations with my friend Helen Mirkovich Kohm, who grew up in Costa Rica and, in her own words, had been nurtured over many years by the Ruhi Institute.[488] Helen, whose father was of Croatian background and a Bahá'í pioneer to Costa Rica, and whose mother was of Indigenous Costa Rican descent, warned me not to see Indigenous peoples as victims, but as people who have lost hope.

Members of all faiths have been congregational to date, Helen said, with a few dominant people, such as clergy, and the rest mainly passive. I come from a Roman Catholic background where the priest acts on behalf of the congregation. This phenomenon of having a few very active people and the rest more passive has also occurred to a certain degree in our Bahá'í communities, particularly before the institute process was firmly established. In a letter written on its behalf to an individual in 2002, the Universal House of Justice acknowledged this.

> Where Bahá'í communities are unable to free themselves from an orientation to Bahá'í life that has long outlived whatever value it once possessed, the teaching work will lack both the systematic character it requires, and the spirit that must animate all effective service to the Cause. To mistakenly identify Bahá'í community life with the mode of religious activity that characterizes the general society — in which the believer is a member of a congregation, leadership comes from an individual or individuals presumed to be qualified for the purpose, and personal participation is fitted into a schedule dominated by concerns of a very different nature — can only have the effect of marginalizing the Faith and robbing the community of the spiritual vitality available to it.[489]

In other words, the whole human race and every people is now at the threshold of empowerment and beginning to break old mindsets of dependency. I had found no space to truly participate while I was a member of the Catholic Church, but this changed when I became a Bahá'í.

I was struck by a passage in Bev Sellars' memoir. The particular context is about the economy, but it seems to me can apply to other aspects of life.

"The churches and governments have reduced once-independent Aboriginal nations to beggars in our own lands. While all the harm and damage cannot be repaired, there is much that can change if non-Aboriginals, individuals, and governments abandon the assumption that they know what is best for Aboriginal people."[490]

This statement provides a cautionary note, I believe, as Baháʼís engage more with Indigenous people. Attitudes of paternalism or of knowing what's best for other people have no place in these interactions. The Universal House of Justice describes the framework of action as "...a process that seeks to raise capacity within a population to take charge of its own spiritual, social and intellectual development." The activities that drive this process (devotional meetings, children's classes, junior youth groups and study circles) "may well need to be maintained with assistance from outside the local population for a time. It is to be expected, however, that the multiplication of these core activities would soon be sustained by human resources indigenous to the neighborhood or village itself—by men and women eager to improve material and spiritual conditions in their surroundings."[491]

***

An article by Holly Hanson in the *Journal of Baháʼí Studies*, entitled "Enacting Thought: Divine Will, Human Agency, and the Possibility of Justice,"[492] reflects further on what is involved in becoming an active participant in a process of social change, such as the one envisioned by the Universal House of Justice through the framework of action. Few of us would disagree that social structures now operating in the world are manifestly unjust, characterized by extremes of wealth and poverty, massive destructive exploitation of the environment, and inequities at every level, from legal and economic, to education and health. Hanson writes that oppressive social structures "are the result of generations of self-interest." In most cases, these structures build on top of each other by imitating the past. In general, most of us have bought into "hegemony," which is defined as the "uncritical assent given by mass society to its own domination by a few."[493] We feel helpless in the face of forces we see as much larger than ourselves and unstoppable.

The Guardian of the Baháʼí Faith, in a letter written on his behalf, speaks about how our inner condition is intimately connected to the environment around us.

"We cannot segregate the human heart from the environment outside us and say that once one of these is reformed everything will be improved. Man is organic with the world. His inner life moulds the environment and is itself also deeply affected by it. The one acts upon the other and every abiding change in the life of man is the result of these mutual reactions."[494]

A rampant materialism characterizes our present economic system and dehumanizes people. Social bonds are replaced with economic ones and people are urged to find satisfaction and happiness through consumption rather than through serving others.[495] The Universal House of Justice explains how such unjust structures can lead over the long term to a condition where oppressed people "lose confidence in their own perception of themselves" and become "drained of that spirit of initiative that is integral to human nature."[496]

Hanson writes that as we align ourselves with the will of God for the age, when "our actions express the love of God which animates us, we create societies characterized by justice."[497] Based on these beliefs, writes Hanson, Bahá'ís recognize "humanity's capacity to transcend oppressive thought and create structures that embody justice using the power of the Word of God."[498]

In the institute process, in particular, human beings learn to make use of the transforming power of the Word of God. Within local contexts, with local people and their cultures, the society-building power of the Word of God can be turned to furthering a vision of social justice. The qualities needed of pure intentions, humility, a sense of responsibility and a deliberate avoidance of distinctions among people can "have influence far beyond their numbers."[499]

As I reflected on these ideas, I found it useful to distinguish between the idea of "charity" and the concept of developing capacity in individuals and institutions. Paul Lample writes:

"The emphasis of the Bahá'í community is not on delivering charity, which so often debilitates the recipient, but on cultivating capacity in individuals and their institutions to participate in their own development."[500]

I was struck by this comment of actor Rainn Wilson, who, in his memoir, distinguishes between education and "charity."

> ...education isn't "charity." I've come to despise that word.
> *Charity* implies *giving out* something to people who are less
> fortunate. It implies "we have" and "you don't have." There's
> a sense of pity attached to doling out to the poor. Education
> empowers. It uplifts. It allows the student to learn to give to
> themselves and their family, country and community with

self-respect and self-determination. Charity makes people dependent. Education makes them independent.[501]

It is in the light of these thoughts that this astounding statement of the Universal House of Justice, that the processes Bahá'ís are engaged in can disable instruments of oppression, makes sense to me.

> It should be apparent to all that the process set in motion by the current series of global Plans, seeks, in the approaches it takes and the methods it employs, to build capacity in every human group, with no regard for class or religious background, with no concern for ethnicity or race, irrespective of gender or social status, to arise and contribute to the advancement of civilization. We pray that, as it steadily unfolds, its potential to disable every instrument devised by humanity over the long period of its childhood for one group to oppress another may be realized.[502]

***

Even if Bahá'ís are not directly involved in Indigenous outreach work, we need to create welcoming, accepting, understanding communities that give space for Indigenous people to fully participate. To do this each of us need to purify our attitudes and eliminate traces of paternalism. Blackfoot Bahá'í Eleanora McDermott told me a story of her experience that provides an example of how someone from the dominant culture can, perhaps unknowingly, seriously discourage local initiative. Eleanora had been asked by the Calgary Spiritual Assembly to teach on the Blackfoot reserve of Siksika Nation. She used to visit there during the week and urged local Bahá'ís to plan their own activities.

"I emphasized that we learn on our own as there are no preachers etc. in the faith, and enough people had gone there to teach, so it was up to them now. Then one day they told (me) they were going to have a feast.

"I had previously explained that our native ancestors were quite spiritual—each morning they would face east and say prayers just as the sun was rising and there were no preachers, which was similar to the Bahá'í Faith...

"On the day of the feast several Calgary members came to the Res. They called it a feast but it was not on a Feast day.

"When we got there, they had everything set up. They said Dwight was going to emcee. They picked out the readings, prayers, and chose who would do the readings, etc. The place was set up and food prepared. They were so happy to say they also invited two non-Bahá'ís.

"This one lady who asked me to pick her up in south Calgary, spoke up very forcefully and told them what they could not do and what they had to do. I cringed, took her outside to explain the situation, but I could not get through to her. We went back in and I told them to go ahead and it was wonderful what they had done.

"They were speaking in Blackfoot, they knew I understood Blackfoot good and they remarked that that woman was bossy and telling them what to do.

"On the way back I asked her if she had done any teaching, she said no. I asked if she knew any natives outside of me and again she said no, but she was adamant they had to do it the proper way, from the start.

"I felt like this little bud poked its head out of the ground and was quickly squished. I have never understood why this happened."

Eleanora's experience reminded me of the "humble posture of learning"[503] needed to put what we believe into action and accompany others to do so in their own cultural context. The Universal House of Justice addressed the need for flexibility, even if there should be mistakes made.

"A wide latitude for action must be allowed them, which means a large margin for mistakes must also be allowed."[504] In addition, respect, sensitivity, tact and wisdom are required in cross-cultural situations. Shoghi Effendi alludes to this in the following advice:

"It is difficult for the friends to always remember that in matter (s) where race enters, a hundred times more consideration and wisdom in handling situations is necessary than when an issue is not complicated by this factor."[505]

***

The Universal House of Justice urges us to "...find those souls longing to shed the lethargy imposed on them by society and work alongside one another in their neighbourhoods and villages to begin a process of collective transformation."[506] Once we find these souls, they begin to build the foundations for a deep transformation, both of themselves and indeed of the community and culture.

Paulette Regan quotes John Paul Lederach in giving advice to non-Indigenous people who wish to work with decolonizing principles.

> This work is not prescriptive; it involves a genuine spirit of inquiry that is respectful of the dignity and humanity of others. Lederach advises us to "focus on people and their experience. Seek a genuine and committed relationship rather than results...Be leery of quick fixes. Respect complexity but do not be paralyzed by it. Think comprehensively about the voices you hear that seem contradictory, both within a person, between people, and across a whole community...No matter how small, create spaces of connection between them. Never assume you know better or more than those you are with that are struggling with the process. You don't. Do not fear the feeling of being lost... Give it time."[507]

Very similar principles are reflected in the Riḍván 2010 message of the Universal House of Justice that reminds us there are "no shortcuts, no formulas" and that the work of creating the nucleus of the glorious civilization enshrined in Bahá'u'lláh's teachings, "will demand centuries of exertion by humanity to bring to fruition."[508]

It took me a long time to realize there is no "magic bullet" to heal social problems. Bahá'ís, especially if we are non-Indigenous, need to recognize that any healing will not necessarily lead to Indigenous communities becoming "more like" the dominant society; they will find their own unique ways to apply the teachings of Bahá'u'lláh to their communities and social issues.

***

With my early experience in the North in the late 1970s, I have felt strongly about the importance of institute training. It has done my heart such good to hear the youth who have returned from intensive study of institute courses speaking of the Manifestations of God, or of having "elevated conversations." At the same time, Daniel Scott, while serving as a member of the Continental Board of Counsellors, cautioned members of our team not to put sole weight on the institute process. He mentioned that, as we have found out, the whole process needs to be bolstered with the gamut of activities one would expect true friends to participate in, such as helping each other with homework, going to movies or on hikes, holding picnics, attending Holy Days and other community activities together or using social media. Indeed, I see the youth forming genuine friendships. As an example, they were instrumental in helping one Nakoda youth to register for university and find a place in Calgary to live while he studies.

For myself, I look for unobtrusive ways to support the initiatives of the youth. One frosty evening, I found myself stuck in a snowbank on Morley while driving some youth home. The youth worked hard to dig me out, and it took quite a while. I was so grateful, I invited them a few weeks later for pizza. Besides helping out by hosting some reflection gatherings, I've also been happy to host some social events, such as a joint birthday party for several youth and a thank you party for the youth director. It's a small way I can support what's going on.

The past few years have seen several intensive Ruhi institute trainings, over weekends and at Christmas break, at Deadman's Flats near Canmore and in Calgary and Rockyview homes. Our team has learned this is an effective way to do training, and is seeking to balance having weekly study circles with intensive campaigns. Several youth have studied Ruhi books 1, 2, 3, 4 and parts of Books 5 and 7 so far. A couple of youth, Gage Beaver and Tyson Bearspaw, have assisted with children's classes and junior youth programs at regional schools. Gage conducted his own children's class from January 2016 to the summer. Because of these efforts, the cluster was able to pass Milestone One (where local people are arising to serve and invite others), and the Stoney Nakoda Nation became its own cluster, which includes the three reserves at Morley, Big Horn, and Eden Valley.

In April 2016, Counsellor Borna Noureddin visited Morley to meet with elders of the community. He showed a film of the services of Indigenous people in Central and South America and how the institute process is gaining momentum and has enabled local people to take spiritual and intellectual matters into their own hands. Those present at the meeting asked questions and supported the budding efforts to firmly establish the core activities.

By the winter of 2016, the youth had held the first youth conference on Morley (modeled on the regional youth conferences in 2013), held one-day camps for children and junior youth, and restarted regular weekly activities for children and junior youth. During the Christmas break, eight Morley youth participated in an intensive Book One study, co-tutored by Tyson Bearspaw and Leva Eghbali. Plans were made to accompany these youth in arising to serve, especially through children's and junior youth activities.

Our Morley team has been part of a collaborating group since it began on Morley. Called the Stoney Nakoda Youth Collaborative (SNYC), it first included former youth director Cathy Arcega and her staff, representatives of the Nakoda Youth Council, the RCMP, Canada Bridges (a Calgary foundation that works with youth on Morley), representation from Alberta Health and Stoney Nakoda Child and Family Services, the Stoney Education Authority and other groups concerned with youth. It has been a wonderful opportunity to collaborate, share information and support each other. While she was director, Cathy Arcega arranged for three retreats for the SNYC group, which served to strengthen our bonds and clarify what each group was offering in service. We Bahá'ís had a chance to offer a facilitator and material about youth development for two of the sessions. Sadly, Cathy's program was shut down in fall 2016, with all the support she offered to youth. Her wish for us, and our own, is to carry on the legacy of collaboration of the past three years and SNYC is continuing to meet.

With the Five Year Plan of 2016-2021, our Morley team has met more systematically to review progress, study guidance and reflect with members of regional institutions. We began having regular three-month cycles. As we move forward into this Five Year Plan, we can be optimistic about the future. The Universal House of Justice has given guidance for programmes of growth in neighborhoods and villages, such as Stoney Nakoda and has stressed the delicate nature of the process.

> Individuals serving in such areas learn how to explain the purpose of those activities, how to demonstrate through deeds the purity of their motives, how to nurture environments where the hesitant can be reassured, how to help the inhabitants see the rich possibilities created by working together, and how to encourage them to arise to serve the

best interests of their society. Yet, recognizing the real value of this work should also increase awareness of its delicate character. An emerging pattern of action in a small area can easily be smothered by too much outside attention; accordingly, the number of friends who move to such locations or visit them frequently need not be great since, after all, the process being set in motion is essentially one that depends on the residents themselves. What is required from those involved, however, is long-term commitment and a yearning to become so familiar with the reality of a place that they integrate into local life and, eschewing any trace of prejudice or paternalism, form those bonds of true friendship that befit companions on a spiritual journey. The dynamic that develops in such settings creates a strong sense of collective will and movement. Over time, the cluster as a whole and its centres of intense activity will infuse one another with the heightened understanding that comes from efforts to apply the teachings in different contexts.[509]

***

I had a dream while we still lived in Yellowknife, of being in the presence of Bahá'u'lláh. He looked as He had in a painting by an Armenian Christian, which one sees in the international archives in Israel while on pilgrimage. In the dream I couldn't look right at His face, despite knowing it was Him, because of His energy and radiance. I was with other people, and we were busy running around doing small acts of service. Bahá'u'lláh was happy with this.

I've never forgotten the dream and the implication that small services count. The Nakoda people, especially the youth and children, will carry forward the material and spiritual betterment of their people and bring their unique contributions to the world community. My life has been greatly enriched by the friendships extended to me and our shared service with the people of Stoney Nakoda. I've learned so much and am immensely grateful to be part of the process.

SUBMISSION OF THE BAHÁ'Í COMMUNITY OF CANADA TO THE TRUTH AND RECONCILIATION COMMISSION

We join countless other Canadians in commending the honourable work of the Truth and Reconciliation Commission to bring to light the personal experiences and untold stories of lives affected by the residential schools. In making this submission, the Bahá'í Community of Canada wishes to express its gratitude to the Commission for inviting our reflections. These arise from a sincere desire to participate in the promotion of justice, reconciliation and healing that will emerge from efforts made by the Commission, those survivors who testify before it, and all who participate in its work.

The establishment of the Commission represents another important step in the process of cultural reconciliation in Canada. Its work builds on the important report of the Royal Commission on Aboriginal Peoples. A submission made by the Bahá'í community acknowledged that the suffering of human beings during the twentieth century has been acutely felt in the lives, families, and communities of the world's Aboriginal or Indigenous Peoples. To right the wrongs experienced by Aboriginal peoples is a daunting challenge.

By bringing to light the suffering and injustice inflicted by the Residential School system, the Truth and Reconciliation Commission will help to right those wrongs experienced by Aboriginal Peoples in Canada. It is essential for us to understand the history and legacy of the Residential School system so that we can heal its deep wounds on our country and its peoples, and build new relationships based on justice and the fundamental oneness of humanity.

Patricia Verge

TRUTH, JUSTICE, AND RECONCILIATION

The grievous, ongoing consequences of the residential schools established within Canada deserve the attention of all Canadians. We are grateful for the testimony of survivors who have shared their experience so that we may know more of the truth about these systematic efforts to dismantle Aboriginal cultures, families and relationships.

The abuses of the Residential School system stand as an affront to its victims' human dignity and inherent nobility. Recent revelations about nutritional experiments conducted on young children reflect the inhumane attitudes that enabled these abuses. The Residential School system was informed by racial ideas that denied the full humanity of Aboriginal people, and it damaged relationships between individuals, families and communities. It remains a painful irony that while this system claimed to be "civilizing" Aboriginal children, often in the name of religion, it promoted ignorance of their culture and spirituality. The purpose of religion, the Bahá'í teachings explain, "is to safeguard the interests and promote the unity of the human race, and to foster the spirit of love and fellowship." The abuses perpetrated by the Residential School system violated the very nature and purpose of religion.

We believe that the pursuit of truth and reconciliation is intimately connected with the principle of justice. Justice is essential to truth and reconciliation alike. Justice is, first, made possible by developing the capacity to seek truth through our own eyes – and not through mere opinion, conventional wisdom, or one-sided views of others. Second, justice is made evident to the degree that unity and reconciliation is reflected in our relationships and social structures. In other words, we must seek to recognize injustice and then see that justice is restored within our society and institutions. Justice also requires that capabilities be developed for universal participation in the process of building a better world.

As the survivors who testify before the Commission help us to understand the truth of what happened within the Residential Schools, we also need to consider how to come to terms with this history. Among other essential elements, the process of reconciliation should involve a clear acknowledgement of responsibility for past crimes. The Residential Schools were also a form of political injustice, and while it is not possible to hold personally accountable

354

those who took decisions that led to violence and trauma, the institutions they represented must bear a degree of historical responsibility.

Justice also involves the provision of reparations or awards to those who have suffered unjustly. While this is difficult in practice because of the passage of time, this element of reconciliation is being addressed to some degree through material means that symbolize what society owes to those who have been dealt with in cruel and devastating ways. Such reparations have included, for example, support for education that respects Aboriginal language and culture and allows Aboriginal people to participate fully in the economy and life of society.

Acknowledging past wounds and offering apologies are essential to reconciliation. The responsibility lies with the perpetrators of injustice; however, where those directly accountable have passed on, the Canadian government and its representatives have spoken on behalf of those who carried out past harmful actions, by which racism, hatred and immorality were either promoted, or duties to protect people were neglected and ignored. Of course, apologies are most effective when followed by actions intended to bring about the restoration of justice within communities and institutions.

The process of reconciliation is aided by magnanimity on the part of all concerned: perpetrators, victims, and even newcomers — all in Canada who have to learn to live together. Without forgetting the injustices of the past, we need a sense of solidarity and resolve as we face the present and the future together. This may be helped by expressions of forgiveness on the part of victims, although no one has the right to require this. Without erasing the memories of past injustice and pain, forgiveness can be a gesture of magnanimity and resilience that reinforces the nobility and courage of those who have suffered.

THE SPIRITUAL PROCESS OF RECONCILIATION

When we speak of reconciliation we are referring to the movement towards peace and unity, and the individual and collective transformation that is required in order to achieve that goal. Reconciliation involves a process that contributes to the achievement of progressively greater degrees of unity and trust. Fundamentally, reconciliation is a spiritual process. It is the process of realizing the essential oneness of humanity in all dimensions of human life.

The pursuit of reconciliation cannot be based upon prejudiced attitudes, achieved through legislation, or undertaken out of fear. It requires engaging with one another in a spirit of selfless love, where misunderstandings are overcome through patient and respectful dialogue, and cultural differences provide an occasion to learn from one another. The Bahá'í teachings call on us to "shut your eyes to estrangement, then fix your gaze upon unity." We should "not be content with showing friendship in words alone," rather, our hearts should "burn with loving kindness for all who may cross your path."

To achieve this goal of unity and reconciliation, we recognize that social divisions need to be healed. We are all part of the same human family. This vision of oneness, and an appreciation of the beauty of our diversity, can guide a process of healing. A passage from the Bahá'í writings illustrates this idea of oneness and harmony:

...let us strive like flowers of the same divine garden to live together in harmony. Even though each soul has its own individual perfume and colour, all are reflecting the same light, all contributing fragrance to the same breeze which blows through the garden, all continuing to grow in complete harmony and accord.

Aboriginal peoples across this continent have long recognized that the natural world is a reflection of attributes of the Creator. We might look to the organic processes of nature for inspiration about the promise of renewal. The winter months are a period of hardship, when a once-vibrant landscape lies dormant and apparently lifeless. However, this period is necessary for the appearance of springtime, when the sweet smells of the earth are regenerated and renewed. The purpose of winter is made clear by the beauty of the spring. Now in this spiritual springtime, when humanity aspires to new standards that reflect the oneness of the human family, our eyes remain focused on the potential of children and youth. Young people have the capacity to bring about constructive change during this bright period of one's life — a time of abundant energy and a desire to contribute to society. Despite the many social forces that would hold them back from pursuing their ideals, they are the fresh and verdant shoots that will flourish and propagate, bringing to life the earnest hopes of their ancestors who endured the winter season.

REBUILDING SOCIAL RELATIONSHIPS

We understand the current, troubled period in human life on this planet, during which Aboriginal peoples have been disproportionally harmed by the destructive forces of history, to be one in which there are also growing constructive forces. These forces are bringing long-separated peoples together into new relationships, where dynamics of prejudice and domination are replaced by the powers of cooperation, reciprocity and genuine love and harmony among diverse peoples. We must do our part to promote those constructive forces while never being so naïve as to ignore the destructive forces that have brought such sorrow and pain to so many.

The process of reconciliation will help us to re-conceptualize and transform the basic relationships that sustain society, to create an environment that promotes individual and collective well-being. Our present relationship with the natural world, based on an unlimited appetite for resources, has produced a deepening environmental crisis. We must recover a balanced and sustainable relationship with the environment, based on moderation and respect for the Earth. The deterioration of the family and home environment has been accompanied by the rise in exploitation of women and children, calling for the need to rethink proper relations within the family unit. The concentration of wealth and power in the hands of the few, while others suffer in conditions of poverty and neglect, reflects ill-conceived relationships that persist within our own country. To truly apply the principle of the oneness of humanity to our common life, then, we need an organic change in the structure of our society.

To talk about rebuilding society, we must also consider the issue of power. Power is often described as a means of domination, or a way of seizing control from someone else. When politics is described as a game, contest or competition, it is often with the goal of seeking power. This model of politics has often proved divisive and destructive. We need to consider a broader view of power that includes the power of unity, of love, of humble service, of pure deeds. These powers of the human spirit can be released and guided to build social relationships based on cooperation and reciprocity, rather than an endless struggle between competing interests. Such a view of power can also inform our approach to politics. Noble goals cannot be achieved by unworthy means. If we seek to build a society based on mutual respect, justice and unity, the means by which social and political change is pursued should reflect these high ideals.

Canada shares the challenge of reconciliation with the rest of the human family. In our international relations, just as in our domestic ones, we need to recognize that we are all parts of an organic whole. How do we forge bonds of unity that respect and draw strength from our diversity? How can we overcome the forces of paternalism and prejudice with the powers of love and justice? What changes do we need to make to the structures of governance and the use of material resources in order to redress past injustices and social inequalities? These are questions that we ask ourselves as citizens of a country that seeks reconciliation. And as we walk this path together in Canada, we will learn lessons and practical measures that will help to guide the healing of other divisions between the world's peoples.

Respectfully submitted by the Bahá'í Community of Canada on September 20, 2013

Central to the Bahá'í teachings is the principle of the fundamental oneness of humankind, which affirms the inherent nobility of every person and calls for the removal of all social divisions and prejudices. In Canada, our challenge is the achievement of unity and reconciliation between the diverse peoples and cultures of this country. Around the world, the Bahá'í community counts members of some 2,100 Indigenous groups, including First Nations, Inuit and Métis, among its adherents. We believe that the creation of a materially and spiritually prosperous global society requires the participation and empowerment of all of humanity.

'Abdu'l-Bahá. *Paris Talks: Talks given by 'Abdu'l-Bahá in 1911-12.* New Delhi, India: Bahá'í Publishing Trust, 2008. Print.

_____.*The Promulgation of Universal Peace.* Wilmette, IL: Bahá'í Publishing Trust, 1982. Print.

_____ . *The Secret of Divine Civilization.* Wilmette, IL: Bahá'í Publishing Trust, 1970. Print.

_____ .*Selections from the Writings of 'Abdu'l-Bahá.* Wilmette, IL: Bahá'í Publishing Trust, 1996. Print.

_____.*Tablets of the Divine Plan: Revealed by 'Abdu'l-Bahá to the North American Bahá'ís.* Wilmette, IL: Bahá'í Publishing Trust, 1993 edition. Print.

Abley, Mark. *Conversations with a Dead Man: The Legacy of Duncan Campbell Scott.* Madeira Park, BC: Douglas & McIntyre Ltd., 2013. Print.

Addison, Donald Francis & Buck, Christopher. "Messengers of God in North America Revisited: An exegesis of 'Abdu'l-Bahá's Tablet to Amir Khan." *Online Journal of Bahá'í Studies,* Vol I (2007) oj.bahaistudies.net/ pp. 180-270. Accessed 16 Feb. 2017.

Aguiar, William and Halseth, Regine. "ABORIGINAL PEOPLES AND HISTORIC TRAUMA: The processes of intergenerational transmission." 2015. https://www.ccnsa-nccah.ca/docs/context/RPT-HistoricTrauma-IntergenTransmission-Aguiar-Halseth-EN.pdf

"Ahousaht First Nation Leads Rescue of Passengers From Capsized B.C. Whale-Watching Boat." 26 Oct. 2015. indiancountrytoday medianetwork.com/2015/10/26/ahousaht-first-nation-leads-rescue-passengers-capsized-bc-whale-watching-boat-162223 Accessed 18 Feb. 2017.

"Alkali Lake." en.wikipedia.org/wiki/Alkali_Lake,_British_Columbia Accessed 16 Feb. 2017.

Amatu'l-Bahá Rúḥíyyih Khánum. *Message to the Indian and Eskimo Baháʼís of the Western Hemisphere.* Toronto, ON: National Spiritual Assembly of the Baháʼís of Canada, August 1969. Print.

Atleo, Shawn A-in-chut. "Daring Greatly Together: Reimagining Canada", Vancouver Island University's inaugural Indigenous Speakers Series. 26 Nov. 2015. www.youtube.com/watch?v=mSwOEu9GFVQ Accessed 17 Feb. 2017.

The Báb. *Selections from the Writings of the Báb.* Haifa, Israel: Baháʼí World Centre, 1976. Print.

Baháʼí Canada, August 2000.

Baháʼí International Community. www.bic.org/ Accessed 16 Feb. 2017.

_____. "Situation of Baha'is in Iran." www.bic.org/focus-areas/situation-iranian-bahais***htjd0SCMfzv6CtUo.97 Accessed 17 Feb. 2017.

bahai.org/beliefs/bahaullah-covenant/ Accessed 16 Jan. 2017.

bahai.org/beliefs/essential-relationships/administrative-order/institution-counsellors Accessed 16 Jan. 2017.

Baháʼí Prayers: A Selection of Prayers Revealed by Baháʼuʼlláh, the Báb and ʼAbduʼl-Bahá. Wilmette, IL: Baháʼí Publishing Trust, 2002. Print.

Baháʼí World Faith: Selected Writings of Baháʼuʼlláh and ʼAbduʼl-Bahá. Wilmette, IL: Baháʼí Publishing Trust, 1976. Print.

Baháʼuʼlláh, *Gleanings from the Writings of Baháʼuʼlláh.* Wilmette, IL: Baháʼí Publishing Trust, 1983. Print.

_____. *Prayers and Meditations by Baháʼuʼlláh.* Wilmette, IL: Baháʼí Publishing Trust, 1974. Print.

_____. *The Hidden Words.* Wilmette, IL: Baháʼí Publishing Trust, 1994. Print.

_____. *Tablets of Bahá'u'lláh Revealed after the Kitáb-i-Aqdas.* Haifa, Israel: Bahá'í World Centre, 1978. Print.

Battiste, Marie, editor. *Reclaiming Indigenous Voice and Vision.* Vancouver, BC: UBC Press, 2002. Print.

"Berger Inquiry." http://indigenousfoundations.arts.ubc.ca/berger_inquiry/

Berger, Thomas R. The Online Guide to Thomas R. Berger. web.uvic. ca/~mharbell/a1/workshop2/index.html Accessed 17 Feb. 2017.

"Blackfoot Crossing." www.blackfootcrossing.ca/ Accessed 17 Feb. 2017.

Borrows, John. www.cbc.ca/8thfire/2011/11/john-borrows.html Accessed 17 Feb. 2017.

Breezes of Confirmation. William Mmutle Masetlha Foundation. Royal Palm Beach FL: Development Learning Press, 2002. Print.

Brown, Toyacoyah. "Ireland pays tribute to Choctaw Nation's Kindness." 15 Mar. 2015. www.powwows.com/2015/03/15/ireland-pays-tribute-to-choctaw-nations-kindness/ Accessed 16 Dec. 2016.

Bushrui, Suheil. *The Wisdom of the Irish: A Concise Anthology.* Oxford England: Oneworld Publications, 2004. Print.

Butala, Sharon. *The Perfection of the Morning: An Apprenticeship in Nature.* Toronto, ON: HarperCollins Publishers Ltd, 1994. Print.

Cahill, Thomas. *How the Irish Saved Civilization: The Untold Story of Ireland's Heroic Role from the Fall of Rome to the Rise of Medieval Europe.* New York, New York: Nan A. Talese/ Doubleday, 1995. Print.

childabusecommission.ie/ Accessed 4 Dec. 2016.

"The Choctaw Nation's Link To The People Of Ireland." 1 Nov. 2011. Mairéad, www.irishamericanmom.com/tag/the-choctaw-nation/ Accessed 26 Feb. 2014.

"Closed Comments on Aboriginal Stories." 1 Dec. 2015. www.cbc.ca/ news/canada/north/cbc-closing-comments-on-aboriginal-stories-reaction-1.3345137 Accessed 15 Feb. 2017.

"Co-dependency". www.mentalhealthamerica.net/co-dependency Accessed 31 Dec. 2016.

Coll, Kenneth M., Freeman, Brenda, Robertson, Paul, Iron Cloud, Eileen, Two Dogs, Rick. "Exploring Irish Multigenerational Trauma and Its Healing: Lessons from the Oglala Lakota (Sioux)." Journal of Rural Community Psychology, Volume E15 (1) file.scirp.org/pdf/AASoci20120200001_81443251.pdf Accessed 16 Feb. 2017.

Compilation of Compilations: Prepared by the Universal House of Justice 1963-1990, Volume 2. Ingleside NSW Australia: Bahá'í Publications Australia, 1991. Print.

Compilation of Compilations: Prepared by the Research Department of The Universal House of Justice, Volume 3. Ingleside NSW Australia: Bahá'í Publications Australia, 2000. Print.

"Constitution Act, 1982 Section 35." http://indigenousfoundations.arts.ubc.ca/constitution_act_1982_section_35/

Covey, Linda S. "Diné Becoming Bahá'í: through the Lens of Ancient Prophecies." Master's Thesis, 2011. bahai-library.com/covey_navajo_becoming_bahai Accessed 16 Feb. 2017.

Crean, Susan. *The Laughing One: A Journey to Emily Carr.* Toronto, ON: HarperCollins Publishers Ltd., 2001. Print.

"Cultural Genocide." 2 June 2015. http://aptnnews.ca/2015/06/02/canada-guilty-cultural-genocide-indigenous-peoples-trc-2/

Danesh, Roshan. "Reconciliation: Meeting the Challenge of Recognition of Aboriginal Title and Rights." 16 Jan. 2016. Uploaded by Jim Flood, 31 May 2016, www.youtube.com/watch?v=iHOlfeRrsq4&t=20s

_____. "Re-Telling Reconciliation." bahaiblog.net/site/2015/02/re-telling-reconciliation-talk-roshan-danesh/ Accessed 17 Feb. 2017.

Daschuk, James. *Clearing the Plains: Disease, Politics of Starvation, and the Loss of Aboriginal Life.* Regina, SK: University of Regina Press, 2013. Print.

Dempsey, Hugh A. *Charcoal's World.* Lincoln NE: Bison Books, 1979. Print.

"Doctrine of Discovery." doctrineofdiscoveryforum.blogspot.ca/ Accessed 15 June 2016.

"Dorothy Maquabeak Francis." bahai-library.com/horton_dorothy_maquabeak_francis Accessed 15 Feb. 2017.

"Dorothy Maquabeak Francis." www.ca.bahai.org/search/content/ Dorothy%20Francis Accessed 15 Feb. 2017.

Esslemont, J.E. *Bahá'u'lláh and the New Era: An Introduction to the Bahá'í Faith*. Wilmette, IL: Bahá'í Publishing Trust, 1980. Print.

Ewing, Tod. *Toward Oneness: A Compilation on Racial and Cultural Issues: Selections from the Writings of Bahá'u'lláh, 'Abdu'l-Bahá, Shoghi Effendi & The Universal House of Justice*. Riviera Beach, FL: Palabra Publications, 1998. Print.

Figley, Dr. Charles. "Compassion Fatigue." www.compassionfatigue.org/ Accessed 5 June 2016.

Fine, Sean and Bonnie Belec. "Residential school survivors in Newfoundland and Labrador seek justice." 9 Nov. 2015. www.theglobeandmail.com/news/ national/residential-school-survivors-in-newfoundland-and-labrador-seek-justice/article27170859/ Accessed 17 Feb. 2017.

Fitzpatrick, Marie-Louise. *The Long March*. Hillsboro, Oregon: Beyond Words Publishing, 1998. Print.

Francis, Daniel. *The Imaginary Indian: The Image of the Indian in Canadian Culture*. Vancouver, BC: Arsenal Pulp Press, 1992. Print.

Freeman, Victoria. *Distant Relations: How My Ancestors Colonized North America*. Toronto, ON: McClelland & Stewart, 2000. Print.

_____. www.cbc.ca/8thfire/2011/11/victoria-freeman.html Accessed 17 Feb. 2017.

Ghadirian, A-M, M.D. *Creative Dimensions of Suffering*. Wilmette, Illinois: Bahá'í Publishing, 2009. Print.

Glimmerings of Hope, Pre-Publication Edition. Royal Palm Beach, FL: Development Learning Press, 2006. Print.

"Haida Case." scc-csc.lexum.com/scc-csc/scc-csc/en/item/2189/index.do Accessed 17 Feb. 2017.

Hanley, Paul. *Eleven.* Victoria, BC: FriesenPress, 2014. Print.

Hanson, Holly. "Enacting Thought, Divine Will, Human Agency, and the Possibility of Justice." *Journal of Bahá'í Studies,* vol.19, no.1/4 March-December 2009, pp. 27-58. Print. Online at bahai-studies.ca /wp-content/uploads/2014/05/19.14-Hanson.pdf

Hatcher, William S. *Love, Power and Justice: The Dynamics of Authentic Morality.* Wilmette, IL: Bahá'í Publishing Trust, 1998. Print.

Hayden Taylor, Drew. "Idle No More isn't dead." 27 Sept. 2014. www. theglobeandmail.com/opinion/idle-no-more-isnt-dead-its-just-resting/ article20795994/ Accessed 15 Feb. 2017.

Helin, Calvin. *Dances with Dependency: Out of Poverty Through Self-Reliance.* Woodland Hills, CA: Ravencrest Publishing, 2008. Print.

Hermann, Duane L. *Fasting: A Bahá'í Handbook.* Oxford, England: George Ronald, 1998.

Hofman, David. *George Townshend.* Oxford, England: George Ronald, 1983. Print.

Hogenson, Kathryn Jewett. *Lighting the Western Sky: The Hearst Pilgrimage and the Establishment of the Bahá'í Faith in the West.* Oxford, England: George Ronald, 2010. Print.

"Hoop dancing and world citizenship: meet Kevin Locke". *One Country* 8.2 (July-Sept. 1996). Quoted in Addison & Buck, "Messengers of God in North America Revisited: An exegesis of 'Abdu'l-Bahá's Tablet to Amir Khan", pp. 225-226. *Online Journal of Bahá'í Studies,* Vol I (2007) oj.bahaistudies.net/

Hornby, Helen Bassett, compiler. *Lights of Guidance: A Bahá'í Reference File.* New Delhi, India: Bahá'í Publishing Trust, 2001. Print.

Horton, Chelsea. "As ye have faith, so shall your powers and blessings be": The Aboriginal-Bahá'í Encounter in British Columbia, Master's Thesis, 2005. summit.sfu.ca/system/files/iritems1/9262/1763.pdf

_____."All is One: Becoming Indigenous and Bahai in Global North America", PhD thesis, 2013. bahai-library.com/horton_indigenous_bahai

Indigenous and Northern Affairs Canada. "Fact Sheet - Urban Aboriginal population in Canada." www.aadnc-aandc.gc.ca/eng/1100100014298/1100100014302 Accessed 17 Feb. 2017.

Insights from the Frontiers of Learning: A document prepared by The International Teaching Centre. Bahá'í World Centre, April 2013.

International Work Group for Indigenous Affairs. "Who are the Indigenous peoples?" www.iwgia.org

Janov, Arthur. *The Primal Scream.* New York City, NY: Dell Publishing Company, 1970. Print.

Jasion, Jan Teofil. *Never Be Afraid To Dare: The Story of 'General Jack'.* Oxford, England: George Ronald, 2001. Print.

Jestes, Roberta."Choctaw nation provides relief to Irish famine victims." 16 Jan. 2014. nativeheritageproject.com/2014/01/16/choctaw-nation-in-1847-provides-relief-to-irish-famine-victims/ Accessed 15 Feb. 2017.

Jonker, Peter. *The Song and the Silence Sitting Wind: The Life of Stoney Indian Chief Frank Kaquitts.* Edmonton, AB: Lone Pine Publishing, 1988. Print.

"Justice Murray Sinclair's remarks on the Truth and Reconciliation report." 15 Dec. 2015. www.macleans.ca/news/canada/justice-murray-sinclairs-remarks-on-the-truth-and-reconciliation-report/ Accessed 17 Feb. 2017.

Kelly, Tom. "Revealed decades ritual child abuse." 21 May 2009. www.dailymail.co.uk/news/article-1184828/Revealed-decades-ritual-child-abuse-Catholic-schools-orphanages-damned-report.html Accessed 4 Dec. 2016.

King, Thomas. *The Inconvenient Indian: A Curious Account of Native People in North America*, Toronto, ON: Doubleday Canada, 2012. Print.

Klein, Christopher. "The Viking Explorer Who Beat Columbus to America." 8 Oct. 2013. www.history.com/news/the-viking-explorer-who-beat-columbus-to-america Accessed 17 Feb. 2017.

Lample, Paul. *Creating A New Mind: Reflections on the Individual, the Institutions and the Community*. Riviera Beach, FL: Palabra Publications, 1999. Print.

"Leif Erikson (11th century)." www.bbc.co.uk/history/historic_figures/erikson_leif.shtml Accessed 17 Feb. 2017.

Lester, Professor Julius. Quoted by Sue Monk Kidd. images.penguingroup.com/Storage/viking/InventionOfWings_BCK_updated.pdf Accessed 17 Feb. 2017.

Lewis-Pert, David. "Canadians Of Colour Talk Racism, Self-Care And Driving Change." 21 Mar. 2016. www.huffingtonpost.ca/2016/03/21/racism-canada-self-care_n_9488774.html Accessed 17 Feb. 2017.

Lindberg, Tracey. *Birdie*. Toronto, ON: HarperCollins Publishers Ltd, 2015. Print.

Loft Watts, Evelyn & Verge, Patricia. *Return to Tyendinaga: The Story of Jim and Melba Loft, Bahá'í Pioneers*. Essex, Maryland: One Voice Press, LLC, 2011. Print.

Lunman, Kim, Mark Lowey and Bob Beatty. "The Stoney Saga: Band mourns 'lost generation'". *Calgary Herald*, 27 December, 1997, pp. A1, A4-A7.

MacEwan, Grant. *Tatanga Mani: Walking Buffalo of the Stonies*. Edmonton, AB: M.G. Hurtig Ltd., 1969. Print.

www.makingtreaty7.com Accessed 17 Feb. 2017.

McCloskey, Molly. Pamphlet for the Listowel Writers' Week, 2014.

"McKenna-McBride Royal Commission." http://www.ubcic.bc.ca/mckenna_mcbride_royal_commission Accessed 17 Feb. 2017.

"Memorial to Sir Wilfred Laurier." shuswapnation.org/to-sir-wilfrid-laurier/ Accessed 17 Feb. 2017.

Milne, Courtney. *W.O. Mitchell Country: Portrayed by Courtney Milne*. Toronto, ON: McClelland & Stewart Inc., 1999. Print.

"Missing and murdered Indigenous women and girls: Understanding the numbers." www.amnesty.ca/blog/missing-and-murdered-indigenous-women -and-girls-understanding-the-numbers Accessed 17 Feb. 2017.

Mosionier, Beatrice Culleton. *In Search of April Raintree: Critical Edition,* edited by Cheryl Suzack. Winnipeg, MB: Peguis Publishers, 1999. Print.

Motlagh, Hushidar, compiler. *The Glorious Journey to God: Selections from Sacred Scriptures on the Afterlife,* 1994. Print.

"Nanaimo Daily News Closing." 23 Jan. 2016. www.cbc.ca/news/canada/ british-columbia/nanaimo-daily-news-closing-1.3417316. Accessed 15 Feb. 2017.

Nature: An Emanation of God's Will. New Delhi, India: Bahá'í Publishing Trust, 2005. Print.

"Numbered Treaties." www.aadnc-aandc.gc.ca/eng/1380223988016/1380 224163492 Accessed 18 Dec. 2016.

Obomsawin, Alanis. *Kanehsatake: 270 Years of Resistance* www.nfb.ca/film/ kanehsatake_270_years_of_resistance Accessed 17 Feb. 2017.

O'Connor, Dr. Garrett. "Breaking the code of silence the Irish and drink." Jan. 2012. irishamerica.com/2012/01/breaking-the-code-of-silence-the-irish-and-drink/ Accessed 15 Feb. 2017.

"October Crisis." www.thecanadianencyclopedia.ca/en/article/october-crisis/ Accessed 15 Feb. 2017.

www.thepasssystem.ca Accessed 17 Feb. 2017.

"Patriation of the Constitution." http://www.thecanadianencyclopedia.ca/ en/article/patriation-of-the-constitution/ Accessed 15 June 2016.

Pember, Mary Annette. "Intergenerational Trauma: Understanding Natives' Inherited Pain." 2016. www.indiancountrymedianetwork.com Accessed 17 Feb. 2017.

Pemberton-Pigott, Andrew. "The Bahá'í Faith in Alberta, 1942-1992: The Ethic of Dispersion." Master's Thesis, University of Alberta, Department of

History, Fall 1992. era.library.ualberta.ca/files/5x21th63w/MM77379.pdf Accessed 15 Feb. 2017.

"Peter and Catharine Whyte." en.wikipedia.org/wiki/Peter_and_Catharine_ Whyte Accessed 16 Feb. 2017.

Popov, Linda Kavelin. *Sacred Moments: Daily Meditations on the Virtues.* Fountain Hills, AZ: Virtues Communications Inc., 1996. Print.

"Racist newspaper letter." 28 Mar. 2013. www.cbc.ca/news/canada/british-columbia/racist-newspaper-letter-sparks-nanaimo-protest-1.1316035. Accessed 15 Feb. 2017.

Ralston Saul, John. *The Comeback.* Toronto, ON: Viking, 2014. Print.

Reed, Hayter. www.biographi.ca/en/bio/reed_hayter_16E.html Accessed 17 Feb. 2017.

Regan, Paulette. *Unsettling the Settler Within: Indian Residential Schools, Truth Telling, and Reconciliation in Canada.* Vancouver, BC: UBC Press, 2010. Print.

Reilly, John. *Bad Medicine: A Judge's Struggle for Justice in a First Nations Community*, Victoria, BC: Rocky Mountain Books, 2010. Print.

_____. *Bad Judgment: The Myths of First Nations Equality and Judicial Independence in Canada.* Victoria, BC: Rocky Mountain books, 2014. Print.

"The Return of the "White Buffalo Calf Woman": Prophecy of the Lakota." Interview of Jacqueline Left Hand Bull by Patricia Locke, 1989. bahai.uga.edu/News/000089.html Accessed 17 Feb. 2017.

"Rioux family genealogy." famillesriou-x.com/publications.html Accessed 15 Feb. 2017.

www.rockymountainnakoda.com/who-we-are Accessed 15 Feb. 2017.

Rogers, Shelagh, DeGagné, Mike, Dewar, Jonathan, and Lowry, Glen. *Speaking My Truth: Reflections on Reconciliation & Residential School.* Ottawa, ON: Aboriginal Healing Foundation, 2012. Print and online speakingmytruth.ca

"Royal Commission on Aboriginal Peoples". www.ca.bahai.org/public-discourse/statements-and-reports.

Royal Commission on Aboriginal Peoples, Volume I Looking Forward, Looking Back. qspace.library.queensu.ca/bitstream/handle/1974/6874 /RRCAP1_combined.pdf?sequence=5&isAllowed=y

Ruhi Institute. *Reflections on the Life of the Spirit.* Book 1. West Palm Beach, FL: Palabra Publications, 2007. Print.

_____. *The Twin Manifestations.* Book 4. West Palm Beach FL: Palabra Publications, 2002. Print.

_____. *Teaching the Cause.* Book 6. Riviera Beach FL: Palabra Publications, 1998. Print.

SaskCulture. www.saskculture.ca/engage/2015/12/1/engage-volume-6-issue-1-fallwinter-2015 Accessed 17 Feb. 2017.

Savage, Candace. *A Geography of Blood: Unearthing Memory from a Prairie Landscape.* Vancouver, BC: Greystone Books, and David Suzuki Foundation, 2012. Print.

"Seigneurial System". www.thecanadianencyclopedia.ca/en/article/seigneurial-system/ Accessed 15 Feb. 2017.

Seligman, Martin E.P. *Learned Optimism: How to Change Your Mind and Your Life.* New York City, NY: Pocket Books, 1992. Print.

Sellars, Bev. *They Called Me Number One: Secrets and Survival at an Indian Residential School.* Vancouver, BC: Talonbooks, 2013. Print.

"Serenity Prayer." en.wikipedia.org/wiki/Serenity_Prayer Accessed 15 Feb. 2017.

Shoghi Effendi. *The Advent of Divine Justice.* Wilmette, IL: Bahá'í Publishing Trust, 1971. Print.

_____. *Bahá'í Administration: Selected Messages 1922-1932.* Wilmette, IL: Bahá'í Publishing Trust, 1974. Print.

_____. *Citadel of Faith: Messages to America 1947-1957.* Wilmette, IL: Bahá'í Publishing Trust, 1970. Print.

_____. *The Faith of Bahá'u'lláh: A World Religion.* A summary of the origin, teachings and institutions of the Bahá'í Faith, prepared in 1947 for the

United Nations Special Committee on Palestine. bahai-library.com/shoghief-fendi_faith_bahaullah Accessed 15 Feb. 2017.

_____. *The World Order of Bahá'u'lláh: Selected Letters*. Wilmette, IL: Bahá'í Publishing Trust, 1991. Print.

Shoghi Effendi and The Universal House of Justice. *A Special Measure of Love: The Importance and Nature of the Teaching Work among the Masses*. Wilmette, IL: Bahá'í Publishing Trust, 1974. Print.

Simon Fraser University. Honorary Degree Citations The Degree of Doctor of Laws, *honorus causa*, conferred on Dr. Mandell, 13 June 2012. www.sfu.ca/content/dam/sfu/ceremonies/HDRs/honorary-degrees/Citation-Mandell-web.pdf Accessed 16 June 2016.

Sinclair, Justice Murray. "Will truth bring reconciliation? Justice Murray Sinclair says not without education." 6 Dec. 2015. www.cbc.ca/radio/unreserved/taking-the-first-steps-on-the-road-to-reconciliation-1.3347611/will-truth-bring-reconciliation-justice-murray-sinclair-says-not-without-education-1.3348070 Accessed 17 Feb. 2017.

Snow, John. *These Mountains Are Our Sacred Places: The Story of the Stoney People*. Calgary AB: Fifth House Ltd., 2005. Print.

Solnit, Rebecca. "Standing Rock protests: this is only the beginning." 12 Sept. 2016. www.theguardian.com/us-news/2016/sep/12/north-dakota-standing-rock-protests-civil-rights Accessed 4 Dec. 2016.

www.stoneynation.com/ Accessed 15 Feb. 2017.

Swanson, Dave. "50 Years Ago: John Lennon's 'Beatles More Popular Than Jesus' Comment Published." 4 Mar. 2016. ultimateclassicrock.com/john-lennon-beatles-more-popular-than-jesus/ Accessed 15 Feb. 2017.

Taherzadeh, Adib. *The Revelation of Bahá'u'lláh: 'Akká, The Early Years 1868-77*. Oxford, England: George Ronald, 1984. Print.

Thanh Ha, Tu and Gloria Galloway. "Ontario judge sides with Sixties Scoop survivors." 14 Feb. 2017. www.theglobeandmail.com/news/national/ontario-judge-sides-with-60s-scoop-survivors-damages-to-be-decided/article34015380/ Accessed 14 Feb. 2017.

Townshend, George. *The Mission of Bahá'u'lláh and other literary pieces.* Oxford, England: George Ronald, 1976. Print.

Treaty 7 Elders and Tribal Council with Walter Hildebrandt, Dorothy First Rider, and Sarah Carter. *The True Spirit and Original Intent of Treaty 7.* Montréal & Kingston: McGill-Queen's University Press, 1996. Print.

"Treaty of Paris, 1763." history.state.gov/milestones/1750-1775/treaty-of-paris Accessed 17 Feb. 2017.

"Trusteeship Council." www.un.org/en/mainbodies/trusteeship/ Accessed 17 Feb. 2017.

Truth and Reconciliation Commission of Canada: *Honouring the Truth, Reconciling for the Future: Summary of the Final Report of the Truth and Reconciliation Commission of Canada,* 2015. Print and online nctr.ca/reports.php

_____. *The Survivors Speak: A Report of the Truth and Reconciliation Commission of Canada,* 2015. Print and online nctr.ca/reports.php

Turning Point: Selected Messages of the Universal House of Justice and Supplementary Material 1996-2006. West Palm Beach Florida: Palabra Publications, 2006. Print.

Twan, Liz. "Tent City." www.williamslakestampede.com Accessed 10 Oct. 2016.

The United Nations Declaration on the Rights of Indigenous People, www.un.org/esa/socdev/unpfii/documents/DRIPS_en.pdf

The Universal House of Justice. *Century of Light: A Publication of the Universal House of Justice.* Haifa, Israel: Bahá'í World Centre, 2001.

_____. Advancement of the Cause an Evolutionary Process, letter dated August 22, 2002, written on behalf of the Universal House of Justice to an individual believer.

_____. Letter dated 19 May 1994 to a National Spiritual Assembly.

_____. Letter dated 24 May, 2001, to Believers Gathered for the Events Marking the Completion of the Projects on Mount Carmel.

_____. Ridván 2008 Message.

_____. Ridván 2010 Message.

_____. Letter dated 28 December, 2010 to the Conference of the Continental Boards of Counsellors.

_____. Letter dated February 8, 2013 to the Bahá'ís of the World, announcing the convocation of 95 youth conferences around the world.

_____. Letter dated April 19, 2013, written on behalf of the Universal House of Justice to a number of individual Bahá'ís resident in Europe.

_____. Letter dated 29 December, 2015 to the Conference of the Continental Boards of Counsellors.

Van den Hoonaard, Will. C. *The Origins of the Bahá'í Community of Canada, 1898-1948*. Waterloo: Wilfred Laurier University Press, 1996. Print.

Verge, Patricia. *Angus: From the Heart*. Cochrane, AB: Springtide Publishing, 1999. Print.

_____. "A Personal Journey Toward Reconciliation." *The Journal of Bahá'í Studies*, vol. 26, no. 3, Fall 2016, pp. 23-42.

Watts, Bob. "Canada's Truth and Reconciliation Commission and Aboriginal Rights." The 2012 Vancouver Human Rights Lecture. thelaurier.ca/lecture-podcasts/ Accessed 17 Feb. 2017.

Wegscheider-Cruse, Sharon. *Another Chance: Hope and Help for the Alcoholic Family*. Palo Alto, CA: Science and Behavior Books, Inc., 1981. Print.

"The White Paper." http://indigenousfoundations.arts.ubc.ca/the_white _paper_1969/

Wilson, Rainn. *The Bassoon King*. New York, NY: Dutton, An imprint of Penguin Random House LLC, 2015.

Wilson Schaef, Anne. *Native Wisdom For White Minds: Daily Reflections Inspired by the Native Peoples of the World*. New York: One World Ballantine Books, 1995. Print.

Youth Conferences, July–October 2013, Participant Materials.

Endnotes

[1] Notes on the Title: Wazin Îchinabi is the Stoney Nakoda word for oneness. The title of the book is partly taken from this quote: "The goal should be all-Indian assemblies, so that these much exploited and suppressed original inhabitants of the land may realize that they are equals and partners in the affairs of the Cause of God, and that Bahá'u'lláh is the Manifestation of God for them." (From letter dated July 28, 1957, written on behalf of Shoghi Effendi to the National Spiritual Assembly of Central America and Mexico), *A Special Measure of Love*, p. 19.

[2] The national governing body of the Bahá'ís of Canada, elected annually.

[3] Bahá'í pilgrimage is primarily for the purpose of visiting the Shrines of the founder and forerunner of the Bahá'í Faith, Bahá'u'lláh and the Báb, as well as other Bahá'í sites, which are located in Israel.

[4] 'Amatu'l-Bahá Rúḥíyyih Khánum (1910-2000) was the wife of the Guardian of the Bahá'í Faith, Shoghi Effendi.

[5] Sellars, *They Called Me Number One: Secrets and Survival at an Indian Residential School*, p. 186.

[6] Bahá'u'lláh is the Prophet-Founder of the Bahá'í Faith. Born in 1817 into a noble family in Persia (today's Iran), He suffered persecution and exile while promoting such teachings as the oneness of humanity and the equality of the sexes. He passed away in Palestine, today's Israel, in 1892.

[7] Butala, *The Perfection of the Morning: An Apprenticeship in Nature*.

[8] McCloskey, from a pamphlet for the Listowel Writers' Week, 2014.

[9] Regan, *Unsettling the Settler Within: Indian Residential Schools, Truth Telling, and Reconciliation in Canada.*

[10] Ibid. p. 29.

[11] Twan, "Tent City." www.williamslakestampede.com

[12] The settlement of Alkali Lake, and the adjoining reserves of the Alkali Lake (Esketemc) Indian Band, get their name from Alkali Lake, which gets its name from an outcrop of alkali on the hillside above it; the lake itself is not an alkali lake. http://en.wikipedia.org/wiki/Alkali_Lake,_British_Columbia

[13] The Wet'suwet'en people have called the Bulkley Valley home for thousands of years. With the neighbouring Gitxsan, they had their Aboriginal title in the area affirmed by the Supreme Court of Canada with its Delgamuukw decision of 1997. (See Chapter Fifteen). The valley is named for the river, which in turn is named for American engineer Charles Bulkley, who oversaw the construction of the telegraph line through the area in the 1860s.

[14] Sellars, p. 85.

[15] Ibid. p. 140.

[16] Mitchell, *"How I Spent My Summer Holidays"*, quoted in *W.O. Mitchell Country: Portrayed by Courtney Milne*, p. 27.

[17] See footnote 93 for an explanation of co-dependency.

[18] Seligman, *Learned Optimism: How to Change Your Mind and Your Life.*

[19] ultimateclassicrock.com/john-lennon-beatles-more-popular-than-jesus/

[20] For more about the October Crisis, please see www.thecanadianency-clopedia.ca/en/article/october-crisis/

[21] For more about the seigneurial system see www.thecanadianencyclope-dia.ca/en/article/seigneurial-system/

There is a Rioux family genealogical society and a Rioux family reunion was held in Trois-Pistoles in August 1987, which drew hundreds of descendants from all over North America. Francois Beaulieu did an extensive genealogy of over 450 pages of the Rioux male descendants from that time, and worked on the female descendants. This genealogy has been updated. For Rioux genealogy see famillesriou-x.com/publications.html

[22] See Chapter Eight.

[23] Janov, *The Primal Scream.*

[24] A Bahá'í who arises and relocates to help establish the Faith in an area needing assistance is called a pioneer.

[25] A fireside is an informal gathering, often in a home, where the principles and practices of the Revelation of Bahá'u'lláh are shared with those investigating the Bahá'í Faith.

[26] There is no ritual associated with becoming a member of the Bahá'í Faith. According to a July 29, 2007, letter of the National Spiritual Assembly of the Bahá'ís of Canada, the "important thing is that the person's heart has been touched with the spirit of the Faith and wishes to become a member of the Bahá'í community." In the process, they must become "basically informed about the Central Figures of the Faith, as well as the existence of laws they must follow and an administration they must obey." Individual applicants may sign an "enrolment card" but there is no requirement for them to do so.

[27] The Báb, *Selections from the Writings of the Báb,* p. 129.

[28] 'Abdu'l-Bahá, *The Promulgation of Universal Peace,* p. 274.

[29] *Bahá'í Prayers,* p. i.

[30] 'Abdu'l-Bahá, *The Promulgation of Universal Peace,* p. 41.

[31] In his Will and Testament, 'Abdu'l-Bahá, who passed away in 1921, appointed his eldest grandson Shoghi Effendi as the Guardian of the Faith. Shoghi Effendi spent 36 years systematically nurturing the development, deepening the understanding and strengthening the unity of the Bahá'í community, as it increasingly grew to reflect the diversity of the entire human race. www.bahai.org/beliefs/bahaullah-covenant/

[32] Shoghi Effendi, *The Faith of Bahá'u'lláh: A World Religion.*

bahai-library.com/shoghieffendi_faith_bahaullah

[33] Bahá'u'lláh, *The Hidden Words*, Arabic #22.

[34] Ibid. Persian #3.

[35] There is no clergy in the Bahá'í Faith. Each Bahá'í has the privilege to serve and to share when someone wishes to learn about its teachings. Spiritual Assemblies–nine-member, non-political councils elected annually–consult and decide on affairs at the local level, in close consultation with community members. There is no nomination or electioneering in Bahá'í elections, which are carried out by secret ballot in an atmosphere of prayer and reflection.

[36] Hands of the Cause of God were Bahá'ís of great capacity who were appointed to assist in the propagation and protection of the Faith.

[37] Auxiliary Board members are appointed by the Continental Boards of Counsellors (see footnote 74) to serve specific geographic areas and territories. They work to stimulate the growth and vibrancy of the Bahá'í community, promoting the development of its spiritual, intellectual, and social life. www.bahai.org/beliefs/essential-relationships/administrative-order/institution-counsellors

[38] Bahá'u'lláh, *Gleanings from the Writings of Bahá'u'lláh,* p. 362.

[39] Greg Johnson passed away in June 2014.

[40] The period of the Bahá'í Fast is March 2 to March 20. Believers from the age of maturity (15 years) abstain from food and drink from sunrise to sundown. Travelers, women who are pregnant or nursing and the ailing are not bound by the Fast. Fasting is "essentially a period of meditation and prayer, of spiritual recuperation...Fasting is symbolic, and a reminder of abstinence from selfish and carnal desires." From a letter on behalf of Shoghi Effendi, 10 January 1936, quoted in Duane L. Hermann, *Fasting: A Bahá'í Handbook,* p. 23.

[41] See Chapter Fifteen for more about Louise Mandell and footnote 227 about "patriation."

[42] 'Abdu'l-Bahá, in Shoghi Effendi, *Citadel of Faith,* p. 16.

[43] Lily Ann and Arthur Irwin had befriended Indigenous people while living in Yellowknife in the 1950s. Early outreach was also done by Bernice and Noland Boss, Bill and Dorothy Carr, Rosemarie (Thrasher) Kirby, Dan and Helen Kelly, Bill and Houri Skuce, Andrew Steen, Marlene Gee, Fran Maclean, Elaine (Holley) Zavitz and others. The history of the Yellowknife Baháʼí community will surely someday be written.

[44] http://indigenousfoundations.arts.ubc.ca/berger_inquiry/

[45] For many years, Alice and Jerry Bathke served at the Native American Baháʼí Institute (NABI) at Houck, Arizona, on the Navajo Nation.

[46] Taherzadeh, *Revelation of Baháʼuʼlláh, Volume Three*, p. 205.

[47] The significance of this sacrifice is described by Adib Taherzadeh. "The death of the Purest Branch must be viewed as Baháʼuʼlláh's own sacrifice, a sacrifice on the same level as the crucifixion of Christ and the martyrdom of the Báb. Shoghi Effendi, the Guardian of the Faith, states that Baháʼuʼlláh has exalted the death of the Purest Branch to the 'rank of those great acts of atonement associated with Abraham's intended sacrifice of His son, with the crucifixion of Jesus Christ and the martyrdom of the Imám Husayn...'... In the Dispensation of Baháʼuʼlláh, it was the Purest Branch who gave his life releasing thereby all the forces necessary for bringing about the unity of mankind." Ibid. p. 211.

[48] ʻAbduʼl-Bahá, *The Promulgation of Universal Peace*, p. 145.

[49] The Universal House of Justice is the supreme governing body of the Baháʼí Faith. It is elected by members of National Spiritual Assemblies at an international convention held every five years.

[50] The Tablet of Aḥmad, along with the daily obligatory prayers and the long Healing Prayer revealed by Baháʼuʼlláh, are prayers invested with "a special potency and significance, and should therefore be accepted as such and be recited by the believers with unquestioning faith and confidence, that through them they may enter into a much closer communion with God, and identify themselves more fully with His laws and precepts." (From a letter written on behalf of Shoghi Effendi, *Baháʼí Prayers*, p. 307.)

[51] Inspired by the *Tablets of the Divine Plan*, the Bahá'ís of the world have shared the message of Bahá'u'lláh through a series of global plans. The Five Year Plan ran from 1974-1979.

[52] See Verge, *Angus: From the Heart*, for a description of outreach efforts in Canada.

[53] Mark Wedge is of Tlingit, Tagish and European background. He has served as an Auxiliary Board member and member of the National Spiritual Assembly of the Bahá'ís of Canada.

[54] Participants in the training institute were Al Vail, Rosa Daniels, Lorayne Menicoche, MaryAnne DeWolf, Larry Swartz, Vicki Swartz, Daphne Greene, Pat Verge, Hazel Lovelace and Mark Wedge.

[55] See Chapter Thirteen.

[56] 'Abdu'l-Bahá, *The Promulgation of Universal Peace*, p. 94.

[57] *Century of Light*, pp. 102-103.

[58] In 2009 the ranch was sold to the Kids Cancer Care Foundation of Alberta who operate Camp Kindle for children with cancer.

[59] The Native Councils "provided an opportunity for the Indian believers to draw strength from each other and arrive at their own sense of responsibility to the teaching work." *Canadian Bahá'í News*, December 1976, quoted in Loft Watts, Evelyn & Verge, Patricia, *Return to Tyendinaga: The Story of Jim and Melba Loft, Bahá'í Pioneers*, p. 147.

[60] Hogenson, *Lighting the Western Sky: The Hearst Pilgrimage and the Establishment of the Bahá'í Faith in the West*, Foreword p. xiv.

[61] Verge, *Angus: From the Heart*, pp. 308-309.

[62] Ibid. p. 52, 70, 308.

[63] Ibid. p. 74.

[64] Andrew Pemberton-Pigott, "The Bahá'í Faith in Alberta, 1942-1992: The Ethic of Dispersion." Master's Thesis, University of Alberta, Department of History, Fall 1992, p. 36.

[65] Melba Loft was the first Canadian Indigenous person to become a Bahá'í on July 18, 1947, while living in the United States. Loft Watts & Verge, *Return to Tyendinaga: The Story of Jim and Melba Loft, Bahá'í Pioneers*, p. 30. Noel Wuttunee became a Bahá'í in Canada in October, 1947. Van den Hoonard, *The Origins of the Bahá'í Community of Canada, 1898-1948*, p. 153.

[66] www.stoneynation.com/

[67] From material on Stoney Nakoda history provided by Duane Mark.

[68] See Chapter Fifteen.

[69] Biographical information about Dorothy Francis can be found at www.ca.bahai.org/search/content/Dorothy%20Francis and bahai-library.com/horton_dorothy_maquabeak_francis

[70] Bahá'u'lláh, *The Hidden Words*, Arabic #27, #26.

[71] Bahá'u'lláh has made obligatory prayer a law for this age. There are three daily obligatory prayers, a short, medium and long prayer. A believer is free to choose any one of the three prayers.

[72] Bahá'u'lláh, *Prayers and Meditations by Bahá'u'lláh*, pp. 271-272.

[73] Popov, *Sacred Moments: Daily Meditations on the Virtues. The Qur'an 12*, January 2 meditation.

[74] Every five years, the Universal House of Justice appoints a total of 81 Counsellors around the world, who organise their work through five Continental Boards. Its members, who have no legislative, executive, or judicial authority, encourage action, foster individual initiative, and promote learning within the Bahá'í community as a whole; this in addition to offering advice to Spiritual Assemblies. www.bahai.org/beliefs/essential-relationships/administrative-order/institution-counsellors

[75] Verge, *Angus: From the Heart*, p. 196.

[76] Joanie and Ted Anderson were the first Bahá'ís to settle in the Yukon Territory during the Ten Year Crusade (global plan from 1953-1963). For this, they earned the title of Knights of Bahá'u'lláh for the Yukon Territory. Joanie Anderson passed away in 2000 and Ted in 2017.

[77] Shoghi Effendi, *The Advent of Divine Justice*, p. 12.

[78] Peggy Ross passed away in 2000. For more on her service with Indigenous peoples, see Verge, *Angus: From the Heart* and Loft Watts & Verge, *Return to Tyendinaga: The Story of Jim and Melba Loft, Bahá'í Pioneers*.

[79] 'Abdu'l-Bahá, *Selections from the Writing of 'Abdu'l-Bahá*, 153.1.

[80] For an explanation of the institute process, see Chapter Thirteen.

[81] en.wikipedia.org/wiki/Serenity_Prayer

[82] See Chapter Seven for the promise made in the *Tablets of the Divine Plan* about the original inhabitants of the Americas.

[83] *Compilation of Compilations: Prepared by the Research Department of The Universal House of Justice, Volume 3*, p. 206, #325. From a letter 5 June 1947 written by Shoghi Effendi to the Bahá'ís of the West.

[84] Wagamese, p. 75, quoted in Mosionier, *In Search of April Raintree: Critical Edition edited by Cheryl Suzack*. From essay by Jo-Ann Thom Episkenew, "The Effect of Readers' Responses on the Development of Aboriginal Literature in Canada: A Study of Maria Campbell's *Halfbreed*, Beatrice Culleton's *In Search of April Raintree*, and Richard Wagamese's *Keeper'n Me*." pp. 302-303.

[85] Wagamese, p. 76, ibid, p. 303.

[86] Thom Episkenew, ibid, p. 303.

[87] See Chapter Thirteen.

[88] See footnote 71 on Obligatory prayer.

[89] See footnote 50 on Tablet of Ahmad.

[90] Ruth Eyford served on the National Spiritual Assembly of the Bahá'ís of Canada, and as an Auxiliary Board member. She passed away in 1996.

[91] Hornby, *Lights of Guidance: A Bahá'í Reference File*, #1171, p. 350.

[92] *Compilation of Compilations: Prepared by the Universal House of Justice 1963-1990, Volume 2*. #1785.

[93] Co-dependency is defined as "a learned behavior that can be passed down from one generation to another. It is an emotional and behavioral condition that affects an individual's ability to have a healthy, mutually satisfying relationship. It is also known as 'relationship addiction' because people with codependency often form or maintain relationships that are one-sided, emotionally destructive and/or abusive." www.mentalhealthamerica.net/co-dependency

[94] *Bahá'í Prayers*, p. 4.

[95] Hornby, *Lights of Guidance: A Bahá'í Reference File*, #391, p. 115. From a letter written on behalf of Shoghi Effendi to an individual believer, February 18, 1954.

[96] Youth Conferences, July - October 2013, Participant Materials.

[97] Johnny Lefthand became a Bahá'í before he passed away.

[98] Bill Wesley passed away in 2013.

[99] Maxwell International Bahá'í School was a co-ed Bahá'í school located on Shawnigan Lake, British Columbia, Canada. It offered boarding students and day students instruction from grades 7-12. Its educational philosophy was based on the principles of the Bahá'í Faith. Students attended from all over the world. The school closed on its 20th anniversary in 2008.

[100] See footnote 35 for explanation of Spiritual Assemblies.

[101] The Riḍván period in the Bahá'í calendar extends for twelve days, from April 21 to May 2, and commemorates the period in 1863 when Bahá'u'lláh first publicly declared His mission as a Manifestation of God to His followers. This took place in the Riḍván garden on the banks of the Tigris River, in Baghdád, Iráq.

[102] Most Assemblies in Indigenous communities did not meet. Among the notable exceptions is the Spiritual Assembly of Eskasoni Reserve in Nova Scotia.

[103] *Bahá'í Prayers*, p. 174. "This prayer appears in "Star of the West", volume 7, number 18 (7 February 1917), page 179, where it is identified as having been taken from a diary entry of Ahmad Sohrab dated 9 May

1914. This has been confirmed by consulting the original diary entry. As no original text for it has been found, this prayer is not considered a part of the authentic Writings of the Faith." From a memorandum dated 29 March 2011 from the Research Department of the Universal House of Justice.

[104] See Chapters Eleven and Twelve.

[105] *Bahá'í Prayers*, p. 113.

[106] Ruhi Book 4 on the Twin Manifestations contains two sections on the subject of crisis and victory. "...the Cause of God advances through a series of crises and victories. The forces of ignorance, injustice, cruelty and fanaticism continually attack the Bahá'í community and give rise to crises. But each time, in accordance with the Will of God, the forces of darkness are defeated and the result is a victory." (p. 101, 105).

[107] Bahá'ís who resided at the Peigan Bahá'í Centre for periods of time included Joyce McGuffie–who had also lived on the reserve much earlier– Ahmad Motlagh, Bill Brewer and Deb Clement.

[108] Among the Bahá'í visitors to Piikani were John Robarts, Hooper Dunbar, Angus Cowan and Dorothy Francis.

[109] The name for this federal government department has changed periodically. On August 28, 2017, the department was split in two. Carolyn Bennett became Minister of Crown-Indigenous Relations and Northern Affairs, while Jane Philpott became Minister of Indigenous Services.

[110] MacEwan, *Tatanga Mani: Walking Buffalo of the Stonies*, pp. 141-142.

[111] Ibid. p. 145.

[112] Ibid. pp. 149-150.

[113] Ibid. p. 154.

[114] Ibid. p. 171.

[115] Ibid. p. 172. Unfortunately, with recent clearcut logging done in the Ghost watershed, destruction of the watershed is a possibility.

[116] Moral Rearmament dissolved in 2001; its successor is Initiatives of Change.

[117] Ibid. p. 181.

[118] Bahá'u'lláh, *Tablets of Bahá'u'lláh Revealed after the Kitáb-i-Aqdas*, p. 142.

[119] MacEwan, p. 182.

[120] Ibid. pp. 201-202.

[121] Ibid. p. 203.

[122] Jonker, *The Song and the Silence, Sitting Wind: The Life of Stoney Indian Chief Frank Kaquitts*, p. 48, pp. 82-89.

[123] Ibid. p. 56.

[124] Ibid. p. 123.

[125] Peter and Catharine Whyte were twentieth-century Canadian artists from Banff, Alberta, known for their landscape paintings of the Canadian Rockies. Their paintings and extensive collection of regional artifacts formed the genesis of what would later become the Whyte Museum of the Canadian Rockies. en.wikipedia.org/wiki/Peter_and_Catharine_Whyte

[126] Jonker, p. 159.

[127] Ibid.

[128] For more about the three bands and the treaties, see Chapter 15.

[129] Ibid. p. 191.

[130] Ibid. pp. 194-195.

[131] Ibid. p. 204.

[132] The story about Sitting Bull's visit is told on Ibid. pp. 205-206.

[133] The potlatch is a gift-giving ceremony practiced by Indigenous peoples of the Pacific Northwest.

[134] See footnote # 76.

[135] Beatrice Poucette passed away on June 29, 2013.

[136] Jacqueline Left Hand Bull now serves on the National Spiritual Assembly of the Bahá'ís of the United States.

[137] This restaurant is on the TransCanada Highway at the Morley town-site turnoff. It existed for at least twenty years before being burned down in 2012 by arson. It has since been rebuilt and now houses an interpretive centre and restaurant.

[138] See Chapter Fifteen.

[139] See Verge, *Angus*, p. 132-133.

[140] www.ca.bahai.org/public-discourse/statements-and-reports

[141] Now the offices of the Town of Cochrane.

[142] *Bahá'í Prayers*, p. 102. See footnote #50.

[143] Warren Harbeck is a linguist who helped translate the Bible into the Nakoda language. He writes a weekly column for the *Cochrane Eagle* newspaper. Mary Anna Harbeck taught school at Morley for many years.

[144] *Calgary Herald*, December 27, 1997.

[145] Reilly, *Bad Medicine: A Judge's Struggle for Justice in a First Nations Community*, 2010; *Bad Judgement: The Myths of First Nations Equality and Judicial Independence in Canada*, 2014.

[146] Bahá'u'lláh, quoted in the Ruhi Institute course, *Reflections on the Life of the Spirit*, p. 9.

[147] Ralph Smith passed away in 2013. He ran a service station on Stoney Nakoda reserve for several years.

[148] Shabnam Tashakour now serves as a member of Continental Board of Counsellors for the Americas.

[149] Four Worlds Centre for Development Learning, owned by Michael and Judie Bopp, worked with the Wesley band for a few years.

[150] Now Shannon Bell.

[151] "Might not this process of steady deterioration which is insidiously invading so many departments of human activity and thought be regarded as a necessary accompaniment to the rise of this almighty Arm of Bahá'u'lláh? Might we not look upon the momentous happenings which, in the course of the past twenty years, have so deeply agitated every continent

of the earth, as ominous signs simultaneously proclaiming the agonies of a disintegrating civilization and the birthpangs of that World Order–that Ark of human salvation–that must needs arise upon its ruins?" Shoghi Effendi, *The World Order of Bahá'u'lláh*, 155.

[152] This section is adapted from "A Personal Journey toward Reconciliation." *The Journal of Bahá'í Studies*, Volume 26, number 3, Fall 2016.

[153] Hornby, *Lights of Guidance: A Bahá'í Reference File*, #350.

[154] 'Abdu'l-Bahá, quoted in Shoghi Effendi, *Bahá'í Administration: Selected Messages 1922-1932*, pp. 15-16.

[155] For an explanation of the Ruhi Institute, see Chapter Thirteen.

[156] *Turning Point: Selected Messages of the Universal House of Justice and Supplementary Material 1996-2006*, p. vi.

[157] Ibid. p. 190.

[158] The Universal House of Justice, letter dated April 19, 2013, written on its behalf to several individual Bahá'ís resident in Europe.

[159] See Chapter Nineteen for background on the persecution of the Bahá'ís in Iran.

[160] See Chapter Twelve, for picnic at Forgetmenot Pond.

[161] Among others who helped out were Helen Kohm, Yassamin Sarvestani, Shamim Alavi, Mehran Imamverdi, Monir Imamverdi, Neda Etemad, Leva, Sama, Beverley Knowlton, Hannon Jaberi, Humeyra Samii, Desiree Morin, and Dan Baker.

[162] Ayyám-i-Há or Intercalary Days, February 26 to March 1, are days of preparation for the Fast, hospitality, charity and the giving of gifts.

[163] The Junior Youth Spiritual Empowerment Program, for youth between the ages of twelve and fifteen, seeks to help them to sharpen their spiritual perception, identify the forces shaping society, and enhance their powers of expression. Through acts of service, they learn together to tangibly contribute to the well-being of society.

[164] The Universal House of Justice, Ridván 2010 Message, paragraph 25.

[165] Hanley, *Eleven*, p. 361.

[166] Ibid. p. 360.

[167] Ibid. p. 359.

[168] Ibid. p. 360.

[169] For example, in both Ruhi Book 3: Children's classes for Grade 3, and in Ruhi Book 9, wisdom from previous religious dispensations is shared.

[170] Hanley, p. 361.

[171] The Universal House of Justice, letter of February 8, 2013, to the Bahá'ís of the World, announcing the convocation of ninety-five youth conferences around the world.

[172] Youth Conferences, July-October 2013, Participant Materials. See footnote #163 for a description of the Junior Youth Spiritual Empowerment Program.

[173] The next fall, 2014, the group was moved to a Sunday time with a different program and facilitators.

[174] *Bahá'í Prayers*, p. 133.

[175] *Insights from the Frontiers of Learning: A document prepared by The International Teaching Centre.* April 2013.

[176] The youth from Morley and beyond who attended included Adam Julian, Dacster Chiniquay, Garrina Amos, Shawyun Refahi, Chan Carlston, Naim Bakhshayesh-Rad, Leva Eghbali, DeAngelo Cecil, Darius Powderface, and Sama Imamverdi.

[177] Bahá'u'lláh, *Tablets of Bahá'u'lláh Revealed after the Kitáb-i-Aqdas*, p. 67.

[178] Wilson Schaef, *Native Wisdom for White Minds: Daily Reflections Inspired by the Native Peoples of the World.* Father Donnchadh O'Floinn, Irish Priest, Sept. 18 reflection.

[179] Thomas Anaquod was the first Indigenous person to serve as a member of the National Spiritual Assembly of the Bahá'ís of Canada. See Verge, *Angus*, pp. 130-131.

[180] Coincidently, when we got back to Canada in 2003, I saw a painting done by good friend visual artist Garry Berteig, of a strikingly similar mountain scene with clouds obscuring the mountain peaks. Garry had painted it during the very time we were in Ireland.

[181] *The Long March*, by Louise-Marie Fitzpatrick.

[182] Some claim the amount was actually $710, although many articles and this book refer to the sum as $170. The Wikipedia page on The Choctaw Nation attributes this error to a misprint in Angie Debo's, *The Rise and Fall of the Choctaw Republic*. Source: nativeheritageproject.com/2014/01/16/choctaw-nation-in-1847-provides-relief-to-irish-famine-victims/ and irishamericanmom.com

[183] www.irishamericanmom.com/tag/the-choctaw-nation/

[184] www.powwows.com/2015/03/15/ireland-pays-tribute-to-choctaw-nations-kindness/

Sculptor Alex Pentek wrote on his Vimeo page: "By creating an empty bowl symbolic of the Great Irish Famine formed from the seemingly fragile and rounded shaped eagle feathers used in Choctaw ceremonial dress, it is my aim to communicate the tenderness and warmth of the Choctaw Nation who provided food to the hungry when they themselves were still recovering from their own tragic recent past.

"I have also chosen feathers to reflect the local bird life along the nearby water's edge with a fusion of ideas that aims to visually communicate this act of humanity and mercy, and also the notion that the Choctaw and Irish Nations are forever more kindred spirits."

[185] Bushrui, *The Wisdom of the Irish*, p. xvi.

[186] Ibid.

[187] Wilson Schaef, *Native Wisdom for White Minds*, April 20 meditation.

[188] Ibid. April 28 meditation.

[189] For background on the abuses, see childabusecommission.ie/; www.dailymail.co.uk/news/article-1184828/Revealed-decades-ritual-child-abuse-Catholic-schools-orphanages-damned-report.html

[190] irishamerica.com/2012/01/breaking-the-code-of-silence-the-irish-and-drink/ Accessed Dec. 5, 2016. O'Connor writes that drinking as a national pastime has historical roots, in religious persecution, land rape, extreme poverty and intermittent abuse of military power by English colonists in Ireland during 700 years of continuous occupation. This history produced a national inferiority complex in Irish Catholics "which I identify as cultural malignant shame, characterized by chronic fear, suppressed rage, self-loathing, procrastination, low self-esteem, false pride and a vulnerability to use alcohol as remission for suffering – past and present."

Dr. O'Connor, in the same article, touches on the subject of spirituality. He quotes John Waters, a controversial and crusading Irish journalist, who stated the following: "Drinking in Ireland is not simply a convivial pastime, it is a ritualistic alternative to real life, a spiritual placebo, a fumble for eternity, a longing for heaven, a thirst for return to the embrace of the Almighty." Irish drinking patterns are, Waters writes, "evidence of a deep hole in the Irish psyche which only alcohol can fill."

[191] Townshend, "The Genius of Ireland." *The Mission of Bahá'u'lláh*, p. 107.

[192] www.rockymountainnakoda.com/who-we-are

[193] Townshend, "The Genius of Ireland." *The Mission of Bahá'u'lláh*, p. 104.

[194] Cahill, *How the Irish Saved Civilization: The Untold Story of Ireland's Heroic Role from the Fall of Rome to the Rise of Medieval Europe.* p. 133, 147.

[195] Ibid. p. 148.

[196] Revelation 21:1.

[197] Hofman, *George Townshend,* p. 50. Letter written by 'Abdu'l-Bahá on Dec. 19, 1920.

[198] See footnote #36 on Hands of the Cause of God.

[199] Townshend, "The Genius of Ireland." *The Mission of Baháʼuʼlláh*, p. 120.

[200] Idle No More is a grassroots movement among Indigenous people in Canada, which was started to protest impending parliamentary bills that would erode Indigenous sovereignty and environmental protections.

[201] *The Globe and Mail*, Sept. 27, 2014. www.theglobeandmail.com/opinion/idle-no-more-isnt-dead-its-just-resting/article20795994/

[202] For more on this subject, see for example, www.cbc.ca/news/canada/north/cbc-closing-comments-on-aboriginal-stories-reaction-1.3345137.

[203] For background on the *Nanaimo Daily News* controversial letters to the editor, see www.cbc.ca/news/canada/british-columbia/racist-newspaper-letter-sparks-nanaimo-protest-1.1316035

[204] After the March letter, the Nuu-chah-nulth Tribal Council, which which had been publishing the *Ha-Shilth-Sa*, Canada's oldest First Nations newspaper, on the *Nanaimo Daily's* press, announced the tribe had economic clout and intended to use it by getting the *Ha-Shilth-Sa* printed elsewhere. Another letter containing similar racist comments was published by the *Daily News* in September 2013, again to outrage. However related, the *Nanaimo Daily News*, which was sold to Black Press in December 2014, stopped publishing on January 29, 2016. Rick O'Connor, Black Press CEO, said the decision to close the paper was not taken lightly. Despite improvements to the content and format of the paper which were well received by existing readers, "they did not translate into an increase in paid circulation or advertising revenue." www.cbc.ca/news/canada/british-columbia/nanaimo-daily-news-closing-1.3417316

[205] Dr. Roshan Danesh received his PhD from Harvard Law School. He is a lawyer, consultant and scholar, who works, teaches, and publishes in the areas of conflict resolution, constitutional law, law and religion, and public law. He has worked extensively with First Nations in Canada on protection and advancement of constitutional rights.

[206] "Reconciliation: Meeting the Challenge of Recognition of Aboriginal Title and Rights." Talk by Dr. Roshan Danesh, January 16, 2016, in Victoria. www.youtube.com/watch?v=iHOlfeRrsq4&t=20s

[207] 'Abdu'l-Bahá, *The Secret of Divine Civilization*, p. 43.

[208] All the Truth and Reconciliation Commission documents can be found at http://nctr.ca/reports.php

[209] Lindberg, *Birdie*.

[210] A report released by the RCMP in May 2014 states that 1,017 Indigenous women and girls were murdered from 1980-2012. Because of gaps in police and government reporting, the actual numbers may be much higher. www.amnesty.ca/blog/missing-and-murdered-indigenous-women-and-girls-understanding-the-numbers. Accessed 23 June 2016.

[211] Culleton Mosionier, *In Search of April Raintree: Critical Edition*, edited by Cheryl Suzack. From essay by Jo-Ann Thom Episkenew, "The Effect of Readers' Responses on the Development of Aboriginal Literature in Canada: A Study of Maria Campbell's *Halfbreed*, Beatrice Culleton's *In Search of April Raintree*, and Richard Wagamese's *Keeper'n Me*", pp. 296-298.

[212] King, *The Inconvenient Indian*, p. 3.

[213] Ibid. p. 12.

[214] Ibid. p. 20.

[215] Ibid. p. 85-89. See also Chapter 14 above about the Removal Act.

[216] Ibid. p. 95.

[217] Ibid. p. 96.

[218] Ibid. p. 201.

[219] Ibid. p. 222.

[220] Ibid. p. 218.

[221] Ibid. p. 234.

[222] Ibid. p. 235.

[223] *Kanehsatake: 270 Years of Resistance* can be seen online at www.nfb.ca/ film/kanehsatake_270_years_of_resistance

[224] King, p. 245.

[225] Ibid. p. 246.

[226] Information from the introduction to the honorary Doctor of Laws, *honoris causa*, conferred on Louise Mandell by Simon Fraser University on June 13, 2012. www.sfu.ca/content/dam/sfu/ceremonies/HDRs/honorary-degrees/Citation-Mandell-web.pdf

[227] "In 1982 Canada 'patriated' its Constitution, transferring the country's highest law, the British North America Act, from the authority of the British Parliament–a connection from the colonial past–to Canada's federal and provincial legislatures...The Constitution was also updated with a new amending formula and a Charter of Rights — changes that occurred after a fierce, 18-month political and legal struggle that dominated headlines and the agendas of every government in the country." http://indigenousfoundations.arts.ubc.ca/constitution_act_1982_section_35/ For more on the implications of Section 35, please see http://indigenousfoundations.arts.ubc.ca/home/government-policy/constitution-act-1982-section-35.html Though many, particularly in government, did not feel at the time of patriation that Section 35 would have influence in changing the law, many successful court cases have been settled in favour of Aboriginal individuals and communities in subsequent decades.

[228] Olive P. Dickason, quoted in the *Royal Commission on Aboriginal Peoples*, Volume 1, p. 20.

[229] Ibid, pp. 50-83. To respect the diversity among Aboriginal nations, RCAP chose to illustrate certain distinctive patterns of culture and social organization by selecting five particular instances from different geographic regions, including Mi'kmaq, Iroquoians, people of the Blackfoot Confederacy, Northwest Coast Indigenous peoples and Inuit.

[230] Another theory about Eriksson's voyage to the new world is that it was planned. "The 'Saga of the Greenlanders'...recounts that Eriksson's voyage to North America was no fluke. Instead, the Viking explorer had heard of a

strange land to the west from Icelandic trader Bjarni Herjolfsson, who more than a decade earlier had overshot Greenland and sailed by the shores of North America without setting foot upon it. Eriksson bought the trader's ship, raised a crew of 35 men and retraced the route in reverse." www.history.com/news/the-viking-explorer-who-beat-columbus-to-america

[231] www.bbc.co.uk/history/historic_figures/erikson_leif.shtml

[232] On a trip to Iceland in 2015, I was fascinated to learn that, contrary to much recorded history, the first European child to be born in the Americas was of Icelandic descent. Snorri Thorfinnsson, born between 1004 and 1013, was the son of Thorfinn and his wife Gudrid, who had reached Newfoundland seven years after Leif Eriksson. They lived there for a few years before returning to Iceland. www.smithsonianmag.com/history/the-vikings-a-memorable-visit-to-america-98090935/

[233] *Royal Commission on Aboriginal Peoples*, (RCAP), Volume I, p. 239.

[234] *Honouring the Truth, Reconciling for the Future: Summary of the Final Report of the Truth and Reconciliation* (HTRF), pp. 49-50.

[235] Ibid. p. 50.

[236] RCAP, Volume I, Part I, pp. 47-48.

[237] http://doctrineofdiscoveryforum.blogspot.ca/ Accessed June 15, 2016.

[238] RCAP, Volume I, p. 95.

[239] Ibid.

[240] Ibid. p. 96.

[241] Ibid. p. 97.

[242] Ibid.

[243] Ibid. p. 21.

[244] "The Treaty of Paris of 1763 ended the...Seven Years' War between Great Britain and France, as well as their respective allies. In the terms of the treaty, France gave up all its territories in mainland North America, effectively ending any foreign military threat to the British colonies there." history.state.gov/milestones/1750-1775/treaty-of-paris

[245] RCAP, Volume I, p. 108.

[246] HTRF, p. 250.

[247] Ibid. p. 252.

[248] Interview, CBC series, The 8th Fire, 2012. www.cbc.ca/8thfire/index. html. John Borrows is a professor and Law Foundation Chair in Aboriginal Justice in the Faculty of Law at the University of Victoria and author of *Canada's Indigenous Constitution.*

[249] United Nations Declaration on Indigenous Peoples, see footnote #368.

[250] HTRF, p. 253.

[251] RCAP, Volume I, p. 133.

[252] Ibid. pp. 114-122.

[253] Ibid. p. 132.

[254] Ibid. p. 165.

[255] Cultural genocide is the systematic destruction of traditions, values, language, and other elements which make one group of people distinct from other groups. http://aptnnews.ca/2015/06/02/canada-guilty-cultural-genocide-indigenous-peoples-trc-2/

[256] Abley, *Conversations with a Dead Man: The Legacy of Duncan Campbell Scott,* p. 187; King, *The Inconvenient Indian: A Curious Account of Native People in North America,* p. 70, 71, 155. Some additional amendments: A 1930 amendment banned Indians from playing pool if they did it too often and wasted their time to the detriment of themselves and their families. In 1985, an amendment known in Parliament as Bill C-31 was passed that allowed Native women who had lost their Indian status through marriage to regain it. King, p. 71.

[257] HTRF, p. 116.

[258] See documentary on the pass system. www.thepasssystem.ca Hayter Reed "brought the discipline and inflexibility of military training to his

work in the Department of Indian Affairs. He is best known for his leadership in shaping and implementing post-rebellion federal Indian policy. But it was a policy that conceived of no native role in a changing Canada, and that caused isolation, economic stagnation, and resentment." By E. Brian Titley. www.biographi.ca/en/bio/reed_hayter_16E.html

[259] See Union of British Columbia Indians, http://www.ubcic.bc.ca/mckenna_mcbride_royal_commission

[260] See Chapter Eleven for more about R. B. Bennett.

[261] Abley, p. 201.

[262] King, p. 73.

[263] http://indigenousfoundations.arts.ubc.ca/the_white_paper_1969/ See also Chapter Eleven, for more about the White Paper.

[264] Flooding also affected many hundreds of people on the Nakoda Nation.

[265] www.blackfootcrossing.ca

[266] Ibid.

[267] HTRF, p. 249.

[268] RCAP, Volume I, p. 121.

[269] Treaty 7 Elders and Tribal Council with Hildebrandt, First Rider, and Carter. *The True Spirit and Original Intent of Treaty 7*. Foreword by Gregg C. Smith, executive director, Treaty 7 Tribal Council.

[270] Ibid. p. 125.

[271] Ibid. p. xi.

[272] In 1869 the Northwest was acquired from the Hudson's Bay Company by the Dominion of Canada. According to the British North America Act, which had passed in 1867, "Indians and lands reserved for the Indians" were to be the exclusive legislative responsibility of the Parliament of Canada. Over the next forty years, eleven numbered treaties were drawn up and signed with the First Nations of Western and Central Canada and the Northwest Territories. They are as follows: Treaty Number 1, 1871,

Lower Fort Garry, Fort Alexander; Treaty Number 2, 1871, Manitoba Post (these first two covered most of southern Manitoba); Treaty Number 3, 1873, North West Angle Treaty (Ontario and eastern Manitoba); Treaty Number 4, 1874, Qu'Appelle Treaty; Treaty Number 5, 1875, Beren's River, Norway House, Grand Rapids; Treaty Number 6, 1876, Fort Carlton, Fort Pitt with Crees and Assiniboines; Treaty Number 7, 1877, Blackfoot Crossing; Treaty Number 8, 1899, 39 First Nation communities in Northern Alberta, Northwestern Saskatchewan, Northeastern British Columbia, and the Southwest portion of the Northwest Territories; Treaty Number 9, 1905, James Bay Treaty in northern Ontario with Ojibwa, Cree, others; Treaty Number 10, 1906, northern Saskatchewan and Alberta; Treaty Number 11, 1921, Northwest Territories. For information on these treaties and for others signed before the numbered treaties, and since, see www.aadnc-aandc.gc.ca/eng/1380223988016/1380224163492

[273] See this chapter, below, Savage, *Geography of Blood*.

[274] MacEwan, *Tatanga Mani: Walking Buffalo of the Stonies*, p. 55.

[275] Treaty 7 Elders and Tribal Council with Hildebrandt, First Rider, and Carter, p. 124.

[276] Ibid, Preface xii and p. 133.

[277] Ibid, Preface xii.

[278] Ibid, p. 25. It has now been more than five generations, as this book was published in 1996.

[279] Bill Mclean, the son of Walking Buffalo, was the oldest person on the Stoney Nakoda First Nation when he passed away in August 2016.

[280] Treaty 7 Elders and Tribal Council with Hildebrandt, First Rider, and Carter, p. 78.

[281] Ibid, p. 130.

[282] Ibid, p. 90.

[283] http://www.makingtreaty7.com / The mandate is described: "The Making Treaty 7 Cultural Society explores the historical significance of the events at Blackfoot Crossing in 1877, while investigating the consequences

and implications of Treaty 7, 137 years later. The Society invites people of all ages and backgrounds to consider an enlightened, sustainable future for everyone – together."

[284] Bahá'u'lláh, *The Hidden Words*, Arabic #2.

[285] Bahá'u'lláh, *Tablets of Bahá'u'lláh*, p. 67.

[286] The name of the band was recorded in the official records as Jacob's Band and changed a number of times over the years. Since 1990 it has been called the Wesley Band, after Chief Peter Wesley. *The True Spirit and Original Intent of Treaty 7*, p. 38.

[287] Ibid. p. 141.

[288] Snow, *These Mountains Are Our Sacred Places: The Story of the Stoney People*, p. 49.

[289] Treaty 7 Elders and Tribal Council with Hildebrandt, First Rider, and Carter, p. 52 and 262.

[290] Snow, p. 60.

[291] Ibid. p. 66.

[292] Ibid. p. 79.

[293] Ibid. pp. 126-127.

[294] Savage, *A Geography of Blood: Unearthing Memory from a Prairie Landscape*, p. 93.

[295] Ibid. p. 81.

[296] Ibid. p. 36.

[297] Ibid. p. 65.

[298] Ibid. pp. 88-89.

[299] Ibid. p. 90.

[300] See also Chapter Sixteen, section "The Benevolent Peacemaker".

[301] Abley, *Conversations with a Dead Man: The Legacy of Duncan Campbell Scott*, p. 58.

[302] Savage, pp. 102-105.

[303] Ibid. pp. 152-153.

[304] Ibid. p. 156.

[305] Ibid. pp. 156-157.

[306] Verge, *Angus: From the Heart*, p. 124.

[307] All TRC documents are available for free at http://nctr.ca/reports.php

[308] HTRF, p. 3.

[309] Ibid. pp. 55-56.

[310] Ibid. pp. 47-48.

[311] Abley, pp. 84-85.

[312] There were some residential schools that were attended by Indigenous children in Newfoundland and Labrador but not run by the federal government, which did not come under the settlement agreement. Efforts are now underway to examine these histories and seek compensation. See, for example, www.theglobeandmail.com/news/national/residential-school-survivors-in-newfoundland-and-labrador-seek-justice/article27170859/

[313] Bob Watts has been involved in many major Indigenous issues in Canada over the past twenty years and led the process, with support from across Canada and internationally, to establish Canada's Truth and Reconciliation Commission. He was Interim Executive Director of the Commission and was a member of the team that negotiated the historic Indian Residential Schools Settlement Agreement. Bob is also a former CEO of the Assembly of First Nations, served as the Chief of Staff to the Assembly of First Nations' National Chief Phil Fontaine, and is a former Assistant Deputy Minister for the Government of Canada. Bob is a graduate of the John F. Kennedy School of Government, Harvard University, a fellow at the Harvard Law School, and an adjunct professor and fellow in the School of Policy Studies, Queen's University. He is from Mohawk and Ojibway ancestry and is a frequent speaker on Indigenous issues. Bob is a recipient of an Indspire award for Public Service.

[314] Loft Watts, Evelyn and Verge, Patricia. *Return to Tyendinaga: The Story of Jim and Melba Loft, Bahá'í Pioneers.*

[315] The 2012 Vancouver Human Rights Lecture, which was featured on CBC Radio's Ideas series, can be found at: thelaurier.ca/lecturepodcasts/

[316] HTRF, p. 8.

[317] *The Survivors Speak: A Report of the Truth and Reconciliation Commission of Canada*, p. 105.

[318] Ibid. p. 44.

[319] Ibid. p. 75.

[320] Ibid. p. 110.

[321] Ibid. p. 112.

[322] Ibid.

[323] Ibid. p. 113.

[324] Ibid. p. 114.

[325] HTRF, p. 112.

[326] HTRF, p. 97.

[327] Abley, pp. 47-48.

[328] HTRF, p. 99.

[329] Abley, p. 57.

[330] Ibid.

[331] Ibid. pp. 49-50.

[332] Dr. Peter Bryce was the first Canadian to be named president of the American Public Health Association. Abley, p. 47.

[333] Ibid. p. 28.

[334] Ibid. p. 36.

[335] Ibid. p. 33.

[336] Quoted in Abley, p. 159.

[337] Quoted in Ralston Saul, *The Comeback*, p. 9.

[338] Ibid.

[339] Abley, p. 156.

[340] Ibid. pp. 156-157.

[341] Ibid. p. 79.

[342] Regan, *Unsettling the Settler Within: Indian Residential Schools, Truth Telling, and Reconciliation in Canada*, pp. 45-48.

[343] http://umanitoba.ca/nctr/

[344] HTRF, p. 186. In October 2017, the federal government announced a $800-million proposed agreement with Sixties Scoop survivors.

[345] Ibid. p. 183.

[346] Ibid. p. 224.

[347] Ibid. p. 204.

[348] Ibid. p. 237.

[349] www.macleans.ca/news/canada/justice-murray-sinclairs-remarks-on-the-truth-and-reconciliation-report/

[350] Crean, *The Laughing One: A Journey to Emily Carr*, p. 146.

[351] Ibid. pp. 177-178.

[352] Ibid. p. 148.

[353] The Trusteeship Council suspended operation on 1 November 1994, with the independence of Palau, the last remaining United Nations trust territory, on 1 October 1994. Major goals of the system were to promote the advancement of the inhabitants of Trust Territories and their progressive development towards self-government or independence. https://www.un.org/en/mainbodies/trusteeship/

[354] Horton, "As ye have faith, so shall your powers and blessings be": The Aboriginal-Bahá'í Encounter in British Columbia," Master's Thesis, 2005. summit.sfu.ca/system/files/iritems1/9262/1763.pdf

[355] Horton, "All is One: Becoming Indigenous and Bahai in Global North America", PhD thesis, 2013. http://bahai-library.com/ horton_indigenous_bahai

[356] International Work Group for Indigenous Affairs. www.iwgia.org

[357] The Universal House of Justice, *Century of Light*, p. 4.

[358] HTRF, p. 53.

[359] For a discussion of the current framework for action, see Chapter Thirteen.

[360] From CBC Radio, www.cbc.ca/8thfire/2011/11/victoria-freeman. html

[361] Freeman, quoted in Regan, *Unsettling the Settler Within: Indian Residential Schools, Truth Telling, and Reconciliation in Canada*, p. 233.

[362] Little Bear, in Battiste, *Reclaiming Indigenous Voice and Vision*, p. 77.

[363] Ibid.

[364] Ibid. p. 82.

[365] Daes, in Ibid. p. 5.

[366] Ibid. p. 7.

[367] Ibid. p. 6.

[368] The United Nations Declaration on the Rights of Indigenous People can be found at www.un.org/esa/socdev/unpfii/documents/DRIPS_en.pdf

[369] Robin Fisher, quoted in Regan, p. 90.

[370] Regan, p. 95.

[371] Ibid. pp. 91-92.

[372] Ibid.

[373] Ibid. p. 96.

[374] Ibid. p. 97.

[375] Ibid.

[376] Ibid. p. 109.

[377] Ralston Saul, quoted in Ibid. p. 71.

[378] Ralston Saul, *The Comeback*, p. 32.

[379] Regan, p. 4.

[380] Ibid.

[381] Ibid. p. 18.

[382] Ibid. p. 47.

[383] Ralston Saul, *The Comeback*, p. 15.

[384] Ibid. p. 46.

[385] Ibid. p. 15.

[386] Ibid. p. 38.

[387] I am indebted to Dr. Roshan Danesh for suggesting the inclusion of these paragraphs and for making helpful suggestions for Chapter Fifteen.

[388] For the judgment in the Haida case, please see scc-csc.lexum.com/scc-csc/scc-csc/en/item/2189/index.do

[389] See Chapter Fifteen.

[390] Ralston Saul, p. 38.

[391] The Universal House of Justice, letter dated 28 December, 2010, to the Conference of the Continental Boards of Counsellors, paragraph 14.

[392] The Universal House of Justice, letter dated 24 May, 2001, to Believers Gathered for the Events Marking the Completion of the Projects on Mount Carmel.

[393] images.penguingroup.com/Storage/viking/InventionOfWings_BCK_updated.pdf

[394] Lample, *Creating A New Mind: Reflections on the Individual, the Institutions and the Community*, pp. 23-24.

[395] www.cbc.ca/radio/unreserved/taking-the-first-steps-on-the-road-to-reconciliation-1.3347611/will-truth-bring-reconciliation-justice-murray-sinclair-says-not-without-education-1.3348070

[396] See Appendix One for full submission.

[397] HTRF, p. 16.

[398] Ibid. pp. 237-238.

[399] Ibid. p. 15.

[400] Shoghi Effendi, *The Advent of Divine Justice*, p. 33.

[401] HTRF, p. 238.

[402] As an example, see SaskCulture's fall/winter 2015 issue www.saskculture.ca/engage/2015/12/1/engage-volume-6-issue-1-fallwinter-2015

[403] HTRF, p. 295.

[404] Ibid. p. 239.

[405] Ibid. pp. 260-261.

[406] Ibid. p. 323.

[407] Ibid. p. 289.

[408] Ibid. p. 18.

[409] speakingmytruth.ca

[410] Rogers, DeGagné, Dewar, and Lowry. *Speaking My Truth: Reflections on Reconciliation & Residential School*, pp. 7-8.

[411] Ibid. pp. 8-9.

[412] Ibid. p. 29, 31.

[413] Ibid. p. 91, 85.

[414] Ibid. p. 161.

[415] The Online Guide to Thomas R. Berger. web.uvic.ca/~mharbell/a1/workshop2/index.html

[416] See footnote #205 on Dr. Danesh. The talk can be found at bahaiblog.net/site/2015/02/re-telling-reconciliation-talk-roshan-danesh/

[417] 'Abdu'l-Bahá, *Paris Talks: Talks given by 'Abdu'l-Bahá in 1911-12*, talk given November 17, 1911, p. 127.

[418] Mr. Ali Nakhjavani and his wife, Violette, were pioneers to Uganda. In 1963, Mr. Nakhjavani was elected to the Universal House of Justice and served this body until 2003.

[419] See Chapter Fifteen.

[420] See footnotes #51 and 82.

[421] Amatu'l-Bahá Rúḥíyyih Khánum, *Message to the Indian and Eskimo Bahá'ís of the Western Hemisphere*.

[422] Ibid.

[423] From a letter dated 11 July 1951 written on behalf of Shoghi Effendi to the National Spiritual Assembly of Meso-America and the Antilles. *Compilation of Compilations Vol III*, p. 208, #332.

[424] From a letter dated 21 September 1951 written on behalf of Shoghi Effendi to the Comite Nacional de Ensenanza Bahai pare los Indigenas, Ibid, p. 209, #334.

[425] Amatu'l-Bahá Rúḥíyyih Khánum, *Message to the Indian and Eskimo Bahá'ís of the Western Hemisphere*.

[426] Jasion, *Never Be Afraid to Dare: The Story of 'General Jack'*, p. 192. From a letter written on behalf of Shoghi Effendi to the Bahá'ís of Sofia, 1 December 1933.

[427] In addition to serving as grand chief of the Assembly of First Nations, Shawn A-in-chut Atleo has also served as chancellor at Vancouver Island University; former regional chief, BC Assembly of First Nations; was appointed by BC Premier Christy Clark to the role of Shqwi qwal

("Speaker") for Indigenous Dialogue at Vancouver Island University. He is a hereditary chief of the Ahousaht First Nation in British Columbia.

[428] Atleo's speech can be found at www.youtube.com/ watch?v=mSwOEu9GFVQ

[429] As of 2017, the University of Winnipeg, Lakehead University in Thunder Bay, Ontario, and Trent University in Peterborough, Ontario, had mandated at least one Indigenous studies course.

[430] indiancountrytodaymedianetwork.com/2015/10/26/ahousaht -first-nation-leads-rescue-passengers-capsized-bc-whale-watching- boat-162223

[431] Douglas White serves as coordinator of Vancouver Island University's Centre for Pre-Confederation Treaties and Reconciliation and is also legal counsel for First Nations across the country. He was appointed to the BC Aboriginal Justice Council by the First Nations Summit in April 2016.

[432] See, for example, Memorial to Sir Wilfred Laurier shuswapnation. org/to-sir-wilfrid-laurier/

[433] See footnote #415.

[434] See Chapter One.

[435] Hatcher, *Love, Power and Justice: The Dynamics of Authentic Morality.*

[436] Recording of talk at Harper Mountain courtesy of Anisa White.

[437] 'Abdu'l-Bahá, *Tablets of the Divine Plan*, p. 93, 95. Tablet revealed on February 21, 1917.

[438] 'Abdu'l-Bahá, *The Promulgation of Universal Peace*, p. 19.

[439] 'Abdu'l-Bahá, *Bahá'í World Faith: Selected Writings of Bahá'u'lláh and 'Abdu'l-Bahá*, p. 359.

[440] Bahá'u'lláh, *Tablets of Bahá'u'lláh revealed after the Kitáb-i-Aqdas*, p. 35.

[441] 'Abdu'l-Bahá, *Lights of Guidance*, p. 145, #483.

[442] Bahá'u'lláh, *The Hidden Words*, Arabic #2.

[443] Loft Watts & Verge, *Return to Tyendinaga: The Story of Jim and Melba Loft, Baháʼí Pioneers*, p. 167.

[444] Baháʼuʼlláh, quoted in Motlagh, *The Glorious Journey to God*, p. 63.

[445] ʻAbduʼl-Bahá, ibid, p. 96.

[446] *Nature: An Emanation of Godʼs Will*, p. 46.

[447] Baháʼuʼlláh, *Prayers and Meditations by Baháʼuʼlláh*, CLXXVI (p. 272).

[448] ʻAbduʼl-Bahá, *Selections from the Writings of ʻAbduʼl-Bahá*, p. 24, #7.4.

[449] Zalida passed away in September 2016.

[450] The extended family has carried on the tradition at the Stampede since Eddie and Elsieʼs passing.

[451] Manufactured at a mill in Pendleton, Oregon, the striking wool blankets have vivid colors and authentic Native American designs.

[452] For a description of the ecumenical councils, see Snow, *These Mountains are Our Sacred Places*, p. 195.

[453] "Hoop dancing and world citizenship: meet Kevin Locke," *One Country* 8.2 (July-Sept. 1996). Quoted in Addison & Buck, "Messengers of God in North America Revisited: An exegesis of ʻAbduʼl-Baháʼs Tablet to Amir Khan," pp. 225-226. *Online Journal of Baháʼí Studies*, Vol I (2007) http://oj.bahaistudies.net/ See also "The Return of the "White Buffalo Calf Woman": Prophecy of the Lakota," interview of Jacqueline Left Hand Bull by National Spiritual Assembly of the United States member Patricia Locke (Lakota). The interview was conducted in 1989 and submitted to public newspapers in the South Dakota area. bahai.uga.edu/News/000089.html

[454] Addison, & Buck. "Messengers of God in North America Revisited: An exegesis of ʻAbduʼl-Baháʼs Tablet to Amir Khan." *Online Journal of Baháʼí Studies*, Vol I (2007), p. 206.

[455] Quoted in Ibid. p. 197.

[456] Quoted in Ibid. p. 252. From a letter dated 21 December 1986, written on behalf of the Universal House of Justice to a National Spiritual Assembly.

[457] Lee Brown PhD has completed a book about the relationship of the teachings of the Peacemaker and those of Bahá'u'lláh.

[458] Quoted in Ibid. pp. 246-247. "Mitakuye Oyasin! We are All Related." Eugene Weekly (2004).

[459] Ibid. p. 183.

[460] HTRF, p. 278.

[461] The United Nations Declaration on the Rights of Indigenous People, http://www.un.org/esa/socdev/unpfii/documents/DRIPS_en.pdf

[462] Bahá'u'lláh, *The Hidden Words*, Arabic #68.

[463] *Compilation of Compilations: Prepared by the Research Department of The Universal House of Justice, Volume 3.* From a letter dated 22 August 1957, written on behalf of Shoghi Effendi to the National Spiritual Assembly of Central America and Mexico. P. 225, #365.

[464] Shoghi Effendi, *The Advent of Divine Justice*, pp. 18-34.

[465] Ibid. pp. 33-34.

[466] Youth Conferences, July - October 2013, Participant Materials, p. 7.

[467] 'Abdu'l-Bahá, *Lights of Guidance*, p. 179, #588.

[468] *Compilation of Compilations: Prepared by the Research Department of The Universal House of Justice, Volume 3.* From a letter dated 25 June 1935, written on behalf of Shoghi Effendi to an individual believer. P.111, #175.

[469] *Teaching the Cause*, Ruhi Institute, Book 6, pp. 140-141.

[470] www.aadnc-aandc.gc.ca/eng/1100100014298/1100100014302

[471] *Compilation of Compilations: Prepared by the Research Department of The Universal House of Justice, Volume 3.* From a letter dated 21 September 1951 written on behalf of Shoghi Effendi to the Comité Nacional de Ensenanza Bahá'í pare los Indigenas de Sud America, pp. 208-209, #334.

[472] From Statement of the Bahá'í International Community www.bic.org/focus-areas/situation-iranian-bahais#htjd0SCMfzv6CtUo.97

[473] The Universal House of Justice, Riḍván 2010, paragraph 33.

[474] Letter to an individual on behalf of the Universal House of Justice, June 23, 2003. Quoted in *Creative Dimensions of Suffering*, by A-M. Ghadirian, M.D. p. 121.

[475] Pilgrim notes are notes taken by believers while on pilgrimage. They are not considered to have authority, as do the writings of the Central Figures of the Faith. "...the notes of pilgrims do not carry the authority resident in the Guardian's letters written over his own signature. On the other hand each pilgrim brings back information and suggestions of a most precious character, and it is the privilege of all the friends to share in the spiritual results of these visits." From a letter written on behalf of the Guardian to the National Spiritual Assembly of the United States. *Lights of Guidance*, p. 439, #1432.

[476] HTRF, p. 360.

[477] Ibid. p. 357.

[478] Covey, "Diné Becoming Bahá'í: Through the Lens of Ancient Prophecies," Masters Thesis, 2011, pp. 35-36. Used with permission. http://bahai-library.com/covey_navajo_becoming_bahai

For a discussion of intergenerational trauma, see "Intergenerational Trauma: Understanding Natives' Inherited Pain" by Mary Annette Pember. www.indiancountrymedianetwork.com

A Canadian perspective can be found in William Aguiar and Regine Halseth, "ABORIGINAL PEOPLES AND HISTORIC TRAUMA: The processes of intergenerational transmission," at https://www.ccnsa-nccah.ca/docs/context/RPT-HistoricTrauma-IntergenTransmission-Aguiar-Halseth-EN.pdf

[479] "Canadians Of Colour Talk Racism, Self-Care and Driving Change," by David Lewis-Peart, March 21, 2016. www.huffingtonpost.ca/2016/03/21/racism-canada-self-care_n_9488774.html

[480] Reggie Newkirk devoted his career to the protection of human rights and has served on the National Spiritual Assembly of the Bahá'ís of Canada, and as an Auxiliary Board member.

[481] Coll, Freeman, Robertson, Iron Cloud, Two Dogs, "Exploring Irish Multigenerational Trauma and Its Healing: Lessons from the Oglala Lakota (Sioux)." file.scirp.org/pdf/AASoci20120200001_81443251.pdf

[482] Ibid.

[483] The Universal House of Justice, Letter dated 29 December 2015 to the Conference of the Continental Boards of Counsellors, paragraph 30.

[484] Dr. Charles Figley, Professor, Paul Henry Kurzweg Distinguished Chair, Director, Tulane Traumatology Institute, Tulane University, New Orleans, LA. www.compassionfatigue.org/

[485] 'Abdu'l-Bahá, *The Promulgation of Universal Peace*, p. 293.

[486] *Compilation of Compilations: Prepared by the Research Department of The Universal House of Justice, Volume 3*. From a letter dated 30 January 1948 written on behalf of Shoghi Effendi to an individual believer, p. 206, #327.

[487] The Universal House of Justice, Riḍván 2010 letter to the Bahá'ís of the World, paragraph 10.

[488] Helen has served as an Auxiliary Board member in both Costa Rica and Alberta and as a translator at many Bahá'í International Conventions; she presently serves as a member of the Regional Bahá'í Council of Alberta.

[489] Letter written on behalf of The Universal House of Justice to an individual, August 22, 2002.

[490] Sellars, p. 189.

[491] The Universal House of Justice, Riḍván 2010 letter to the Bahá'ís of the World, paragraph 5.

[492] *The Journal of Bahá'í Studies*, Volume 19, number 1/4 March-December 2009. Online at bahai-studies.ca/wp-content/uploads/2014/05/19.14-Hanson.pdf

[493] Ibid. p. 27, 31, 28.

[494] Quoted in Hanson, p. 30.

[495] Ibid. p. 50, 52.

[496] Universal House of Justice, Letter to the Followers of Bahá'u'lláh in the Cradle of the Faith, 26 November 2003, quoted in Ibid. p. 33.

[497] Ibid. p. 31.

[498] Ibid. p. 29.

[499] Ibid. p. 41.

[500] Lample, *Creating A New Mind: Reflections on the Individual, the Institutions and the Community*, p. 107.

[501] Wilson, *The Bassoon King*, p. 277. Rainn Wilson is best known for his role as Dwight Schrute on the television series, The Office. He is the founder of the digital media company SoulPancake.

[502] Universal House of Justice, Letter dated 28 December 2010 to the Conference of the Continental Boards of Counsellors, paragraph 34.

[503] Universal House of Justice, Riḍván 2008, paragraph 3.

[504] Universal House of Justice, Letter dated 19 May 1994 to a National Spiritual Assembly.

[505] On behalf of Shoghi Effendi, quoted in Ewing, *Toward Oneness: A Compilation on Racial and Cultural Issues*, p. 29.

[506] Universal House of Justice, Riḍván 2010, paragraph 6.

[507] Regan, p. 234.

[508] Universal House of Justice, Riḍván 2010, paragraph 25.

[509] Universal House of Justice, Letter dated 29 December 2015 to the Conference of the Continental Boards of Counsellors, paragraph 17.

About the Author

Patricia Verge is a writer and editor who lives in the foothills of the Rocky Mountains in Alberta. She is the co-author, with Evelyn Loft Watts, of *Return to Tyendinaga: The Story of Jim and Melba Loft, Bahá'í Pioneers*, and the author of *Angus: From the Heart*, both stories of the history of Indigenous people and the Bahá'í Faith.

Printed in Canada